This volume surveys Iberian interr ... century, with particular emphasis o ... on changes brought by the Christian ... Spain (al-Andalus) in the thirteenth century.

From the tenth to the thirteenth cen ... in the Iberian peninsula were closely linked to markets elsewher ... the Islamic world, and a strong east–west Mediterranean trading network linked Cairo with Cordoba. Following routes along the North African coast, Muslim and Jewish merchants carried eastern goods to Muslim Spain, returning eastwards with Andalusi exports. Situated at the edge of the Islamic west, Andalusi markets were also emporia for the transfer of commodities between the Islamic world and Christian Europe. After the thirteenth century the Iberian peninsula became part of the European economic sphere, its commercial realignment aided by the opening of the Straits of Gibraltar to Christian trade, and by the contemporary demise of the Muslim trading network in the Mediterranean.

Cambridge studies in medieval life and thought

TRADE AND TRADERS IN MUSLIM SPAIN

Cambridge studies in medieval life and thought
Fourth series

General Editor:
D. E. LUSCOMBE
Professor of Medieval History, University of Sheffield

Advisory Editors:
R. B. DOBSON
Professor of Medieval History, University of Cambridge, and Fellow of Christ's College

ROSAMOND MCKITTERICK
Reader in Early Medieval European History, University of Cambridge, and Fellow of Newnham College

The series Cambridge Studies in Medieval Life and Thought was inaugurated by G. G. Coulton in 1920. Professor D. E. Luscombe now acts as General Editor of the Fourth Series, with Professor R. B. Dobson and Dr Rosamond McKitterick as Advisory Editors. The series brings together outstanding work by medieval scholars over a wide range of human endeavour extending from political economy to the history of ideas.

For a list of titles in the series, see end of book.

TRADE AND TRADERS IN MUSLIM SPAIN

The commercial realignment of the Iberian peninsula, 900–1500

OLIVIA REMIE CONSTABLE

CAMBRIDGE
UNIVERSITY PRESS

Published by the Press Syndicate of the University of Cambridge
The Pitt Building, Trumpington Street, Cambridge CB2 1RP
40 West 20th Street, New York, NY 10011-4211, USA
10 Stamford Road, Oakleigh, Melbourne 3166, Australia

First published 1994
Reprinted 1995
First paperback edition published 1996

Printed in Great Britain at the University Press, Cambridge

A catalogue record for this book is available from the British Library

Library of Congress cataloguing in publication data

Constable, Olivia Remie.
Trade and traders in Muslim Spain: the commercial realignment of the Iberian peninsula, 900–1500 / Olivia Remie Constable.
p. cm. – (Cambridge studies in medieval life and thought: 4th ser., 24)
Includes bibliographical references.
ISBN 0 521 43075 5
1. Spain – Commerce – History. 2. Muslims – Spain – History.
3. Merchants – Spain – History. 4. Spain – History – 711–1516.
I. Title. II. Series.
HF3685.C66 1994
380.1'0946–0902 – dc20 93–15165 CIP

ISBN 0 521 43075 5 hardback
ISBN 0 521 56503 0 paperback

DX

For Evhy and Owen

CONTENTS

ILLUSTRATIONS

ACKNOWLEDGMENTS

Many people have helped with this project, some with a timely word and others with their constant presence and support. Special thanks are due to Avram Udovitch and Mark Cohen, who encouraged me to use the Geniza and who were among those who read, re-read, or commented on my manuscript. Also to David Abulafia, Jonathan Berkey, Thomas Glick, Martha Howell, William Jordan, David Luscombe, David Nirenberg, Teofilo Ruiz, Amy Singer, and Christopher Taylor whose advice, expertise, suggestions, and editorial good sense have saved me from many pitfalls.

My thanks are also due to many others for their erudition, ideas, hospitality, encouragement, and friendship. Among these are Margaret Alexander, Caterina Baglietto, Derek and Dorothy Bell, Muhammad Benaboud, Corinne Blake, John Boswell, Robert Burns, Caroline Bynum, Mounira Chapoutot, Bill and Lynn Courtney, Heath Dillard, Elizabeth and Muhammad El-Khattabi, Mercedes García-Arenal, Eduardo Grendi, Francisco Hernández, Jonathan Katz, Hilmar C. Krueger, Bernard Lewis, Victoria Lord, David Nicholle, Catherine Otten-Froux, Wim Phillips, Vito Piergiovanni, Geo Pistarino, John Pryor, Adeline Rucquoi, Robert Somerville, Wim Smit, Alan Stahl, Muhammad Talbi, Joaquin Vallvé, and David Wasserstein. Special thanks, also, to William Davies and Anne Rix at Cambridge University Press, and to Eliza McClennen who drew the maps for this volume.

My thanks go likewise to the archives and libraries where I have worked, and whose staff assisted me in my research. In Genoa, the Archivio di Stato in Genoa and Societá Ligure della Storia Patria. In Tunis, the National Library. In Madrid, the Real Academia de la Historia; the Instituto Miguel de Asín, CSIC; the Real Biblioteca del Escorial; the Biblioteca Nacional; the Casa de Velázquez; and the Instituto Hispano-Arabe. In

Rabat, the National Library. In the United States, the Columbia University Library, Princeton University Library, Yale University Library, and University of Wisconsin Library, Madison. Also the S.D. Goitein Geniza Research Laboratory at Princeton University and the American Numismatics Society in New York City.

I am grateful for generous financial support from Princeton University and from the Council on Research and Faculty Development in the Social Sciences at Columbia University, and for fellowships from the Fulbright-Hays Foundation, the Social Science Research Council, the Josephine De Kármán Foundation, and the Mrs. Giles Whiting Foundation.

Finally, my special love and thanks to Giles and Matthew.

ABBREVIATIONS

AHDE	*Anuario de la historia del derecho español*
AHR	*American Historical Review*
Annales: ESC	*Annales: économies, sociétés, civilisations*
Antonin	Antonin Collection, St. Petersburg(*)
ASG	Archivio di Stato, Genoa
ASLSP	*Atti della Societá ligure di storia patria*
BAH	*Bibliotheca arabigo-hispana* (ed. F. Codera)
BGA	*Bibliotheca geographorum arabicorum* (ed. M. J. de Goeje)
BM	British Museum, London(*)
Bodl	Bodleian Library, Oxford(*)
BRABLB	*Boletín de la real academia de bellas letras de Barcelona*
BRAH	*Boletín de la real academia de la historia* [*Madrid*]
BSOAS	*Bulletin of the School of Oriental and African Studies*
DK	David Kaufman Collection, Budapest(*)
Dropsie	Dropsie College, Philadelphia(*)
ENA	Elkan N. Adler Collection, Jewish Theological Seminary of America, New York(*)
Firkovitch	Firkovitch Collection, St. Petersburg(*)
Gottheil-Worrell	*Fragments from the Cairo Genizah in the Freer Collection*. ed. R. Gottheil and W.H. Worrell, New York, 1927(*)
JAOS	*Journal of the American Oriental Society*
JESHO	*Journal of the Economic and Social History of the Orient*
Mosseri	Jack Mosseri Collection(*)
Madrid: MDI	*Maʿhad al-dirasāt al-islamiyya* [*Madrid*]
MGH	*Monumenta germaniae historica*

ROMM	*Revue de l'Occident musulman et de la Méditerranée*
Sassoon	David S. Sassoon Collection, Letchworth(*)
TS	Taylor-Schechter Collection in the University Library, Cambridge(*)
ULC	University Library Collection, Cambridge(*)
Westminster College	Westminster College Collection, Cambridge(*)

(*) indicates collections of Geniza manuscripts cited according to the standard system used by Goitein and others. The shelfmark indicates their collection, and sometimes their size, volume, and folio. Thus, a document cited as TS 10 J 12.7 comes from the Taylor-Schechter collection in the University Library, Cambridge, England. It is folio seven in volume twelve of the series of volumes ten inches long. TS manuscripts kept in glasses are catalogued differently (TS 12.251 designates number 251 of the series of glasses twelve inches long). Each collection uses a different system of shelfmarks for Geniza manuscripts. For further explanation and description, see S.D. Goitein, *A Mediterranean Society*. [Berkeley, 1967–88], I, pp.xix–xxvi.

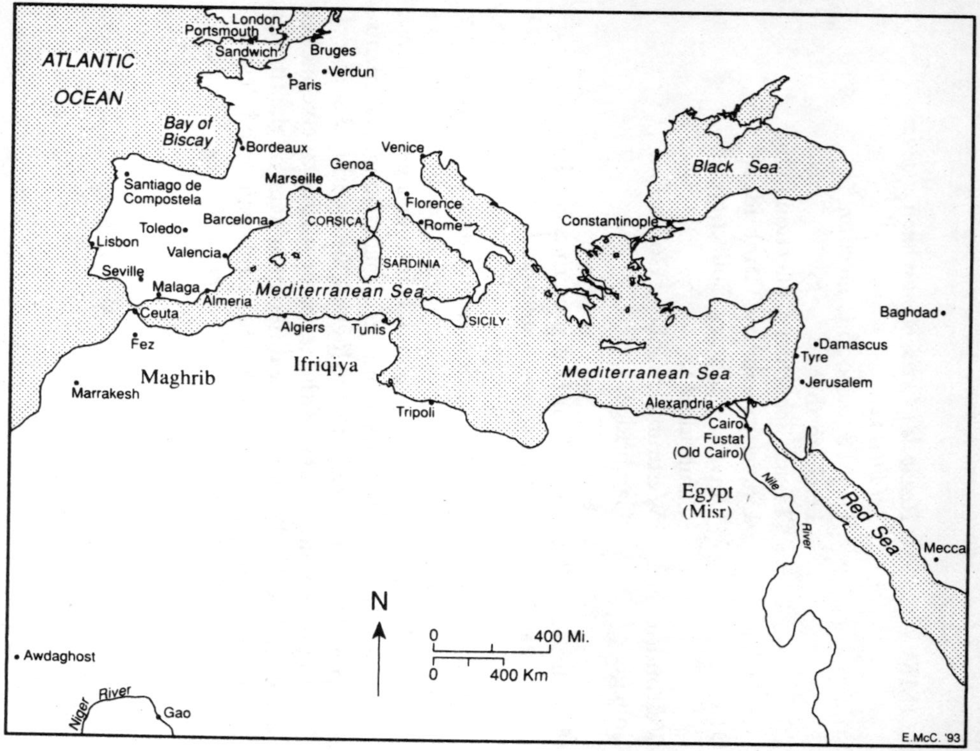
ATLANTIC
OCEAN
Bay of Biscay
London
Portsmouth
Sandwich
Bruges
Paris
Verdun
Bordeaux
Santiago de Compostela
Toledo
Lisbon
Seville
Valencia
Barcelona
Malaga
Almeria
Ceuta
Fez
Marrakesh
Maghrib
Marseille
Genoa
Venice
Florence
Rome
CORSICA
SARDINIA
SICILY
Mediterranean Sea
Algiers
Tunis
Ifriqiya
Tripoli
Constantinople
Black Sea
Mediterranean Sea
Alexandria
Cairo
Fustat
(Old Cairo)
Egypt
(Misr)
Nile
River
Red Sea
Mecca
Tyre
Damascus
Jerusalem
Baghdad
Awdaghost
Niger
River
Gao
N
0
400 Mi.
0
400 Km
E.McC. '93

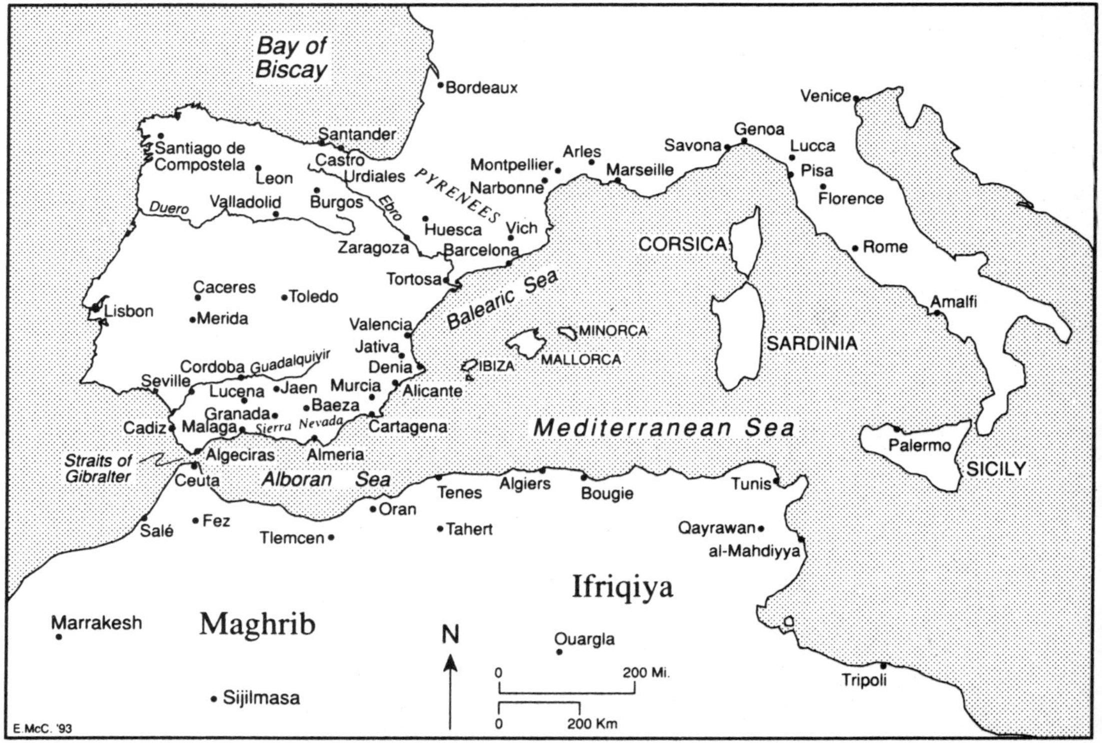
Bay of Biscay
Bordeaux
Santiago de Compostela
Santander
Castro Urdiales
Leon
Burgos
Valladolid
Duero
Ebro
PYRENEES
Huesca
Zaragoza
Vich
Barcelona
Tortosa
Montpellier
Narbonne
Arles
Marseille
Savona
Genoa
Lucca
Pisa
Florence
Venice
Rome
Amalfi
CORSICA
SARDINIA
SICILY
Palermo
Lisbon
Caceres
Merida
Toledo
Valencia
Jativa
Denia
Alicante
Murcia
Cartagena
Cordoba
Guadalquivir
Seville
Lucena
Jaen
Baeza
Granada
Sierra Nevada
Malaga
Cadiz
Almeria
Algeciras
Straits of Gibralter
Ceuta
Balearic Sea
MINORCA
MALLORCA
IBIZA
Mediterranean Sea
Alboran Sea
Tenes
Algiers
Bougie
Tunis
Oran
Tahert
Salé
Fez
Tlemcen
Qayrawan
al-Mahdiyya
Ifriqiya
Maghrib
Marrakesh
Sijilmasa
Ouargla
Tripoli
N
0
200 Mi.
0
200 Km
E.McC. '93

PREFACE

Reconstructing the patterns of Muslim Spanish (*Andalusi*) international trade is like trying to piece together a jigsaw puzzle of unknown design, in which many of the pieces are missing and some of the available pieces are borrowed from other apparently similar puzzles. No primary sources deal specifically with the topic of Andalusi commerce and few provide more than a handful of useful references. This meagerness has made it necessary to cull information from a wide variety of materials. It is possible to view the spectrum of routes, merchants, and commodities in Andalusi trade only by combining many sources, yet gaps still remain.

Among sources in Arabic, works of geography and travel, legal materials, and biographical dictionaries (*tarājim*) have yielded the most useful data, with supportive information added from chronicles, poetry, and professional treatises. Medieval geographers and travelers provided detailed descriptions of Andalusi cities and exports, including accounts of routes of trade and regions of production. Their books have proved invaluable to this study, although they vary in accuracy and originality. Some writers, including Ibn Ḥawqal, Ibn Jubayr, and Benjamin of Tudela, actually journeyed through the places that they described in their works. In contrast, many other writers remained at their desks, cribbing from earlier books or recording the reminiscences of contemporary travelers. These sedentary geographers are not necessarily less accurate than their more energetic counterparts, but they tend to be less up-to-date. When a writer mixed data from different periods, as in the case of Idrīsī who wrote in the middle of the twelfth century but incorporated earlier materials into his work, it seems that at least some of the information dates from the time of writing. By and large, I have accepted the information provided by geographers unless it is clearly inaccurate or entirely derivative, and I have dated it to the time of writing.

Legal materials present a different array of complications, particularly since books of Islamic law, handbooks of formulae for writing contracts (*wathā'iq*), and manuals for the instruction and guidance of market inspectors (*ḥisba* books) tend to be prescriptive. Nevertheless, they contain many valuable details relating to commercial practice. Collections of juridical rulings (*fatwas*) addressed specific legal queries, with the answer attributed to a particular legal scholar (thus indicating the period and place of delivery). Many *fatwas* appear to record real commercial situations and merchant disputes. Biographical dictionaries describing the lives and travels of Muslim scholars are also of service because they mention scholars who were also merchants. These merchant-scholars may not be representative of all Muslim merchants, but they are virtually the only Muslim traders for whom we have any personal information.

The Judeo-Arabic documents in the Cairo Geniza collection have been among the most important sources for this study. This cache of materials, including thousands of medieval letters and other papers, were preserved in a sealed room of a synagogue in Old Cairo where they were discovered in the late nineteenth century. Written in Arabic, but using Hebrew characters, many Geniza letters pertain to the affairs of Jewish merchants trading to and from Egypt during the eleventh and twelfth centuries. Over two hundred of them contain references to Andalusis, Andalusi goods, and travel to Andalusi ports. The Geniza also includes Hebrew responsa and Jewish court records that show Andalusi Jewish merchants and their partners involved in suits which parallel those detailed in Muslim *fatwas*. Although there is some question as to the degree to which Geniza materials represent general trading patterns in the contemporary Mediterranean, or merely Jewish trading patterns, at the very least they provide data on the movement of Jewish traders and their goods to and from Andalusi ports. I have had access to Geniza materials not only through published editions and translations, but also through the unpublished notes, transcriptions, photographs, and microfilms donated to Princeton University by the late S.D. Goitein, whose pioneering work demonstrated the value of this source.

Latin and vernacular documents fill in the picture of Andalusi commercial contact with Christian Spain and other areas of Europe. Town charters (*fueros*) from Castile, Aragon, and Portugal often include tariff schedules, demonstrating the kinds of goods (Andalusi and otherwise) that were traded in northern markets. Similar lists of commercial tolls are available from Italian and Provençal cities, and later from ports in northern Europe. Notarial registers are also of value, since they record contracts for merchant voyages to Iberian ports or sales of Andalusi commodities. The earliest surviving registers, dating back to the 1150s, are preserved in the Archivio di Stato in Genoa, and later contracts are available in Marseille, Savona, Vich, and other cities. Christian chronicles, legal and royal decrees, diplomatic materials, records of ecclesiastical donations, and secular literature also provide data on Andalusi commercial activity.

Physical evidence from the fields of archeology, art history, and numismatics also yields clues about Andalusi international commerce and economic contacts. For example, the Pisan *bacini* (ceramic dishes or fragments used in architectural decoration) demonstrate the diffusion of Andalusi and Christian Spanish ceramics to Italy from the eleventh to fifteenth centuries. The nature of their material strongly suggests that these items arrived in Italy through commerce. In contrast, the wide diffusion of Andalusi coinage may result from economic and commercial contact or from some other means of transfer.

It is difficult to evaluate and use these disparate pieces of information. On the one hand, it can be argued that the relative scarcity of data relating to Andalusi trade indicates that commercial exchange was neither important nor widespread. I believe otherwise. Although it is impossible to quantify precisely the numbers of merchants, size and value of cargoes, or frequency of commercial voyages in any given year, there is much to be gained from looking at a variety of documentation. Even a few references to trade, if scattered, are likely to reflect a larger reality. There is little source material attesting to trade between Muslim Spain (*al-Andalus*) and Pisa, for instance, yet its existence is proved in the diverse bits of information that survive. There is a Pisan tariff schedule from the second half of the twelfth century noting levies on vessels arriving from Andalusi ports, and there are contemporary diplomatic documents drawn up between Almohad rulers and Pisa that refer to commercial matters. Chronicles likewise note Pisan maritime expeditions in Andalusi waters, while the Pisan *bacini* mutely testify to the transfer of ceramics between Spain and Italy. No notarial contracts survive to record Pisan mercantile expeditions to Andalusi ports, but here we may extrapolate from the Genoese notarial data. Since Genoa and Pisa had similar commercial aspirations (creating competition between the two cities) and because Genoese records parallel those cited above for Pisa, it is probable that Pisan merchants formed partnerships and made voyages very like those shown in the Genoese contracts.

By examining the network of commercial routes to and from Iberian ports, the different types of merchants, and the variety of commodities exported from the peninsula, it is possible to reconstruct the quality of international trade, even without being able to quantify the volume of trade in any given period. Nevertheless, the patch-work of data does allow an educated guess as to changes in volume of trade between periods. Although lack of evidence does not necessarily prove that something did not exist, a sharp decrease or sudden increase in material may well signal a real change. This is particularly true in cases where there is external evidence supporting an observed variation in data. The scarcity of Geniza records after the middle of the twelfth century, for example, gives the impression of a decline in Jewish activity in Andalusi trade. It would be difficult to accept this evidence alone as indicative of a real phenomenon without the accounts of contemporary persecution of Jews in al-Andalus and the concurrent appearance of Italian merchants in Andalusi trade. Likewise, when sources documenting Andalusi trade with Muslim ports decline in the second half of the thirteenth century, this probably reflects a true shift in trade because at the same period quantities of data suddenly appear showing traffic between the Iberian peninsula and Europe.

This book is concerned primarily with international trade, not with the internal Andalusi economy. To some extent, the distinction between international commerce and internal economy is artificial, since the former was an extension of the latter and dependent in many respects on local markets and regional production. International commerce is set apart by the fact that it formed its own profession, however, and the merchants who handled this trade specialized in buying and selling goods over long distances rather than at the local level. International trade may thus be considered independently as an instrument of contact between the internal Andalusi economy and the wider European–Mediterranean sphere.

The terms long distance, international, and cross cultural, all carry their own particular connotations and associations. For the purposes of this study, long-distance trade is the most general term since it applies to virtually all of the commercial activity under consideration whether between Iberian cities only a few days journey apart or between al-Andalus and the Near East. International trade is used for external Andalusi commerce with both Europe and other regions of the Islamic world (*dār al-Islām*). Because medieval frontiers were not perceived in the same way as modern national borders, the term international here applies not only to trade between regions under different political regimes, such as two kingdoms within the peninsula, but also to trade between traditional geographical regions such as the Iberian peninsula, North Africa, Egypt, and Europe. Cross cultural, on the other hand, is used for trade across a multiple frontier of language, religion, cultural heritage, and ethnicity.[1] Andalusi trade was cross cultural when it involved traffic with northern Spain, Europe, or Byzantium. In contrast, trade with other areas of the Islamic world was often long distance and international without being cross cultural.

The diversity of the Iberian peninsula, with its heritage of multiple religions, cultures, and languages, poses terminological difficulties. These begin with the name Spain itself, which is used here for reasons of simplicity and convenience to mean the entire Iberian peninsula, unless modified as Christian or Muslim (or Islamic). The preferable term for Muslim Spain, however, is the Arabic *al-Andalus*. Al-Andalus is used in contrast to Andalusia (southern Castile in the later middle ages), and Andalusi (pertaining to al-Andalus) in contrast to Andalusian (pertaining to Andalusia). A number of conventional geographical designations (Europe, the Near East, the Mediterranean world, and the Muslim world) are used, even though their borders are vague or variable. Wherever possible, however, I have favored more specific designations, such as Castile, Aragon, Portugal, or Granada.

[1] This is similar to the definition laid out by P. Curtin in *Cross-Cultural Trade in World History* (Cambridge, 1984).

Other terms also present difficulties, particularly when religious, ethnic, or linguistic designations are stretched to apply to political or geographical entities. The Muslim world, for example, encompasses all regions under the administration of Muslim rulers, although Christians and Jews lived within its borders. Similarly, Muslim trade generally means trade carried out by Muslims as opposed to trade in the Muslim world (which had many participants). Arab trade likewise means commerce among Arabs, whereas Arabic trade is conducted in Arabic (thus including many non-Arabs and non-Muslims). Analogous problems may arise with the terms Christian and Latin.

It is almost impossible to be entirely consistent in the use of place names and personal names, but where an English form exists I have almost always chosen to use it. Thus, I prefer Castile over Castilla; Old Cairo or Fustat over Fusṭāṭ; Almeria over both Almería and al-Mariyya. Despite this general rule, some names are used in their original language for the sake either of specificity or variety. Most personal names have likewise been anglicized where there is a common equivalent. Iberian monarchs have become James (thus avoiding the confusions of Jaime/Jaume), Peter, and Ferdinand, but Alfonso retains its Castilian spelling. Latin first names have also generally – but not invariably – been rendered in English. Names in Arabic and Hebrew present a slightly different problem, and most have retained their original spellings following the system of transliteration laid out in the *International Journal of Middle East Studies*. Thus, I use Muḥammad (rather than Mohammed), ʿAlī, and so forth. Names like Ibrāhīm, Yūsuf, or Yaʿqūb are given in their Arabic forms, whether they belonged to Muslims or Jews, if references come from Arabic or Judeo-Arabic texts. A few eccentricities persist, nonetheless, as with such well-known names as Moses b. Maimon (or Maimonides) or Benjamin of Tudela. Where a *nisba* (that part of an Arabic name that denotes a person's place of origin, such as Andalusī, Baghdadī, etc.) is used, it is written without the final long *ī* (thus, Andaluṣi and Baghdadi) unless the full name is given.

Except for the place names al-Andalus and al-Mahdiyya, the initial *al-* (the definite article) has been dropped, so that al-Idrīsī becomes merely Idrīsī, al-Maqqarī becomes Maqqarī, al-Rāzī becomes Rāzī, and so forth. The definite article has been retained however, but not elided, when it appears in the middle of a name (i.e., ʻAbd al-Raḥmān, not ʻAbd ar-Raḥmān). The use, or abuse, of the definite article presents a special problem in the context of names such as Almoravid (from *al-Murābiṭ*) and Almohad (*al-Muwaḥid*) in which the Arabic definite article has been incorporated into the English form of the name. Technically, it is redundant to refer to *the* Almoravids or *the* Almohads, but it usually sounds odd to use these names in English without the article. Likewise, there is the nicety that, in Arabic, a term such as *dār al-Islām* or Sharq al-Andalus (eastern al-Andalus) should not be preceded by the definite article because this is already implied. Again, for the sake of English grammar, I write of the *dār al-Islām* and the Sharq al-Andalus.

In the interests of familiarity, I have as a rule favored the Christian system of dating, but in a few cases a Muslim date is also given to reflect a citation from an Arabic text.

Chapter 1

THE MARKET AT THE EDGE OF THE WEST

For most of the medieval period, the Iberian peninsula experienced the paradox of an existence between two worlds. Situated at the western edge of the Muslim Mediterranean and the southern edge of Christian Europe, it was part of both – yet not fully part of either. Distance continually accentuated the peninsula's liminality, while at the same time the region remained an accepted element within both Muslim and Christian views of the world. From the eighth to the fifteenth centuries, the peninsula belonged to two spheres, Christian in the north and Muslim in the south, with a border which shifted southward over the centuries. As a frontier, Spain (by which I intend the entire peninsula) provided a gateway between Christian and Muslim worlds, giving passage to diplomats, scholars, refugees, soldiers, and merchants.

This book will concentrate on the passage of merchants and their goods to and from Muslim Spain (*al-Andalus* in Arabic) from the tenth through the twelfth century. International trade and traders helped to preserve ties between al-Andalus and other regions of the Mediterranean world, both Muslim and Christian. During these three centuries, the peninsula formed a distinct political, cultural, and economic entity incorporated within the larger Muslim world (*dār al-Islām*). Although geographically distant from Cairo and Baghdad, Mecca and Jerusalem, Andalusi cities remained in close contact with the Muslim east, and al-Andalus was very much part of the Islamic Mediterranean mental, religious, and commercial sphere. Even in times of political discord between Muslim regimes in east and west, communications remained open as travelers, letters, and commodities passed back and forth with ease and regularity. Merchant ships and their cargoes traveled across the Mediterranean between east and west with sufficient frequency to render a commercial voyage from

Egypt to al-Andalus something of "a humdrum experience".[1]

In most respects, Andalusi international trade during these three centuries matched wider patterns in the medieval Mediterranean economy. The structure of Andalusi commerce was similar to contemporary trade elsewhere, and there was nothing particularly unusual in Iberian commercial techniques, merchant relations, shipping, governmental attitude toward trade, or market forces. As Braudel has observed, over the long term there were "identical or near-identical worlds ... on the borders of such countries as far apart and in general terms as different as Greece, Spain, Italy, North Africa ... [worlds which could] live at the same rhythm ... [with] men and goods ... able to move from one to another without any need for acclimatization".[2]

For all these similarities, however, al-Andalus differed from other Muslim regions. The Iberian peninsula was on the border between Muslim and Christian spheres, and it was the only region of the Mediterranean world to remain a frontier for eight centuries. Al-Andalus played a unique role in western Mediterranean commerce, serving as an economic transit zone and an emporium through which commercial connections stretched across the border between the Muslim world and the Latin west. From an Islamic Mediterranean viewpoint, al-Andalus was the market at the edge of the west: a consumer of eastern imports, an exporter of Andalusi goods, and a way-station for commodities coming southward from Europe into the *dār al-Islām*. From a Christian European perspective, al-Andalus was a point of contact with the Islamic trading domain and one of the channels through which desirable luxuries – eastern spices, precious metals, textiles, paper, and other items – might be obtained. Before the expansion of European commercial horizons and mercantile activity in the central middle ages, nearby Andalusi markets could supply many of the good things in Latin Christian life.

This unique commercial function disintegrated in the first half of the thirteenth century, when the progress of Spanish Christian victories, together with parallel trends toward Christian military and commercial expansion elsewhere in the Mediterranean

[1] S.D. Goitein, *A Mediterranean Society. The Jewish Communities of the Arab World as Portrayed in the Documents of the Cairo Geniza.* [Berkeley, 1967–88] 1, p. 42.

[2] F. Braudel, *The Mediterranean and the Mediterranean World in the Age of Philip II.* [New York, 1966] 1, p. 231.

world, permanently realigned power in the peninsula. Economic changes went hand in hand with territorial conquest, as the peninsula reoriented its trade northward to Christian Europe and away from the Muslim world.

A brief survey of Andalusi history is necessary in order to demonstrate the repercussions of political and economic events on the structure of Andalusi international trade. Al-Andalus became part of the Islamic world in 711, when a Muslim army crossed the Straits of Gibraltar, conquered the Visigoths, and established most of the peninsula as a western province under the rule of the Umayyad caliph in Damascus. When the Umayyads were ousted by the Abbasids in the middle of the next century, the center of eastern Muslim political, cultural, and economic power shifted to Iraq and al-Andalus became marginalized. Perched at the edge of the Islamic west, al-Andalus took on an autonomous existence under the rule of its first amir, ʿAbd al-Raḥmān I (756–88), one of the few surviving members of the Umayyad family.

Despite the new independence of his realm, ʿAbd al-Raḥmān did not claim the title of caliph (though the ʿAbbasids were not acknowledged in Andalusi Friday prayers) and the peninsula remained culturally aligned with the larger *dār al-Islām*. For two centuries, intellectual and religious developments in al-Andalus closely followed trends set in the east. Baghdadi poets and scholars were read and admired in the peninsula, though eastern readers paid little attention to western writings. Likewise, the inhabitants of ninth-century Cordoba, the Umayyad capital, were renowned for their slavish adherence to the fashions and manners of Baghdad, while Andalusi merchants, scholars, and pilgrims journeyed eastward seeking profit, learning, and religious fulfillment.

During the eighth and ninth centuries, al-Andalus also communicated with Christian territories, both within the peninsula and beyond. Andalusi borders (*thughūr*) with Christian Spain remained fairly stable in this period, but Muslim armies held the upper hand. Although the Christian idea of reconquest (or *reconquista*, a crusade to win back territories lost to the Muslims in 711) may have taken root as early as the eighth century, it would not come to fruition for two centuries. Outside the peninsula, Umayyad interests extended as far as Byzantium, as shown by diplomatic contact between Cordoba and Constantinople in the ninth century, but there is more evidence for relations between Cordoba and Aachen at this period. After Carolingian expansion into the Spanish March and their rout by Basques at Roncevalles (commemorated indelibly, if inaccurately, in the *Song of Roland*), embassies were exchanged between the Umayyad and Carolingian courts. Later diplomacy is also recorded between Umayyad and Ottonian rulers.[3]

Commerce came along with other contacts, and Andalusi markets began to serve as channels through which Muslim commodities, from the peninsula and further east, found their way to consumers in northern Spain and elsewhere in the Latin west. In commercial terms, al-Andalus could take a more dominant role in its relations with Christian regions than with the *dār al-Islām*. A skilled Andalusi workforce, with well-developed industries and sophisticated agriculture, had much to offer to the rural and less technologically developed northern kingdoms.

Political developments in the tenth century brought an end to the somewhat subservient status of al-Andalus in relation to the eastern Islamic world. When the Umayyad ruler ʿAbd al-Raḥmān III declared himself caliph in 929, Muslim Spain became a major player on the stage of Mediterranean politics and commerce. The declaration of an Andalusi caliphate was sparked by the contemporary decline (though not disappearance) of Abbasid power in Iraq and the rise of the Fatimids, a Shiʿite dynasty that had taken the unprecedented step of establishing the first rival caliphate in Tunisia in 909 (and in Egypt after 969). In assuming the title of caliph, ʿAbd al-Raḥmān positioned al-Andalus as an influential entity within the Muslim Mediterranean, and he backed his claim with military and diplomatic force. During the 920s and 930s, Umayyad armies captured several ports along the North African coast, which served as buffers against the Fatimids, provided termini for Andalusi trade, and gave access to the gold-producing regions of West Africa. When Andalusi mints began to produce gold dinars for the first time in 929, these coins served to proclaim Umayyad economic and political power both at home and abroad.

With the declaration of an Umayyad caliphate in al-Andalus, the appearance of a Fatimid caliphate in Tunisia and Egypt, and

[3] E. Lévi-Provençal, "Un échange d'ambassades entre Cordoue et Byzance au IXe siècle," *Byzantion* 12(1937), pp. 1–24; A.A. el-Hajji, *Andalusian Diplomatic Relations with Western Europe during the Umayyad Period*. [Beirut, 1970].

the decline of the ʿAbbasids in Iraq, the Mediterranean world took on a renewed vigor in the tenth century. Economic opportunities and merchant enterprise won out over political and religious antagonisms as a commercial network emerged to link markets in al-Andalus, Sicily-Tunisia, and Egypt. The demise of Baghdad as a critical trading hub allowed Mediterranean port cities (particularly Almeria, Tunis, al-Mahdiyya, and Alexandria) to become focal markets for trade along a busy east–west Mediterranean axis. The appearance of this energetic new commercial system signaled a renaissance in Mediterranean trade, which had been depressed though by no means made extinct during the previous two centuries. Demand in the Mediterranean channeled eastern goods coming by sea from the Indian Ocean away from the Persian Gulf and into routes up the Red Sea to Egypt. From Egypt, goods were disseminated along the east–west trunk route to markets in Ifriqiya and al-Andalus, and from there along spur routes to Christian lands and other satellite markets. Andalusi markets were a crucial western component in this system, since not only did they consume and distribute eastern imports, but they also exported Iberian goods back to the eastern Mediterranean. Andalusi agriculture and industries were well developed and diversified by the tenth century, allowing a reasonable balance of trade between east and west.

The period from the tenth to the late twelfth century, during which this Muslim Mediterranean commercial system remained functional, marked a phase of relative stability for Andalusi international trade. The integration of Muslim Spanish commerce within the Mediterranean trading axis gave it strength, and thus Andalusi markets were able to maintain their far-flung trading contacts and retain their function even in the face of three major obstacles. The first was distance (both perceived and actual), the second was the turmoils of internal Andalusi politics, and the third was the shifting balance of Christian and Muslim power in the peninsula and wider Mediterranean world. The first two could be overcome, but the addition of the third would eventually destroy Andalusi trade and the Muslim Mediterranean network.

Before continuing the survey of political history, a discussion of perceptions of distance draws attention to the position of al-

Andalus within the Muslim thought world during the Umayyad period and after. Merchants and other travelers knew that physical distance could be traversed and that a trip from Almeria to Alexandria might be accomplished in a couple of months. Conceptual distances were harder to conquer, however, and al-Andalus remained at the western edge of the Islamic mental map. Geographical writings emphasized this Andalusi paradox of being both part, and yet not fully part, of the *dār al-Islām*. Arab geographers in the ninth and tenth centuries provided descriptions and maps that portrayed the Iberian peninsula hovering at the western edge of the earth. In the early tenth century, the eastern geographer Ibn al-Faqīh described the inhabited world as all that "is known between al-Andalus and China".[4] By the middle of the twelfth century the techniques of map-making had improved, but although the geographer Idrīsī (writing ca. 1150) was careful to depict al-Andalus accurately, with rivers and cities clearly sited, the peninsula still marked the farthest western point of the known world with an empty ocean beyond. Within a hundred years of the creation of Idrīsī's map, this perceived liminality became real. By the middle of the thirteenth century, most of the peninsula had slipped out of the Muslim sphere and the functional Islamic frontier shifted southward across the sea to North Africa.

Not only distance, but also the unique position of al-Andalus as a long-term frontier inhibited the peninsula's full incorporation within an Islamic world view. Geographical descriptions emphasized the role of al-Andalus as a border territory. According to the tenth-century geographers Iṣṭakhrī and Ibn Ḥawqal, al-Andalus had two borders, one along its frontier with Christian Spain ("the land of the unbeliever") and the other along its coastline.[5] Because the Arabic term *thughūr* could apply to either a land frontier or a sea coast, al-Andalus was entirely surrounded by borders and even its access to the rest of the Islamic world necessitated a sea journey across the Straits of Gibraltar. Port cities in the south, including Seville, Malaga, and Almeria, were channels of connection to other Muslim regions. Northern cities, such as Barcelona and Tarragona, were "the gates of al-

[4] Ibn al-Faqīh, *Kitāb al-buldān*. [ed. M.J. de Goeje, *BGA*, 2nd edn, v, Leiden, 1967], p. 50.

[5] Iṣṭakhrī, *Kitāb al-masālik wa al-mamālik*. [ed. M.J. de Goeje, *BGA*, 2nd edn, I, Leiden, 1967], p. 41; Ibn Ḥawqal, *Kitāb ṣūrat al-arḍ*. [ed. J.H. Kramers, Leiden, 1938], p. 109.

Andalus".[6] Tudela (north of Zaragoza along the Ebro) was "the furthest frontier of the Muslims" and a point at which merchants and other travelers might cross into the "lands of the infidel".[7] Some authors took a dismal view of the Andalusi situation, with Ibn Bassām (d. 1147) lamenting that the people of al-Andalus live "close to the Christians, in a land which is at the extremity of those conquered by Islam and quite removed from the influence of Arab traditions, surrounded by the vast sea . . ."[8]

In literary imagery likewise, al-Andalus stood on the perimeter of the Muslim world. One anonymous author, in a fanciful mood, related an anecdote in which King Solomon questioned a cloud regarding its course, and learned that it traversed the sky from "one gate of Paradise, called al-Andalus, in the far west," to Abbadan in the east.[9] In a similar vein, the eastern author Yāqūt (d. 1229) recalled the verses: "I asked the people about Anas, and they replied: [He is] in al-Andalus, and al-Andalus is far away."[10] Perhaps the eleventh-century Andalusi scholar Ibn Ḥazm best summed up the Andalusi paradox of distance and unity when he wrote that

> if [my beloved] were in the most distant eastern region of the civilized world, while I remained in the furthest western region, with the whole length of the inhabited world [between us], yet there would still be only the distance of a single day's journey between him and me, for the sun rises at daybreak in the extreme east, and sets at the end of every day in the extreme west.[11]

Al-Andalus was certainly far away, but the passage of people and ideas ensured that the peninsula was never out of touch with the Islamic east. After the twelfth-century Jewish poet Judah Ha-Levi wrote "my heart is in the east and I am at the edge of the west . . . it would be easy for me to leave behind all the good

[6] Isḥāq b. al-Ḥusain, "Il compendio geografico arabo di Isḥāq ibn al-Ḥusayn," [ed. and trans. A. Codazzi and C.A. Nallino] *Rendiconti della R. academia nazionale dei Lincei* [Rome] 6th series, 5(1929), p. 411.

[7] Ibn Ghālib, "Naṣṣ andalusī jadīd qaṭʿia min kitāb farḥa al-anfūs li-Ibn Ghālib," [ed. L. ʿAbd al-Bādī] *Majalla maʿhad al-makhṭūṭāt al-ʿarabiya* 1(1955), p. 287.

[8] H.E. Kassis, "Muslim revival in Spain in the 5th/11th Century," *Der Islam* 67 (1990), p. 83.

[9] L. Molina (ed.), *Una descripción anónima de al-Andalus.* [Madrid, 1983], p. 17.

[10] Yāqūt, *Muʿjām al-buldān.* (*Jacut's Geographisches Worterbuch.*) [ed. F. Wüstenfeld, Leipzig, 1873] 1, p. 375.

[11] Ibn Ḥazm, *Ṭawq al-ḥamāma.* [ed. T.A. Makki, Cairo, 1975], p. 135.

things of Spain; it would be glorious to see the dust of the ruined shrine . . ." he fulfilled his desire and traveled to the Holy Land in 1140.[12] When he arrived, he was eagerly greeted by eastern friends and admirers, whose enthusiasm marked a significant change from an earlier period. During the tenth century, al-Andalus began to emerge as a more equal participant in the Arabic intellectual world. Andalusi scholarship flourished in the eleventh and twelfth centuries, producing such figures as Judah Ha-Levi, Moses b. Maimon, Ibn Rushd, Ibn Ḥazm, and Ibn Ṭufayl. Increasingly, Andalusi learning and literature were studied and appreciated in the Near East, and western scholars began to journey east to teach as well as to learn.

Changes in the relationship between al-Andalus and the wider world, both Muslim and Christian, were also evident in the political sphere. The eleventh and twelfth centuries witnessed major upheavals in internal Andalusi politics, although not sufficient to destroy the Mediterranean trading axis. After nearly two and a half centuries of relatively stable centralized Umayyad rule in al-Andalus, the dynasty crumbled in the early eleventh century (usually dated to 1031) in the face of disputes over succession and civil war. In its place, smaller independent states emerged called Taifas or *Mulūk al-ṭawā'if* ("Party Kingdoms"). Life in these smaller states emphasized the ethnic differences that had always existed in Andalusi society. For example, an Arab dynasty, the ʿAbbadids, ruled in Seville; two Berber dynasties, the Ḥammūdids and the Zīrids, controlled Malaga and Granada respectively; while the so-called *ṣaqāliba* (or Slavs) held power in the coastal cities of Almeria, Valencia, and Tortosa.[13]

The disintegration of the Umayyad state into these smaller kingdoms weakened Andalusi cohesion along the land frontier, and provided an opportunity for northern Christian rulers (in Galicia, Castile, Leon, Navarre, Aragon, and Catalonia) to gain advantage. Since individual Muslim rulers were no longer able to defend their borders against either Christian armies or each other, many sought alliance with northern states. In return for security of their borders, Taifa states paid monthly or annual

12 *The Penguin Book of Hebrew Verse.* [ed. and trans. T. Carmi, London, 1981], p. 347.

13 On the Taifa states, see D. Wasserstein, *The Rise and Fall of the Party Kings: Politics and Society in Islamic Spain, 1002–1086.* [Princeton, 1985].

tribute (*paria*) to Christian rulers.[14] This was in stark contrast to the situation in the tenth century, when Christian Spanish kingdoms had paid tribute to the Umayyads. *Parias* were first paid to Ramon Berenguer I of Catalonia during the 1040s, and soon became a widespread phenomenon. Some Taifa states paid multiple *parias*, notably the kingdom of Zaragoza, which owed tribute to Catalonia, Urgel, Navarre, Castile, and Aragon, with each of whom it shared a border, while more isolated Taifas owed only a single payment.

The payment of tribute to northern rulers was a drain on the coffers of Taifa rulers, but it does not seem to have damaged Andalusi international trade. Evidence from the Cairo Geniza and elsewhere indicates that commerce remained vigorous in the middle of the eleventh century, with many merchants trafficking along the trunk routes between Almeria and Alexandria. Indeed, it may have been the very success of Andalusi international trade in this period, and particularly the profits derived from Andalusi exports of silk, which allowed Taifa rulers to keep up with their *paria* payments.

Tribute did not ensure peace, however, and Christian armies began to push south, shattering Muslim confidence by capturing Toledo in 1085. The loss of Toledo made clear the need for military assistance, and an invitation was extended to the Almoravids, a Berber dynasty based in Marrakesh. Almoravid armies arrived in the peninsula in 1086, soon halted the Christian advance at the Battle of Zallaqa, and shortly thereafter established Almoravid control over both the peninsula and North Africa. Unified Almoravid rule marked the end of Taifa diversity, and established al-Andalus as part of a huge single kingdom. The new centralization strengthened Andalusi military organization so that most *paria* payments stopped and Christian incursions were slowed, although Muslim armies never managed to retake Toledo. Internal dissent gradually led to the disintegration of Almoravid power in the early twelfth century and the brief reappearance of Taifas before another Berber dynasty, the Almohads, incorporated al-Andalus into their North African empire in 1147.

[14] The term *paria* derives from either the Arabic *bara'* (to be free, acquitted, cleared [of a debt]) or *bara'* (which in some forms means to donate, give, or concede). Chapter 2 contains a more detailed discussion of *paria* tribute.

The vast extent of Almoravid and Almohad territories, which stretched from al-Andalus eastward across much of North Africa (and included regions traversed by the routes of gold traffic coming from West Africa), gave these two dynasties unprecedented economic weight in the Mediterranean world. The influence of the Almoravid regime, in particular, is attested by the diffusion and imitation of their gold dinars (*murabiṭūns*) throughout Christian Spain and southern Europe. Under the caliph 'Abd al-Mu'min (1130–63), the Almohads held ports stretching from Valencia to Tripoli. The dynasty also controlled the critical maritime passage through the Straits of Gibraltar from their Andalusi capital at Seville. With the cooperation of the Ayyubid dynasty in Egypt, Almohad hegemony helped to maintain the Muslim Mediterranean trunk route between Egypt and al-Andalus, although the network was beginning to fray by the second half of the twelfth century. The reasons for this disintegration lay not only within the Islamic world, where mercantile interests in Egypt were starting to turn eastward toward the Indian Ocean, but also outside the *dār al-Islām*, with contemporary developments in Europe and the Christian Mediterranean.

Changes in commerce were only one element in a slow but profound shift taking place in Europe and the Mediterranean world from the tenth to the fourteenth century. Parallel trends in political, military, demographic, and economic strength combined to redefine the balance between Christianity and Islam, north and south, east and west. The burgeoning of European population, industries, and trade all contributed to shift the foci of power in the Mediterranean world. In particular, the growth of southern European city states in the eleventh and twelfth centuries, including Genoa, Pisa, Venice, Florence, Marseille, and Barcelona, created substantial new players on the western Mediterranean stage. These cities emerged as naval and commercial powers that Muslim rulers, both in al-Andalus and elsewhere, could not ignore.

In parallel with Christian military conquests in the Iberian peninsula, there were Christian advances elsewhere in the Mediterranean. Sicily came under Norman rule in the 1060s and 1070s, shortly before the First Crusade was launched to Palestine. In support of their commercial concerns, Italian cities lent their fleets to naval endeavors, with Pisa attacking al-Mahdiyya in 1087, and both Pisa and Genoa assisting in Christian campaigns in the Iberian peninsula during the 1090s. Just as internal disunity in al-Andalus during the Taifa period had paved the way for the Castilian conquest of Toledo in 1085, events elsewhere in the Muslim world opened the way for these Christian advances. In the central Maghrib, the middle of the eleventh century marked a period of disruption after the Fatimids moved to Egypt. Nomadic incursions in Ifriqiya, followed by Norman invasions, disturbed commerce and agriculture in the southern-central Mediterranean, providing a further opening for Christian mercantile opportunism. Muslim states in the Near East were also in flux at this time, as the Seljuqs took control of Baghdad in 1055, challenged Fatimid rule in Syria, and defeated Byzantine armies at Manzikert in 1071.

Aided by Christian military advances in the eleventh and twelfth centuries, European merchants began to exploit Mediterranean markets and routes previously controlled by Muslim and Jewish traders. Maritime routes along the east-west trunk route that had once been the domain of Muslim and Jewish trade were gradually taken over by Christian shipping, or displaced by more northerly routes that shifted business away from Muslim ports. The incorporation of Mediterranean islands (including the Balearics, Corsica, Sardinia, Sicily, and Crete) into the Latin Christian sphere allowed Italian, French, and Catalan shipping to control the safer and faster routes along the northern Mediterranean shores and avoid the reefs and contrary winds along the North African coastline.[15] Meanwhile, the growth of cities, population, and commercial interests in Italy, southern France, and Catalonia supplied a new merchant community to Mediterranean trade. These traders thrived on the nascent commercial opportunities presented as northern European consumers began to clamor for Mediterranean goods and buyers in the Mediterranean became aware of European industries and exports.

In the peninsula, Spanish Christian conquests during the first half of the thirteenth century brought an end to Muslim rule in most of the south. After his grandfather's watershed victory at Las Navas de Tolosa in 1212, Ferdinand III of Castile took

[15] These shifts are the theme of J. Pryor's *Geography, Technology, and War: Studies in the Maritime History of the Mediterranean, 649–1571*. [Cambridge, 1988].

Cordoba in 1236 and Seville in 1248. Meanwhile, James I of Aragon conquered Mallorca in 1229–30 and Valencia in 1238. Political unification and expansion also gave new economic, demographic, and territorial clout to northern Christian rulers. By the late 1230s, Ferdinand III ruled a united Castile and Leon, while Aragon, Catalonia, and Valencia were incorporated within the Crown of Aragon. Only the Kingdom of Granada, encompassing the south coast from Gibraltar to just east of Almeria and stretching north into the Sierra Nevada, remained in Muslim hands under the Nasrid dynasty.

If it is relatively easy to accept the basic fact of a shift from Muslim to Christian dominance in the Mediterranean world, it is much harder to find an explanation for this change. Theories range from crude cultural superiority to subtler hypotheses involving differential technological and agrarian development, political and military structure, metallic and commercial balance, or demographics and reaction to the Black Death. Many economic explanations, including Lopez's perception of a commercial revolution taking place in Europe between 950 and 1350, assume that the change had to do with something new emerging in the Christian west at this period.[16] Some combination of internal European developments, some new western energy sparked urban, agrarian, and commercial growth, and propelled Europe to military and economic supremacy in the Mediterranean. Other theories, notably that of Abu-Lughod, reject this eurocentric viewpoint, looking instead at developments in other parts of the medieval world that may have created a situation conducive to the creation of "European hegemony" by the late fourteenth century. From this perspective, western access to power had nothing to do with anything inherently European but rather with setbacks and a lack of necessary dynamism elsewhere.[17] Neither theory includes the role of the Iberian peninsula, with its position on the Muslim–Christian frontier and its critical control of the Straits of Gibraltar, in helping to explain the shift in world balance.

The analysis of Iberian international trade holds clues, though

[16] R.S. Lopez, *The Commercial Revolution of the Middle Ages 950–1350*. [New York, 1971].

[17] J. Abu-Lughod, *Before European Hegemony, The World System A.D. 1250–1350*. [Oxford, 1989].

not full answers, to the problem of shifting economic balance and military advantage. It also presents a new perspective on an otherwise fairly familiar landscape. The peninsula (with or without its trade) has been strikingly neglected by modern scholars, who have perpetuated the paradoxical image of Spain as a marginal element in the medieval world. Iberian history has been perceived as removed from mainstream medieval European history, nor has it been central to the concerns of historians studying the Islamic world. After the coming of Islam, the Iberian peninsula lapsed into a historiographical no-man's land, a border territory which fell between two fields. Thus, medievalists have tended to concentrate on isolation, difference, and the unique nature of Spain, without seeking to integrate the peninsula within a wider context. Textbooks on medieval Europe abandon their coverage at the Pyrenees (with perhaps a passing reference to the Compostela pilgrimage), and even works devoted to the medieval encounter between Christianity and Islam tend to neglect the western frontier after a brief mention of Poitiers, Roncevalles, and translators in Toledo. In contrast, the brilliance of Andalusi culture usually wins it a nostalgic place in textbooks on Islamic history, but the brief chapter on Muslim Spain often seems awkwardly grafted into a book otherwise devoted to Near Eastern affairs. Even books seeking to emphasize a "world system" in the middle ages conspicuously remove the Iberian peninsula from integration – or even contact – with other regions.[18] Only in a later period, with Braudel's perception of a "Mediterranean world", does Spain emerge as an integral element in the European–Mediterranean scene.

Two Iberian factors contribute to make this vision of an all-embracing Mediterranean world seem more possible in the sixteenth century than in the twelfth century. First, the fact that by the sixteenth century the Iberian peninsula was no longer betwixt and between, but had become part of Europe. Second, the control of the Straits of Gibraltar by Christian Iberian rulers allowed for the maritime union of northern Europe and the Mediterranean. Before Christian victories in Spain, this union had been impossible. After it was achieved, an entirely new north–south commercial system emerged, with the peninsula at

[18] See, for example, Abu-Lughod's map of the world system in the 13th century (Abu-Lughod, *Before European Hegemony*, p. 34).

its southern edge. Christian victories in the eleventh, twelfth and early thirteenth centuries destroyed al-Andalus and the Muslim Mediterranean trading axis, but they made way for the realignment of the Iberian peninsula with Europe and for the opening of the Atlantic.

For almost exactly five hundred years, from 711 to 1212, al-Andalus had been a Muslim country, the western edge of a world which stretched eastward as far as India. The focus of Andalusi life had been on the Mediterranean and the Near East, with scholars traveling to Baghdad and Cairo, merchants trading with Alexandria and Tunis, and pilgrims making their way to Mecca and Jerusalem. By the late thirteenth century, Iberian society and economy had been refocused toward the Atlantic and northern Europe. Al-Andalus had virtually ceased to exist, and the peninsula was now a largely Christian domain, an aspiring southern adjunct to the European cultural and commercial sphere, learning a new orientation toward Paris, Bruges, London, Genoa, and Rome. The peninsula remained a part of the Mediterranean world, yet its Atlantic coasts took on a new dimension as sea routes connected the Mediterranean with the Bay of Biscay and the North Sea. Meanwhile, without the Mediterranean axis, traders in the Muslim world shifted their international business eastward to the Red Sea and Indian Ocean, away from the Mediterranean.

The function of Iberian markets also changed with the opening of the Atlantic and the commercial realignment of the peninsula toward Europe. Once, Andalusi markets had served both indigenous and foreign merchants, exported a wide variety of goods, imported eastern commodities, and functioned as points of commercial access linking Christian trade with the Muslim Mediterranean system. In the thirteenth to fifteenth centuries, in contrast, trade between northern Europe and markets in Castile, Aragon, and Granada was less well balanced. By this period, peninsular commerce had fragmented between different trading zones, with those of the south almost completely controlled by foreign traders. To a large extent, the peninsula's economy was now dependent on the economy of northern Europe. Spain no longer produced a variety of raw and manufactured goods, but instead peninsular exports narrowed to a limited number of raw materials geared to meet foreign demand (and mostly produced in competition with superior varieties from elsewhere). At the same time, Iberian consumers continued to demand a wide range of imports from both northern Europe and the Mediterranean. Southern Iberian ports still functioned as markets for sale and transfer, but they were no longer important termini nor did they control their own commerce. By the fourteenth century, they served mainly as points of transshipment along the route between the Mediterranean and the Atlantic. Ironically, the peninsular paradox had intensified by the late middle ages, and Iberian commerce from the thirteenth to the fifteenth century was less well integrated within the European economy than had been Andalusi trade within the Islamic world from the tenth to the late twelfth century. Now at the southern tip of the western Christian world, the Iberian peninsula had become part – yet not fully part – of Europe.

Chapter 2

AL-ANDALUS WITHIN THE MEDITERRANEAN NETWORK: GEOGRAPHY, ROUTES, AND COMMUNICATIONS BEFORE THE THIRTEENTH-CENTURY

ANDALUSI GEOGRAPHY AND PORTS

Geography, routes, and patterns of communication hold the key to understanding the role of al-Andalus within the network of medieval Mediterranean trade. Until the early twelfth century, the northern Mediterranean littoral was the realm of Christian coastal trade, while the southern shores were entirely in Muslim hands. The Iberian peninsula was one of the two places in the western Mediterranean, together with the nexus of Ifriqiya–Sicily, where Christian and Muslim shipping routes met. Thus, several advantages combined to maintain the region as a strategic participant in Mediterranean commerce throughout the medieval period: first, its role as a commercial frontier and transfer zone between the Islamic and Christian trading spheres; second, its geographical potential to benefit from or even manipulate this trade; and lastly its own economic consumption and productivity.

Most commercial itineraries to and from Andalusi ports relied upon maritime routes. Except in the case of Andalusi commerce with the Christian Spanish kingdoms to its north, for which there is significant evidence of overland transit, merchants from other regions of the Islamic world and southern Europe almost always made their way to and from al-Andalus by sea. Medieval navigators generally preferred to keep their vessels close to the coast, and thus the safest and most convenient north–south routes between northern Italy, southern France, and North Africa lay along the Iberian coast, passing through the Balearic Sea. Because the east coast of the peninsula was so well suited as a shipping channel, routes along this coast remained virtually unchanged throughout the period of Islamic rule.

The tenth-century geographer Ibn Ḥawqal described this coastal route in his notes on southern Europe, and the historian Rāzī, his contemporary, likewise remarked that in order to reach al-Andalus from Europe it was necessary to pass through the channel between Mallorca and the mainland.[1] In the early twelfth century, when Italian merchants were beginning to play a role in Andalusi trade, a Genoese boat sailing home from Almeria plotted a course running "between Barcelona and the Balearic Islands".[2] Later in the century, the Andalusi Jewish traveler Benjamin of Tudela would follow a similar coastal itinerary, as did the Englishman Roger of Hoveden in the 1190s.[3] Control of this *route des îles*, and of the Balearic islands which defined it, was critical to the development of Muslim and later Christian commercial shipping.[4] The channel between the Balearics and the mainland was carefully monitored and patrolled by fleets from Valencia, Denia, Barcelona, and Mallorca, and it was often necessary for other maritime powers to negotiate their access to the waterway.

"Al-Andalus possesses a number of remarkable sea ports on its Atlantic and Mediterranean coasts," wrote Rāzī, and these "are frequented by many ships, bringing in merchandise from abroad and carrying away [goods purchased in Iberian markets]."[5] Andalusi ports were well situated to benefit from coastal shipping through the Balearic Sea, the Alboran Sea, and the Straits of

[1] Ibn Ḥawqal, *Kitāb ṣurat al-arḍ*. [ed. J.H. Kramers, Leiden, 1938], p. 194; Rāzī, "La 'Description de l'Espagne' d'Ahmad al-Rāzī" [trans. E. Lévi-Provençal], *Al-Andalus* 18(1953), p. 60.

[2] Petrus Guillelmus, *Miracula beati Aegidii*. [ed. P. Jaffé, MGH Scriptores (in folio), Hanover, 1856] XII, p. 321.

[3] Benjamin of Tudela, "The Itinerary of Benjamin of Tudela" [trans. M.N. Adler], *Jewish Quarterly Review* 16(1904), pp. 467–70; Roger of Hoveden, *Cronica*. [ed. W. Stubbs, London, 1868–71] III, pp. 46–52. Roger's journey followed an identical route to that which we find in Arabic geographies. In fact, this route is so traditional that J. Vernet has suggested that Roger borrowed his account from an earlier text ("La cartografía náutica, ¿Tiene un origen hispano-árabe?" *Madrid: MDI* 1(1953), p. 67).

[4] On the importance of the *route des îles*, see J. Pryor, *Geography, Technology, and War*. [Cambridge, 1988], pp. 109–11, and J. Ruiz Domenec, "Ruta de las especias/ruta de las islas: apuntes para una nueva periodización," 10(1980), pp. 689–97.

[5] Rāzī, "Description" (English translation from French translation by Lévi-Provençal), p. 63.

Gibraltar. Maritime travelers along the eastern and southern Andalusi coast had a wide choice of harbors in which to stop for trade, supplies, repairs, shelter, or commercial information. Cities generally provided the best markets for international business, a fact recognized in a twelfth-century anecdote in which an Arab merchant admonished his son to "take your goods to the large cities even if you believe that you will sell there more cheaply".[6] Among the most important Iberian ports in the medieval period, working northward along the Mediterranean coast from Gibraltar, were Algeciras, Malaga, Almeria, Cartagena, Alicante, Denia, and Valencia. To the south-west, Seville, with access into the Atlantic, dominated the western coast and Straits of Gibraltar. The naval use and commercial popularity of these different ports fluctuated over time, but most remained active throughout the Muslim period.

Almeria (*al-Mariyya*) was the premier Mediterranean port of Muslim Spain, and described by one twelfth-century Arab geographer as the "key" to Andalusi commerce.[7] The maritime importance of Almeria is demonstrated not only by lavish descriptions in geographical literature, but also in Arabic and Latin chronicles and Jewish merchant letters from the Cairo Geniza collection.[8] The economy of Muslim Almeria was based on two industries, commercial shipping and the production of silk. Already in the early tenth century, Rāzī had reported that Almeria was a locus of ship building and silk weaving.[9] As regards the importance of Almerian shipping, an Andalusi poet once explained: "I was asked whether [the city] had any means of subsistence, and I replied, '[Yes,] if the wind blows'."[10] The city achieved the

[6] Petrus Alfonsi, *The "Disciplina clericalis" of Petrus Alfonsi*. [trans. P.R. Quarrie, London, 1977], p. 135.

[7] Ibn Ghālib, "Naṣṣ andalusī jadīd qaṭʿīa min kitāb farḥa al-anfūs li-Ibn Ghālib" [ed. L. 'Abd al-Badī], *Majalla ma'had al-makhṭūṭāt al-'arabiya* 1(1955), p. 283.

[8] A brief selection of recent studies on Almeria includes a lengthy work by J.A. Tapia Garrido, *Almería musulmana*. [Almeria, 1986] and briefer survey by A.A. Salim, *Ta'rīkh madīnat al-Mariyya al-Andalusiyya*. [Alexandria, 1984]; as well as articles by E. Molina López, "Algunas consideraciones sobre la vida socio-económica de Almería en el siglo XI y primera mitad del XII," *Actas del IV Coloquio hispano-tunecino* [*Palma, 1979*]. [Madrid, 1983], pp. 181–96; and L. Torres Balbás, "Almería islámica," *Al-Andalus* 22(1957), pp. 411–53.

[9] Rāzī, "Description," p. 67.

[10] Ḥimyarī, *La Péninsule ibérique au moyen âge d'après le 'Kitāb ar-rawḍ al-mi'ṭār fī habar al-akhtār*." [ed. E. Lévi-Provençal, Leiden, 1938], p. 183.

apex of its commercial success in the eleventh and twelfth centuries, when Geniza letters amply demonstrate its importance as an international port. Several letters mention foreign mercantile shipping in Almeria, or refer to the arrival in Egypt of ships from this city.[11] Maqqarī recorded that "boats belonging to both Muslim and non-Muslim merchants" called at Almeria between 1069 and 1091, and the geographer ʿUdhrī (d. 1085) similarly stated that "ships arrive at her harbor and leave from there to the Maghrib and the rest of the world".[12] In the next century, Idrīsī (ca. 1154) reported that ships put into Almeria from Alexandria and Syria, and other geographers confirmed his information. Zuhrī (writing in the middle of the twelfth century) called Almeria "the harbor of al-Andalus, to which ships set off from the east and from Alexandria", adding that the city was "the emporium [*qayṣārīya*] of al-Andalus, and its shipyard", while Yāqūt (d. 1229) stated that "merchants embark [from Almeria] and here their ships arrive to engage in commerce". Saqaṭī (probably writing 1210–20) also mentioned that Almeria was a port of call for "merchants and travelers".[13]

After Almeria, Malaga (*Mālaqa*) also prospered from international commerce, and its location made it particularly suitable as a holding port for vessels awaiting a favorable wind to sail westward through the Straits of Gibraltar to Seville. The geographer Iṣṭakhrī remarked on Malaga's shipping and commerce in the tenth century, and two centuries later, Idrīsī reported that "its markets are flourishing, its commerce has a [good] turnover, and it has many advantages".[14]

On the eastern Andalusi coast, the port of Denia (*Dāniya*) handled much of the commerce with the Balearics, as well as traffic to and from the eastern Mediterranean. The biographer

[11] See, for example, TS 13 J 16.19; TS 8 J 20.2; TS 8 J 18.1; Bodl d74.41.

[12] Maqqarī, *Nafḥ al-ṭīb min ghuṣn al-Andalus al-raṭīb*. [Cairo, 1949] v, p. 110; or *Analectes sur l'histoire et la littérature des arabes d'Espagne*. [ed. R. Dozy, Leiden, 1855–60] II, pp. 386–7. ʿUdhrī, "Nuṣūṣ ʿan al-Andalus" [in *Tarḍīʿ al-akhbār wa tanwīʿ al-'athār*. ed. A.A. Ahwānī, Madrid, 1960], pp.85–6.

[13] Idrīsī, *Opus geographicum*. v, [Rome-Naples, 1975] p. 562; Zuhrī, "Kitāb al-djaʿrāfiyya" [ed. M. Hadj-Sadok] *Bulletin des études orientales* 21(1968), p. 206; Yāqūt: *Muʿjam al-buldān*. (*Jacut's Geographisches Worterbuch*.) [ed. F. Wüstenfeld, Leipzig, 1873] IV, p. 517; Saqaṭī, *Kitāb al-faqīh al-ajall al-ʿālim al-ʿārif al-awḥad* [*Un manuel hispanique de ḥisba*). [eds. G.S. Colin and E. Lévi-Provençal, Paris, 1931], p. 55.

[14] Iṣṭakhrī, *Kitāb al-masālik wa al-mamālik*. [ed. M.J. de Goeje, *BGA*, 2nd edn, I, Leiden, 1967], p. 42; Idrīsī, *Opus*, v, p. 565.

Ibn al-ʿAbbār mentioned a scholar setting off on a pilgrimage to Mecca from Denia in the early eleventh century, and Geniza letters cited boats arriving in Alexandria from Denia during the 1060s and 1070s.[15] The twelfth-century Jewish historian Abraham ben Daud also remarked that at roughly this period, "Denia was fully settled, and possessed mastery over the sea."[16] Later, Idrīsī wrote that "boats travel to this city, and many of them are built [in Denia] because there are shipyards. Fleets leave from here for raids, and ships set out from here for the distant east."[17] One such vessel was mentioned in a letter sent from Alexandria to Old Cairo, ca. 1156, reporting that "the ship from Denia has just arrived, carrying the rest of the goods, including silk and mercury . . ."[18]

North of Denia, Valencia (*Balansiya*) became an important port during the Taifa period. The city served as a center for Andalusi coastal trade, and an outlet for the rich agricultural regions inland, but there is little evidence that it participated in direct shipping to the Maghrib or Near East while under Islamic rule. It is probable, however, that the city took part in trade along the Levant coast, to the Balearics, and later to southern Europe. Certainly, when Ibn Ḥazm (d. 1064) wanted to travel quickly from Almeria to Valencia, he went by ship.[19] Although Valencia does not appear in Geniza letters, Idrīsī cited the city's "many merchants . . . its markets and commercial activity, and [the] departure and arrival [of ships?]" to the city.[20] By the middle of the twelfth century, Genoese merchants included Valencia in their commercial circuit, and their contracts indicate that the city served as an outlet for Andalusi goods exported to Christian ports along the north-west Mediterranean rim.

The location of Malaga, Almeria, Denia, Valencia, and the smaller towns along the Mediterranean coast gave these ports

[15] Ibn al-ʿAbbār, *Kitāb al-takmila li-kitāb al-ṣila*. [ed. F. Codera, *BAH*, v, Madrid, 1886], p. 118, # 409; TS 13 J 16.19 and TS 10 J 16.17.

[16] Abraham ben Daud, *Sefer ha-qabbalah* [*The Book of Tradition*]. [trans. G.D. Cohen, Philadelphia, 1967], pp. 82–3.

[17] Idrīsī, *Opus*, v, p. 557.

[18] T.S. 10 J 14.16.

[19] Ibn Ḥazm, *Ṭawq al-ḥamāma*. [ed. T.A. Makkī, Cairo, 1975], p. 156. A passage from Alfonso X's *Primera crónica general de España*, said to be a translation from the Valencian author Ibn al-Qama (1036–1107), extolled the economic importance of Valencia's harbor (ed. R. Menéndez Pidal [Madrid, 1906, reprint 1977] II, p. 578).

[20] Idrīsī, *Opus*, v, p. 556.

importance both as Andalusi markets and as places to stop along a longer Mediterranean itinerary. In contrast, the geographical position of Seville (*Ishbīliya*), the largest port west of the Straits of Gibraltar, supported a different function. Control of ports to the west of the Straits allowed control of the passage through the Straits themselves, and this made Seville strategically valuable. Under the Almohads, Seville became the Andalusi capital, and in consequence it was the Christian conquest of Seville in 1248, rather than the fall of Cordoba twelve years previously, which marked the apex of Castilian expansion in the thirteenth century.

In order to reach Seville from the Mediterranean, ships had to sail westward through the Straits, a journey that was often made difficult by adverse winds and currents. Unless the vessel were equipped with oars, or could wait in a holding port east of the Straits for a favorable wind, the passage into the Atlantic could be slow and arduous. Ships emerging from the Mediterranean had little recourse, except retreat, if they found a hostile fleet waiting on the Atlantic side.[21] Nevertheless, Seville was clearly part of the larger network of Islamic Mediterranean trade, which suggests that merchant vessels were permitted to traffic freely through the Straits. It is possible that some merchants arrived in al-Andalus through one of the Levant ports, came overland to Seville, then took a ship from there for the relatively easy return journey eastward into the Mediterranean. However, such a pattern could not have predominated in Sevillian trade. Geniza letters show Seville in direct commercial contact with the eastern Mediterranean by the eleventh century. A letter written ca. 1055–60 noted the transit of a Sevillian boat from Alexandria to the west, and another, from ca. 1140, indicated that it was possible to sail from Gabes to Seville in as little as eight days.[22] Maimonides (d. 1204) also remarked on boats traveling between Seville and Alexandria.[23] Genoese merchants

[21] The complications of westward transit through the Straits have been described by A. Lewis, "Northern European Sea Power and the Straits of Gibraltar, 1031–1350 AD," *Order and Innovation in the Middle Ages: Essays in Honor of Joseph R. Strayer.* [Princeton, 1976], pp. 139–65.

[22] T.S. 8 J 27.2. This boat is called *al-markab al-ishfīlī*, which could mean either "the Sevillian boat" or "the boat belonging to a man from Seville." It is possible that the boat was not actually from the city itself, but merely belonged to a Sevillian trading in the Near East.

[23] Moses b. Maimon, *Responsa.* [ed. J. Blau, Jerusalem, 1957] II, p. 576.

were trading with Seville in the early thirteenth century, as were the Catalans by 1227.

Seville was esteemed as "one of the best ports in al-Andalus," even though the city was situated fifty miles from the sea on the Guadalquivir River (*Wādi al-kabīr*).[24] Other Andalusi rivers were also exploited for trade, but the Guadalquivir carried by far the largest volume of goods.[25] Commodities coming upriver were destined not only for Seville, but also for markets further inland.

One of these markets was Cordoba, the Umayyad capital, located along the Guadalquivir upstream from Seville. As Idrīsī remarked, "anybody who wants to travel to Cordoba from Seville [can] get on a boat and travel upstream by river."[26] River traffic provided a boon for the city, and brought more business to Cordoban markets than to any other inland Andalusi city. Umayyad Cordoba was the largest urban center in the peninsula, and tenth-century geographers marveled at the size and splendor of this flourishing metropolis. According to Ibn Ḥawqal, Cordoba had "no equal in the Maghrib, or in the Jazira, or Syria, or Egypt, to approximate the size of its population, extent of its territory, area of its markets, cleanliness of its inhabitants, construction of its mosques, and number of its baths and hostelries." Muqaddasī also commented favorably on the markets and extensive commercial activity found in Cordoba, while Ibn Ḥayyān and Masʿūdī remarked on the many boats traveling up and downstream past the city.[27] Umayyad Cordoba was also a hub for travel, since most of the principal Andalusi routes passed through the capital. The city's strategic importance was enhanced by the fact that, since Roman times, Cordoba had been the site of the best bridge over the Guadalquivir.

Although Cordoba was an important commercial center

[24] Rāzī, "Description," p. 93.

[25] Muslim geographers note a number of smaller Andalusi rivers, including the Ebro, Tagus, Duero, and Guadiana, as arteries for trade. Many of these were only navigable by small barges, not large ships, but remained important routes of access to the interior. Visigothic law codes also indicate the use of Iberian rivers in the sixth and seventh centuries.

[26] Idrīsī, *Opus*, v, p. 574.

[27] Ibn Ḥawqal, *Kitāb*, p. 111; Muqaddasī, *Description de l'occident musulman au IVe = Xe siècle*. [ed. C. Pellat, Paris, 1950], pp. 33–5; Ibn Ḥayyān, *Muqtabis*. II [ed. M.A. al-Makkī, Beirut, 1973], p. 19; Masʿūdī, *Kitāb at-tanbih wa al-ishrāf*. [ed. M.J. de Goeje, *BGA*, 2nd edn, VIII, Leiden, 1967], p. 68.

within the Andalusi trading sphere, it was never an international market on the scale of Seville or Almeria. Nor was Cordoba ever described as a port, since river passage along the Guadalquivir above Seville was not accessible to sea-going vessels. In consequence, it appears that fewer foreign merchants came to Cordoba than to the Andalusi maritime cities. Goods coming up the Guadalquivir to the capital would have been transshipped to smaller river barges at Seville, and were probably handed over to local merchants at that time. After the demise of Umayyad power in the early eleventh century, Cordoba's commercial influence declined, and later sources only describe the city briefly, providing little commercial information other than noting the presence of various ateliers, markets, and hostelries.[28]

ANDALUSI SHIPPING

Andalusi port cities were of particular importance to international trade because most goods and merchandise traveled to and from the peninsula by sea. Any contact with the Muslim world involved a maritime journey, and most traders from Europe also preferred to come by water. Almeria, Seville, and other Andalusi ports were as famous for their shipyards and harbors as for their warehouses and markets, and they served as both naval and mercantile centers. Thus, before describing the maritime routes that linked these cities with other regions of the Mediterranean, it will be useful to look briefly at the ships that traveled these routes.

Most Mediterranean merchant ships were powered by sails, and they tended to be larger, rounder, and slower than the oar-powered galleys which made up naval squadrons. Galleys, in contrast to round ships, had long narrow hulls, making them fast and highly maneuverable, although their shallow draft rendered them unsuitable for the transport of cargo or for use in heavy seas. Merchant ships were more stable, yet even they tended to avoid winter travel. Triangular, or lateen, sails were commonly used by both Arab and Christian ships in the medieval Mediterranean. These sails were preferred for their versatility, although square sails were not unknown. Studies of the

[28] Idrīsī, *Opus*, v, p. 575; Ḥimyarī, *Péninsule*, p. 153; Yāqūt, *Mu'jām*, iv, pp. 58–61. On Cordoba in the Taifa period, see M.A. Khallāf, *Qurṭuba al-islāmiyya*. [Tunis, 1984].

length of commercial voyages suggest that merchant vessels relied almost exclusively on the wind for their power, despite the fact that some Mediterranean ship types (notably the *tarida*) were designed for the use of both sails and oars. While propelled by sails, merchant ships could be directed by one or two steering oars in the rear of the vessel.[29]

Aside from more general Mediterranean data, we have evidence on Andalusi shipping from a variety of sources, both written and pictorial.[30] The latter tend to be more informative, yet they are harder to pin down in terms of date and provenance. Several of the Pisan *bacini* (ceramic dishes used for architectural ornamentation) depict ships. Of these, two eleventh-century bowls made in the Balearics show three-masted ships with lateen sails (in one case the rear sail is not rigged), each with a high stern-castle and curved prow. In the foreground we see smaller oared boats, one with a single mast and lateen sail, perhaps carrying passengers to or from the larger ship.[31] These vessels must be similar to those launched by Ibn Mujāhid, the ruler of Denia (1044–75), who figures as a ship-owner in Geniza documents.

Arabic documents provide a wealth of maritime vocabulary and technical names for the vessels that carried merchants be-

[29] A. Udovitch, "Time, the Sea and Society: Duration of Commercial Voyages on the Southern Shores of the Mediterranean during the High Middle Ages," *La navigazione mediterranea nell'alto medioevo*. [Spoleto, 1978], p. 517.
Medieval Mediterranean shipping and maritime technology has been described by J. Pryor, *Geography, Technology, and War*. See also E.H. Byrne, *Genoese Shipping in the Twelfth and Thirteenth centuries*. [Cambridge, Mass., 1930]; B. Kreutz, "Ships, Shipping, and the Implications of Change in the Early Medieval Mediterranean," *Viator* 7(1976), pp. 79–107; R.W. Unger, *The Ship in the Medieval Economy (600–1600)*. [London, 1980]; A. Lewis and T. Runyon, *European Naval and Maritime History 300–1500*. [Bloomington, Indiana, 1985].

[30] I know of no data on Andalusi vessels derived from underwater archeology, although information on wrecks has been of great value to our knowledge of medieval shipping in other areas of the Mediterranean. Investigations of the early medieval Yassi Ada ship and the eleventh-century Serçe Liman vessel have told much about shipping in the eastern Mediterranean. An Arab wreck (probably tenth century) has also been found off the French coast near Cannes. Much of its cargo has been retrieved, including ceramics, but there is no proof of an Andalusi connection. See M.J.P. Joncherey, "Le navire de Bataiguier," *Archéologia* 85(1975), p. 43.

[31] J.H. Pryor and D. Nicolle link these *bacini* dishes depicting ships to the Balearics (or possibly Tunisia). See J.H. Pryor, "The Medieval Muslim Ships of the Pisan Bacini," *The Mariners Mirror* 76(1990), pp. 99–113; D. Nicolle, "Shipping in Islamic Art: Seventh through Sixteenth Century AD," *The American Neptune* 49 (1989), pp. 172–3. In contrast, G. Berti and L. Tongiorgi note these two *bacini* as unusual, and perhaps Spanish, but they do not mention the Balearics (*I bacini ceramici medievali delle chiese di Pisa*. [Rome, 1981], pp. 191–2).

1 Dish showing three-masted Muslim ship, probably from the Balearics, eleventh century (Soprintendenza ai Beni Ambientale, Architettonici, Artistici e Storici di Pisa)

tween Andalusi ports and other areas of the Mediterranean. However, it is not always possible to determine the type of vessel merely from the word used to describe it. In some cases this is because authors (landlubbers, in many cases) were imprecise in their terminology, but often we simply do not know the precise application of maritime terms. Andalusi Muslim sources cite a variety of vessels. For example, in a sample contract for the hire of boats, the jurist Jazīrī (d. 1189) referred to *shānī*, *kharrāq*, *dughaiyaṣ*, and *zawraq* (respectively translatable as a galley, sailing boat, transport vessel, and skiff), but made no

2 Dish showing three-masted Muslim ship, probably from the Balearics, eleventh century (Soprintendenza ai Beni Ambientale, Architettonici, Artistici e Storici di Pisa)

particular differentiation between them in terms of use or legal status.[32] On top of this, names for ships varied with time and place, so that the term for a large sailing vessel in one port might signify a small barge in another. In Arabic and Judeo-Arabic materials, ships were often referred to by the generic terms *markab*, *qārib*, or *safīna*, but we also find many other types of

[32] Jazīrī, *Maqṣūd al-maḥmūd fī talkhīṣ al-ʿuqūd*. [Miguel Asín Institute, CSIC, Madrid] ms. 5, fol. 47v. For *shānī* and *dughaiyaṣ* see R. Dozy, *Supplément aux dictionnaires arabes*. [Leiden, 1881] 1, pp. 447, 717.

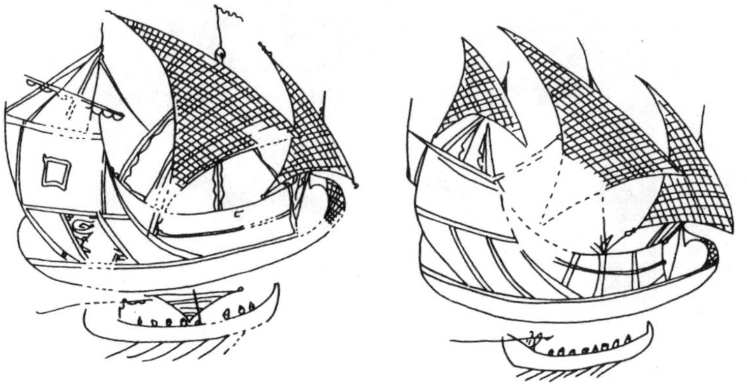

3 Drawing of the two Bacini ships (courtesy of D. Nicolle, *The American Neptune* 49 (1989) p. 172)

vessel. A Geniza letter from the 1130s notes the fact that a *shaḥṭūra* had reached Almeria from Alexandria in sixty-five days, arriving ahead of two sailing ships that had left Egypt at the same time. Goitein speculated that a *shaḥṭūra* – the term appears frequently in Geniza records – was a type of open barge propelled by oars and used in Mediterranean trade during the summer (this particular vessel reached Spain in early July).[33] In another instance, a barge seems to have proved more sturdy than a sailing vessel, since when the two were journeying in convoy between Tripoli and Seville, ca. 1140, the larger ship sank, leaving the barge to rescue its unfortunate passengers.[34]

Nevertheless, sails remained the norm. Geniza writers often remark on the winds, as in the letter from Alexandria complaining that no ships "except one large Andalusi one" had arrived for over a month, since the winds had been uncooperative, blowing "from neither east or west."[35] The expectation, clearly, was that merchant vessels were powered by the wind. In another example, Judah Ha-Levi was delayed in Egypt for several days waiting for a west wind to carry him to Palestine, although ships heading eastward to Spain, Sicily,

[33] Bodl d74.41; S.D. Goitein *A Mediterranean Society*. [Berkeley, 1967–88] 1, pp. 305, 325.

[34] TS 16.54. Goitein, *Mediterranean Society*, 1, pp. 305–6.

[35] S.D. Goitein, "The Unity of the Mediterranean World in the 'Middle' Middle Ages," *Studia Islamica* 12 (1960), p. 40.

4 Thirteenth-century Castilian merchant ship from the *Cántigas de Santa María*, CLXXII (courtesy of the Patrimonio Nacional, Madrid)

and the Maghrib had already departed on a favorable east wind.[36]

Mediterranean vessels varied in size, and a ship described as "large" may have held several hundred passengers. In the middle of the eleventh century, Usamah b. Munqidh mentioned a ship carrying four hundred pilgrims from the Maghrib to the eastern Mediterranean.[37] Geniza letters from the next century confirm these numbers. One mentioned a boat traveling to Seville with "thirty-six or thirty-seven Jews and nearly three hundred Muslims," while another referred to a ship bringing four hundred people from Palermo to Alexandria.[38] At about the same time, Ibn Jubayr described a Genoese ship carrying two hundred Maghribi pilgrims home from Egypt.[39]

[36] ULC Or1080 J 258; S.D. Goitein, "The Biography of Judah Ha-Levi in the Light of the Cairo Geniza Documents," *Proceedings of the American Academy for Jewish Research* 28 (1959), p. 55.

[37] Usamah b. Munqidh, *Kitāb al-ʿitibār*. (*Ousāma ibn Mounkidh, un émir syrien au premier siècle des croisades* [*1095–1188*].) [ed. H. Derenbourg, Paris, 1886–93] 1.2, p. 61.

[38] Goitein, *Mediterranean Society*, 1, p. 315.

[39] Ibn Jubayr, *The Travels of Ibn Jubair*. [trans. R.J.C. Broadhurst, London, 1952] p. 362.

We know somewhat more about the Christian ships that traveled to and from Iberian ports during the twelfth and thirteenth centuries. Spanish ships are depicted in the famous thirteenth-century Castilian *Cántigas de Santa María*, which includes several tales of merchants, crusaders, or pilgrims rescued from shipwreck by divine intervention, as well as other stories involving ships. Most of the vessels illustrated are round ships with two or three masts rigged with either square or lateen sails, again with high curved stern-castles, and a rear steering oar.[40] These Castilian vessels are clearly from the same tradition of maritime architecture as the Muslim Balearic ships depicted on the *bacini*. Genoese notarial contracts also refer to sailing ships, usually with the generic term *navis* or, more rarely, *bucius*.[41] Italian round ships generally had two masts, lateen sails, and several decks to hold passengers and cargo.[42] Overall, these vessels were probably quite similar to the ships illustrated in the *Cántigas de Santa María*, particularly since Castilian shipping was largely controlled by the Genoese at the time this manuscript was created. Until the end of the thirteenth century, the design of Muslim and Christian merchant ships in the Mediterranean retained similarities born of common heritage. This would change with the establishment of regular shipping routes through the Straits of Gibraltar at the end of the century, as Christian Mediterranean ships began to adopt the characteristics of their sturdier, square-sailed, counterparts from northern Europe.

AL-ANDALUS AND THE MUSLIM MEDITERRANEAN COMMERCIAL NETWORK

Goods and merchants traveled far afield from Andalusi ports, and there is evidence of Andalusi commercial contact with most regions of the Mediterranean world. The position of the Iberian peninsula in international trade was nothing new; it had been an integral element in the Roman trading sphere (leading Pliny to

[40] Boats are pictured in *Cántigas* numbers 9, 5, 23, 25, 35, 36, 65, 95, 112, 115, 172, 176, 183, and 193. See J. Guerrero Lovillo, *Las Cántigas, estudio arqueológico de sus miniaturas*. [Madrid, 1949], pp. 324–39.

[41] H.C. Krueger has suggested that the *bucius* was only employed in the western Mediterranean for trading runs to Sicily, Spain, and North Africa (*Navi e proprietà navale a Genova secondo metà del secolo XII*. [Genoa, 1985], pp. 25–7).

[42] R.W. Unger, "Warships and Cargo Ships in Medieval Europe," *Technology and Culture* 22 (1981), pp. 236–7.

praise the dye-stuffs of Merida and other Iberian exports), and the peninsula maintained its commercial importance into Visigothic times.[43] Iberian sources mention the presence of foreign merchants in Visigothic territories, and Gregory of Tours cited maritime traffic between Iberia and Marseille.[44] An early seventh-century source later reported that "some Greek merchants came in ships from the Orient . . . and landed upon the coasts of Spain."[45] There is even evidence for an Atlantic trade route between the Mediterranean and Britain, before the sixth century, which would have passed through the Straits of Gibraltar and along the Iberian coast.[46]

Just as the peninsula was very much a part of the late antique commercial sphere, so it was quickly incorporated into the Islamic Mediterranean world. Travel between al-Andalus and other regions of the Mediterranean world is well attested from soon after 711, when armies, fugitives, pilgrims, diplomats, and scholars left traces of their journeys. A party of merchants are recorded as traveling from al-Andalus to Mecca, by way of Qayrawan, as early as 763.[47] Ibn Khurradādhbih described the itineraries of Jewish merchants traveling between the peninsula and the Near East in the ninth century, and in the next century, Muqaddasī remarked that "the inhabitants . . . of al-Andalus are [among] the people most experienced with the sea . . . they have routes across this sea to Egypt and Syria."[48]

Southward from al-Andalus and across the sea lay the Maghrib

[43] On the role of Spain in Roman trade, see M. Grant, *The Ancient Mediterranean.* [New York, 1969], pp. 264–5. Pliny, *Natural History.* [ed. H. Rackham, Cambridge, Mass., 1983] Book IX, lxv, p. 258. On Visigothic trade, see P.D. King, *Law and Society in the Visigothic Kingdom.* [Cambridge, 1972], pp. 194–9.

[44] Gregory of Tours, *Historia Francorum.* [eds. W. Arndt and B. Krusch, *MGH* Scriptores rerum Merovingicarum I.I, Hanover, 1884] IX.22, p. 380

[45] *Vitas sanctorum patrum Emeretensium.* [ed. A. Maya Sánchez, Corpus Christianorum: Series latina, 116; Turnhout, 1992], p. 31.

[46] R. Hodges, *Dark Age Economics. The Origins of Towns and Trade AD 600–1000.* [New York, 1982], pp. 33–4. Hodges claims that this route disappeared after the late sixth century, leaving little evidence of traffic between the Mediterranean and northern Europe until the tenth and eleventh centuries. On land routes linking the peninsula and Europe in this period, see M. Rouche, "Les relations transpyrénéennes du Ve au VIIIe siècle," *Les communications dans la péninsule ibérique au moyen âge.* (Actes du Colloque de Pau, 28–9 mars 1980) [Paris, 1981], pp. 13–20.

[47] Nuwayrī, *Historia de los musulmanes de España y Africa por en-Nuguari.* [ed. M. Gaspar Remiro, Granada, 1917] Arabic text p. 5. The long gap in time between this report and the period which it describes necessitates some caution in accepting its veracity.

[48] Ibn Khurradādhbih, *Kitāb al-masālik wa al-mamālik.* [ed. M.J. de Goeje, *BGA*, 2nd edn. VI, Leiden, 1967], pp. 153–5 (M. Lombard provides an excellent map of the

(the "West") as North Africa was usually designated in Arabic. Andalusi shipping connections with ports along the Maghribi coast provided the primary link between Muslim Spain and the rest of the Islamic world. Although the sea could be choppy and unpleasant to cross in bad weather, the straits between the peninsula and North Africa are so narrow that in some places one can see the opposite coast on a clear day.[49] The eleventh-century geographer ʿUdhrī noted that ships sailed from Almeria to "the other side [of the straits] (*al-ʿidwa*) and the rest of the world," while a legal opinion (*fatwa*) of the Andalusi jurist Ibn Rushd (d. 1126) described a boat held jointly between two Andalusi merchants, one of whom wished to travel across the straits to the land on the other side (*barr al-ʿidwa*).[50]

The Maghrib was both a market for Andalusi trade and a place for transit and transshipment. Many Andalusi commercial voyagers probably traveled by sea only as far as the facing shore, then proceeded overland by caravan to their final destination. In this way, al-Andalus could remain in commercial contact with other regions of the Islamic world even in winter, when lengthy sea crossings were risky or impossible.

A medieval traveler could choose among a number of routes to make the crossing from the Iberian peninsula to the North African shore and beyond. Muslim geographers took considerable pains to enumerate these options, leaving a record of many different itineraries utilized between the ninth and fourteenth centuries. Queasy sailors might wish to employ the shortest crossing possible, embarking from Algeciras and arriving at Ceuta (a day), whereas the more seaworthy might choose a lengthier trip from Denia to Algiers (about a week), or even the long haul between Almeria and Alexandria (one or two months).[51] Some ships and their passengers made the longer

various Rādhānite routes in *The Golden Age of Islam*. [Oxford, 1975], p. 210); Muqaddasī, *Description*, p. 15.

[49] The Granadan poet Ibn Mālik (1163–1249) remarked that it was sometimes possible to see from Algeciras to Ceuta. His poem was collected by Ibn Saʿīd al-Gharnāti, *Rāyāt al-mubarrazīn wa ghāyāt al-mumayyzīn*. [Cairo, 1393/1973], pp. 85–6.

[50] ʿUdhrī, "Nusūs," p. 85; Ibn Rushd, *Fatāwā Ibn Rushd*. [ed. Ibn al-Tāhir al-Talīlī, Beirut, 1407/1987,] p. 836.

[51] The longer the journey, the more variable the length. One Geniza letter (Bodl d74.41, written ca. 1130) reported that the trip from Alexandria to Almeria took sixty-five days, while Idrīsī (*Opus*, v, p. 582) cited thirty-six days for the transit from Spain to Antioch. J. Mann noted that a letter sent between Umayyad Spain and Iraq

voyages direct, while others dropped into various ports along the way. However, even if the trip was only a brief hop from shore to shore, voyages to and from Andalusi ports were legally classed as sea journeys rather than coastal travel. Yaḥyā b. ʿUmar, a ninth-century Tunisian jurist, outlined an explicit distinction relating to the hire of ships for voyages from Tunisia to Egypt, Sicily, and al-Andalus. According to his ruling (which was frequently cited by later jurists), a trip to Egypt went along the coast (*rīf*), while a journey to Sicily or al-Andalus went by sea (*ʿalā al-baḥr*). Because of this differentiation between coastal and open-sea travel, the captain of the hired vessel had different rights and responsibilities according to his destination and the type of route followed.[52]

The popularity of particular routes and ports varied over time. Tunis, for example, was not a popular destination for Andalusi ships during the tenth century, perhaps owing to Umayyad-Fatimid hostilities before 969, but had become an important market for Andalusi goods and merchants by the eleventh century. At this period, the geographer Bakrī reported many more maritime routes across the Alboran Sea (roughly the triangle of sea with corners at Gibraltar, Algiers, and Denia) than seen previously.[53] The complications of Taifa politics may explain this apparent proliferation of sea crossings in the eleventh century, because unlike the relatively stable Umayyad regime (which utilized only a few controlled and established ports), the individual Taifa kingdoms developed a number of smaller ports and diversified their trading contacts. The number of routes between al-Andalus and North Africa may have declined somewhat in the Almoravid and Almohad periods, for Idrīsī cited many fewer routes in the twelfth century than those noted by Bakrī in the century before. It is probable that the Berber dynasties sought to control traffic to and from their territories by concentrating merchant access to a certain number of specified ports. Nevertheless, despite the

could take a year to arrive ("The Responsa of the Babylonian Geonim as a Source of Jewish History," *Jewish Quarterly Review* 7 (1916–17), p. 486).

52 The first citation which I have found to this *fatwa* is in the Ibn Abī Firās, *Kitāb akriyat al-sufun*. [ed. M.A. Tahir] *Cahiers de Tunisie* 31 (1983), p.28. It is also cited by Jazīrī (d. 585/1189) in his *Maqsud al-maḥmūd*, fol. 55r; and by Wansharīsī, *Miʿyār al-muʿrib wa al-jāmiʿ al-maghrib*. [ed. M. Hajjī, Rabat-Beirut, 1981] VIII, pp. 310–11.

53 Bakrī, *Description de l'Afrique septentrionale par Abou-Obeid El-Bakri*. [ed. M. de Slane, Paris, 1911 (reprint 1965)] Arabic text pp. 89–99.

reduction in active ports, commerce between Muslim Spain and the Maghrib appears to have flourished under these regimes, presumably aided by the fact that the entire area was controlled by a single authority.

The Moroccan inland cities of Fez and Marrakesh had long been part of the Andalusi trading sphere, but commerce probably increased after the late eleventh century with their growing prestige under the Almoravid and Almohad regimes. Fez, in particular, was well situated to maintain trading ties with al-Andalus. In the middle of the twelfth century, an Andalusi Jewish merchant wrote home to his father in Almeria to say that he had arrived safely in Fez, with five camel loads of goods. This journey would have taken about a week from Ceuta, according to Idrīsī.[54] Another Geniza missive, written ca. 1110, noted a purchase made in Fez with Andalusi coins.[55] The geographer Zuhrī likewise noted that "goods of great worth and commodities of high cost [were imported] from Yemen, Iraq, Syria, and al-Andalus" to twelfth-century Fez.[56] When a goldsmith in Fez ordered a pair of Andalusi weights and scales in 1141, he probably wanted them in order to do business more conveniently with Andalusi clients.[57]

During the same period, Geniza documents allow us to follow Andalusi merchant itineraries further inland from Fez to Marrakesh, or in the other direction from Tlemcen to Fez to al-Andalus. In the filial letter noted above, the Almerian merchant in Fez wrote that he planned to "join the first company setting out for Marrakesh." Nearly a century later, an Andalusi refugee fleeing from Seville in 1224, followed a similar overland itinerary from Ceuta to Marrakesh.[58] In another Geniza letter, sent from Fez to al-Andalus ca. 1138, Halfōn b. Nethanel (an Egyptian merchant well-known from his extensive Geniza correspondence) remarked that he had traveled from Tlemcen to Fez and intended to continue from there to Almeria.[59] By Idrīsī's reckon-

[54] TS 12.435; Idrīsī, *Opus*, v, p. 532. See also R. Le Tourneau, *Fez in the Age of the Marinids*. [Norman, Oklahoma, 1961], p. 113.

[55] Bodl d66.52; A purchase of perfume was paid for in "Andalusī *mithqāls*." Whether or not these coins had arrived in Fez with the purchaser, their circulation in Morocco shows economic contact between al-Andalus and this city.

[56] Zuhrī, "Kitāb," p. 193.

[57] TS 13 J 21.12.

[58] Ḥimyarī, *Péninsule*, p. 86.

[59] TS 12.435 and TS 8 J 19.28.

ing, his trip from Tlemcen to Fez would have taken about nine days.[60]

Economic links also existed between al-Andalus, Fez, Marrakesh, and regions still further to the south, as testified by a coin hoard discovered near the probable site of Awdaghost, containing four Andalusi dinars from the period 1107–16, three struck in Murcia and one from Malaga. Likewise, marble stelae found in Gao, and dating from the same period (1100–10), were carved in stone imported from Almeria.[61] Such finds do not prove direct trade between the peninsula and the sub-Saharan interior, but they show that there was contact by the early twelfth century.

Many other ports further east along the Maghribi coast also received commercial maritime traffic from al-Andalus. Oran, for example, had "markets, industry, and commerce . . . much of the provisioning of the Andalusi coast [came] from here . . . prices are low and ships come here from al-Andalus."[62] Further east, the cities of Tenes, Cherchell, and Algiers also maintained close contacts with facing Andalusi ports. Tenes, particularly, had long-standing Andalusi contacts attributable to the tradition that the town had been established by Andalusi pirates in the ninth century.[63]

All ships and caravans in transit between the eastern and western basins of the Mediterranean had to pass through the central hub of Sicily and Tunisia. Political and military events frequently disrupted trade in the area, particularly after the eleventh century, but its geographical position maintained it as a crucial point of transit in all east–west Mediterranean itineraries. There is abundant evidence of Andalusi merchants and goods

[60] Idrīsī, *Opus geographicum*. III [Naples-Rome, 1972], pp. 243, 246.

[61] M. Brett, "Ifrīqiya as a Market for Saharan Trade from the 10th to the 12th C. AD," *Journal of African History* 10 (1969), p. 358; J. Devisse, "Routes de commerce et échanges en Afrique occidentale en relation avec la Méditerranée: Un essai sur le commerce africain médiéval du XIe au XVIe siècle," *Revue d'histoire économique et sociale* 50 (1972), p. 67. See also C. Vanacker, "Géographie économique de l'Afrique du Nord selon les autors arabes du IXe siècle au milieu du XIIe siècle," *Annales: ESC* 28 (1973), p. 680. On the Gao stelae: J. Sauvaget, "Les épitaphes royales de Gao," *Al-Andalus* 14 (1949), pp. 123–41, and another article by the same title in *Bulletin de l'Institut français de l'Afrique Noire* 12 (1950), pp. 421, 424, 429.

[62] Idrīsī, *Opus*, III, p. 252.

[63] T. Lewicki, "Les voies maritimes de la Méditerranée dans le haut moyen âge d'après les sources arabes," *La navigazione mediterranea nell'alto medioevo*. [Spoleto, 1978], p. 460.

coming through this region, and we may conjecture an even greater volume of traffic than the documents record. Commodities from the eastern Islamic world were continually available in al-Andalus and must have passed westward through the nexus of Ifriqiya and Sicily. Andalusi exports likewise found their way into Egyptian and Tunisian markets, showing that trade ran in the opposite direction too.

Andalusi merchants often established a base in the central Mediterranean, either in Tunisia or pre-Norman Sicily, from which to run their businesses and oversee shipments of goods traveling between the Iberian peninsula and the Near East. Several Andalusi Jewish merchants whose primary occupation was the shipment of silk and flax between Egypt and the central Mediterranean lived in Palermo and al-Mahdiyya in the first half of the eleventh century. Letters from these merchants and their colleagues demonstrate the supervisory position of Ifriqiya–Sicily in Mediterranean trade. A Geniza letter written in Qayrawan, ca. 1000, remarked that a shipment of brazilwood received from Egypt had been sent to al-Andalus, and in 1015 a document needed in Egypt was reported to have gone astray between Almeria and Tunisia. Five years after this, some eastern pearls and textiles were passed on to al-Andalus from Tunisia because there was no market for them locally, and in 1040 a Tunisian merchant reported that goods had been shipped to Egypt on "Andalusi ships."[64] Andalusi economic influence was also apparent inland at roughly the same period, when a merchant in Qayrawan remarked that "the dirhams of al-Andalus are in great quantity [here], and all prices are based on them."[65] Even after the Norman conquest of Sicily, the region continued to play a pivotal role in Mediterranean trade, and Genoese merchant itineraries routinely included a stop in Sicily on the way to Egypt, or on circular routes beginning in Genoa and traveling to or from Andalusi ports.[66]

By way of this central Mediterranean channel, Andalusi ports maintained commercial contact with Egypt, the rest of the eastern Muslim world, and beyond. Iberian contacts with the eastern Mediterranean were already well established in Umayyad

[64] DK 13; TS 13 J 36.1; TS 8.12; Bodl a2.17.
[65] TS 12.282.
[66] D. Abulafia, *The Two Italies: Economic Relations between the Norman Kingdom of Sicily and the Northern Communes.* [Cambridge, 1977], pp. 162, 229.

times, when Jewish Rādhānite merchants trafficked along complex itineraries linking east and west. Meanwhile, Andalusi merchant-scholars sought learning and business in the Hijaz, Iraq, and Aden during the ninth and tenth centuries.[67] An anonymous tenth-century geography, the *Ḥudūd al-ʿālam* assumed commercial contact in its statement that "whatever is produced in . . . al-Andalus" was brought to Syria, while on the Andalusi side, the Umayyad courtier Hasday b. Shaprūt observed the arrival of merchants from Egypt and Khurasan in Cordoba.[68] Ibn Ḥayyān likewise remarked that merchants came to al-Andalus from both Egypt and Iraq.[69] Perhaps some of these men sought passage on a large Andalusi ship which traveled to Egypt in 955 and returned to al-Andalus from Alexandria loaded with goods.[70]

Andalusi merchants traveled even farther afield in the Umayyad period – according to both legend and more reliable report. As told in one tenth-century tale, a ship foundering in the China Sea, after sailing from Siraf with "a crowd of merchants . . . from every country," was brought to safety through the wisdom of "an old Muslim from Cadiz" who happened to be on board.[71] Biographical data on other traders support the possibility of some truth in this story. There is, for example, the case of Abū Bakr Muḥammad b. Muʿāwiya al-Marwānī, a merchant-scholar who left his native Cordoba to go on pilgrimage in 908, then traveled on commercial business as far as India.[72]

Sources from the eleventh and early twelfth centuries also show commerce between Muslim Spain and Egypt. A Geniza

[67] Ibn al-Faraḍī, *Kitāb ta'rīkh 'ulama' al-Andalus*. [ed. F. Codera, *BAH*, Madrid, 1890] I, pp. 51–2, 53, 68–9, 130–1, 179–81.

[68] *Ḥudūd al-ʿālam: "The Regions of the World," A Persian Geography*. [trans. V. Minorsky, London, 1970], p. 148; D.M. Dunlop, *The History of the Jewish Khazars*. [Princeton, 1954], pp. 134–5; and W. Heyd, *Histoire du commerce du Levant au moyen âge*. [Leipzig, 1885] I, p. 148.

[69] Ibn Bassām (d. 1147/8), *Dhakhīra fī maḥāsin ahl al-jazīra*. [Cairo, 1358/1939–1364/1945] IV/1, p. 65. Ibn Bassām attributed this information to Ibn Ḥayyān.

[70] Ibn al-Athīr, *Kāmil fī al-ta'rīkh*. [ed. C.J. Tornberg, Leiden, 1851–76] VIII, pp. 384–5; [trans. E. Fagnan, *Annales du Maghreb et de l'Espagne*. Algiers, 1898], pp. 358–9.

[71] Buzurg b. Shahriyar, *The Book of the Wonders of India*. [trans. G.S.P. Freeman-Grenville, London, 1981], pp. 13–18. The story is fiction, yet there is no reason to believe that the mention of an Andalusi on board was part of the wonder related. The storm, not the unfortunate travelers, was the subject of the tale. As in *The Arabian Nights*, the genre of *'ajā'ib* literature usually contains enough of daily life to properly set off the wonders described.

[72] Ibn al-Faraḍī, *Kitāb*, p. 363, no. 1287; E. Lévi-Provençal, "Le 'Kitāb nasab Quraysh' de Musʿab al-Zubayrī," *Arabica* 1(1954), p. 95.

merchant writing in the 1040s mentioned that a friend was leaving for al-Andalus, while three other documents, dating 1050–70, noted the arrival of ships from Almeria and Denia in Alexandria.[73] In a later letter, sent from Alexandria ca. 1110, a merchant wrote at length of commodities, and alluded briefly to his recent arrival from al-Andalus.[74] Likewise, Halfōn b. Nethanel sailed from Almeria to Egypt ca. 1138, while his friend the poet and philosopher Judah Ha-Levi completed a similar trip shortly thereafter, arriving in Alexandria in 1140.[75]

Andalusi ships bound for Egypt could often be spotted off the western Egyptian coast before their arrival, allowing news of their coming to be transmitted to Old Cairo even before they docked in Alexandria. Thus, a number of Geniza missives dispatched to Cairo from the coast report the imminent arrival, or non-arrival, of Andalusi vessels. One letter, written at the beginning of the twelfth century, bewailed the fact that "no one has arrived from the west except the ship from al-Andalus . . . [and only one other] ship from al-Andalus is expected." Likewise, in the middle of the century, a more cheerful partner wrote from Alexandria to the capital to report that "the ship from Denia has just arrived, carrying the rest of the goods."[76] Parallel information was provided in a third letter, this time from the peninsula (written in Almeria, 1138), advising that "a barge [had] arrived from Alexandria . . . [and the] merchants who had traveled in it said that they had left behind two [other] ships ready to sail for Almeria."[77] Sometimes there are even references to specific Andalusi boats. Several letters from Egypt refer to "the ship of the *qā'id*," a vessel which Goitein associated with the Almoravid Qā'id Ibn Maymūn of Almeria.[78]

[73] TS 13 J 28.9; TS 13 J 16.19; TS 8 J 20.2; TS 10 J 16.17. See also TS 10 J 11.13 and Gottheil-Worrell 27 for other references to Egyptian-Andalusi trade in the 1060s.

[74] Bodl d66.52.

[75] TS 8 J 19.28; TS 13 J 15.16.

[76] ULC Or1080 J 178 (trans. Goitein, *Mediterranean Society*, I, p. 320); and TS 10 J 14.16. Departures, as well as arrivals, were reported. Another letter from Alexandria to Cairo (ULC Or1080 J 258, dated 1141) noted that the "ships bound for al-Andalus, al-Mahdiyya, Tripoli, Sicily, and Rūm have departed."

[77] Bodl d74.41. The translation is adapted from S.D. Goitein, *Letters of Medieval Jewish Traders*. [Princeton, 1973], p. 263. Other Geniza documents from the twelfth century that mention traffic between Spain and Egypt include TS 13 J 22.30; TS 8 J 18.1; and TS 12.285.

[78] TS 12.290; TS 13 J 14.21; and JTS Geniza misc. 13. See also Goitein, *Mediterranean Society*, I, p. 310.

In contrast to this plethora of data on trade contacts between Egypt and al-Andalus in the eleventh and early twelfth centuries, Geniza evidence for Andalusi–Egyptian commerce becomes scarce after the middle of the twelfth century. Nevertheless, some record of later commercial contact is continued in other sources. Zuhrī, for one, noted that "the luxury goods of Hind, Sind, and Iraq" were exported "to Ifriqiya and al-Andalus" through Egypt. Benjamin of Tudela (ca. 1165) confirmed that Alexandria was "a commercial market for all nations" when he traveled there, with merchants arriving from many regions, including al-Andalus, to make their purchases there.[79] The philosopher Maimonides, himself of Andalusi origin, likewise reported that shipments of Sevillian olive oil came regularly from the west to Alexandria in the late twelfth century.[80]

AL-ANDALUS AND THE CHRISTIAN COMMERCIAL NETWORK

Commercial contacts also existed between al-Andalus and the Christian world, although these were not so extensive or well attested as connections with the Islamic Mediterranean sphere. Whereas Andalusi markets were fully integrated into the Muslim trading network, so that Andalusi goods and merchants were well established in the central and south-eastern Mediterranean (and even ventured as far east as the Indian Ocean), links with Christian trade were more limited. This section will address, first, data on links between al-Andalus, the Christian Mediterranean, and northern Europe, and second, the evidence for Andalusi overland trade with Christian Spain.

Records from Byzantium and Venice indicate little, if any, economic contact with al-Andalus, and Andalusis are rarely found in the north-eastern Mediterranean. Unlike traders in the western Mediterranean, where Andalusi markets played a strategic role in the distribution of Andalusi exports and other Muslim goods, Byzantine merchants had more direct channels of access to Muslim commodities. At the same time, Byzantium had its own industries producing silk and other goods in competition with exports from Muslim Spain. Although there are a few references to Andalusi goods arriving in Constantinople, these

[79] Zuhrī, "Kitāb," p. 257; Benjamin of Tudela, "Itinerary," p. 686.
[80] Moses b. Maimon, *Responsa*, II, p. 576.

items tended to come as diplomatic gifts rather than commodities.[81]

In contrast to this dearth of trade with eastern Christian markets, al-Andalus was an influential adjunct to the Latin Christian trading sphere. Andalusi markets attracted Christian merchants from northern Spain and other regions of Europe, although the Andalusi economy remained directed toward the Muslim commercial world and Andalusi traders concentrated on traffic with Islamic ports. A few Jewish merchants (and even fewer Muslims) traded with Christian Spain, but they rarely ventured into European regions north of the Pyrenees, particularly after the Umayyad period. Instead, most contacts came through the influx of Latin Christian merchants into Andalusi markets and ports, and the outflow of Muslim commodities and coins into Christian lands.

In line with the contemporary development of European urban centers and growing commercial engagement in the Mediterranean, documentary and numismatic data suggest that commercial connections grew over time. Patchy Carolingian records give way to more substantial documentation by the twelfth and thirteenth centuries. For the period before the eleventh century, coins provide the most concrete proof of contact between al-Andalus and Latin Europe, but this evidence must be used with caution since the mere movement of coins does not indicate trade. As Morrison has warned, "documenting the existence of a . . . trade route by means of coin finds is like documenting the existence of the griffin by means of gargoyles and heraldry. Indeed, the case is stronger for the griffin." Although movement through trade cannot be ruled out, coins could travel for many reasons – as gifts, tribute, booty, ransom, or other purposes – unconnected with commerce.[82]

Whatever the means of transfer, numismatic data show that coins moved between al-Andalus and Europe during the eighth, ninth, tenth, and early eleventh centuries. Early hoards contain

[81] A survey of customs records (usually such a fruitful genre for clues to commercial links) shows no Byzantine contact with Muslim Spain (H. Antoniadis-Bibicou, *Recherches sur les douanes à Byzance*. [Paris, 1963]).

[82] K. Morrison, "Numismatics and Carolingian Trade: A Critique of the Evidence," *Speculum* 38(1963), p. 432; P. Grierson, "Commerce in the Dark Ages: A Critique of the Evidence," *Transactions of the Royal Historical Society* 9(1959), pp. 123–40.

Andalusi silver coins, which is not surprising since there was little Andalusi gold to circulate before the reforms of ʿAbd al-Raḥmān III in 929. One literary reference, from Arles ca. 798, mentions Muslim gold coins, but with no indication of their provenance.[83] The proximity of Arles to the peninsula suggests that these may be Andalusi dinars, yet the lack of material evidence has led Grierson to conclude that Iberian gold penetrated no further than southern France (if at all), and that any wide circulation of Arab gold in Europe before 1100 must "be regarded as unproven, and indeed in the highest degree unlikely."[84]

One school of thought contends that Carolingian coinage reforms were triggered by the need to combat the flow of superior Andalusi silver into Carolingian territories.[85] If this were the case, circulation of Muslim currencies in Gaul must have been considerably greater than either archeological or textual evidence have yet shown. A few Andalusi silver dirhams (struck between 777 and 807) have been found in France, in Britain (dated 869 and 999), and a small number of late Umayyad coins have come to light in Scandinavian and eastern European hoards.[86] Although surviving examples are scarce, Andalusi dirhams must have been sufficiently familiar in Europe to engender re-use and imitation. A curious silver coin found in a Polish hoard bears an Arabic inscription naming Hishām II (976–1009)

[83] Theodulfus, *Versus contra iudices*. [ed. E. Dümmler, *MGH* Poetae latini medii aevi, 1. 2, Berlin, 1881], p. 498. For other documentary data on coinage transfer, see J. Duplessy, "La circulation des monnaies arabes en Europe occidentale du VIIIe au XIIIe siècle," *Revue numismatique* 5th series, 18(1956), pp. 121–52.

[84] P. Grierson, "Carolingian Europe and the Arabs: The Myth of the Mancus," *Revue belge de philologie et d'histoire* 32(1954), pp. 1064, 1074.

[85] H. Pigeouneau, *Histoire du commerce de la France*. [Paris, 1885], pp. 86–7; On Carolingian reforms, see R. Doehaerd, "Les réformes monétaires carolingiennes," *Annales: ESC* 7(1952), pp. 13–20.

[86] M. Barceló, "Why and How did Andalusian coins travel to Europa during the Emirate and the Caliphate from 98/716–17 to 403/1012–13," *ROMM* 36(1983), p. 10; A.D. Longpérier, "Monnaie andalouse trouvée à Contres," *Revue numismatique* n.s. 8(1863), pp. 14–16; A. Canto García and A.M. Balaguer, "Al-Andalus y los carolingios, un singular testimonio monetario," *Gaceta numismatica* 85(1987), p. 48; N.M. Lowick, "The Kufic Coins from Cuerdale," *The British Numismatic Journal* 46(1977), pp. 21–5; R.H.M. Dolley, "A Spanish Dirham found in England," *The Numismatic Chronicle* 17(1957), pp. 242–3.

Andalusi dirhams make up only 1 percent of Islamic coins found in Eastern Europe, and the numbers in Scandinavia are even smaller. Scandinavian hoards contain coins from the period 724–999, but all Andalusi coins in Eastern European hoards (Poland, Russia, and the Ukraine) date from the reign of Hishām II (976–1009).

on one face, and a Latin inscription naming Henry II (1002–24) on the other.[87]

Opinions vary on the route by which these Andalusi coins arrived in northern European hoards. Did they come directly from the peninsula, or by a more circuitous route through the Near East and along the Volga?[88] Because southward numismatic diffusion is attested by Iberian hoards yielding Carolingian coins (which surely did not arrive via the Near East), it seems likely that most Andalusi coins came into Europe by the shorter northward route.[89]

Building on the ambiguous evidence provided by coins, written sources indicate commercial contact between Europe and al-Andalus before 1000. Hārūn b. Yaḥyā, a Muslim captured by Christians in the ninth century, observed a sea route between the peninsula and Italy.[90] In the tenth century, Ibn Ḥayyān noted diplomatic and commercial delegations arriving in Cordoba from Amalfi, while the contemporary Andalusi traveler Ibrāhīm

[87] T.S. Noonan, "Andalusian Umayyad Dirhams from Eastern Europe," *Acta numismatica* 10(1980), p. 87.

[88] On routes of traffic, see articles by U.S. Linder Welin, "Spanish-Umaiyad Coins found in Scandinavia," *Numismatiska Meddelanden* 30(1965), pp. 15–25; T.S. Noonan, "Andalusian Umayyad Dirhams," pp. 81–91; T.S. Noonan, "Ninth-century dirham hoards from European Russia: A preliminary analysis," *Viking-Age Coinage in the Northern Lands*. [ed. M.A.S. Blackburn and D.M. Metcalf, Oxford, 1981], pp. 47–117. Regarding the dirhams found in Britain, Lowick ("Kufic Coins," pp. 21–5) insists that an 869 coin from Cuerdale did not arrive in England directly from al-Andalus, but came instead by way of the Near East. Dolley, in contrast, believes that a dirham struck by Hishām II in 390/999–1000 must have come to England through Europe ("Spanish Dirham," pp. 242–3).

[89] Andalusi hoards mainly contain Muslim coins, rarely Christian pieces. One collection, found in 1866, contained coins dating from 884–986, minted in Toulouse, Quentovic, Orleans, Tours, and elsewhere. Another, discovered near Cordoba in 1950, included seven whole Carolingian pennies and bits of others, mainly struck in the Spanish March under Louis the Pious and Charles the Bald. On these finds and others see S. de los Santos Jener, "Monedas carolingias en un tesorillo de dirhemes del emirato cordobés," *Numario hispánico* 5(1956), pp. 79–87; E. Gariel, *Les monnaies royales de France sous la race carolingienne*. [Strasbourg, 1883] 1, p. 136; K. Morrison, "Numismatics and Carolingian Trade," p. 428. An intriguing Umayyad dirham (struck in 230/844–5) with a bit of a Carolingian penny (struck under Louis the Pious, 814–40) inserted into it, is discussed by A. Canto García and A.M. Balaguer, "Al-Andalus y los carolingios," pp. 41–9. Six Anglo-Saxon coins minted under Ethelred II (978–1013) have also been discovered near Roncevalles, but these were almost certainly brought by pilgrims (F. Mateu y Llopis, "El hallazgo de 'pennies' ingleses en Roncevalles," *Principe de Viana* 11(1950), pp. 201–10).

[90] Hārūn b. Yaḥyā's account was recorded by Ibn Rustah, *'Alaq al-nafīsah* [ed. M.J. de Goeje, *BGA*, 2nd edn, VII, Leiden, 1967], p. 129.

b. Ya'qūb reached Mainz and other towns in northern Europe.[91] Oddly, little evidence exists for trade between al-Andalus and Europe for most of the eleventh century. This is in spite of the fact that there was clearly economic contact between Taifa rulers and the northern Spanish kingdoms, and the pilgrimage route to Santiago was gaining fame at this time.

Whatever its import, this lack of eleventh-century evidence contrasts with the sudden growth of documentation, mostly in Latin, for European–Andalusi trade in the twelfth century. The most important participants in this commerce were Italians, particularly merchants from Genoa and Pisa. Because of their similar commercial interests these two cities were often rivals, although Pisa never came close to achieving Genoa's commercial success in Iberian trade. In April 1149, however, they concluded a fifteen-year treaty of alliance valid throughout the western Mediterranean, including *Barbariam . . . Garbum et . . . totam Yspaniam.*[92]

At least one Genoese boat anchored in Malaga during the late eleventh century, and another of the city's ships sailed home from Almeria ca. 1120.[93] This latter vessel could hardly have been unique, since by 1143 Genoese tariff schedules included tolls on ships arriving from Almeria.[94] By the late twelfth century, Genoa was preeminent in western Mediterranean trade, leading Zuhrī to observe that "the city of Genoa is among the greatest cities of [Europe] . . . they are a merchant people, [trading] by sea between Syria and al-Andalus. They have control of the sea."[95] Genoese notarial registers provide a particularly valuable source of information on Italian–Iberian trade. Registers from the second half of the twelfth century contain roughly

[91] Ibn Ḥayyān, *Muqtabas*. v [eds. P. Chalmeta, F. Corriente, M. Subh, Madrid, 1979] pp. 478,485. On Ibrāhīm b. Ya'qūb, see A. Miquel, "L'Europe occidentale dans la relation arabe d'Ibrāhīm b. Ya'qūb (Xe s.)," *Annales: ESC* 21(1966), pp. 1048–64. The *Ḥudūd al-'ālam* (p. 158) contains the surprising statement that Britain (*Baritīniya*) was "an emporium of Rūm and Spain;" no other evidence suggests that commercial ties existed between Britain and Spain in the tenth century.

[92] Imperiale di Sant'Angelo, Cesare (ed.), *Codice diplomatico della repubblica di Genova*. [Rome, 1936–42] I, pp. 243–7. *Yspania*, in this context, almost certainly refers to al-Andalus.

[93] R. Arié, *La España musulmana siglos VII–XV*. [Barcelona, 1982], p. 152; Petrus Guillelmus, *Miracula beati Aegidii*, p. 321.

[94] L.T. Belgrano (ed.), "Il registro della curia arcivescovile di Genova," *ASLSP* 2(1862), p. 9. A Genoese ruling from 1142 also noted a tariff levied on vessels going to Spain (Imperiale, *Codice*, I, p. 141).

[95] Zuhrī, "Kitāb," pp. 229–30.

fifty contracts for Genoese voyages to Andalusi ports or for sales of Andalusi goods. In 1160, for example, a Genoese merchant agreed to transport Andalusi textiles from Genoa to Bougie, while another promised to carry goods from Genoa to Bougie, Oran, Ceuta, or *Yspania* in 1197.[96]

Diplomatic records also show Italian trading interests in al-Andalus. During the second half of the twelfth century, Genoa and Pisa worked to extend their commercial power through treaties with Muslim rulers in Valencia, Denia, and the Balearics.[97] Both cities likewise negotiated with the Almohads for trade privileges in their domains. The Genoese may have come to terms with the Almohad caliph ʿAbd al-Mu'min as early as 1153 (shortly after the Almohad arrival in Spain), and an alliance was certainly in place by 1161. Almohad treaties with Genoa appear to have been renewed at roughly fifteen-year intervals through 1223, and generally included clauses guaranteeing safe conduct for shipping, tariff reductions for Genoese traders, and the right to maintain hostelries (*funduqs*) in Almohad ports.[98] Similar treaties were drawn up between the Almohads and Pisa in the late twelfth century, although Pisan merchants had to pay higher tariffs, and Pisan access to Almohad ports may have been more limited than that accorded to the Genoese.

Despite the military upheavals in the peninsula in the early thirteenth century, the Genoese had uncanny success in maintaining, and even in strengthening, their commercial ties with the region. After the final Almohad departure in 1228, Genoa reached an accord with the amir of Seville by 1231.[99] Furthermore, when Ferdinand III of Castile captured the city in 1248,

[96] Giovanni Scriba, *Il Cartolare di Giovanni Scriba.* [eds. M. Chiaudano and M. Moresco, Rome, 1935] II, p. 4, #812; ASG, *Diversorum 102*, fol. 84r.

[97] Genoa and Pisa arranged parallel accords with Ibn Mardānish, the ruler of Valencia, in 1149 and 1150. Under threat of attack, Ibn Mardānish promised Genoa money, tariff exemptions, and hostelries in both Valencia and Denia (Imperiale, *Codice*, I, pp. 247–9; and *Liber iurium reipublicae genuensis.* [ed. M.E. Ricotti, *Historia patria monumenta*], VII, pp. 152–3). The Pisan treaty promised hostelries and safe-conduct, but said nothing of money (M. Amari (ed.), *I diplomi arabi del R. Archivio Fiorentino.* [Florence, 1863], pp. 239–40). Genoa apparently renewed its commercial treaty with Ibn Mardānish in 1161 (Caffaro, *Annali genovesi di Caffaro.* [ed. L.T. Belgrano, Genoa, 1890] I, pp. 61–2). Genoa likewise sought diplomatic ties with the Balearics in the 1180s (Imperiale, *Codice*, II, pp. 341–3; M. Amari, "Nuovi ricordi arabici su la storia de Genova," *ASLSP* 5(1867), pp. 600–6).

[98] H.C. Krueger, "Genoese Trade with Northwest Africa in the 12th century," *Speculum* 8(1933), p. 379.

[99] Caffaro, *Annali genovesi*, III, p. 57.

he granted extensive trade privileges to the Genoese in Seville and, in 1251, throughout his realm. These concessions paved the way for a new phase in Genoese–Iberian relations, and firmly implanted the Genoese as participants in the later trade of southern Castile.[100]

Although the evidence is more limited, other Christian cities in the western Mediterranean were also in communication with Andalusi ports. A treaty negotiated in 1155 between Genoa and Arles referred to "boats coming and going from Arles to *Yspania* by sea," while another accord from this year documented much the same for Montpellier.[101] Montpellier would later receive special permission from James I of Aragon, in 1231, to trade with Andalusi ports.[102] Catalans also traded with the south, and a commercial contract written in Barcelona, in 1211, concerned a sea voyage to Muslim Spain (*Yspania*).[103] By the middle of the thirteenth century, with the progress of Christian victories and the growth of Catalan mercantile interests, traffic to the south (particularly maritime traffic) increased rapidly.

Merchants also moved back and forth along overland routes between Andalusi cities and the markets of Castile, Leon, Navarre, Galicia, and Portugal. Although Lévi-Provençal once lamented *le manque absolu de documents* relating to Iberian overland trade,[104] brief references nevertheless indicate the existence of trade between north and south. Evidence for long-distance overland commerce and economic contact may be gleaned from information on overland routes, diplomatic or regulatory citations to commercial traffic, financial-numismatic data, and other references to merchants and goods moving across the *thughūr*. Owing to their common border, relations between al-Andalus and its northern Christian neighbors differed from those with other European states. In many ways, commercial interchange within the Iberian peninsula was less formal than trade in other

[100] The text of this 1251 treaty and subsequent renewals are edited in the *Liber iurium*, pp. 1060–4, 1392–3.

[101] Imperiale, *Codice*, I, pp. 316–20.

[102] F. Fabrège, *Histoire de Maguelone*. [Paris-Montpellier, 1894–1900] II, p. 238.

[103] S. Bensch, "From Prizes of War to Domestic Merchandise: Slaves in the Towns of Eastern Iberia," unpublished paper presented at the annual meeting of the Medieval Academy [Princeton, NJ, May, 1991], p. 6.

[104] E. Lévi-Provençal, *L'Espagne musulmane au Xème siècle: Institutions et vie sociale*. [Paris, 1932], p. 183.

spheres, since it did not necessarily involve large cargos or expensive commodities. Even in times of conflict, when passage through the border regions may have been hazardous, traffic continued.

Arabic geographers, particularly Idrīsī, were evidently familiar with the commerce of northern Spanish cities, although they did not cite the presence of Andalusis trading there. As the pilgrimage to Santiago de Compostela grew popular in the eleventh and twelfth centuries, so did the towns along its route, including Burgos (*Burghush*) and Leon (*Liyūn*), which Idrīsī described as containing "markets and merchants," and Santiago (*Shant Yāqūb*) itself was famous for its "markets, sales, and purchases." Further east, Huesca (*Washqa*) was also "a fine and civilized city with commercial activity and flourishing markets."[105] At roughly the same period, ca. 1140, a pilgrimage guide to Santiago noted Muslim textiles among items sold in local markets.[106] These fabrics (whether of Andalusi or eastern manufacture) probably arrived through trade with al-Andalus, since another contemporary source mentioned merchants traveling between Santiago and Valencia.[107]

Roads between northern cities provided routes for overland trade, as attested by documents referring to transit *per ipsam viam mercadarium* (noted in 925), *per viam mercati* (1058), and *per via mercatera* (1076).[108] Christian rulers supported and protected commerce along these roads, so that under Alfonso VI of Leon-Castile (1065–1109) "merchants and pilgrims traveling through his entire realm feared nothing for themselves or their goods." Likewise the twelfth-century *Usatges* of Barcelona ruled that the roads should be safe, so that all men, including "merchants and businessmen, going and coming along them, may go and come securely and quietly, with all their goods and without fear."[109] Roads between Christian and Muslim regions could also be protected, as when Sancho IV of Navarre and Muqtadir of

[105] Idrīsī, *Opus geographicum*. VII [Naples-Rome, 1977], pp. 732, 728, 733; Ḥimyarī, *Péninsule* (p. 174) provided information on Leon which he attributed to Idrīsī.

[106] *Le guide du pèlerin de Saint-Jacques de Compostelle*. [ed. J. Vielliard, Macon, 1950], pp. 32–3.

[107] Herman of Tournai, "Epistola de corpore S. Vincentii diaconi," *Analecta bollandiana* 2(1883), p. 246.

[108] L. García de Valdeavellano, *Sobre los burgos y burgueses de la España medieval*. [Madrid, 1960], p. 60.

[109] J.,O'Callaghan, *A History of Medieval Spain*. [Ithaca, 1975], pp. 294, 297.

Zaragoza agreed in 1069 that "the roads which run between [their two kingdoms] should be secure and safe, so that no impediment or harm come to any [of the people] who travel along them."[110] Although this accord does not specifically note commercial traffic, other rulings ensuring the safety of merchants traveling overland indicate that this was among the primary intentions for maintaining the security of roads.

Portazgos, the tariff lists frequently appended to urban charters, provide information on overland trade across the Christian-Muslim border.[111] Except in special cases, tariffs were not designed to regulate trade with particular regions, but rather to raise revenues. Many of those towns with a *portazgo* citing trade with Muslim territories were situated in southern Castile close to the Andalusi frontier. This may indicate a differentiation between Castile, with its long-established physical and economic connections to al-Andalus, and more northerly Iberian kingdoms with fewer contacts. One *portazgo* from the Castilian town of Alarilla, dating to the late twelfth century, set a charge of one *morabetino* on "a loaded beast arriving from [the land of] the Moors" and a similar tax on people "going to the land of the Moors."[112] Likewise, a *portazgo* from 1173 stipulated that a sum must be paid to the order of Calatrava on flocks and goods traded with Moorish lands (*terras maurorum*). The fee was to be rendered at Consuegra, another Castilian town close to the Andalusi border.[113] Later, when the frontier had been pushed further south after the Christian victory at Las Navas de Tolosa in 1212, a 1226 *portazgo* from Ocaña (north-east of Toledo, and thus no longer in a true border region) still regulated taxes on "all goods which go to the land of the Moors and which come from the land of the Moors."[114] Further to the west, the 1231 *fuero* of Caceres also indicated the existence of overland routes when it

[110] J.M. Lacarra, "Dos tratados de paz y alianza entre Sancho el de Peñalén y Moctádir de Zaragoza (1069–1073)," *Colonización. parias, repoblación, y otros estudios.* [Zaragoza, 1981], p. 92.

[111] On the institution of *portazgo* see C. González Minguez, *El portazgo en la edad media. Aproximación a su estudio en la Corona de Castilla.* [Bilbao, 1989] and J. Gautier-Dalché, "Les péages dans les pays de la Couronne de Castille état de la question, réflexions, perspectives de recherches," *Les communications dans la péninsule ibérique au moyen âge.* (Actes du Colloque de Pau, 28–9 mars 1980) [Paris, 1981], pp. 73–8.

[112] J.L. Martín Rodríguez, "Portazgos de Ocaña y Alarilla," *AHDE* 32(1962), p. 524.

[113] J. González, *El Reino de Castilla en la época de Alfonso VIII.* [Madrid, 1960] II, p. 297.

[114] Martín, "Portazgos," p. 526.

stipulated that merchants from both Moorish and Christian lands be allowed to trade at an annual fair.[115] Three years after this, in 1234, Pope Gregory IX granted permission for a castle in the region of Toledo to trade with Muslim territories.[116] This permission, in view of Gregory's numerous other attempts to restrict Christian–Muslim commerce, serves as one more indication of the persistent and long-standing nature of the Iberian border trade.

References to Andalusi commodities available in Christian markets also point to the existence of cross-border trade. Northern literature and documents are full of references to Muslim textiles, leather, paper, spices, and other imports. In contrast, references to northern goods in Muslim Spain are less varied, mainly citing traffic in slaves and furs. Related to commodities, the adoption of Andalusi units of weight and measurement in Christian Spain points to commercial exchange between north and south. Most of the common Arabic units found their way into one or all of the Iberian romance languages. As early as 989, the *qafīz* (a measure of weight) appeared in Catalonia as the *kaficio*, and later the *qadah* (a large measure for grain) became *alcadafe* in Castilian, *alcadefe* in Portuguese, and *cadaf* or *cadufa* in Catalan.[117]

Evidence for the circulation of Andalusi coins in northern Spain likewise attests to the existence of overland Iberian contacts, although (as elsewhere) it need not imply commerce. The complications of numismatic diffusion are particularly evident in the Iberian peninsula where, during most of the medieval period, commercial traffic in *both* gold coinage and luxury goods flowed from south to north. Northern Christian rulers did not mint their own gold until the thirteenth century, yet various gold coins were used in the north throughout the medieval period.[118] Andalusi currency was certainly transported across the frontier from as early as the eighth century.

Latin documentary references to Andalusi coins in Christian

[115] T. González (ed.), *Colección de privilegios, franquezas, exenciones y fueros.* [Madrid, 1833] IV, p. 94.

[116] R.I. Burns, "Renegades, Adventurers, and Sharp Businessmen: The 13th century Spaniards in the Cause of Islam," *Catholic Historical Review* 58(1972) p. 363.

[117] J. Vallvé, "Notas de metrología hispano-árabe II, Medidas de capacidad," *Al-Andalus* 42(1977) pp. 91–8. Vallvé has calculated that the *qafīz* weighed roughly 56–64 pounds, although it could vary widely by region.

[118] P, Grierson, "Carolingian Europe," p. 1065.

Spain rarely mention trade with the south, but instead concern local religious donations, house sales, and other expenditures for which sums are stated in Andalusi currency. In 915, for example, Ordoño II of Leon bequeathed five hundred *mectales ex auro purissimo* to the Church of Santiago.[119] Here, the combined specification of *mectales* and gold makes it almost certain that the sum was composed of Andalusi dinars (which are referred to as *mithqāls* in Andalusi sources). Andalusi dirhams also appear in Christian documents, usually under the guise of *solidos mahometi, solidos de argento Kazimi*, or *solidos hazimi*. Chalmeta has cited twenty-two references to these *qāsimī* dirhams dating between 933 and 1078, primarily from Catalan and Portuguese sources, though Andalusi coins also appear in texts from Leon and Galicia. It is possible that these Latin references to *qāsimī* dirhams applied to money of account or units of weight, rather than true specie, in which case the appearance of *qāsimī* dirhams in northern Spain would demonstrate economic contact, but not the transfer of actual coinage.[120] Nevertheless, when the minting of Andalusi dirhams became irregular after the death of the Andalusi ruler Manṣūr in 1002, imitation dirhams began to be struck in Barcelona.[121] This new production may be explained by some degree of dependence on southern currency and a need to compensate for its declining availability.

During the eleventh century, Taifa gold circulated widely in Christian Spain, but its diffusion owed more to tribute payments (*parias*) than to trade. The sums in question were large, and their

[119] C. Sánchez-Albornoz, *Estampas de la vida en León durante el siglo X*. [Madrid, 1934], p. 37.

[120] P. Chalmeta, "Précisions au sujet du monnayage hispano-arabe (dirham qāsimī et dirham arbaʿīnī)," *JESHO* 24(1981), pp. 316–18; also C. Sánchez-Albornoz, "La primitiva organización monetaria de Léon y de Castilla," *AHDE* 5(1928) p. 308; and E. Lévi-Provençal, *Histoire de l'Espagne musulmane*. III [Paris, 1953], p. 257. The term *solidus*, once applicable to a gold coin, was often used in Spain as a translation for dirham, and the term *kazimi/hazimi* is thought to derive from the name of Qāsim b. Khālid, a director of the Umayyad mint in Cordoba under ʿAbd al-Raḥmān III. Another, perhaps more convincing, explanation for the term *qāsimī* has been put forward by J. Vallvé ("Notas de metrología hispano-árabe III," *Al-Qantara* 5(1984), p. 165), who equated this unit with the dirham *arbaʿīnī* which, at a weight of thirty-six grains, divided (*qasama*) a dinar in half. On the circulation of these coins, see also L. García de Valdeavellano, "Economía natural y monetaria en León y Castilla durante los siglos IX, X, y XI," *Moneda y crédito* 10 (1944), pp. 37ff.

[121] Grierson, "Carolingian Europe," p. 1064. F. Mateu has published photographs of these Barcelona dinars in "Hallazgos numismáticos musulmanes," *Al-Andalus* 12(1947), pp. 481–4.

payment over the years is thought to have considerably altered the balance of wealth between Muslim and Christian Spain. ʿAbd Allah b. Buluggīn of Granada (1073–90), for example, paid an initial *paria* of 30,000 *mithqāls* to Alfonso VI of Castile (1065–1109), followed thereafter with 10,000 *mithqāls* annually. During the 1090s, other kingdoms including Lerida, Tortosa, and Denia, sent 50,000 *mithqāls* a year to the Cid, as representative of Alfonso VI, and Valencia paid an even higher annual tribute of 100,000 *mithqāls*.[122]

Sums for the payment of *parias* were invariably specified in gold, but it is probable that they were frequently delivered in silver, or even in kind. Increasing shortages of gold in the late eleventh century brought open recognition of the necessity of substitution, as evident in a treaty drawn up in 1073 between Sancho IV of Navarre and the Taifa of Zaragoza which specified an acceptable rate of exchange.[123] In the absence of either sufficient gold or silver, Taifa states such as Almeria sometimes rendered tribute in silk or other domestically produced goods.[124]

The impact of *paria* tribute on the medieval Iberian economy has been a subject of much debate. *Parias* probably decreased the availability of precious metals in Muslim Spain, causing inflation and currency devaluation, but they may have stimulated Taifa commerce as well. Glick sees a "goodly portion" of *paria* monies being "ineluctably drained away" from the Christian north and returned to al-Andalus in exchange for Muslim goods.[125] In this way, tribute payments could actually have stimulated Islamic industries and promoted inter-Iberian trade.

[122] J.M. Lacarra, "Aspectos económicos de la sumisión de los Reinos de Taifas (1010–1102)," *Colonización, parias, repoblación, y otros estudios.* [Zaragoza, 1981], pp. 71–2. Because of the variations in currency and the rapid devaluation of some eleventh-century coins, it is difficult to know the true value of these sums. M. Benaboud has pointed out that, in roughly the same period, 5,000 *mithqāls* was noted as the price of complicity in a plot to overthrow the ruler of Granada, while the same sum was awarded to a poet in Seville ["Tendances économiques dans al-Andalus durant la période des Etats-Taifas", *Bulletin économique et social du Maroc* 151–52 (1983), p. 24]. On a more practical level, one could buy a house in late eleventh-century Cordoba for 50–280 *mithqāls*, and at the start of the century, 100 kg. of wheat sold for 1.52 dinars (see E. Ashtor, "Prix et salaires dans l'Espagne musulmane aux Xe et XIe siècles," *Annales:ESC* 20(1965), pp. 665, 669).

[123] Lacarra, "Aspectos," p. 62.

[124] Molina López, "Algunas consideraciones sobre la vida socio-económica de Almería," p. 186.

[125] T. Glick, *Islamic and Christian Spain in the Early Middle Ages.* [Princeton, 1979], pp. 126–7.

Alternatively, while *paria* payments boosted the amount of currency in circulation throughout the peninsula, they may have fostered an inflationary spiral, leading to higher prices and little increase in Andalusi production.[126] Even if some tribute money returned to the south through overland trade, northern Christian building campaigns and fortifications, military and naval improvements, and ecclesiastical donations all provided other outlets for the redistribution of *paria* gold.[127]

Most *paria* payments ceased with the arrival of the Almoravids in 1085, putting an end to the tributary status of southern al-Andalus, but not to the availability of Muslim gold in the northern peninsula. *Murabiṭūns* (Almoravid dinars) already appear in Christian Spanish documents in 1084, and clearly circulated throughout the northern kingdoms until the late twelfth century.[128] Murcia continued to mint dinars of the Almoravid type until the region was conquered by the Almohads in 1172. Within the next year or two, Alfonso VIII of Castile began striking the *morabetino alfonsino* or *maravedí*.[129] As with the Barcelona dirhams in the previous century, the introduction of Alfonso's *morabetino* indicates that Castile was accustomed to the regular presence of Muslim gold. The new Castilian issue was indisputably based on the *murabiṭūn*, since early versions still bore an Arabic inscription, and the name *morabetino* was clearly derivative. Following the example of its namesake, the Castilian *maravedí* gained great popularity, even outside of Christian Spain, and although minting ceased in 1221, reckoning in this currency (whether actual coinage or a unit of account) continued into the fifteenth century.[130]

[126] This theory has been suggested by M. Benaboud, "Tendances économiques," p. 22.

[127] Using *paria* monies, Alfonso VI doubled the annual Castilian donation to Cluny, and the treasuries of Spanish cathedrals, including Santiago de Compostela, were filled with Muslim specie by the late eleventh century. C.E. Dufourcq and J. Gautier Dalché, *Histoire économique et sociale de l'Espagne chrétienne au moyen âge*. [Paris, 1976], pp. 70–1.

[128] Devisse, "Routes de commerce," p. 63. Devisse noted the wide distribution of the *murabiṭūn* in Christian Spain, also citing references from Castile (1112), Asturias (1127), Santander (1136), Leon (1141), and Galicia (1166).

[129] Reports vary as to whether Alfonso VIII introduced his new coinage in 1172, 1173, or 1175. J. Todesca favors 1173 ("The Monetary History of Castile-Leon (ca. 1100–1300) in Light of the Bourgey Hoard," *American Numismatic Society Museum Notes* 33 (1988), pp. 136–7).

[130] P. Spufford, *Handbook of Medieval Exchange*. [London, 1986], p. 155.

In summary, maritime routes preserved the integration of Andalusi ports and markets within the Islamic Mediterranean trading network from the late eighth to the early thirteenth centuries. Communications remained open as merchants (and other travelers) carried goods back and forth between the eastern and western Mediterranean, traveling by ship as far as the Maghrib to meet up with overland caravans, or embarking on longer sea journeys to Tunis or Alexandria. Along the way, it was common to make interim stops to buy and sell, to rest, to seek supplies and repairs, and to collect commercial information. Andalusi ports were also in economic contact with Latin Europe and the western Mediterranean, but apparently not with Venice or the Greek east. Most of this commerce was maintained by non-Andalusi Christian merchants, who came to the peninsula by sea or overland in search of Muslim goods. This Christian traffic increased over time, particularly after the eleventh century and the European "Commercial Revolution" when Genoese and other Italians began to invest in commerce with the peninsula.

Beside the array of references to commercial routes and contacts between al-Andalus and other regions of the Mediterranean world, data on merchants doing business in Andalusi markets, and on the commodities they traded, provide the best information on the mechanics of trade in Muslim Spain. Information on traders and goods delineates the ways in which the peninsula fitted into larger commercial networks and regional trading systems before and after the Muslim period. These merchants and their merchandise are the subject of the following chapters.

Chapter 3

THE MERCHANT PROFESSION IN MUSLIM SPAIN AND THE MEDIEVAL MEDITERRANEAN

MERCHANT TYPOLOGY AND ASSOCIATION

Merchants came from all over the medieval Mediterranean world to do business in the markets of Muslim Spain, while Andalusi traders, in their turn, ventured far afield in search of commercial opportunities. This chapter will examine the affiliations and allegiances of these international traders, the overlapping commercial spheres of different merchant groups, and the structure of their partnerships.

The Arabic word for merchant, *tājir* (pl. *tujjār*), includes different merchant types within its scope. It can refer to a dealer in local trade, but is more frequently applied to merchants involved in long-distance international commerce. In a classic description of merchants operating in the medieval Islamic world, the eastern author Abū Faḍl al-Dimashqī cited three basic categories of *tujjār*. His first category was the *khazzān*, or stapler, a sedentary merchant who stocked goods when their price was low for later resale when the price rose. Next came the *rakkāḍ*, who traveled on business for himself or in partnership, perhaps with the third variety of merchant, the *mujahhiz*, a sedentary importer/exporter.[1] Of the three, the latter seems to have operated on the largest scale, frequently acting as the central organizer for a wide network of traveling and sedentary partners in distant places. Although this tripartite typology originally described Muslim merchants working in the Near East, it also fits well with data on Andalusi traders.

[1] Dimashqī, Abū Faḍl Ja'far, *Kitāb al-'ashāra ilā maḥāsin al-tijāra.* [Cairo, 1318/1900] pp. 48–52. The dates of this author are disputed; he may have lived as early as the ninth century or as late as the eleventh century. On Muslim merchants generally, see M. Rodinson, "Le marchand musulman," *Islam and the Trade of Asia.* [ed. D.S. Richards, Philadelphia, 1970] pp. 21–35.

We find examples of two of Dimashqī's merchant types in contemporary Geniza records describing trade between Egypt and al-Andalus. Of those engaged in international traffic, Ibn ʿAwkal and Nahray b. Nissīm were well-known Jewish merchants who conducted most of their business from a central base in Old Cairo, thus conforming to the profile of a *mujahhiz*. The twelfth-century Halfōn b. Nethanel, on the other hand, is known to have traveled extensively, and could be more accurately described as a *rakkāḍ*. The majority of data on merchants active in Andalusi international commerce show men conforming to the category of the *rakkāḍ*, but this abundance may be misleading, since it was probably the very fact of their travels that earned these traders a place in the historical record. The *khazzān* probably had as important a role in maintaining the flow of international trade as his itinerant counterparts, but he has left fewer traces in the historical record.

Merchants often changed their status and sphere of activities at different stages of their professional careers. Thus, a young man just starting out in the business might have journeyed widely, gaining experience of trade and establishing his own contacts. In contrast, an older and experienced merchant was more likely to play the sedentary role of *mujahhiz*. However, many counter-examples to this pattern can be found, and some respected traders, including the influential Halfōn b. Nethanel himself, traveled throughout their lives.

Aside from Dimashqī's three categories, other types of merchant were active in Andalusi trade, though they may not have been so directly involved in international business. Among these were a variety of agents, brokers, and other middle-men engaged in foreign commerce. On a lower level, there were also itinerant peddlers who traveled outside of the fixed commercial networks and routes used by more established merchants. The early thirteenth-century market inspector Saqaṭī discussed these merchants, calling them either *tujjār musāfirīn* (traveling merchants) or *tujjār mutajawilīn* (wandering merchants).[2] Traders of this sort probably carried goods across the borders between Christian and Muslim regions, but the scope of their commerce seems to have been limited to relatively inexpensive household articles. Seden-

[2] Saqaṭī, *Kitāb al-faqīh al-ajall al-ʿālim al-ʿārif al-awḥad* (*Un manuel hispanique de ḥisba*). [eds. G.S. Colin and E. Lévi-Provençal, Paris, 1931], pp. 1, 15, 17.

tary local merchants (shop keepers and the like) are not of concern here. Although they may have dealt in international commodities, their personal sphere of action was limited. Only in the frontier regions were they engaged in anything approximating long-distance or international traffic.[3]

Evidence on merchants and merchant affairs is extremely fragmentary because there are no medieval treatises devoted to Andalusi merchants as a subject in themselves. Collections of juridical rulings (*fatwas*) may discuss the intricacies of mercantile activities, but rarely mention individual merchants by name. The same is true of urban documents and handbooks on economic affairs. Tombstones, on the other hand, tend to record only the names and death dates of merchants. Biographical dictionaries (*tarājim*) likewise mention the names of Muslim merchant-scholars, their death dates, and something of their travels, but the authors of these books were primarily interested in their subjects' scholarly careers, not their business affairs.

Overall, sources tell us very little about the commercial specialization, personal life, business associates, training, social status, or day-to-day operations of the Andalusi merchant community. Only in special cases do we hear from the merchants themselves, in their letters, contracts, accounts, and lawsuits. The letters from the Cairo Geniza provide illuminating confirmation for the claim that "there is no better key to the psychology of the merchant than his correspondence."[4] Geniza letters constitute the principal source for the information presented here on Jewish merchants trading to and from al-Andalus. Geniza materials are also used, to some extent, for more general extrapolations regarding medieval Mediterranean mercantile organization. In a later period, notarial records and other Latin legal documents become a useful tool for tracing the voyages of Latin Christian merchants to Andalusi ports.

Other factors, besides the paucity of data, make it difficult to define the status of merchants in Andalusi society. It appears to have been common for merchants to maintain other careers

[3] Local merchants, markets, and trade in al-Andalus have been extensively treated by P. Chalmeta in his *El señor del zoco en España: edades media y moderna, contribución al estudio de la historia del mercado*. [Madrid, 1973].

[4] R.S. Lopez and I.W. Raymond (eds.), *Medieval Trade in the Mediterranean World*. [New York, 1955], p. 378.

alongside their commercial activities, so that many merchants were also ship-owners, doctors, soldiers, government officials, or scholars. Sources enhance this impression of professional duality because few mere businessmen were sufficiently important to merit inclusion in chronicles or other records. Muslim merchant-scholars, for instance, found their place in biographical dictionaries owing to their learning, not their trade.[5] Merchants and others who made their living through commerce seem to have been more widely spread through the social hierarchy of the medieval Islamic world than that of the Latin west. As is

[5] Biographical dictionaries were generally written for the specific purpose of recording the lives and scholarly connections of learned men in order to verify the transmission of religious knowledge. These books were not intended to record individual professions aside from those connected to scholarship. Other problems also arise with their use. First of all, a person with *al-tājir* as part of his name was probably, but not necessarily, a merchant. It may have been a family profession. Only in cases where he is described as "making his living as a merchant" or coming to a place "as a merchant" (*tājiran*), is his trade certain. I have only included examples of the latter type in this study. Secondly, one finds a high percentage of people coming to al-Andalus "as merchants" from the east, but very few Andalusis going east for the same purpose. The reasons for this are obvious: trade was a reasonable explanation for a journey to al-Andalus, but biographers preferred to cite pilgrimage as the motivation for Andalusis venturing to the east. If these Andalusis were also trading on the side, it is not mentioned.

The primary works used here are Ibn al-Faraḍī (d. 1013) *Kitāb ta'rikh 'ulama' al- Andalus.* [ed. F. Codera, *BAH*, Madrid, 1890]; Ibn Bashkuwāl (d. 1183) *Kitāb al-ṣila fī ta'rīkh al-immat al-Andalus.* [Cairo, 1955]; Aḥmad al-Ḍabbī (d. 1202) *Kitāb bughyat al-multamis fī ta'rikh rijāl ahl al-Andalus.* [ed. F. Codera, *BAH*, Madrid, 1885]; and Ibn al-'Abbar (13th c.) *Kitāb al-takmila li-kitāb al-ṣila.* [ed. F. Codera, *BAH*, Madrid, 1886]. The *Ṣilat al-ṣilah.* by Ibn al-Zubayr (d. 1308) [ed. E. Lévi-Provençal, Rabat, 1938] contains no merchants among the scholarly ranks. One further source is the *Akhbār wa tarājim Andalusīya.* of Silafī (d. 1180), of which the section on Andalusis traveling in the east has been edited separately by I. 'Abbās [Beirut, 1963]. See also A.I. Rozi, "The Social Role of Scholars ('Ulamā') in Islamic Spain. A Study of Medieval Biographical Dictionaries (Trājim)." [Ph.D. Dissertation, Boston University, 1983], pp. 349–71, 410. Sufi scholars may have been less involved in lucrative international business. Ibn 'Arabi cited only small-scale jobs (tanner, capmaker, cobbler, etc.) as means of livelihood for scholars described in his *Sufis of Andalusia. The Rūḥ al-quds and al-Durrat al-fākhirah of Ibn 'Arabī.* [trans. R.W.J. Austin, Berkeley, 1977], pp. 76, 84, 97, 115, 118, 124, 140.

Merchant-scholars were by no means unique to al-Andalus. In a study of the professional affiliations of eastern scholars through the eleventh century, H.J. Cohen has found that 4,200 out of 14,000 entries describing scholars in biographical dictionaries contained information on their trade. Among these, 22 percent were employed as merchants or artisans in the textile industry, 13 percent in foods, 4 percent in jewels, 4 percent in perfumes, 4 percent in leather-work, 4 percent in books, 3 percent in metals, 2 percent in wood, 2 percent in general commerce, and 9 percent in other commodities. Besides these traders, 3 percent acted as bankers and 2 percent were middlemen or commercial agents ("The Economic Background and Secular Occupations of Muslim Jurisprudents and Traditionists in the Classical Period of Islam," *JESHO* 13(1970), pp. 26–31).

made clear by the existence of Muslim merchant-scholars, who combined religious learning with commercial expertise, and by the letters preserved in the Cairo Geniza, many merchants were literate and even highly educated. They could be religious as well as economic leaders in their communities. These individuals may not be entirely representative of the majority of traders, yet they are the merchants who have left a record of their existence.

There is also the important fact that the merchant community was not a unified block, but was segregated along the lines of religion, ethnicity, geographical origin, and business dealings. Dimashqī's description of merchant types rests on an assumption of varying personalities and professional interests. This kind of differentiation was later adopted by Ibn Khaldūn, who perceived two distinct merchant types: the crafty, tenacious, devoted businessman, who dealt with all aspects of trade, and the aristocratic merchant, who provided financial backing and guidance but did not handle daily transactions. According to Ibn Khaldūn's observations, since "a merchant must concern himself with buying and selling, earning money and making a profit," it was generally necessary that he have "cunning, willingness to enter into disputes, cleverness, and great persistence." However, as the historian went on to point out, there also "exists a second kind of merchant . . . those who have the protection of rank and are thus spared [from] . . . having anything to do personally with such [business manipulations]."[6] This contrast flirts with caricature, yet Ibn Khaldūn's descriptions probably signal a genuine distinction, as valid for merchants in al-Andalus as in the author's native North Africa. Certainly, Andalusi data indicate considerable diversity among those involved in commerce, from simple tradesmen to aristocratic investors.

Andalusi international traders must have had dealings with other types of merchant. A traveling merchant, for example, would have traded through a sedentary partner, and foreign traders bought and sold from local merchants. The specific structures of partnership and cooperation between merchants will be discussed in the final section of this chapter. Mercantile interaction and partnerships did not mean, however, that the businessmen trading to and from al-Andalus formed an open community. On the contrary, by their choice of associates,

[6] Ibn Khaldūn, *The Muqaddimah.* [trans. F. Rosenthal, New York, 1958] II, pp. 343–5.

merchants separated themselves into groups based on geographical origin and, more importantly, on religion. The ties of allegiance and identity apparent in the merchant community were in line with more general trends in Andalusi society, since economic collaboration often grew out of social and religious interaction. To some degree, it appears that Andalusis – merchants and otherwise – were bound together by their common regional identity. Andalusis abroad were usually identified by their *nisba* (that part of an Arabic name which denotes origin),[7] and tended to associate with others from their homeland.[8]

While on one level there existed a strong bond of Andalusi affiliation, religious and ethnic diversity tended to override geographical solidarity. Merchants operating within the Andalusi trading sphere, as elsewhere in the medieval Mediterranean world, preferred to group themselves along religious lines: Muslim, Jewish, and Christian. An example of this tendency can be found in a letter written by Moses Maimonides to his son Abraham, cautioning the latter to beware of strangers on his travels, and not to "befriend intimately any group except our own loving brethren of Spain, who are known as Andalusis."[9] By this, Maimonides intended that Abraham should be friendly with Andalusi Jews, not necessarily with Andalusi Muslims or Christians. In keeping with the sentiment expressed by Maimonides in his paternal counsel, documents from the Geniza show Andalusi Jews keeping company to the point that Goitein has

[7] A *nisba* may derive from a place name (al-Andalusī, al-Fāsī, al-Qurṭubī), tribe, family, or other affiliation. It was a common method of identification, particularly for merchants and other people traveling far from their homes. The *nisba* was employed by many Arabic speakers, no matter what their religion, and may be helpful in identifying certain groups. However, *nisbas* can be unreliable in identifying geographical origin since they frequently refer not to the bearer's own birthplace, but to that of an ancestor.

[8] The issue of Andalusi solidarity (*ʿaṣabīya*) has been much debated. See, D. Wasserstein, *The Rise and Fall of the Party Kings: Politics and Society in Islamic Spain 1002–1086.* [Princeton, 1985], p. 165, and N. Roth, "Some Aspects of Muslim-Jewish Relations in Spain," *Estudios en homenaje a D. Claudio Sánchez-Albornoz.* II, [Buenos Aires, 1983] p. 203. Also, M. Benaboud, "ʿAsabiyya and Social Relations in al-Andalus during the Period of the Taifa States," *Hespéris-Tamuda* 19(1980–1), pp. 5–45; M. Shatzmiller, "The Legacy of the Andalusian Berbers in the 14th-century Maghreb," *Relaciones de la península ibérica con el Magreb [siglos XIII–XIV]*. [eds. M. García-Arenal and M.J. Viguera, CSIC, Madrid, 1988], pp. 205–36; P. Guichard, *Structures sociales "orientales" et "occidentales" dans l'Espagne musulmane.* [Paris, 1977].

[9] Moses b. Maimon, *Letters of Maimonides.* [trans. L.D. Stitskin, New York, 1977], p. 157. Stitskin's text has "Andalusians" where I have "Andalusis."

noted that Jewish Andalusi merchants working abroad formed "a kind of closed club, known to each other" in which non-Jews and non-Andalusis did not generally participate.[10] It is probable that Muslim and Christian Andalusis subscribed to a similar religious clannishness. Thus, although geographical origin was important, causing merchants and other travelers to seek out the company of their compatriots, they identified themselves first and foremost with their own religious communities.

This pattern of religious segregation was true of society throughout the Islamic world, and shows up clearly in the differentiation of sources. It is rare, for instance, to find a genre or individual source which contains general information on merchants of different religions. Further evidence for religious segregation is provided by data on routes of travel and commodity specialization.[11] Christian shipping routes, for instance, were rarely the same as those followed by Muslims and Jews. In general, merchant ships from Latin Europe tended to prefer routes along the northern Mediterranean littoral, bordering Christian territories, while merchants from the Islamic world favored more southerly itineraries.[12] Nor did merchant groups carry identical cargoes, although most medieval merchants dealt in a wide spectrum of goods. For example, both Christians and Muslims – but apparently not Jews – traded in timber, even in the face of religious prohibitions against purveying shipping materials to "the enemy". Similarly, in most cases merchants would not sell or transport slaves of their own religion: Muslims bought and sold Christian slaves, while Christians did the same with Muslims.

Separate identification on the grounds of religion and geographical origin remained the norm, in spite of strongly similar traits which inevitably existed between the individual merchant groups. Businessmen of different religions certainly had contact with one another, particularly in exchanging commercial information, acquiring goods, and organizing marine transportation.

[10] S.D. Goitein, *Letters of Medieval Jewish Traders*. [Princeton, 1973], p. 184, n.21.

[11] For more on the professional specialization of different religious and ethnic groups in Andalusi society (although not relating to international merchants) see M. Shatzmiller, "Professions and Ethnic Origins of Urban Labourers in Muslim Spain," *Awrāq* 5–6(1982–3), pp. 149–59.

[12] J. Pryor has described this trend in *Geography, Technology, and War*. [Cambridge, 1988].

Likewise, these merchants engaged in individual commercial transactions, but they never – or very rarely – formed lasting interfaith partnerships. By and large, they preferred commercial dealings and partnerships with their co-religionists.

Geographically, Muslim, Jewish, and Christian traders operated within separate but overlapping commercial spheres. They all took part in Mediterranean international commerce, all did business in Andalusi markets, yet each group was subject to different constraints. It was characteristic throughout the medieval Mediterranean world to find Jews and Christians trading with all regions, while Muslim merchants generally restricted their sphere of operation to Islamic markets. Muslim merchants traded freely throughout the southern Mediterranean, both in al-Andalus and elsewhere within the *dār al-Islām*. Further to the east, however, they pursued their commercial activities as far away as India and China. In contrast, Muslim traders are strikingly absent from the markets of Latin Europe. Several explanations have been proposed to explain this disparity, though none are fully satisfactory. European markets may have been less enticing than those of Muslim lands, since they had less to offer in the way of exports. In any case, most northern products could be easily obtained from the Christian merchants who flocked in growing numbers to Islamic ports. Perhaps Muslim travelers also found Christian cities uncongenial to their needs, particularly in terms of facilities for bathing and eating, and shunned them in consequence. These considerations would have been less of a hindrance to Jewish merchants, who could rely on the existence of a resident Jewish community in most destinations.

Islamic law also discouraged (*makrūh*) Muslims from traveling to or trading with non-Islamic lands, although these excursions were usually not forbidden (*ḥarām*).[13] However, Muslim jurists in al-Andalus and North Africa, following the Mālikī school of Islamic law, tended to adopt a more rigid stance against travel and trade to the *dār al-ḥarb* (non-Islamic lands) than did jurists elsewhere. The jurist Saḥnūn (ninth century) cited Mālik as having a "strong repugnance" for Muslim commercial activity in non-Muslim territories, and later Andalusi legal scholars, including Ibn Ḥazm (d. 1064) and Ibn Rushd (d. 1126), also

[13] B. Lewis, *The Muslim Discovery of Europe*. [New York, 1982], p. 61.

ruled against trade to non-Muslim lands.[14] The unusual strictness of these opinions was surely a consequence of the close proximity between al-Andalus and Christian Spain. Because of the Iberian frontier, the opportunities for Muslim merchants to trade in Christian lands were considerably greater than in most other areas of the Islamic world.

As with most legal evidence, however, there may have been considerable disparity between judicial theory and commercial reality, since repeated prohibitions often indicate non-compliance. Thus, although modern historians have traditionally placed trade across the Andalusi frontier in the hands of Christian and Jewish traders, it appears that Muslim merchants also trafficked along the Iberian overland routes, in spite of judicial sanctions. Muslim traders were present in northern Iberian markets, but they rarely ventured north of the Pyrenees. Twelfth century Castilian and Aragonese town charters (*fueros*) frequently included tariff lists that cited people and goods coming "from the land of the Moors". The 1166 Fuero of Evora, for example, listed "Christian, Jewish, as well as Moorish, merchants and travelers" among those people affected by its rulings.[15] Likewise, another late twelfth-century *fuero*, from Santa Maria de Cortes, promised that "free saracens will be secure if they come to this town for the purpose of trading in animals".[16] As already noted in the preceding chapter, the 1231 *fuero* of Caceres permitted Christians, Jews, and Muslims to come to an annual fair, whether from Christian or Muslim territories.[17]

The trading sphere of Jewish merchants was more comprehensive

[14] Saḥnūn, *Mudawwana al-kubrā*. [Cairo, 1323/1905] x, p. 102; Ibn Ḥazm, *Maḥallī*. [Cairo, 1347/1928–9] vii, pp. 349–50; Ibn Rushd, *Kitāb al-muqaddimāt al-mumahhidāt*. [Cairo, 1325/1907] ii, p. 285; (Ibn Ḥazm was a Ẓāhirī, not a Mālikī). A later Maghribi scholar, Ibn Juzayy (d. 1340) was also strict on this matter, ruling that "it is not permitted to trade to the *dār al-ḥarb*" (*Qawānin al-aḥkām al-sharʿiya*. [Beirut, 1968], p.319). See also M. Khadduri, *War and Peace in the Law of Islam*. [Baltimore, 1955]; J. Yarrison, "Force as an Instrument of Policy: European Military Incursions and Trade in the Maghrib, 1000–1355." [Ph.D. Dissertation, Princeton University, 1982], pp. 269ff.

[15] *Portugaliae monumenta historica: Leges et consuetudines*. i, [Lisbon, 1856] p. 393. Also in the same volume, the *Fuero* of Mós (1162) referred to Moorish textiles, p. 391.

[16] A. Ballesteros y Beretta, *Historia de España y su influencia en la historia universal*. [Barcelona, 1920] ii, p. 529.

[17] T. González, *Colección de privilegios, franquezas, exenciones, y fueros, concedidos a varios pueblos y corporaciones de la Corona de Castilla, copiados de orden de S.M. de los registros del Real archivo de Simancas*. [Madrid, 1833] iv, p. 94.

than that of Muslim merchants, and Jewish commercial networks linked al-Andalus with markets all over the Mediterranean world and beyond. The commercial success of Jewish traders, both Andalusi and otherwise, during the early middle ages has been attributed to several different causes. Among these, the ubiquitous presence of Jewish communities around the Mediterranean littoral, their easy communications through ties of family and partnership, their non-military status, and their lenient attitude toward institutions of credit were all conducive to building strong commercial connections.

Jewish traders controlled a major portion of Andalusi commerce from the early middle ages until at least the middle of the twelfth century, during which time Geniza letters show traffic between Andalusi ports and those in the Maghrib, Egypt, and Palestine. Many letters written in the east refer to particular merchants traveling to or from al-Andalus, or simply include a brief comment to the effect that "the Andalusis have arrived" or "we are waiting for the Andalusis".[18] Jewish businessmen were also an integral part of the internal Andalusi economy. One eleventh-century *fatwa* dealing with a complaint about Jewish peddlers (and particularly about their easy access to women in households where they came to sell their wares) provides insight into the special abilities of Jewish merchants to move throughout Andalusi society and even to enter the women's quarters of a private home.[19]

Jews also maintained commercial links across the Iberian frontier. An eleventh-century anecdote cited by several Andalusi authors indicates that Jewish businessmen probably enjoyed a freedom and flexibility of travel not found among other merchant groups in the Iberian peninsula. The story tells of a Jewish merchant who was hired by a Muslim to try to rescue the latter's daughters who had been captured by Christians at the siege of Barbastro in 1064. Although the attempt was unsuccessful, the Jewish merchant has survived in legend as an example of

[18] Geniza documents referring to the arrival of Andalusi people and boats include: Bodl b3.20 (ca. 1042); TS 12.794 (1050–5); TS 13 J 16.19 (1050s); TS 13 J 19.20 (1062); TS 16.163 (ca. 1063); TS 8 J 20.2 (ca. 1065); TS 10 J 16.17 (late 1000s); ULC Or 1080 J 178 (ca. 1100); TS 13 J 15.16 (1140).

[19] R.H. Idris, "Les tributaires en occident musulman médiéval d'après le *Mi'yār* d'al-Wansharīsī," *Mélanges d'islamologie: Volume dédié à la mémoire de Armand Abel.* [Leiden, 1974], p. 180.

a highly mobile and non-aligned entity, admirably suited to operations of this sort.[20]

Jewish commerce across the Andalusi frontier may have been a particularly important area of Jewish trade, since there is virtually no other evidence of direct commercial contact between Jews in the eastern Islamic world and those in Europe.[21] It is possible that Andalusi Jewish merchants played a mediating role in the Jewish trading sphere similar to that played by al-Andalus in the wider Mediterranean commercial world. Evidence from the Geniza and elsewhere suggests – though it cannot prove – that this was the case. Certainly, Jewish merchants traded regularly between al-Andalus, the Maghrib, and the Near East, taking advantage of well-developed commercial and communal ties throughout the eastern Mediterranean. Similarly, Andalusi Jews had contacts across the Iberian frontier into northern Spain and Europe. This is shown in an early period by the activities of Jewish slave traders and of travelers such as Ibrāhīm b. Yaʿqūb, and is later indicated by the fact that Benjamin of Tudela seems to have known a number of his co-religionists in French and Italian coastal cities. The Jewish communities of the western Mediterranean probably had a communications network not unlike the system existing in the eastern Mediterranean. The point of contact between these two networks lay in the Andalusi Jewish community.

Although Christian merchants also traded in Andalusi markets, they were neither influential nor numerous before the middle of the twelfth century. Unlike Andalusi Muslims and Jews, indigenous Christians, the Mozarabs, seem to have had little interest in commerce. It is often assumed that Mozarabic merchants forged a vital commercial and cultural link between north and south across the Iberian frontier, but the texts do not provide much support for this. There are only a handful of references to Mozarab merchants active in Andalusi trade during the Umayyad period, and no later data.[22] Refugee Mozarabs may

[20] E. Ashtor, *The Jews of Moslem Spain.* [Philadelphia, 1973–84] III, p. 202.

[21] This dearth of data has been discussed, with an attempt at explanation, by A.O. Citarella, "A Puzzling Question Concerning Relations Between the Jewish Communities of Christian Europe and those represented in the Geniza Documents," *JAOS* 91 (1971), pp. 390–7.

[22] Ashtor believed that Mozarabs carried luxury goods throughout Spain, and both Arié

have had influence in northern Spanish trade (for instance, a number of Mozarab merchants are found living in Toledo in the twelfth and thirteenth centuries), but there is no reason to believe that they engaged in commerce with their abandoned homeland.[23] An explanation for the lack of Mozarab commercial activity in the south – if this was indeed the case – may rest in the low status of trade as a profession in the eyes of Iberian Christians during much of the medieval period. This is in contrast to the greater respect accorded to merchants in Muslim and Jewish society, where trade was frequently combined with other callings, such as politics, scholarship, or medicine. In Visigothic Spain, merchants had fallen to the bottom of the social heap, victims of an attitude which was preserved in Castile into the thirteenth century. Indigenous Andalusi Christians probably saw no reason to compete for a profession which they despised and which was willingly assumed by others. Thus, the few Christian traders at work in Umayyad markets tended to be foreigners, drawn from northern Spain and Europe by the desire for Andalusi products and other Muslim luxury goods.

Most traffic between al-Andalus and Christian regions remained in the hands of Jewish and Muslim traders until the dramatic shifts initiated by European commercial expansion in the eleventh and twelfth centuries. With the development of Italian maritime power, and the southward progress of Christian Spanish conquests, Andalusi international trade came increasingly into the control of Christian traders from northern Spain, southern France, and Italy. By the middle of the thirteenth century, Iberian trade was an almost exclusively Christian concern, and even the trade of Nasrid Granada was largely controlled by foreign Christian merchants.

The slow start to Christian traffic with al-Andalus probably owed more to Christian commercial disinterest and disorganization in the early middle ages than to specific legal or religious impediments in the Muslim world. Although Islamic law discouraged Muslim merchants from trafficking in Christian lands, it

and Verlinden consider them to have been very active in medieval commerce. See E. Ashtor, *The Jews of Moslem Spain*, I, p. 278; R. Arié, *España musulmana*. [Barcelona, 1982], p. 251; C. Verlinden, "The Rise of Spanish Trade in the Middle Ages," *Economic History Review* 10 (1940), p. 47.

[23] A. González Palencia, *Los mozárabes de Toledo en los siglos XII y XIII*. [Madrid, 1926–8], pp. 79, 126, 127, 162.

placed few obstacles in the path of incoming Christian traders. Non-Muslim foreigners traveling within the *dār al-Islām* were required to obtain a certificate of safe-conduct (*'amān*), and adhere to guidelines set for all non-local merchants.[24] An *'amān* was generally valid for between four months and a year, and allowed a non-Muslim to live and work in Islamic territories during this period without assuming the status of a resident non-Muslim (*dhimmī*). Even with the proper documentation, however, it was rare for European merchants to penetrate the internal commercial networks of Muslim lands. After Christian trade became well established in the twelfth and thirteenth centuries, Christian merchants still usually limited their contact to certain port cities where, if permitted, they might establish a trading house (*funduq*) and a small community of their countrymen. With a few exceptions, foreign merchants could traffic in any merchandise.[25] If Christian merchants faced restrictions on their traffic to Islamic lands, these tended to be imposed by their own rulers and religious authorities, rather than by their Muslim hosts. By the thirteenth century, at least, it was common policy for Christian authorities to reiterate sanctions against traffic with "enemy" Muslim territories.

The lack of Muslim legal strictures may stem from the fact that Muslim jurists – and Muslim and Jewish merchants – appear to have regarded Christian merchants with a certain disdain. Not only were foreigners seen as uncouth, but they were considered gullible and naive. The Andalusi market inspector Ibn 'Abd al-Ra'ūf (writing ca. 950–75) quoted the caliph 'Umar in support of his opinion that "foreigners ought not to sell in our market[s] unless they understand [our] religion, [for] it is preferable to trade with people of learning and refinement . . ."[26] In other cases we find Christian foreigners becoming a local joke. A partner in Alexandria wrote to Nahray b. Nissīm in

[24] The nature of this institution is further outlined by J. Wansbrough, "The Safe-Conduct in Muslim Chancery Practice," *BSOAS* 34(1971), pp. 20–35, and by Khadduri, *War and Peace*, pp. 163–4.

[25] Only a few items were restricted. For example, Ibn Rushd (d. 1126) ruled that a Christian merchant could not sell Muslim slaves in the *dār al-Islām* (*Kitāb al-muqaddamāt*, pp. 274–6).

[26] Ibn 'Abd al-Ra'ūf, *Risāla*. in E. Lévi-Provençal (ed.), *Documents arabes inédits sur la vie sociale et économique en occident musulman au moyen âge*. [Cairo, 1955], pp. 84–5. Ibn 'Abd al-Ra'ūf attributed this quotation merely to 'Umar; it is not clear whether he intended 'Umar I or 'Umar II.

Old Cairo, ca. 1075, detailing the idiocies of the Christian merchants who "do not discriminate between first-class and inferior goods. It appears to be all the same to them and they pay the same price . . . they buy the poor quality for the same price as the excellent variety, and are not prepared to pay more for the latter."[27]

As early as the tenth century, Christian merchants from northern Spain and other regions of Europe came to Andalusi markets. Muslim jurists generally advocated protection of these traders, particularly in the Umayyad period. Ibn Abī Zayd (d. 996) recalled a ruling of the ninth-century Mālikī scholar Saḥnūn that "regarding Christian ships which arrive . . . it is not permitted to capture them if [they carry] merchants known for their commercial relations with the Muslims . . ."[28] The safety of those Christian merchants who trafficked in Andalusi territories varied with the shifting climate of relations between Christian kingdoms and Andalusi rulers. In times of truce, mercantile safe passage under the protection of an *'amān* was guaranteed by law, in theory if not always in fact. In confirmation of this general precept, Wansharīsī cited a tenth-century *fatwa* concerning an escaped Christian captive who later returned as a merchant to the Andalusi town of his captivity. The judge adjudicating this case ruled that, in time of peace, this man and other Christians like him were secured against re-capture.[29] This man's early captivity and later security demonstrate the changeable nature of Umayyad–Christian relations, and indicate the effect of politics (and periods of formal truce) on trade. Later, the hostilities of the reconquest and the arrival of the Almoravids and Almohads increased the insecurity of overland commerce across the Iberian frontier. A question brought before the Almoravid amir Tamīm b. Yūsuf b. Tāshufīn (d. 1127) asked whether a party of Christian

[27] BM Or 5546.27; trans. A.L. Udovitch, "A Tale of Two Cities, Commercial Relations between Cairo and Alexandria during the Second Half of the 11th Century," *The Medieval City*. [eds. H. Miskimin, D. Herlihy, A. Udovitch, New Haven, 1977], p. 156. Muslim disdain for western Christians, both merchants and others, has recently been discussed by A. Al-Azmeh, "Barbarians in Arab Eyes," *Past and Present* 134(1992), pp. 3–18.

[28] M. Talbi, "Intérēt des oevres juridiques traitant de la guerre pour l'historien des armées médiévales ifrīkiennes," *Cahiers de Tunisie* 4(1956), p. 291. This English translation is taken from Talbi's French translation of a passage from an unpublished manuscript of Ibn Abī Zayd, *Kitāb al-nawādir*. [Tunis, Zaytuna ms. 5191, fol. 287r].

[29] H.R. Idris, "Les tributaires en occident musulman," p. 174.

merchants from Toledo, coming to Cordoba in peacetime, might be taken hostage against the return of some recently captured Muslims. The answer was positive: the merchants and their goods could be held until the captives were restored, after which point the broken truce would be renewed.[30] The professional risks inherent in overland commerce are also seen in other sources. One eleventh-century tale described the miraculous rescue of a Catalan merchant, Arnold, who was waylaid by Muslims while journeying from his home in Cardona (in Central Catalonia) to Balegaris (near Lerida). Another story told of a monk seeking to travel to Valencia in the twelfth century. After being told that most routes were impassable owing to war, he was advised to go to Santiago instead, where he might join up with merchants who had paid tribute in return for protection on the journey to Valencia.[31] Despite (or perhaps because of) the insecurity of overland trade, Italian maritime traffic with Andalusi ports began to flourish in this period. Access to ports was easier to control than land routes, and Almoravid and Almohad rulers appear to have encouraged Christian sea trade (through diplomatic treaties with Italian cities) at the same time that they hampered the traffic of merchants coming overland from the enemy regions of northern Spain.

The differing diplomatic status of Christian regions, some of whom were at war with al-Andalus while others were not, tended to divide the Christian merchant population. Unlike Muslims and Jews, Christian merchants did not form a strong cohesive group, since by the time they gained significant influence in Iberian trade in the late twelfth century, their ranks were segregated along regional, or proto-national, lines. Although they certainly viewed themselves as part of a larger Christian community, Genoese tended to associate with Genoese and Catalans with Catalans, so that one regional group often viewed another as a rival in trade. This differentiation was encouraged by Christian rulers, who legislated in the interest of their own subjects at the expense of foreign traders.

[30] Wansharīsī, *Mi'yār al-mu'rib wa al-jami' al-maghrib.* [ed. M. Hajjī, 13 vols., Rabat-Beirut, 1401/1981] IX, pp. 598–9.

[31] *Liber miraculorum Sancte Fidis.* [ed. A. Bouillet, Paris, 1897] Appendix, p. 243 (Bouillet dated this manuscript to the mid-eleventh century, certainly before 1060, p. viii); Herman of Tournai, "Epistola de corpore S. Vincentii diaconi," *Analecta bollandiana* 2(1883), p. 246.

The Christian merchant population was also divided by differing access to Andalusi markets. Merchants from Castile or Navarre would have come by overland routes, whereas Italians and other European traders, including Catalans, usually came by sea. For this reason, traders from the northern-central peninsula often penetrated more deeply into the Andalusi interior than did other Christian merchants. However, aside from these overland ventures to Andalusi markets, Castilian international trade hardly existed before the thirteenth century. There was some small-scale commerce through the Atlantic ports of Laredo, Santander, Castro Urdiales, and San Vicente de la Barquera, but these ports would not become crucial to the Castilian economy until the end of the thirteenth century.[32] In contrast, Aragon-Catalonia, with its lengthy Mediterranean coastline, achieved earlier and greater recognition as a maritime power. The relative ease of sea transport led to considerable commercial expansion in Catalonia during the twelfth and thirteenth centuries, when Barcelona began to rival the Italian maritime powers. Differences in mercantile development in Catalonia and Castile may also have stemmed, in part, from different perceptions of the social status of merchants. Whereas the Catalan mercantile persona developed along similar lines to Italian and southern French conceptions, creating what some have seen as a commercial bourgeoisie, the merchant in Castile (like his Visigothic and Mozarab counterparts) had a lower status. No Castilian of social standing would have considered a commercial profession during the twelfth or early thirteenth centuries, and they were happy to leave their commercial affairs in the hands of foreign traders, particularly the Genoese.

MERCHANT PARTNERSHIPS

Despite religious divisions within the Andalusi merchant population, commerce was a gregarious profession, and merchants were bound to each other by ties of cooperation and partnership. The distinction between partnership and cooperation was vague, for many instances of cooperation, including favors between

[32] T. Ruiz, "The Transformation of the Castilian Municipalities: The Case of Burgos 1248–1350," *Past and Present* 77(1977), p. 12; L. García de Valdeavellano, *El mercado en León y Castilla durante la edad media.* [2nd edn., Seville, 1975], p. 154.

friends or personal letters containing business tips, might be considered as a type of informal partnership. A formal partnership, in contrast, was generally a legal and binding arrangement, understood to hold for the duration of a commercial enterprise or longer. Formal partnerships could exist between two people, or within a large network of family members, business associates, and agents. Partners served many functions. They could receive, send, carry, buy, and sell goods, they could transfer money, and they kept other members of the partnership or commercial firm informed of local prices, conditions, and availability of commodities.

Muslim, Jewish, and Christian merchants operated side-by-side in medieval Mediterranean trade, and they frequently cooperated with each other on an informal basis. Cooperation was evident in the passage of goods and information between different merchant groups. For instance, a Jewish merchant writing from al-Andalus to Morocco in 1138 reported that he had received information from Muslim merchants who had recently arrived from Alexandria.[33] Likewise, a Genoese merchant sailing to Ceuta or Bougie might stop along the way in a southern Andalusi port to obtain news from local traders on current commercial conditions in North Africa.[34]

Interaction between different merchant groups was particularly apparent in sea travel and shipping, where the same ship might carry many different traders, and in overland transport. Geniza letters show Jewish merchants traveling between al-Andalus and the east on Muslim vessels. In several cases, these ships are identified as belonging to Muslim rulers such as the *sulṭān*, or the *qāʿid*, or to an apparently ordinary Iberian Muslim, such as ʿAbd Allah al-Andalusī. Judah Ha-Levi traveled to Egypt on an official ship (*markab al-sulṭān*) in 1140. Other ships, of unknown ownership, carrying both Jewish and Muslim passengers are mentioned in the Geniza. One vessel was shipwrecked on the voyage from Libya to Seville in the mid-twelfth century with thirty-seven Jews and three hundred Muslims on board. Only a few of the passengers survived.[35] Jews might also travel overland with Muslim traders, as shown in an eleventh-century

[33] Bodl d74.41.

[34] A *naulizo* contract written in 1253 allowed for an interim stop in Malaga en route from Genoa to North Africa (ASG Cart. 29, fol. 164r).

[35] TS 16.54.

responsum of Rabbi Alfasi that mentioned an Andalusi Jewish merchant returning to al-Andalus with a caravan of the *Isma'īlīm*.[36]

By the middle of the twelfth century, as Italian shipping began to dominate western Mediterranean routes, it became common for Jewish and Muslim merchants to seek passage on Christian boats.[37] The Andalusi traveler Ibn Jubayr, for instance, sailed to the Near East and back on Christian ships in the 1180s, although he remarked that Muslim and Christian passengers did not mix while on board.[38] Indeed, Christian transport was so common by this period that the Almohad caliph Abū Yūsuf Ya'qūb al-Manṣūr thought it worthwhile to include a clause in an 1186 treaty with Pisa to specifically prohibit the city from carrying Muslim passengers on its ships.[39] Despite such strictures, the Muslim merchant Muḥammad b. Mahalam, who sailed from Ceuta on a Genoese vessel in 1222, was surely only one of many non-Christian merchants to avail themselves of Italian and Catalan transport in the thirteenth century.[40]

In spite of inter-faith cooperation, commercial partnerships rarely crossed religious boundaries. Jewish merchants generally formed partnerships with other Jews, Muslims with other Muslims. In the early eleventh century, however, the Egyptian merchant Ibn 'Awkal is known to have worked with both Muslim and Jewish agents.[41] Christian Genoese merchants may have entered into partnerships with Jewish merchants, although it appears that partnerships between Christians and Muslims were rare.[42] Partnership forms and expectations may also have

[36] Alfasi, Isaac b. Jacob, *She'elot u-teshuvot*. [Bilgoraj, 1935 (reprinted Jerusalem, 1973)] no. 72.

[37] Bodl c28.60; This letter mentions two merchants who set out from al-Mahdiyya for Sicily on an Italian boat.

[38] Ibn Jubayr, *The Travels of Ibn Jubair*. [trans. R.J.C. Broadhurst, London, 1952], pp. 26, 325, 353.

[39] M. Amari (ed.), *I diplomi arabi del R. Archivio Fiorentino*. [Florence, 1863], p. 21.

[40] Salmon, *Liber magistri Salmonis sacri palatii notarii (1222–1226)*. [ed. A. Ferretto] *ASLSP* 36(1906), p. 100, 283. See also C.E. Dufourcq, *L'Espagne catalane et le Maghrib aux XIIIe et XIVe siècle*. [Paris, 1966], p. 576.

[41] N.A. Stillman, "The Eleventh-Century Merchant House of Ibn 'Awkal (A Geniza Study)," *JESHO* 16(1973), p. 23.

[42] Uncertainty regarding the religion of certain merchants appearing in Genoese contracts makes it difficult to ascertain the extent of Genoese interfaith partnerships. The views of E.H. Byrne "Easterners in Genoa," *JAOS* 38(1918), pp. 176–87, and B. Nelson "Blancard (the Jew?) of Genoa and the Restitution of Usury," *Studi in onore di Gino Luzzato*. [Milan, 1949] 1, pp. 96–116, are now outdated. C. Cahen addressed the question of Muslim-Christian partnerships in Egypt in "Douanes et commerce

placed obstacles in the path of inter-faith ventures. In general, evidence suggests that long-term commitment to a partnership was more common among Muslim and Jewish merchants working in the southern Mediterranean than it was among European Christians. Formal partnerships in the Arab world tended to be of longer duration than the Christian contracts, which usually remained valid for only one commercial venture.

Several varieties of formal partnership co-existed in the medieval Mediterranean world.[43] In the Islamic sphere, the terms *shirka* or *khulta* were often used to describe a partnership in which two or more people invested both capital and labor towards economic gains. All profits were then split among the partners according to each individual's investment. A more elaborate arrangement was the *qirāḍ* (also *muḍaraba*), in which the first party, the investor(s), provided the capital while the second party, the factor(s), did the work. The profits were unevenly divided, with the most common pattern allotting two-thirds to the first party – in recompense for economic risks taken – and one-third to the second party – for physical risks taken. Although at first glance this system perhaps seems best suited to the scenario of wealthy sedentary merchant investors lending to impecunious traveling factors, it also allowed more marginal investors to invest small amounts of money or goods to be carried in partnership by a well-known and successful merchant.

Similarity of partnership forms around the Mediterranean has given rise to speculations on inter-faith trading connections and the fluidity of exchange in mercantile ideas and techniques. In many respects, the *qirāḍ* (which appeared in Islamic law by the eighth century) was similar to the pre-existing partnership forms of the Jewish *ʿiṣqa* and the Byzantine *chreokoinonia*. However,

dans les ports méditerranéens de l'Egypt médiévale d'après le 'Minhādj d'al-Makhzūmī'," *JESHO* 7(1964), p. 270.

[43] For a more complete description of partnership forms see S.D. Goitein, *Mediterranean Society*. [Berkeley, 1967–88] 1, pp. 164–83, and his earlier article "Commercial and Family Partnerships in the Countries of Medieval Islam," *Islamic Studies* 3(1964), pp. 315–37. Also, E. Bach, *La cité de Gênes au XIIe siècle*. [Copenhagen, 1955], pp. 16–20; A.L. Udovitch, *Partnership and Profit in Medieval Islam*. [Princeton, 1970]; J.H. Pryor, "The Origins of the 'Commenda' Contract," *Speculum* 52(1977), pp. 5–37. Also of interest are the economic models proposed by A. Greif, "The Organization of Long-Distance Trade: Reputation and Coalitions in the Geniza Documents and Genoa during the 11th and 12th centuries." [Ph.D. Dissertation, Northwestern University, 1989].

the *qirāḍ* was distinguished by the fact that it exempted the factor, in most cases, from responsibility for loss of capital. It is possible that the *qirāḍ* was adopted in western Europe as the Latin *accomendatio* (or *commenda*), of which the earliest surviving example is a Venetian contract dating from 1072.[44] The structure of these two partnership forms is substantially the same, although the *qirāḍ*, unlike the *commenda*, was often of long duration and could be applied to overland trade as well as the maritime ventures favored by the *commenda*.[45] Whether or not their similarity derived from a direct link, it shows the parallel interests of mercantile business, and suggests exchange between the trading techniques of Muslim, Jewish, and Christian merchants in this period. Also, if the *commenda* did originate in the *qirāḍ*, it is noteworthy that the idea was adopted from the Arab commercial world just as the Muslim Mediterranean trading axis was beginning to weaken.

Prior to their use of the *commenda*, European merchants had favored the sea loan (*foenus nauticum*) and the *societas* as forms of commercial partnership. The three existed simultaneously through the twelfth century, but most of the early Genoese contracts for merchant voyages to Spain were phrased as a *societas* (*cum hac societate laboratum ire debet Yspaniam . . .*).[46] Of the three forms, the sea loan was the oldest, having been used in Roman commerce, but its medieval use was limited both by its open reliance on the payment of interest in return for money lent and also by the fact that the loan need only be repaid upon safe arrival of the ship and cargo. Because of the latter condition, the insecurity of medieval shipping once the Mediterranean was no longer a Roman lake encouraged high rates of interest and diminished the returns on a sea loan investment.[47] The *societas*, on the other hand, like the *qirāḍ* and *commenda*, was safer and

[44] This text is translated in R.S. Lopez and I.W. Raymond, *Medieval Trade*, pp. 178–9.

[45] A.L. Udovitch, "At the Origins of the Western Commenda: Islam, Israel, Byzantium?" *Speculum* 37(1962), pp. 198–207. In contrast to Udovitch's views, J.H. Pryor ("The Origins of the 'Commenda' Contract") argues that the *commenda* was largely derived from pre-existing western partnership forms.

[46] See, for example, contract dated January 16, 1160, in Giovanni Scriba, *Cartolare di Giovanni Scriba*. [eds. M. Chiaudano and M. Moresco, Rome, 1935] 1, p. 327, 603.

[47] Particular notarial care was needed in the wording of contracts for sea loans in order to escape the censure of canon law. For more on the sea loan see C.B. Hoover, "The Sea Loan in Genoa in the 12th Century," *Quarterly Journal of Economics* 40 (1925–6) pp. 495–529, and Pryor, "The Origins of the 'Commenda' Contract," pp. 22–3.

more secure since it relied on the distribution of profits from the commercial endeavour rather than the payment of interest (a practice as much frowned upon by Islam as Christianity). Unlike the *commenda*, however, a simple *societas* required that both parties invest capital in the venture: the investor contributed two-thirds, the factor gave one-third, and the profits were divided equally. In some cases, one finds that an extra sum (belonging to either partner) was carried over and above the joint investment.[48] In contrast, the *commenda* resembled the Muslim *qirāḍ* in the division of investment between investor(s) (100 percent) and factor. The distribution of profits was slightly different, and tended to be weighted 75 percent to the investor (*commendator*), 25 percent to the factor (*tractator*). Although there is an apparent shift in the notarial record from a preference for the *societas* in the middle of the twelfth century to a preference for the *commenda* by the beginning of the thirteenth century, it is uncertain whether these forms were clearly distinguished in the minds of the merchants who made the contracts. Their use of the terms *societas* and *commenda* can be vague and interchangeable, to the point that (as Pryor has remarked) it may be best to consider them as, respectively, bilateral and unilateral forms of the same type of partnership.[49] By extension, then, the same might be argued for the relationship between the *shirka* and the *qirāḍ*.

Partnerships between Andalusi merchants, or between foreign merchants organizing trips to the peninsula, show no differences from partnerships between merchants trading in other regions of the Mediterranean. An Andalusi jurist from Toledo, Ibn Mughīth (d. 1067), detailed a classic Islamic contract in which "Partner A and Partner B make a *shirka* for commerce. Partner A takes a certain sum from his assets and Partner B takes a like

[48] E. Rottenburger, "Genoese Relations with Mediterranean France and Spain and the Balearic Islands, 1155–1164." [MA Thesis, University of Cincinnati, 1947], p. 108. It is also common to find these extra privately owned sums being carried in *shirka*, *qirāḍ*, or *commenda*.

[49] H.C. Krueger estimated that in the middle of the twelfth century, *societas* contracts made up 57 percent of all commercial contracts in Genoa, *commendas* 22 percent, and sea loans 21 percent. By 1200, the figures were, respectively, 13 percent, 72 percent, and 15 percent ("Genoese Merchants, their Associations and Investments, 1155–1230," *Studi in onore di Amintore Fanfani*. [Milan, 1962] 1, p. 421). Pryor, "Origins of the 'Commenda' Contract," pp. 6–7.

sum, and they mingle [the money] so that they have one purse for joint trading in such-and-such a market in such-and-such a region . . ."[50] In another example, Goitein cited a "model partnership" between two Jewish merchants, both (rather confusingly) named Ibrāhīm b. Mūsā, one of whom was from Mallorca. In this basic *shirka*, each partner contributed two hundred dirhams for a voyage to an unspecified place. The money was put "into one purse" and the two partners promised to "sell, buy, take and give and do business with their capital and their bodies." The profits, presumably, were to be split equally.[51] Such joint action and pooled resources could provide greater capital, reduce the risks, and increase the total profits of commercial ventures.

There were exceptions and variations to these basic partnership forms, both among Andalusis and others. In an unusual bilateral contract for a commercial trip from Fez to Almeria in January 1138, Halfōn b. Nethanel invested "sixty good Murabitī *mithqāls*" in partnership with Yūsuf b. Shuʿayb, who contributed forty of the same and traveled to al-Andalus as factor. The proceeds of this expedition were to be divided equally.[52] In many ways, this arrangement was more similar to a *societas* than to a *qirāḍ*, and thus demonstrates the fluidity and variability of such arrangements.

The relationship between investor and factor may not always have fulfilled the requirements of a formal partnership, but the tale of one Ḥabīb Aḥmad al-Lahmī illustrates the importance of financial backing for success in international trade. Named Qāḍī of Cordoba in 904, Ḥabīb originally became rich through the assistance of a patron. In his *History of the Judges of Cordoba*, Khushanī related that "the fortunes of Ḥabīb, in as much as money was concerned, were exclusively due to the Qāḍī Sulaymān b. Aswad, who showed great solicitude towards [him] . . . demonstrated to him the basics of commerce, and urged him to [become a merchant]. But Ḥabīb replied that one must have money in order to go into trade, and he had none. After hearing this, Sulaymān let a few days pass, then called [Ḥabīb] to him, and gave him five thousand dinars, saying 'take these and trade

[50] Ibn Muqhīth, *Muqniʿ fī ʿilm al-shurūṭ*. [Real Academia de la Historia, Madrid, Gayangos ms. 44], fol. 71r. The original text refers to each party as *fulān*.

[51] TS 8 J 11.14; See Goitein, *Mediterranean Society*, 1, pp. 173, 442.

[52] TS 12.830.

with them on your own' (*li-nafsika*)."[53] Although no stipulations were made for the future division of profits, this tale may be read as a standard *qirāḍ* contract rather than merely a story of the generosity of an elder toward a younger man.

Sulaymān's final words indicate that he expected Ḥabīb to employ his own brains and initiative to make a profit on this investment. The exercise of independent action was possible (and even encouraged) within a partnership, although the autonomy of the members varied with the relationship between them. Usually, if one of two partners were absent or occupied, the other was free to do business on his own account. Between trusted long-time colleagues one often finds the admonition, in letters, to "do as you think best," whereas stricter instructions might be issued to a more junior associate. Injunctions like the following, addressed by an Andalusi merchant in Tyre to his partner in Egypt, were common: "Do not let idle with you one single dirham of our partnership, but buy whatever God puts into your mind and send it on the first ship sailing." In such a case, the recipient might act as he chose. A similar trust was evident in a letter sent from Fez to Almeria in 1141, in which it was left to the Andalusi partner to decide whether to buy an item in individual units or *en bloc*.[54] However, such leeway was not always permitted. The Egyptian merchant Ibn ʿAwkal was obviously angry with a partner in Qayrawan for sending a shipment of brazilwood to al-Andalus against instructions, as shown by the partner's indignant letter of explanation written ca. 1000.[55]

Letters exchanged between partners reveal the extent of trust, cooperation, and responsibility that was necessary to maintain a successful relationship. Information (*akhbār*) on changing prices and products was one of the most valuable items exchanged in letters between partners, and its importance implies a fluctuating market, with shifting and sensitive prices, that needed constant

[53] Khushanī, *Historia de los jueces de Córdoba por Aljoxaní.* [ed. and trans. J. Ribera, Madrid, 1914], pp. 175–6, 216–17.

[54] TS 8 J 41.2 (Goitein translated this passage in *Mediterranean Society*, 1, p. 200) and TS 13 J 21.12.

[55] DK 13; This letter is fully translated by Goitein in *Letters*, pp. 29–33. The writer of the letter does not make it absolutely clear whether Ibn ʿAwkal had sent brazilwood for sale in al-Andalus which was then mistakenly sold in Ifriqiya, or whether it was intended for Tunisian sale and was shipped on to al-Andalus. Goitein interpreted an insinuation, on the part of Ibn ʿAwkal, that his Tunisian partner had worked a fiddle for his own personal gain.

regional monitoring by merchants and their agents. One eleventh-century writer complained bitterly of a slump in the Tunisian pepper market, and related the details of the situation to a partner in Egypt:

The pepper, however, was dead. No one offered it. The price was down to 130 [quarter dinars per pound], but still no one bought. [Eventually] all the foreigners either sold everything they had for 130–132, and regarded this as a boon, or bought and loaded. But my heart did not let me sell for such a price and I held it until the time when the sailing of the ships approached, in the hope that it would rise. However, the slump got worse. Then I was afraid that suspicion might arise against me and sold your pepper to Andalusi merchants for 133 . . .

. . . while I am writing this letter – it is now the night before the sailing of the ships – pepper has become much in demand, for the foreigners had sold all they had, while boats (with customers) arrived and only local people had some left. Thus, it was sold for 140–142. I took collateral for the sale of my pepper at 140–142. But, brother, I would not like to take the profit for myself. Therefore I transferred the entire sale to our partnership.[56]

As his words make clear, the writer was selling pepper both on his own behalf and in partnership with an Egyptian colleague who had, we presume, originally sent the pepper westward. While the price was low, sellers were unwilling to part with their goods. However, a later influx of new customers, particularly after much of the available pepper had been reluctantly sold at a low price, drove the price up. Our merchant ultimately received a middling profit on his sale, having prudently sold his partner's pepper to Andalusi merchants at 133, slightly above the lowest rate, then luckily recouping a higher price on his own goods. In order to avoid any suspicion that he had not acted in the best interests of his partner, the writer promised that the difference would be split between them.

Another passage taken from a letter of 1141, sent from Fez to Almeria, detailed the volatile alum market, the variations in product quality, and the necessity that a merchant be constantly vigilant in attention to his own and his partner's affairs. One partner wrote from Morocco to al-Andalus:

Please take notice that in the shipment of alum that I sent you there are seven bales of particularly good quality, each *qinṭār* costing more than the regular price by a quarter of a *mithqāl*. The remaining quantities are

[56] Bodl a3.13. With minor changes, the translation is from Goitein, *Letters*, pp. 122–3.

of different values, but the whole purchase was at a low price . . . You may either sell each quality by itself or mix them, you know the market better and are able to act in accordance with the situation . . . had I had the courage, I would have sent you 100 *qinṭārs*. But I did not dare, since there was a great demand for it . . . the bearer of this letter is the packer who was present when the alum was packed. He knows which is the good quality and which the excellent one.[57]

It is not clear whether the writer was afraid to send more alum to al-Andalus because there was a great demand in Morocco and the price was very good, or because there was a demand among other Andalusi merchants and he was afraid that they would also send alum to Almeria, causing the price to fall in al-Andalus. The former option seems a more straightforward interpretation. Either way, the information and instructions relayed between partners were a crucial element in the commercial success of their endeavor.

Partners were often widely dispersed geographically, and since some of the evidence for their affairs is preserved in records concerning law suits, this creates a (perhaps mistaken) impression that long-distance partnerships were fraught with difficulties. Among such legal suits, a case brought before the Babylonian Gaon in the late tenth century involved a dispute between two partners – one in Qayrawan and the other in al-Andalus. In the next century, the Cordoban jurist Ibn Sahl noted numerous problems arising from absentee partners, while Wansharīsī's *Mi'yār* contained several later examples of far-flung disgruntled partners who brought their woes to court.[58] Likewise, Saqaṭī described the relationship between international merchants and their local agents in early thirteenth-century Malaga. He suggested that although agents were indispensable, merchants should keep a sharp eye on their activities, because partnership relationships were very open to fraud.[59]

Owing to the necessity of careful investigation and clarifica-

[57] TS 13 J 21.12 (trans. Goitein, *Letters*, p. 267).

[58] Tenth-century dispute: Ashtor, *The Jews of Moslem Spain*. I, p. 278. Hebrew text in S. Assaf, *Gaonica. Gaonic Responsa and Fragments from Halachic Literature*. [Jerusalem, 1933], p. 1; Ibn Sahl, *Aḥkām al-kubrā*. [General Library, Rabat, ms 838Q] fols. 180, 183–6, 189, 190; Wansharīsī notes cases concerning a partner absent for four years in Fez, al-Andalus, and Tlemcen (*Mi'yār*, VIII, p. 90–1); a question about what happens if a partner dies abroad in Fez or al-Andalus (*Mi'yār*, VIII, p. 204); and a debt between a man in Cordoba and a partner in Fez (*Mi'yār*, X, p. 443).

[59] Saqaṭī, *Kitāb al-faqīh*, pp. 391ff.

tion, court records often provide invaluable information on the exact structure of partnerships and the obligations they entailed. Two examples from the Geniza illustrate this point. The first presents a complicated case that came to the Jewish court in Denia in 1083. It involved a suit brought by Isḥāq b. Ibrāhīm against a certain Abū al-Ḥasan Qāsim, whose servant had mismanaged the sale of a cargo of cinnabar sent from Denia to al-Mahdiyya. The servant, as traveling agent, was charged with having sold the goods himself rather than delivering them to another partner, Ḥassān b. Ḥassān, in al-Mahdiyya. The court found the case to be unproven, but it remains interesting both as an example of commercial method and, as the names seem to indicate, of a Jewish-Muslim partnership.[60]

A second more poignant example concerned a woman in Tunisia, who sued her deceased father's partner, one Musāfir b. Samuel (then living in Egypt), for money formerly held in partnership with her father. The latter, Japheth Abū al-Riḍā, had perished in a shipwreck while returning from al-Andalus, and three hundred dinars of a *shirka* originally worth one thousand dinars had been lost with him. Using her husband as her agent, the daughter sought to retrieve three hundred and fifty of the remaining seven hundred dinars now held by Musāfir. Apparently both partners originally put five hundred dinars into the *shirka*; each partner thus owned one hundred and fifty dinars of the three hundred lost in the shipwreck and half of the surviving seven hundred. Unfortunately, the court's reply to her plea does not survive, leaving only the original petition, written ca. 1085, and one other record to tell of this case. Nonetheless, we can clearly discern the structure of this partnership, the expectation of mutual financial risk, and (not to be overlooked) the physical dangers involved in maritime commerce.[61]

[60] TS 12.570; this document is edited by E. Ashtor in "Documentos españoles de la Genizah," *Sefarad* 24(1964), pp. 76–7.

[61] ENA 4010.31 and TS 20.162. Goitein mentions this case in *Mediterranean Society*, III, p. 280.

Chapter 4

THE MERCHANTS IN ANDALUSI TRADE

Our knowledge of merchant groups, religious or otherwise, derives from scattered data on individuals trading to and from Andalusi ports. Most of these men are known only because their names appear briefly in biographical dictionaries, in chronicles and letters, or as participants in commercial contracts. Only in rare cases, as with the prominent Geniza businessmen or wealthy Genoese investors, do these people appear in more than one record. Even more rarely is it possible to know much of their life or activities beyond the particular commercial ventures on record.

Nevertheless, isolated references to individual traders allow us to build a larger picture of Andalusi commerce. These were the men who carried the goods and trafficked the routes between Andalusi ports and other regions of the Mediterranean world. Analysis of their activities reveals several important points. First, merchants were continuously engaged in Andalusi trade, so that there was no period in which commerce noticeably languished. Even in the early Muslim period, from the eighth century, people traded to and from Andalusi ports, and traffic continued through the period of Christian Spanish victories in the thirteenth century. Yet while trade persisted, the identity of the merchant population shifted over time. Likewise, the volume of their business appears to have fluctuated with shifts in political regime, maritime security, and the progress of the Christian reconquest.

Under Umayyad, Taifa, and Almoravid regimes, Andalusi Muslims and Jews traded throughout the southern Mediterranean, while merchants from other regions of the Islamic world regularly came to trade in Andalusi ports. In contrast, Christians had little role in Andalusi trade before the middle of the twelfth century, when the growth of Italian maritime interests brought Genoese, Pisan, and Provençal traders to the peninsula. These newcomers to Andalusi trade flourished, gradually shifting the balance of merchant activity into Christian hands. Christian commercial success may have been aided, in part, by support from the newly arrived Almohad dynasty, since Italian–Almohad treaties conceded tariff reductions and safe conduct to Italians trafficking in specified Andalusi and Maghribi ports. Christians began to trade in al-Andalus at the same time that Almohad religious intolerance was reducing Jewish mercantile activity in the peninsula. Records of Jewish traders in al-Andalus become scarce after ca. 1150, when it is probable that many Jews shifted their business northward to Christian markets or into the eastern Mediterranean and Indian Ocean.

These two factors, the new presence of Christian traders and the decline of the Jewish mercantile influence, suggest a watershed in the structure of Andalusi trade in the middle of the twelfth century. A second major shift in the Andalusi merchant population would come a century later, when Christian victories virtually eliminated the Jewish and Muslim mercantile presence in Andalusia, leaving a vacuum readily filled by Italian traders, who were later joined by Castilian and Catalan merchants. In keeping with this chronological pattern of merchant distribution and power, this chapter deals first with the period of Muslim and Jewish commercial hegemony before the middle of the twelfth century, then looks at the period of increasing Christian dominance after 1150.

MERCHANTS IN ANDALUSI TRADE UNTIL CA. 1150

Muslims

Arabic sources provide only sporadic data on individual Muslims active in Andalusi trade, yet they indicate that the final century of Umayyad rule in Cordoba was a fertile period for mercantile activity in al-Andalus. The centralizing power of the dynasty under ʿAbd al-Raḥmān III (912–61), together with the internal economic stability and productivity of the peninsula in the tenth century, were conducive to international commerce and merchant security. Before this time, data are too patchy to show much more than the clear existence of some level of trade, but the evidence becomes more solid in the tenth century, when geographers and other writers mention Andalusi merchants trafficking throughout the Muslim world. Ibn Ḥawqal referred to

Andalusis trading in Tabarca and to an Andalusi merchant colony in Tripoli. By 972, ʿIsā b. Aḥmad Rāzī noted another businessman, Muḥammad b. Sulaymān, plying similar routes between al-Andalus and Ifriqiya.[1] Ibn Ḥawqal may himself have worked as a merchant, trading between the peninsula and North Africa, when he came to al-Andalus as an agent of the Fatimids, and Rāzī also came from a merchant family.[2] At roughly the same period, Andalusis were also trafficking in the eastern Mediterranean and beyond. Ibn Ḥayyān noted that the scholar ʿAbd Allah b. Massara had worked as a merchant when he was young (he was born in 882), traveling with his brother on commercial business in the Near East before turning to scholarship.[3] Another merchant-scholar, Abū Bakr Muḥammad b. Muʿāwiya al-Marwānī (d. 968), reached the markets of Iraq and India where he amassed 30,000 dinars through trade before losing everything in a shipwreck on the way home to al-Andalus. Unlike most of his commercial colleagues, Marwānī is noteworthy for the fact that his name conveys something of his family and social status. Not only was he clearly Muslim and Arab, he was also a member of the ruling Umayyad family. Within the complex mélange of tenth-century Andalusi society, this lineage would have carried some weight.[4] Compilers of biographical dictionaries, including Ibn al-Faraḍī, Ḍabbī, Ibn Bashkuwāl, and Ibn al-ʿAbbār, mentioned many other Andalusis who traveled and traded in Syria, Egypt, and the Near East during the late ninth and tenth centuries.[5] Some, however, never got that far. Ṣāliḥ b. Muḥammad al-Murādī (d. 914), a merchant from

[1] Ibn Ḥawqal, *Kitāb ṣurat al-arḍ*. [ed. J. H. Kramers, Leiden, 1938], p. 78. See also C. Courtois, "Remarques sur le commerce maritime en Afrique au XIe siècle," *Mélanges d'histoire et d'archéologie de l'occident musulman: Hommage à Georges Marçais*. [Algiers, 1957], p. 54. Rāzī, *Anales palatinos del califa de Córdoba al-Ḥakam II, por ʿIsā b. Aḥmad al-Rāzī*. [trans. E. García Gómez, Madrid, 1967], p. 110.

[2] Muḥammad b. Mūsā al-Rāzī worked as a merchant during the reign of amir Muḥammad I (852–86) (Ibn Hayyān, *Muqtabis*. [ed. M.ʿA. al-Makkī, Beirut, 1973] II, p. 267). See also A. I. Rozi, "The Social Role of Scholars (ʿUlamā) in Islamic Spain." [Ph.D. Dissertation, Boston University, 1983], p. 358.

[3] Ibn Ḥayyān, *Muqtabas*. V [eds. P. Chalmeta, F. Corriente, M. Subḥ, Madrid, 1979], p. 35.

[4] Ibn al-Faraḍī, *Kitāb ta'rīkh ʿulamā' al-Andalus*. [ed. F. Codera, *BAH*, Madrid, 1890], p. 363, #1287.

[5] Ibn al-Faraḍī, *Kitāb*, pp. 51–2, #181; p. 53, #184; pp. 68–9, #235; pp. 130–1, #453; pp. 179–80, #650. Ibn Bashkuwāl, *Kitāb al-ṣila fī ta'rīkh al-immat al-Andalus*. [Cairo, 1955], p. 31, #43; p. 456, #1042 (no date). Aḥmad al-Ḍabbī, *Kitāb bughyat al-multamis fī ta'rīkh rijāl ahl al-Andalus*. [ed. F. Codera, *BAH*, Madrid, 1885], pp.186–7, #455. Ibn al-

Huesca, was travelling to Mecca on pilgrimage when his merchandise was stolen in Qayrawan. This left him without financial support and he had to make his way back to al-Andalus.[6] Despite his penniless state, Ṣāliḥ's fate was better than that of another Andalusi Muslim trader whose tombstone shows that he died in Qayrawan in 862.[7]

Andalusi merchant-scholars continued to travel during the early eleventh century, well after the heyday of Umayyad hegemony. Ibn al-ʿAbbār noted a Cordoban who died in Valencia in 1028, and Ibn Bashkuwāl cited two further Andalusi traders, both from Seville, who were active at this time. One, clearly of Arab origin (bearing the name al-Qaysī), was reported to have "wandered for a time through the lands of Ifriqiya and al-Andalus, searching for knowledge and trading" before his death in 1033. The other man, perhaps of Berber heritage, also traded in Ifriqiya.[8]

In contrast to these stories of Andalusis abroad, biographical dictionaries include fewer references to eastern merchant-scholars arriving in Andalusi ports during the Umayyad period. This may be because eastern scholars, unlike Andalusis traveling eastward, lacked the added incentive of pilgrimage to lure them westward. Ibn al-ʿAbbār noted one eastern merchant, Muḥammad b. Mūsā (d. 886), who worked in al-Andalus. Later, Ibn al-Faraḍī mentioned a tenth-century trader from Ceuta who, after wide travels through North Africa and the Near East, lived for a period on the Andalusi frontier earning a living as a merchant and soldier.[9] Likewise, Ibn Bashkuwāl cited a Baghdadi merchant-scholar who arrived in al-Andalus in 966, and two more (one of whom was particularly renowned for his excellent

ʿAbbār, *Kitāb al-takmila li-kitāb al-ṣila*. [ed. F. Codera, *BAH*, Madrid, 1886] 1, p.96, #320. Ibn Bashkuwāl mentioned a further Cordoban, probably of this period, whom I have not included among these seven since the author provides no dates and lists his name, not necessarily his profession, as *tājir* (p. 492, #1135).

[6] Ibn al-Faraḍī, *Kitāb*, pp. 167–8, #600.

[7] B. Roy, P. Poinssot, and O. Poinssot, *Inscriptions arabes de Kairouan*. [Paris, 1950] 1, p. 114.

[8] Ibn al-ʿAbbār mentioned Khalīl al-Qurṭubī as being "by profession a merchant" (*Takhmila*, 1, p. 59, #187). Ibn Bashkuwāl referred to Naẓār b. Muḥammad b. ʿAbd Allah al-Qaysī and Marwān b. Sulaymān b. Ibrāhīm b. Mūraqāt al-Ghāfiqī (d. 1027) (*Kitāb al-ṣila*, p. 606, #1407; p. 581, #1347).

[9] Ibn al-ʿAbbār, *Takhmila*, 1, p. 366, #1048; Ibn al-Faraḍī, *Kitāb*, p. 61, #1604. No dates are given for this second man, Yaḥyā b. Khalaf al-Sadafī, but it is reasonable to assume that he lived during the tenth century, as did most of those described by Ibn al-Faraḍī.

grasp of commercial matters) who came from Egypt and Qayrawan early in the next century.[10]

Non-scholars also arrived from the east to trade in the markets of Umayyad Spain. Writing during the reign of the caliph ʿAbd al-Raḥmān III, Hasday b. Shaprūt extolled the natural wealth of al-Andalus, and listed the merchants who flocked to the peninsula for trade. Among these, he particularly noted Egyptians (who brought perfumes, precious stones, and other luxuries) and the "merchant-envoys of Khurasan."[11] At about the same time, Ismaʿīlīs (including the geographer Ibn Ḥawqal noted above) were coming to al-Andalus to spread Shīʿism, although the eleventh-century jurist Ibn Sahl reported that they hid "their true purpose under the pretext of legitimate activities such as commerce, or science, or itinerant Sufism."[12] Toward the end of the Umayyad period, under the rule of Muẓaffar (1002–7), Ibn Ḥayyān recorded the presence in al-Andalus of foreign merchants from Egypt, Iraq, and elsewhere.[13]

During the Taifa period, a number of Muslim Spanish businessmen were involved in commerce with Maghribi ports, but there are fewer references to Andalusis trafficking with more distant destinations. The geographer Bakrī, writing in the 1060s, mentioned the appearance of Andalusi traders in al-Mahdiyya and provided detailed and varied itineraries for their crossings of the channel between al-Andalus and North Africa.[14] Other more general indications of Andalusi commerce with the Maghrib are also found in legal documents and in geographical works from

[10] The three men noted by Ibn Bashkuwāl are ʿAbd al-ʿAzīz b. Jaʿfar al-Baghdādī (*Kitāb al-ṣila*, pp. 356–7, #802); ʿAbd al-Raḥmān b. Muḥammad al-Miṣrī, who arrived in al-Andalus from Egypt in 1003–4 (*Kitāb al-ṣila*, p. 337, #756); and Muḥammad b. al-Qāsim al-Qarawī, who came to al-Andalus in about 1010 (*Kitāb al-ṣila*, pp. 564–5, #1309).

[11] W. Heyd, *Histoire du commerce du Levant au moyen âge*. [Leipzig, 1885] 1, p. 49; D.M. Dunlop, *The History of the Jewish Khazars*. [Princeton, 1954], pp. 134–5. There has been considerable debate concerning the authenticity of Hasday's correspondence. Dunlop considered that the letters written by Hasday himself were genuine, although the replies may be later fabrications (p. 120ff). It is not certain that these merchants were Muslim, but since Hasday was addressing a Jewish reader, he probably would have noted them as co-religionists had this been the case.

[12] Ibn Sahl, *Thalāth wathāʾiq fī muḥārabat al-ahwāʾ wa al-bidaʿ fī al-Andalus*. [ed. M.A. Khallāf, Cairo, 1981], p. 44.

[13] Ibn Bassām, *Dhakhīra fī maḥāsin ahl al-jazīra*. [Cairo, 1358/1939–1364/1945] IV/1, p. 65. Ibn Bassām attributed his information to Ibn Ḥayyān.

[14] Bakrī, *Description de l'Afrique septentrionale*. [ed. and trans. M. de Slane, Paris, 1911], p. 67.

this period. We often learn in passing of traveling merchants when their absence caused family members or acquaintances to take cases to court. Ibn Sahl recorded several suits of this type, including one, dated 1066, in which a man came to a judge in Cordoba after trying in vain to locate a commercial partner in Fez.[15]

Overall, there are considerably less data on Spanish Muslim merchants active in the Taifa states than under Umayyad rule. This apparent slowing in local Muslim commerce may be due to political unrest and insecurity in the peninsula in the early eleventh century. There is, in particular, a marked reduction in references to Andalusi merchant-scholars traveling abroad in this period, but this may be a scholarly rather than a mercantile trend. A study of all scholarly travel (whether for pilgrimage, commerce, or other purpose) has shown less scholarly mobility during the 1030s and 1040s than in the previous half century.[16] We may hypothesize that the disunity of Taifa politics and the necessity of *paria* payments confused earlier economic structures, hindered communications, and generally hampered long-distance trade.

Nevertheless, although Taifa economies seem to have discouraged the activities of indigenous Muslim entrepreneurs, foreign traders continued to arrive in Andalusi ports during the eleventh century. Even as Taifa coffers were drained to pay tribute to northern Spanish rulers, commercial revenues from abroad ensured that Andalusi markets flourished and ports remained functional. In contrast to the paucity of data on Andalusi merchant-scholars traveling eastward, Ibn Bashkuwāl provides a startling abundance of biographical data on merchant-scholars arriving in Islamic Spain between the years 1023 and 1041. His biographical dictionary records the names of at least twenty-two foreign merchant-scholars active during this short period – although it contains the names of only two foreigners trading in al-Andalus later in the century. The Muslim traders whom he

[15] Ibn Sahl, *Aḥkām al-kubrā*. [General Library, Rabat, ms. 838Q] fols. 180, 183–6, 189–90

[16] M.L. Avila has determined the percentage of scholars journeying abroad from biographical evidence: 961 (29 percent); 970 (34 percent); 980 (38.4 percent); 990 (35.5 percent); 999 (38.4 percent); 1009 (37.6 percent); 1019 (36.5 percent); 1029 (34.6 percent); 1038 (23.4 percent); 1048 (24.1 percent) (*La sociedad hispano-musulmana al final del califato [aproximación a un estudio demográfico]*. [Madrid, 1985], p. 83).

cites hailed from all over the Islamic world. A few had origins as far away as Yemen and Iraq, some came from North Africa, while the majority had traveled to al-Andalus from Syria and Egypt.[17] The time frame here is intriguing, because the twenty years in question span the gap between the final years of the Umayyad dynasty and the emergence of the early Taifa states, an era thought to have been troubled by civil war. One might expect to see a decrease in commercial activity during this period (as indeed is suggested by the relatively scarce data on native Andalusi traders), yet Ibn Bashkuwāl's data indicate that foreign Muslim merchant-scholars continued to arrive in Andalusi markets during this period of political turmoil and weak government control. It is impossible to know why Ibn Bashkuwāl's records contain such a dramatic increase in references for these years. They may reflect a change in commercial activity or merely a variation in the biographer's source material. Perhaps his information was for some reason more comprehensive for this period, and thus these numbers – in fact a more accurate reflection of merchant demographics – should be taken as a model for other years.

There is always the question, however, as to whether the activities of merchant-scholars may be taken as representative of general trends in the Muslim merchant population. Sources on scholars do not always show parallel trends as those describing ordinary traders. In the late eleventh century, for example, biographical evidence on scholars declines while other sources show continuing commercial activity among other Muslim traders. If the decrease in data reflects a real reduction in the travels of merchant-scholars, then this should probably be attributed to non-commercial causes, most likely the arrival of the Almoravid dynasty in al-Andalus in 1086. The religious and economic policies of this regime are under debate, but their reputed hostility to the Andalusi intellectual elite may have put a damper on scholarly travel to and from ports under their control. Their

[17] Ibn Bashkuwāl, *Kitāb al-ṣila*, entries 779, 652, 528, 674, 1314, 1406, 285, 957, 1311, 948, 1313, 1402, 1312, 269, 1366, 654, 960, 1400, 247, 1316, 1338, 1445. These are arranged chronologically according to the date when the travelers arrived in al-Andalus, and origins are based on *nisba*. The phrasing which Ibn Bashkuwāl generally uses reads: "he came to al-Andalus as a merchant in the year . . ." Ibn Bashkuwāl also noted a later merchant-scholar who arrived from Syria in 1073 (*Kitāb al-ṣila*, p. 602, #1399).

presence may explain why Ibn Bashkuwāl cited only two merchant-scholars active in the Almoravid period. One was an Iraqi who traveled to al-Andalus in 1090, the other was an Andalusi from Almeria who died in 1136.[18] Likewise, Ibn al-ʿAbbār mentioned only one later Maghribi scholar (d. 1172) who visited al-Andalus as a merchant and one Denian businessman, who died in 1152.[19]

Although the Almoravid arrival may have affected the movement of merchant-scholars, the new regime does not seem to have hindered the activities of ordinary Muslim traders. Making assumptions from patchy data, general commercial business apparently continued unabated in Andalusi cities. Market handbooks describe apparently normal market procedures under Almoravid rule, and references to Muslim merchants continue to show up in a variety of sources. A legal ruling by the jurist Māzarī (d. 1141) concerned a Maghribi selling goods in al-Andalus earlier in the century, and Geniza letters from 1138 and 1140 reported that Muslim merchants had arrived in Muslim Spain from Alexandria and Libya.[20] Three epitaphs from Almeria, dated 1125, 1133, and 1145, also attest to the mercantile presence in the first half of the twelfth century. The Quranic quotations on their tombstones show that the deceased were all Muslim, and one was certainly of Andalusi origin, as shown by his *nisba*, al-Shātibī (from Jativa). Another, named Ibn Ḥalīf, was a merchant from Alexandria, who presumably died while on a voyage to al-Andalus.[21]

Jews

In contrast to the limited data on Muslim merchants in Andalusi trade, we know considerably more about their Jewish counterparts, and this relative abundance is largely owing to the records of the Cairo Geniza. As in the case of Muslim commerce, there are clear chronological trends in Jewish mercantile activity, one

18 Ibn Bashkuwāl, *Kitāb al-ṣila*, p. 599, #1391; p. 410, #927. This author also recorded two further non-Andalusis arriving in Muslim Spain [*Kitāb al-ṣila*, p. 113, #264; p. 409, #924] but included no dates.

19 Ibn al-ʿAbbār, *Takmila*, p. 370, #1054; pp. 193–5, #669.

20 H.R. Idris, *La Berbérie orientale sous les Zirides*. [Paris, 1962] p. 678. Bodl d74.41; TS 16.54.

21 E. Lévi-Provençal, *Inscriptions arabes d'Espagne*. [Paris, 1931], pp. 121, 127, 116.

of the most striking being the apparent decrease in the presence of Jewish traders in Andalusi markets by the middle of the twelfth century. Through the eleventh and the early twelfth century, we know of many individual Andalusi Jewish merchants, as well as something of the larger family partnerships and trade networks existing among Iberian Jews. In contrast to these rich materials, there is almost no information regarding Jewish businessmen in Andalusi trade after ca. 1140. This change in data coincides both with the arrival of the Almohad regime in al-Andalus in 1147 and with the rise of Italian trade (the earliest Genoese notarial records date to the 1150s). However, it also occurred at a time when the Geniza records become less plentiful. Thus, it is difficult to know whether there was a real reduction in Jewish trade – a product of Almohad persecutions, Italian commercial competition, or some other cause – or whether there is merely a lack of sources documenting the presence of Jews.

Jewish merchants were already well established in the Iberian peninsula during the Visigothic period, when legal statutes note their presence, especially as ship-owners, slave traders, and marine merchants.[22] However, in keeping with other anti-Jewish legislation during this period, most Visigothic rulings relating to Jewish businessmen sought to limit their sphere of action, and particularly heavy economic sanctions were imposed on Jewish commerce by King Egica (687–702). Although the extent of Visigothic intolerance toward Iberian Jews has been debated, it is probable that the Muslim conquest in 711 provided a better environment for Jewish life.[23]

It is likely that Islamic rule also created a favorable atmosphere for Jewish commercial growth. By the ninth century, Ibn Khurradādhbih described the Rādhānite merchants who trafficked between the east and the west, speaking many languages (among them *Andalusī* – probably an Iberian Romance dialect), and carrying goods of all varieties – including "Andalusi slave girls."[24] The origin of the Rādhānites is unclear, and several

[22] *Lex Visigothorum*. [ed. K. Zeumer, *MGH* Leges (in quarto) I. I, Hanover-Leipzig, 1892] XII, 2, 18, p. 427.

[23] For more on Jewish life in the peninsula at this period, see S. Katz, *The Jews in the Visigothic and Frankish Kingdoms of Spain and Gaul*. [Cambridge, Mass., 1937], p. 22.

[24] Ibn Khurradādhbih, *Kitāb al-masālik wa al-mamālik*. [ed. M.J. de Goeje, *BGA*, 2nd edn, VI, Leiden, 1967], pp. 153–5. R.S. Lopez and I.W. Raymond provide an English

possibilities have been proposed based on the evidence of their collective name and their itineraries. Because one of their trade routes began in France or on the Iberian peninsula, then proceeded south through the Maghrib to Egypt, some scholars have traced their original home to either southern France or al-Andalus.[25]

Aside from these Rādhānite itineraries, little is known of Andalusi Jewish merchants before the late tenth century when one Andalusi traveler, Ibrāhīm b. Yaʿqūb al-Ṭurṭūshī, left an account of his journeys to Italy and northern Europe ca. 960. His name, his itinerary, and his detailed descriptions of European commerce and commodities suggest that he may have been a Jewish merchant. ʿUdhrī (d. 1085), who preserved parts of Ibrāhīm's account, certainly believed that he was Jewish, since he added *al-Israīlī* to his name.[26] Other Andalusi Jews also traded back and forth across the Iberian frontier during the same period. A tenth-century Andalusi rabbi was consulted, for example, concerning a merchant who had been absent for over six years in a Christian country, most likely in one of the northern Spanish kingdoms.[27] Another rabbi, Hanokh b. Moses of Cordoba (d. 1014), was questioned about a man who was away in "the land of the Christians."[28] Under Hishām II (976–1009), a Jew called Yaʿqūb b. Jau was briefly assigned the position of tax

translation of this passage on the Rādhānites in their *Medieval Trade in the Mediterranean World.* [New York, 1955], pp. 30–3.

[25] De Goeje, Ashtor, and Cahen all favored Western origins for the Rādhānites, as did Lombard, who suggested that their name derived from the Rhone River (*The Golden Age of Islam.* [Oxford, 1975], p. 209). M. Gil, however, in his study "The Radhanite Merchants and the Land of Radhan" (*JESHO* 17(1974), pp. 299–328) strongly favored Iraq as the Rādhānite homeland.

[26] The rest of Ṭurṭūshī's work was preserved by Qazwīnī, who gave his full name as Ibrāhīm b. Aḥmad al-Ṭurṭūshī, a name more applicable to a Muslim than a Jew (though it might belong to a Muslim of Jewish heritage). It is not entirely clear whether the two Ibrāhīms of ʿUdhrī and Qazwīnī were indeed the same person. This question has been explored by A.A. El-Hajji in his article "Andalusia e Italia altomedievale," *Rivista storica italiana* 79(1967), pp. 158–73. El-Hajji also suggested that Ṭurṭūshī may have been a slave merchant, a view shared by H. Mones, "Al-jughrāfīya wa al-jughrāfīyūn fī al-Andalus," *Madrid: MDI* 7–8(1959–60), p. 220. Another useful source is A. Miquel, "L'Europe occidentale dans la relation arabe d'Ibrāhīm b. Yaʿqūb (Xe siècle)," *Annales: ESC* 21(1966), pp. 1048–64.

[27] J. Müller (ed.), *Teshuvot geonei mizrah u-ma'arav* (*Responsen der Lehrer des Osten und Westens.* [Berlin, 1888 (repr. Jerusalem, 1966)], no. 192. Müller also noted this responsum in his *Die Responsen der spanischen Lehrer des 10. Jahrhunderts.* [Berlin, 1889], p. 37, no. 57. This reference is also cited by E. Ashtor, *The Jews of Moslem Spain.* [Philadelphia, 1973–84] 1, p. 278.

[28] Müller, *Teshuvot*, #191.

collector among the Jews of the Umayyad Empire (which then stretched as far south as Sijilmasa). Abraham ben Daud, who related this information in his *Sefer ha-qabbalah*, described Ya'qūb and his brother Yūsuf as "merchants [and] manufacturers of silk" textiles.[29] Perhaps Ya'qūb's duties as an administrator were aided by his commercial connections.

The activities of Andalusi Jewish traders become much clearer in the eleventh century, largely owing to the data provided by the Cairo Geniza. Because of the politically fragmented nature of the peninsula during the Taifa Period, however, it is difficult to make generalizations regarding the status and condition of Andalusi Jews, whether merchants or otherwise. Jews seem to have prospered in the first half of the century, when the famous Jewish vizier, Samuel b. Naghrīla (d. 1056), rose to power at the court of Granada. Ibn Naghrīla was himself a trader at one point in his life, occupying himself "in very modest circumstances as a spice-merchant" in Malaga.[30] Jews also immigrated to al-Andalus in the eleventh century. We know of these people through their children, such as Yūsuf b. al-Shāmī (d. 1141), the son of a Syrian immigrant, and through letters of recommendation addressed to Jewish communities in al-Andalus.[31] In 1066 however, ten years after the death of Ibn Naghrīla, there were bloody riots against the Jews of Granada. Although similar uprisings did not occur in other Taifa states, the Granada riots may have reflected more widespread anti-Jewish feeling.[32]

The earliest Geniza references to individual Jews trading to and from al-Andalus are found in the eleventh-century correspondence between the Egyptian merchant Yūsuf Ibn 'Awkal and his partners. Ibn 'Awkal's business house concerned itself exclusively with Mediterranean trade, including commerce with al-Andalus. The firm employed several Andalusi associates in the first decades of the eleventh century, including Khalaf b. Ya'qūb

[29] Abraham b. Daud, *Sefer ha-qabbalah (The Book of Tradition)*. [trans. G.D. Cohen, Philadelphia, 1967], pp. 68–9.

[30] Abraham b. Daud, *Sefer ha-qabbalah*, p. 72.

[31] TS 10 J 24.4; see also Ashtor, *Jews of Moslem Spain*, III, p. 186. One example of a recommendation letter is TS 13 J 36.13, edited by Ashtor in "Documentos españoles de la Genizah," *Sefarad* 24(1964), pp. 68–71. This eleventh-century recommendation was carried to the Jewish community in Algeciras, and is the earliest known reference to Jews in this city.

[32] N.A. Stillman, "Aspects of Jewish Life in Islamic Spain," *Aspects of Jewish Culture in the Middle Ages*. [ed. P. Szarmach, Albany, 1979], p. 69.

al-Andalusī, whose name crops up frequently in Ibn ʿAwkal's correspondence, and who appears to have worked as a commercial agent in al-Mahdiyya. In a bill of lading from 1015, Khalaf was mentioned shipping hides to Egypt, and the *al-Andalusī* sending another shipment of hides in the following year (this time used as packaging for a parcel of silk) was probably also Khalaf.[33] Later, a long non-commercial letter sent from Palermo to al-Mahdiyya praised Khalaf and his son, who had been influential in engineering the release of some Jewish prisoners and obtaining salvage rights for goods from a shipwreck.[34] Other Andalusi associates of Ibn ʿAwkal were also dealers in silk, probably because Muslim Spain was a major center for Mediterranean silk production. A letter to Ibn ʿAwkal in Egypt, written from Tunisia ca. 1010, remarked "... I have sent silk to ... Abī Ibrāhīm al-Andalusī ... it is held in partnership between myself and him and [another]. My wish in this matter is for a speedy and easy sale."[35] Presumably Abū Ibrāhīm was resident in Egypt and connected in some manner with Ibn ʿAwkal's trading network. We learn of yet another Andalusi partner in a letter sent from Palermo in the 1020s–1030s, in which a partner wrote to Ibn ʿAwkal: "I am sending silk in a boat in which Marwān al-Andalusī and I – God willing – are traveling to al-Mahdiyya the day after tomorrow. I appreciate the extent of your love for him, your desire for 'friendly relations' with him, and your firm confidence in him ..."[36] Perhaps this Marwān was a younger partner being groomed for a position of trust and responsibility in the firm.

As well as trading in Andalusi goods, and with Andalusi

[33] TS 13 J 16.23 (1015) and TS 10 J 9.26 (1016). In the earlier document, Khalaf is referred to by name, but not by *nisba*. However, his full name is known from elsewhere. N.A. Stillman assumed that the two shippers mentioned in these letters were the same man ("The Eleventh-Century Merchant House of Ibn ʿAwkal (A Geniza Study)," *JESHO* 16(1973), p. 71).

[34] TS 24.6, this letter is discussed by S.D. Goitein in *A Mediterranean Society*. [Berkeley, 1967–88] II, pp. 60–1. A Yaʿqūb b. Khalaf al-Andalusī later turned up as a witness in Egypt in 1040; it is possible that he was the son of the earlier Khalaf (Mosseri L 101, ed. M. Gil, *Palestine during the First Muslim Period*. [Tel Aviv, 1983] II, pp. 336–9, #193).

[35] TS 12.171.

[36] TS Arabic Box 5.1; trans. N.A. Stillman, "East-West Relations in the Islamic Mediterranean in the Early Eleventh century – A Study in the Geniza correspondence of the House of Ibn ʿAwkal." [Ph.D. Dissertation, University of Pennsylvania, 1970], p. 344.

partners, Ibn ʿAwkal's firm also sent non-Andalusi merchants to trade in Muslim Spain. Among these were four brothers from the Tāhertī family of Qayrawan, of whom at least one, Abū al-Faḍl Ṣāliḥ, did business between Egypt and al-Andalus. In a letter sent to Ibn ʿAwkal in Cairo in either 1015 or 1024, a relative reported that Abū al-Faḍl Ṣāliḥ had just returned from al-Andalus, bringing with him goods belonging to a number of different investors.[37] Later, in the 1050s, an associate of the prominent Egyptian businessman Nahray b. Nissīm wrote from Sicily to say that he had contracted with another partner named Abū al-Faḍl to travel to al-Andalus. If, as is conceivable, this was the same man found earlier in Ibn ʿAwkal's correspondence, his reappearance suggests that business firms based in Old Cairo commonly engaged specialists in Andalusi trade for commercial ventures in that region. However, since the name in question is not rare, this identification cannot be made with certainty.[38] Nahray must have had other eastern partners who traveled and did business for him in western Mediterranean markets, since another letter written to him from Sicily in 1053–7 mentioned a fellow merchant who was absent in al-Andalus.[39]

Many Andalusi Jewish merchants were active in the east in the eleventh century, either working for large eastern trading houses or in smaller networks. Most of these men only appear in passing, such as an Andalusi in Cairo who was accused of taking a case to a Muslim judge in 1027, instead of to a Jewish court. This merchant argued that the Jewish court had not been able to handle his case at the time.[40] Other Andalusi businessmen traded in Palestine. Among these, Yehuda b. Yūsuf b. al-Hānī al-Andalusī wrote repeatedly from Jerusalem to a partner in Egypt, in the 1040s, requesting an exact balance and accounting of their transactions.[41] Another eleventh-century Andalusi merchant was mentioned in a letter that described a frightening trip from Alexandria to Tripoli, Lebanon, during which "water seeped into the ship and . . . each man had to bail fifty buckets of

[37] Bodl d65.9; trans. Stillman, *East-West Relations*, p. 212.

[38] Bodl c28.61; It also appears that the man was holding a bale of flax jointly with one of the Tāhertīs, who had close business relations with Nahray b. Nissīm. The mention of the Tāhertī family lends weight to the identification of the Abū al-Faḍl in this letter with the one mentioned in Bodl d65.9.

[39] DK 22.

[40] Bodl b13.42.

[41] TS K 6.189; Goitein, *Mediterranean Society*, I, p. 451.

water in a shift . . . Abū al-Faraj b. Yūsuf al-Andalusī also took his turn . . ."[42] One is led to imagine this Abū al-Faraj as a respected, perhaps elderly, figure who nevertheless helped to bail when the ship was in danger.

It is often difficult to know how closely these Andalusis operating in the eastern Mediterranean remained tied to their homeland. In some cases the connection seems minimal, as with the eleventh-century family of Ya'qūb al-Andalusī, a clan that particularly stands out in the Geniza records of expatriate Andalusis doing business in the central and eastern Mediterranean. Several dozen letters written to, from, and about different members of this family have survived from the 1040s to 1060s, and they allow us a more intimate view of a merchant dynasty at work. Although the patriarch himself never appears in these letters, his son, son-in-law, grandsons, and even great-grandsons were active in eastern trade. The exact relationships within this Andalusi clan are not certain, but their family tree may be plausibly constructed as follows:

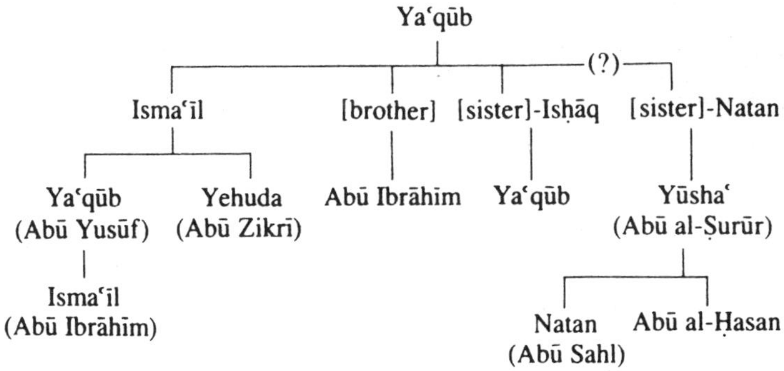

This family never formed an independent merchant house, but its members were associated with Nahray b. Nissīm and his trading firm. It is clear that they had close ties to Nahray (though probably of friendship rather than blood) because many letters mention family matters and personal details as well as commercial information. Goitein has proposed that the two brothers-in-law, Isma'īl and Natan, left al-Andalus in the early

[42] TS 12.241; trans. Goitein, *Mediterranean Society*, I, p. 321.

eleventh century, with one settling in Ifriqiya-Sicily and the other in the eastern Mediterranean.[43] Perhaps Isma'īl and Natan left al-Andalus in search of promising economic opportunities in the east, or perhaps their departure was caused by the threat of civil war in the peninsula during the late Umayyad period. Whatever the reason, both men built permanent connections abroad and apparently never returned to al-Andalus. Their sons Ya'qūb, Yehuda, and Yūsha' continued the family partnership. Ya'qūb (about whom we know most) operated mainly in Ifriqiya-Sicily and handled shipments of goods going back and forth to Egypt. His brother Yehuda acted as a traveling partner and was often mentioned in Ya'qūb's letters as having just arrived from (or departed to) Egypt. Yūsha', their cousin, did business primarily in Egypt, and a number of letters mention Abū al-Ṣurūr (as Yūsha' was called) journeying between the capital and the Egyptian countryside to oversee the flax harvest. However, Yūsha''s wife and family lived in Jerusalem, where he was a well-known member of the community by 1046.[44] These three were not the only family members to be merchants. Their cousins Ya'qūb b. Isḥāq and Abū Ibrāhīm were also associated with trade but appear in only a few letters. Likewise, the third generation followed in the family profession, and Yūsha''s son, Abū Sahl, must already have entered the business when he acted as a courier for Nahray between Cairo and the flax-growing region of Busir in the late 1050s.[45]

In spite of the fact that members of this family were frequently cited with their *nisba*, al-Andalusī, they apparently had very little direct contact with al-Andalus. Indeed, there is no evidence that Ya'qūb b. Isma'īl, Yehuda, or Yūsha' ever visited the peninsula, and their business seems to have been confined to the eastern Mediterranean. Although they trafficked in a wide variety of merchandise – silk, flax, textiles, pearls, oil, wheat, pepper, sugar, cinnamon – none of these commodities had a specified Andalusi origin or destination. Either this Andalusi family had become completely and exclusively incorporated into the eastern Mediterranean sphere, or if there was a western half of their business the records for this half were not preserved

[43] S.D. Goitein, *Letters of Medieval Jewish Traders*. [Princeton, 1973], p. 111.
[44] TS 20.9. See Goitein, *Letters*, p. 112.
[45] Mosseri L190.

in Cairo. Possibly the elusive cousins Abū Ibrāhīm and Yaʿqūb b. Isḥāq were active in the west, trading between Tunisia and Andalusi ports, and this would explain their infrequent mention.

Jewish merchants continued to travel between al-Andalus and the east through the first half of the twelfth century, although the arrival of the Almoravids in al-Andalus seems to have reduced the commercial opportunities open to the local Jewish population. References to Andalusi Jewish merchants decrease in the late eleventh century, a period that may have seen increasing religious intolerance and persecution. The year 1090 brought another purge in Granada (reminiscent of the riots in 1066), and toward the end of the Almoravid regime, in 1135, the Jewish quarter in Cordoba was sacked and burned.[46] In spite of these troubles for Andalusi Jews, Jewish traders continued to do business with Andalusi ports and markets under Almoravid rule. In about 1110, an Egyptian businessman named Abū al-Khulayf described recent transactions that he had made in al-Andalus and Morocco.[47] Another trader – bringing Andalusi copper and textiles to sell, and looking to buy oriental spices – arrived in Alexandria in the 1140s, and in November of 1141 a man in Alexandria noted the arrival of his nephew from Almeria.[48] About this period we also learn of the arrival in Alexandria of the "son of Ben Lukhtūj" from Denia. Samuel b. Uhtūsh was an Andalusi relative of the influential Egyptian merchant Halfōn b. Nethanel, and may have been a regular commuter between al-Andalus and Egypt.[49]

Halfōn b. Nethanel himself was something of a twelfth-century globe-trotter. By means of his extensive correspondence, it is possible to track Halfōn's journeys to al-Andalus and the Maghrib in 1128–30, to India in 1132–4, and back to the west in 1138–9. Many of the letters he sent during his periods of travel in Muslim Spain concerned commercial transactions between east and west, and negotiations with Andalusi partners. His far-flung connections led one Iberian friend and admirer to describe him as "a unifier of the dispersed great of his time, as a leader of his own community [i.e., the Egyptian] as well as ours [the

[46] J. O'Callaghan, *A History of Medieval Spain.* [Ithaca, 1975], p. 286.

[47] Bodl d66.52; Goitein, *Letters*, p. 50.

[48] TS Arabic Box 40.113; TS 10 J 24.4.

[49] TS 10 J 16.17. See also Goitein, *Mediterranean Society*, III, p. 439.

Andalusi]."[50] Halfōn's connections with al-Andalus may have been particularly close owing to family ties in the peninsula and his friendship with the philosopher and poet Judah Ha-Levi. His exhausting travels took their toll, however, as we learn from a letter to a Jewish notable in Lucena, in which Halfōn apologized for not having written earlier and pleaded a long illness suffered as a result of hardships endured on land and sea during his time in al-Andalus and the Maghrib.[51]

Halfōn was not the only Jewish trader to travel widely in the twelfth century. With the growth of the India trade, we find merchants operating in Aden one year and in Almeria the next. One such merchant, another Egyptian-based businessman and seasoned India trader, Makhlūf b. Mūsa Nafūsī, traveled to al-Andalus at the turn of the twelfth century then noted his return to Egypt in a letter sent from Alexandria to Cairo.[52] A few Andalusi merchants also traded in India, as indicated by a cryptic Geniza fragment sent (probably) from ʿAydhab on the east African coast, ca. 1100, which referred to the arrival of a certain *al-Qurṭubī* (presumably a merchant of Cordoban origin) bringing commercial goods from al-Mahdiyya.[53] In another example, a letter written in Aden in 1137 addressed to Halfōn in Egypt provided accounts from the previous year of shipments from India, some in partnership with a certain Mubārak from Malaga.[54] Two other western colleagues of Halfōn were with him in ʿAydhab ca. 1134.[55] Perhaps the best known twelfth-century India trader, by association, was the Andalusi David b. Maimon, the brother of Maimonides, who died in a shipwreck on the Indian Ocean in 1168.[56]

[50] ULC Or 1080 J 94; trans. and glosses by Goitein "The Biography of Judah Ha-Levi in the Light of the Cairo Geniza Documents," *Proceedings of the American Academy for Jewish Research* 28(1959), p. 43.

[51] ENA NS 18.30; Data comes from Goitein's unpublished *India Book* notes.

[52] ULC Or1080 J 178; This man is found trading with India in other letters, including TS 24.78.

[53] ENA 2730.7; margin, lines 1–2. My reading is taken from Goitein's transcription of the text.

[54] TS 24.37; Data from Goitein's unpublished transcript and *India Book* notes.

[55] TS Arabic Box 48.270. These two merchants are known from an earlier letter, TS 13 J 17.22, in which Judah Ha-Levi sent greetings to them via Halfōn. Goitein believed them to be either Andalusi or Maghribi, but they must certainly have traveled in al-Andalus at some point to have made the acquaintance of Judah Ha-Levi.

[56] L. Rabinowitz, *Jewish Merchant Adventurers: A Study of the Radanites*. [London, 1948], p. 62.

After Halfōn's journeys to and from the peninsula in the late 1130s, we lose track of foreign Jewish merchants trading in al-Andalus. Geniza evidence ceases and twelfth-century Andalusi chronicles, *ḥisba* books, responsa, and Arabic legal materials do not contain enough information on Jewish traders to fill this gap. It is unclear whether the apparent disappearance of Jewish merchants from Andalusi trade in the middle of the twelfth century is owing to the decrease in documentation or to a genuine decline in their business. Contemporary events support the latter conclusion, since changes in Andalusi politics and western Mediterranean mercantile power after the arrival of the Almohads in the peninsula are likely to have had a direct influence on Jewish traders working in Muslim Spain.

During the twelfth century, persecution of Andalusi Jews may have increased, convincing many Jews to leave the peninsula.[57] The evidence is contradictory, however, and opinions vary regarding the extent of Almohad oppression.[58] Early Almohad policies may not have extended further than a strict enforcement of the traditional restrictions placed on *dhimmīs*, but Geniza letters from the 1140s contain descriptions of massacres of Jews in Morocco. The situation may have been worse in the Maghrib than in al-Andalus, for an Almerian Jewish merchant traveling in Fez at this period wrote home that "hatred (of Jews) is rampant in this country to a degree that, in comparison with it,

[57] Stillman, "Aspects," p. 73. Abraham b. Ezra (who left in 1137) and Judah Ha-Levi (1141) have been cited as notable departures. Their actions, however, seem to have been motivated by personal desire rather than political necessity, since both men had already left by the time the Almohads arrived in the Peninsula in 1147.

[58] The theory of Almohad persecution is widely accepted, although D. Corcos-Abulafia has argued that the Almohad period did not represent a time of unmitigated Jewish persecution. He saw a period of forced conversions and repression only under the rule of Abū Ya'qūb Yūsuf I (1163–84) (Corcos-Abulafia, "The Attitude of the Almohadic Rulers towards the Jews," *Zion* 32(1967), pp. 137–60). Stillman considered this attempt at revision to be "not altogether convincing," but Roth has called Corcos-Abulafia's theory "brilliant" (Stillman, "Aspects," p. 73; Roth, "Some Aspects of Muslim-Jewish Relations in Spain," *Estudios en homenaje a D. Claudio Sánchez Albornoz*. [Buenos Aires, 1983], II p. 179). Other scholars, including R. Le Tourneau, have proposed that Jewish persecutions continued beyond 1184, and certainly extended through the reign of Abu Yūsuf Ya'qūb (1184–99) (Le Tourneau, *The Almohad Movement in North Africa in the 12th and 13th Centuries*. [Princeton, 1969], pp. 57,77). H.Z. Hirschberg, on the other hand, considered that by the middle of the twelfth century, after the first years of Almohad rule, Jewish tribulations had abated (*A History of the Jews in North Africa*. [Leiden, 1974], p. 136).

Almeria is a place of salvation!"[59] However, the fact that the family of Maimonides fled from Cordoba to Fez a few years later, in 1159 or 1160, suggests that persecution in North Africa and al-Andalus was neither constant nor universal. His family's further departure for Egypt in 1165, on the other hand, could signify overall worsening conditions. The situation may have been doubly difficult for the Jewish merchant community, since at the same time that Almohad rulers made life difficult for Jews living in and moving through their territories, they also allowed foreign Christians to trade in Almohad ports.

Christians

The appearance of Christian commercial competition in the middle of the twelfth century was a new phenomenon, since Christians had had little influence in Andalusi markets before this period. Although Christian traders certainly did business in al-Andalus during the Umayyad and Taifa periods, they were much less important than their Muslim and Jewish counterparts. The lack of an indigenous Christian merchant community within al-Andalus partially explains this imbalance. Only a couple of early Mozarab merchants appear in the records. The ninth-century Christian preacher Eulogius is supposed to have had two brothers who were merchants, both engaged in trade to Europe ca. 849, and in 850 a Christian merchant called Joannes was whipped and imprisoned for invoking the name of the Prophet while selling his wares.[60] As noted in the previous chapter, the dearth of Mozarab traders may be explained by the low status of merchants in Iberian Christian society in contrast to the higher regard for the profession among Muslims and Jews.

Early data on foreign Christian traders are also scarce, despite ongoing diplomatic and economic contact between the Umayyads and Carolingians. Several Latin authors, including Liutprand of Cremona (949) and John of Gorze (978–84), commented on

[59] Sassoon 713, written from Egypt to Aden in December of 1147, tells of widespread killings in Tlemcen, Sijilmasa, and Marrakesh; also in Meknes, Fez, and again in Marrakesh [margin]. "Andalusiīn" are mentioned among the dead [right margin, 1.24]. This letter is edited by H.Z. Hirschberg in I.F. Baer Jubilee Volume. [Jerusalem, 1961], p. 142. On hatred: TS 12.435 (trans. Goitein, *Letters*, p. 55). Goitein dates this letter to the 1140s.

[60] E. Florez, *España sagrada*. [Madrid, 1753], X p. 416. See also K. Wolf, *Christian Martyrs in Muslim Spain*. [Cambridge, 1988], p. 12.

the infamous merchants from Verdun, .who were reputed to carry Christian slaves between Europe and Muslim Spain.[61] Less reliably, a Catalan tale (probably written in the thirteenth century but set in 986) told of a man who traded between Christian Barcelona and Muslim Mallorca, and his rescue of an abbess held captive by Muslims through hiding her in his cargo on the journey back to Barcelona.[62]

Foreign Christian merchants also appear in a handful of Arabic sources. Ibn Ḥayyān mentioned a treaty for peace and commercial security negotiated between the Umayyads and the Counts of Barcelona in 939, and described a visit to Cordoba by Amalfitan merchants in 942. Ibn Ḥayyān went on to say that, after this successful Amalfitan visit, "their successors" continued to come to al-Andalus and make great profits.[63] Far from the peninsula, an anonymous Persian geographer referred to *Rūmī* traders who did business in Ecija, Jaen and other southern cities in the tenth century.[64] An anonymous fourteenth-century source (thus suspect in terms of chronology) also noted the presence of foreign merchants in al-Andalus during the early Umayyad period.[65] Collectively, this information sheds doubt on Ibn Khaldūn's later statement that "not a single Christian board floated on [the Mediterranean]" in the tenth century.[66] A few Christian merchants clearly arrived in Andalusi ports during the Umayyad period, although Christians would not appear in al-Andalus in any number until the middle of the twelfth century, when the European commercial revolution was well underway.

[61] Liutprand of Cremona, *Antapodosis.* [in *Opera*, ed. J. Becker, MGH Scriptores in usum scholarum, Hanover-Leipzig, 1915], p. 156; John of Gorze, *Vita.* [ed. G.H. Pertz, MGH Scriptores IV (in folio), Hanover, 1841], pp. 370,375. *Virdunensis negociatores* are also noted trading with the peninsula in the *Liber miraculorum S. Bertini Abbatis.* [*Acta Sanctorum*, September 5, II, Antwerp, 1748], pp. 597.

[62] This incident is mentioned in M. Coll i Alentorn, "La crónica de Sant Pere de les Puelles," *II Colloqui d'historia del monaquisme catala.* [Santas Creus, 1967] II, p. 39. The story is told in A. Yepes, *Coronica general de la Orden de San Benito.* [Valladolid-Pamplona, 1609–21] III, pp. 345–8. My thanks to H. Dillard for this citation.

[63] Ibn Ḥayyān, *Muqtabas*, V, pp. 478,485. Chalmeta read these references to *malfatānīn* and *malfiyyīn* as Amalfitans ("La Méditerranée occidentale et al-Andalus de 934 à 941: les données d'Ibn Ḥayyān," *Rivista degli studi orientali* 50(1976) pp. 341–2,351).

[64] *Ḥudūd al-ʿālam: "The Regions of the World", A Persian Geography.* [trans. V. Minorsky, London, 1937 (reprinted 1970)], p. 155.

[65] Ibn Sammāk, "Al-zahrāt al-manthūra fī nakt al-akhbār al-ma'thūra" [ed. M.A. Makki], *Madrid:MDI* 21(1981–2), p. 55.

[66] Ibn Khaldūn, *The Muqaddimah.* [trans. F. Rosenthal, New York, 1958] II, p. 42.

MERCHANTS IN THE PENINSULA 1150–1250: THE CHRISTIAN COMMERCIAL CONQUEST

The growing influence of European merchants in Andalusi markets signals a new era in the Mediterranean mercantile sphere, as Genoese, Pisans, and other Christians took over trade and trade routes from other merchant groups. During the twelfth century, this phenomenon can be observed all over the Mediterranean, and developments in Andalusi markets must be seen as complementary to the new European commercial presence in Alexandria, Tunis, Bougie, Ceuta, and elsewhere. Analysis of Genoese notarial records shows that Andalusi ports were never a primary destination for Genoese traffic, at least in comparison with ports in North Africa or the Near East, but they remained a consistent element in the Genoese trading network. If we look at Genoese registers from 1191 and 1253, for example, we find that in both years roughly 3.5 percent of Genoese commercial contracts were written for voyages to *Yspania* (i.e., al-Andalus) or other Iberian destinations.[67] Nevertheless, the total number of Genoese voyages increased considerably between the middle of the twelfth and the middle of the thirteenth century, so that from the Iberian viewpoint, Genoese traders (and other Italians) must have represented an increasingly important component of the merchant population. The following analysis considers Genoese interests in both Christian and Muslim Spain, since Christian Spanish ports, especially Barcelona, often served as points of export for Andalusi goods. At the same time, this was the period in which increased Christian commercial activity in the peninsula began to shift the balance of traffic toward Christian markets.

Notarial contracts provide information not only on the Iberian destinations of Genoese commercial voyages, but also on the men and women who were engaged in this trade. They record the names of over two hundred and fifty people involved in trade with Andalusi ports in the period between 1156 and 1253. Even so, these people represent only a fraction of those referred to in the Genoese records, again emphasizing the relatively minor role of the peninsula in the Genoese commercial sphere as compared to other regions of the Mediterranean.

[67] O.R. Constable, "Genoa and Spain in the twelfth and thirteenth centuries," *Journal of European Economic History* 19(1990), pp. 643–4.

Genoese contracts for Iberian voyages also suggest that merchants did not specialize in this region. Although a traveling merchant might make several voyages to Iberian ports, or an investor might risk a few moderate sums on such trips, they each continued to maintain other – and usually more substantial – commercial interests elsewhere in the Mediterranean. In the century after 1150, there are no names that appear regularly over the years in contracts to Iberian destinations, and only eighteen that are found in more than one document. Of these eighteen, eight were investors, all of whom operated in the second half of the twelfth century.[68] Among these eight, three merchants invested in three ventures to Spain, but only one made contracts for four voyages. In contrast, no contracts drawn up by thirteenth-century notaries show an investor sending more than two investments to Iberian destinations.

One of the more prominent twelfth-century investors in Iberian trade was Soloman of Salerno, a Genoese merchant who traveled and invested in both the eastern and the western Mediterranean. His name appears in at least forty records written by the notary Giovanni Scriba in the 1150s and 1160s, and the variety of his interests suggests that – despite being Genoese – he might fit the model of the *rakkāḍ* outlined in al-Dimashqī's merchant typology.[69] Soloman invested in three Iberian ventures between the years 1156 and 1158, including £103 sent to *Yspania* in 1158 on the ship of Henry Nivetella.[70] Two years later, Soloman's wife, Eliadar, is found making a very complicated contract for trade to Spain.[71] While Soloman invested in the peninsula and the western Mediterranean, he also conducted business in eastern markets. As Abulafia has observed, the fact that "Soloman was financially able to maintain simultaneous ventures to both extremities of the Mediterranean. . .speaks for the diversity of his commercial interests no less than for his wealth." He has even been called a "merchant prince."[72] Nevertheless, Soloman's commercial network seems almost parochial

[68] Not all of the remaining ten merchants were factors, since some names appear on other types of contract.

[69] For a detailed analysis of Soloman's life and activities, see D. Abulafia, *The Two Italies*. [Cambridge, 1977], pp. 237–54.

[70] Giovanni Scriba, *Cartolare di Giovanni Scriba*. [eds. M. Chiaudano and M. Moresco, Rome, 1935] 1, pp. 226–7, #176; I, pp. 264–5, #495; 1, p. 267, #500.

[71] Giovanni Scriba, *Cartolare*, 1, p. 339, #625.

[72] Abulafia, *Two Italies*, pp. 244, 254.

in comparison with the extensive trading interests maintained by Halfōn b. Nethanel two decades previously.

It has been proposed that a number of the merchants operating in Genoa in the twelfth century were foreigners and Jews rather than native Genoese, and Soloman of Salerno is a case in point. Byrne and several others believed that Soloman was a Jew from southern Italy, although Abulafia has argued that he was Genoese.[73] In fact the name of only one investor in Iberian trade, Joseph Iudeus (who made a contract for a voyage to *Yspania* in 1162), strongly suggests that he was not Christian.[74] However, several other merchants trading with Iberian ports are of disputed origin. Bonus Johannes Malfiiaster, for example, may have been of Greek extraction – though long established in Genoa by the middle of the twelfth century. We know of four of his Iberian investments made between 1156 and 1160. In 1156 he ventured £20 on a voyage to Almeria, while a contract made in 1159 showed him sending £150 to *Yspania*, and a further £40 to the same destination in the following year.[75] During this period, Bonus Johannes was also very active in other arenas of Mediterranean commerce, investing in ventures to Sicily, Alexandria, Sardinia, Syria, and North Africa. Blancardus, another merchant of controversial origin, contracted three partnerships for Andalusi commerce during the middle of the twelfth century. One of these, drawn up in 1162, stated that he entrusted £120 to Johannes the son of Albericus, who was traveling to *Yspania*. In the following year he dispatched £40 to Ibiza, and, in 1164, £50 to Seville.[76]

Whether or not Soloman of Salerno, Bonus Johannes Malfiiaster, and Blancardus were "insiders" or "outsiders" in Genoese society, they are set apart by being three of the four merchants to make repeated investments in voyages to Spanish destinations.

[73] Abulafia, *Two Italies*, p. 237; In this regard, my statements in *Journal of European Economic History* 19(1990), pp. 648–9 should be revised.

[74] Giovanni Scriba, *Cartolare*, II, p. 104, #1011.

[75] Giovanni Scriba, *Cartolare*, I, p. 120, #224; p. 295, #550; pp. 338–9, #624; and pp. 73–4, #141. See also E.H. Byrne, "Easterners in Genoa," *JAOS* 38(1918), pp. 176–87, and as a corrective to Byrne, Abulafia, *Two Italies*, pp. 236–7.

[76] Giovanni Scriba, *Cartolare*, II, pp. 78–9, #967; II, p. 141, #1084; II, pp. 229–30, #1269. The heritage of Blancardus is uncertain. Byrne believed him to be Jewish, but B. Nelson raised serious doubts in his article "Blancard (the Jew?) of Genoa and the Restitution of Usury in Medieval Genoa," *Studi in onore di Gino Luzzatto* [Milan, 1949] I, pp. 96–116. Abulafia has likewise questioned Blancardus' Jewish heritage (*Two Italies*, p. 235).

The fourth was a well-known Genoese ship-owner named William Rataldo. Three contracts survive for William's Iberian investments between 1191 and 1192, two to Catalonia and one to Castile.[77] Like Soloman of Salerno, William also had interests in other areas of Mediterranean commerce. In 1190, for instance, he sent money to Syria in a *societas* with Fulco, the son of the rich and influential merchant and statesman Fulco de Castello.[78] In all, Krueger has calculated that William Rataldo's investment in traffic to Ultremare totalled £3,165 for the years 1179–1200.[79] In contrast, his Iberian expenditures come to just over £400.[80]

Members of prominent twelfth-century Genoese families, such as the de Volta, Burone, Mallone, and Vento clans, also made occasional contributions toward Iberian ventures, although they were primarily interested in commerce with the Levant. Overall, their investments in the western Mediterranean tended to be considerably smaller than those in the east. The de Volta family, for example, were recorded by Giovanni Scriba as sending a total of £16,800 to the Levant, £3,800 to the Maghrib, and £4,800 to the Iberian peninsula and France during the period 1155–62.[81] Likewise, William Vento put £1,200 toward Levantine voyages and £170 into western ones, of which just over £102 was taken up in a commercial voyage to Seville in 1161.[82] Sometimes investors combined their eastern and western interests, as did William Burone in August 1160, when he invested

77 *Guglielmo Cassinese (1190–1192).* [eds. M. Hall, H.C. Krueger, R.L. Reynolds, Turin, 1938] I, p. 88, #218; II, p. 37, #1199; II, pp. 183–4, #1573. Note that these investments were to Christian Spanish markets, not to al-Andalus.

78 H.C. Krueger, *Navi e proprietà navale a Genova, seconda metà del secolo XII.* [Genoa, 1985], p. 80. Many people who appear prominently in Genoese commerce were also influential in Genoese politics. Fulco de Castello acted as a consul for the city in 1188, 1195, 1207, and 1215, and many other prominent "merchants" trading in Spain and elsewhere also followed this career path (Krueger, *Navi e proprietà*, p. 148).

79 Krueger, *Navi e proprietà*, p. 124.

80 A number of other Genoese investors also added Iberian investments to a portfolio of wider interests, but their names do not appear in more than two contracts. They include the merchants Iordanno Crerico, Oberto Notario, Baiamonte Barlaira, and Roland de Caneto.

81 H.C. Krueger, "Post-War Collapse and Rehabilitation in Genoa (1149–1162)," *Studi in onore di Gino Luzzatto.* [Milan, 1949], pp. 127–8. Genoese investments during the twelfth century have been extensively studied and documented by E. Bach, *La cité de Gênes au XIIe siècle.* [Copenhagen, 1955]. Many of the merchants noted here are described in more detail by Bach, pp. 103–39.

82 H.C. Krueger, "Genoese Trade with Northwest Africa in the 12th century," *Speculum* 8(1933), pp. 387–8. Giovanni Scriba recorded the 1161 venture (*Cartolare*, II, p. 32, #859).

£100 in a voyage to Constantinople and Alexandria, with the instructions that the ship should return to Genoa by way of Bougie or *Yspania*. A month earlier, he had shared an investment of £200 with Ido Mallone and others for a similar voyage directed first to Alexandria, then on to either al-Andalus (*Yspaniam ultra Barchinoniam*) or Bougie.[83]

In most cases, members of prominent Genoese families were investors in voyages to Andalusi ports, but they sometimes acted in the capacity of traveling partners. In 1159, Marchio de Volta acted as factor in a *societas* to *Yspania*, and a century later, in 1253, Raymond de Volta made a *commenda* in which he agreed to travel to Mallorca.[84] Likewise, we find three contracts (dated 1160, 1198, and 1237) in which members of the Mallone family invested in expeditions to *Yspania* and Catalonia, but another, from 1182, in which Henry Mallone accepted £40 for a voyage to the Balearics.[85]

Younger family members sometimes worked as traveling agents in partnership with older relatives – often their fathers. This arrangement seems not unlike the familial ties of partnership that we see in the Cairo Geniza. In 1160, for example, Otto de Castro commissioned his stepson Johannes to travel to Alexandria, then Spain.[86] Somewhat later, in 1179, Fulco de Castello arranged for his son, "Fulchino," to carry £20 to Mallorca.[87] As we saw above, the younger Fulco later became an investor in his own right, sending money to Syria in a *societas* with William Rataldo twelve years later. In 1203, William de Petra accepted money from his brother Johannes for traffic to Barcelona.[88] We may speculate that there were similar family partnership arrangements at work in 1191, when William Cavarunco agreed to travel to Mallorca with money belonging to Philip Cavarunco, and in 1252, when Ansaldo Letanelo contracted with five differ-

[83] Giovanni Scriba, *Cartolare*, 1, pp. 404–5, #752; 1, p. 380, #705.

[84] Giovanni Scriba, *Cartolare*, 1, p. 292, #544; ASG Cart. 29, 220r.

[85] (1160) Giovanni Scriba, *Cartolare*, 1, p. 380, #705; (1198) *Bonvillano (1198)*. [eds. J.E. Eierman, H.C. Krueger, R.L. Reynolds, Turin, 1939] p. 50, #108; (1237) ASG Cart. 56, 168v; (1182) ASG Cart. 2, 17r (Henry Mallone also appears on the same page as an investor in Mallorcan trade).

[86] Giovanni Scriba, *Cartolare*, 1, pp. 404–5, #752.

[87] ASG Diversorum 102, 11r. In 1201, another member of the family, Obertus, acted as a factor carrying cloth to Catalonia (*Giovanni di Guiberto [1200–1211]*. [eds. M. Hall, H.C. Krueger, R.L. Reynolds, Turin, 1940], p. 210, #442).

[88] *Lanfranco (1206–1226)*. [eds. H.C. Krueger, R.L. Reynolds, Genoa, 1951] 1, p. 151, #375.

ent investors (including Henry and William Letanelo) for a voyage to *Yspania*.[89] Although members of the influential Guercio family were primarily interested in traffic with the eastern Mediterranean, particularly Byzantium, Simon, the son of Johannes Guercio, carried £50 to Catalonia for a female relative, Johanna, in 1243.[90]

Family partnerships and investments were not confined to the investor–factor relationship. In several cases Genoese brothers or cousins pooled resources to finance a Spanish voyage, as did the two members of the Letanelo clan in 1252. The following year, Materino de Guisulfo entrusted £60 pounds to Simon Cicada, who was traveling to Mallorca, then immediately made a second contract with Simon for another £60 on behalf of his brother, Johannes de Guisulfo.[91] Likewise, Ingo Galleta made two contracts in 1252 for trade to Mallorca. The first, for £25, was made with his own money; the second, for £41, was made with money from his sister, Sibilia.[92]

As in the cases of Simon Cicada and Ansaldo Letanelo, it was common for Genoese factors to collect money from several investors before embarking on a voyage to the Iberian peninsula or any other destination. For this reason, the names of individual factors are likely to appear more frequently in contracts than those of investors. A few factors seem to have specialized in western voyages, since their names appear in contracts for different trips, to different Iberian ports, in different years. Two such merchants were Vassallus Raviolo and Fulco de Predi, who twice worked together on voyages to al-Andalus. In August, 1163, they traveled to Ibiza and Bougie, with £40 invested by Blancardus. The following year they carried another sum for Blancardus, together with money from other investors, to Seville.[93] In the 1160s, these two may have been young men, just starting out in the business. Twenty years later, however, in 1182, Vassallus Raviolo is listed as a ship-owner in a contract made to Sicily and the Maghrib.[94] Another traveling partner

[89] (1191) *Guglielmo Cassinese*, II, p. 69, #1287; (1252) ASG Cart. 24, 166r.

[90] ASG Cart. 26/II, 92v. Johanna was the wife of the influential Balduinus Guercio (Krueger, *Navi e proprietà*, pp. 49, 89, 138, 150–2).

[91] ASG Cart. 18/I, 81r–v.

[92] ASG Cart. 24, 169v.

[93] Giovanni Scriba, *Cartolare*, II, p. 141, # 1084; II, pp. 229–30, #1269.

[94] Krueger, *Navi e proprietà*, p. 66.

and ship-owner, Henry Nivetella, worked with Soloman of Salerno in 1158, carrying an investment of nearly £350 to Spain, Sicily, and Provence.[95] Four years later, another contract indicates that Henry went to Spain again in 1162.[96] Henry may have specialized in western Mediterranean traffic at this point in his career, but his ships are found carrying goods to Alexandria, Syria, and Constantinople by the 1180s and 1190s.[97]

The appearance in contracts of Eliadar, the wife of Soloman of Salerno, Johanna, the wife of Balduinus Guercio, and Sibilia, the sister of Ingo Galleta, indicates a further group of Genoese investors in Andalusi commerce. Their presence is unique in Andalusi trade, since there are no records of female investors in either the Muslim or Jewish merchant communities. Genoese women enjoyed considerable financial independence, and often used their money to commercial advantage. A dozen women are found investing in Iberian trade, although like their male relatives they were usually also involved in commercial transactions in other areas of the Mediterranean. As well as investing her own money (she had sent £18 to Spain in 1160), Eliadar acted as her husband's agent in his absence and handled Soloman's business affairs in Genoa while he traveled.[98] Other women – usually identified as the wives, widows, or sisters of merchants appearing elsewhere in the notarial records – also conducted business in Spain. Adalaxia, the wife of Fulco de Castello, sent £50 to Mallorca in 1182.[99] In August 1201, Drua and Montanara (both married to members of the Streiaporco family) entrusted small sums to different factors who were traveling to Catalonia on a ship called the Diana. Another woman, Mabilia, sent £7 to Catalonia in the same month, perhaps on the same ship.[100] Overall, individual investments

[95] Abulafia, *The Two Italies*, p. 244; The contract for Spain is recorded by Giovanni Scriba, *Cartolare*, I, p. 267, #500.

[96] Giovanni Scriba, *Cartolare*, II, p. 104, #1011.

[97] Krueger, *Navi e proprietà*, pp. 72, 86, 90.

[98] On Eliadar, see Abulafia, *The Two Italies*, pp. 241.

[99] ASG Cart. 2, 6r. This is probably the wife of the senior Fulco, since a reference from 1213 discusses the dowry of one Aimelina the wife of a Fulco de Castello – presumably the younger Fulco (S. Epstein, *Wills and Wealth in Medieval Genoa 1150–1250*. [Cambridge, Mass., 1984], pp. 105–6).

[100] Drua and Montanara: *Giovanni de Guiberto*, p. 221, #470; p. 230, #494. Mabilia: ASG Cart. 4, 110v. Also on Genoese women, see G. Pistarino, "Le donne d'affari a Genova nel secolo XIII," *Miscellanea di storia italiana e mediterranea per Nino Lamboglia*. [Genoa, 1978] pp. 157–69.

made by women in Spanish trade tended to be somewhat smaller than investments made by men, although plenty of men also made contracts for very minor sums.

There is little material on merchants trading with the peninsula from other European cities, because their archives lack the wealth of early notarial data preserved in Genoa. What minimal evidence exists all comes from north-western Italy and southern France, for despite their extensive commercial network, the Venetians showed no interest in Iberian trade at this period. Pisan diplomatic treaties with Andalusi rulers indicate the existence of commercial traffic between Pisa and al-Andalus in the twelfth and early thirteenth centuries, but there are no records of individual Pisan businessmen traveling to or from the peninsula before the middle of the thirteenth century. In 1245, however, fourteen Pisans in Mallorca pooled together to rent a ship belonging to a Lombard merchant, and records of Pisan commerce with Catalonia and the Balearics become abundant by the end of the thirteenth century.[101] Documents from other Italian and southern French cities are likewise unrevealing. Records from Savona include a *commenda* made in 1183 in which the factor was permitted to go anywhere *except* Provence or Catalonia (perhaps voyages to these destinations were usually acceptable), and a shipment of six pieces of cordoban leather from Savona to Genoa three years earlier may indicate commercial contact with the peninsula.[102] Early thirteenth-century registers of the Savonese notary Martin contain a few contracts to the Balearics, including two to Ibiza in 1203 and 1205, but none of these references tell us much about the individual Savonese merchants involved.[103] Contracts from Marseille, written in the middle of the thirteenth century, also mention Iberian goods (including alum, cordoban, and Muslim slaves) coming through that city, but say nothing about the merchants transporting these goods.[104]

[101] D. Herlihy, *Pisa in the Early Renaissance.* [New Haven, 1958], pp. 171–3, 177.

[102] A. Cumano, *Il Cartulario di Arnaldo Cumano e Giovanni di Donato (Savona, 1178–1188).* [ed. L. Balletto, Rome, 1978] p. 561, #1118; p. 336, #618.

[103] Martin of Savona, *Il Cartulario del notaio Martino, Savona, 1203–1206.* [ed. D. Puncuh, Genoa, 1974] p. 100, #277; p. 122, #365. There are also three contracts to *Melonica* (probably Mallorca) #440, 805, 808.

[104] L. Blancard (ed.), *Documents inédits sur le commerce de Marseille au moyen âge.* [Marseille, 1884–5] I, pp. 58–9, 63–4, 161–2; II, pp. 268, 313, 317, 326; III, pp. 196–203.

Italian and French traders were not the only Christians to do business in Andalusi markets in the twelfth and thirteenth centuries. Castilians and other merchants from inland Spanish kingdoms also trafficked with al-Andalus, in spite of the dangers of overland travel across the Iberian frontier. A *portazgo* list from Toledo, dated 1137, described tolls due from merchants traveling from that city to al-Andalus, and other tariff lists from urban charters of the same period referred to items, particularly textiles, imported *de tierra de moros.*[105] The influential *Fuero* of Cuenca, granted to the city by Alfonso VIII between 1177 and 1189, addressed the problem of how to prove whether a certain commodity had been purchased "in the land of the Moors," being thus subject to a different tax than local goods.[106] Since it was the origin of the commodity that was in question, rather than that of the merchants, it seems likely that the latter were Christians. A similar matter was raised in the economic legislation of the Cortes of Toledo (1207), which enforced local price controls on merchants leaving Toledo to buy goods in other regions. It also forbad Toledan traders to import textiles from other Christian kingdoms but allowed them to bring these goods from across the Pyrenees or from the land of the Moors.[107]

Despite this overland activity, Castilian merchants were overshadowed by the maritime ventures of their Catalan and Aragonese colleagues. Traders from the Crown of Aragon were aided by the conquests of Mallorca (1229–30) and Valencia (1238), which gave them control over the strategic *route des îles*, but Catalan vessels had traded with the south before this, as shown by a commercial contract (dated 1211) for a sea voyage between Barcelona and *Yspania.*[108] Protectionist legislation also aided Catalan trade. In 1227, for example, James I passed a

[105] T. Muñoz (ed.), *Colección de fueros municipales.* [Madrid, 1847 (reprint 1971)] 1, p. 375. For other *fueros*, see J.L. Martín, "Portazgos de Ocaña y Alarilla," *AHDE* 32(1962), p. 525.

[106] *Fuero de Cuenca.* [ed. A. Valmaña Vicente, Cuenca, 1978] pp. 268–9. This *fuero* became the model for many later charters.

[107] Although this last could also refer to other Islamic countries, the most likely application is al-Andalus. F.H. Hernández, "Las Cortes de Toledo de 1207," *Las Cortes de Castilla y León en la Edad Media.* [Valladolid, 1988], p. 244.

[108] S. Bensch, "From Prizes of War to Domestic Merchandise: Slaves in the Towns of Eastern Iberia," unpublished paper presented at the annual meeting of the Medieval Academy [Princeton, NJ, May, 1991], p. 6.

decree that foreign merchants could not ship goods out of Barcelona if a Catalan merchant were willing to make the trip.[109] Apparently some merchants were willing, and in the same year a Catalan merchant ship sailed to Seville – only to be attacked by pirates from Mallorca on the way home.[110] In 1231, a contract from Vich allowed the traveling partner to go to Murcia, Valencia, and Ceuta, and when James I granted a *leuda* to the town of Tamarit in 1243, it included mention of boats traveling to al-Andalus with goods.[111] The extent of Catalan commercial exchange with al-Andalus appears to have created controversy, since in 1237 Pope Gregory IX complained that despite three warnings Catalan merchants were still shipping contraband goods to Ibiza, whence they reached al-Andalus.[112]

Catalan merchants also appear in notarial registers from Italian and southern French cities, and these traders probably provided a channel for the export of Andalusi goods to European markets. In 1248, Arnold, "a Catalan from Tortosa," agreed to carry £14 in Genoese currency to Catalonia, and at least a dozen other Tortosan merchants appear in Genoese records at this period.[113] At the same time, Pisan tariff registers from 1247 note tax discounts granted to traders from the Crown of Aragon.[114] Genoese registers also cite a number of merchants bearing names of apparent Iberian origin (such as *de Cartagenia* or *de Barcellonio*), although their contracts did not necessarily pertain to commerce with Spain. It is not clear, for example, whether Bernard de Barcellonio, whose name appears in a contract from 1191, was merely making a brief stop in Genoa or whether he lived there.

[109] G. de Reparez, "L'activité maritime et commerciale du royaume d'Aragon au XIIIe siècle," *Bulletin hispanique* 49(1947), pp. 425–6; and A. Capmany y de Monpalau, *Memorias históricas sobre la marina, comercio y artes de la antigua ciudad de Barcelona.* [new edn, Barcelona, 1961–3] II, pp. 12–13.

[110] A. Schaube, *Handelsgeschichte der romanischen völker des Mittelmeergebiets bis zum ende der kreuzzüge.* [Munich-Berlin, 1906], p. 328.

[111] A. García, "Contractes comercials vigatans de principis del segle XIII," *Ausa* (Vich) 43(1963), p. 336; M.D. Sendra Cendra, *Aranceles aduaneros de la Corona de Aragón (siglo XIII).* [Valencia, 1966], p. 36.

[112] R.I. Burns, "Renegades, Adventurers, and Sharp Businessmen: The 13th century Spaniards in the Cause of Islam," *Catholic Historical Review* 58(1972), pp. 359–60. The growth of Aragonese and Catalan commercial power in the late thirteenth and fourteenth centuries has been thoroughly chronicled elsewhere. See especially C.E. Dufourcq, *L'Espagne catalane et le Maghrib aux XIIIe et XIVe siècles.* [Paris, 1966] and other works by the same author.

[113] ASG 26/II, 140v.

[114] Herlihy, *Pisa in the Early Renaissance*, p. 202.

Similar doubts arise about Oberto Ferrario de Valencia and his son William, who figured in a number of Genoese contracts from 1213, and about Ogerio de Cartagenia, who was mentioned in a Savonese will in 1179.[115] In many cases, closer examination shows that these merchants had no direct or contemporary connections with the Iberian regions from which they took their names. The de Cartagenia clan, for instance, though originally from the peninsula, had done business in Genoa for years and may have considered themselves Genoese.[116] More complex difficulties arise with the name *de Valencia*, since, as Lopez has pointed out, it is impossible to distinguish, in Latin, between the native of Valencia (Spain), Valenza (Piedmont), or Valence (France).[117]

The rise of Christian mercantile strength after the middle of the twelfth century challenged the earlier Muslim and Jewish commercial hegemony in Andalusi ports. Muslims and Jews appear much less frequently in economic records after the middle of the twelfth century, although some non-Christian traders continued to do business in the peninsula. Jews from the northern peninsula may have traded across the Iberian frontier, and references to Jewish merchants continue to appear regularly in *fueros* and other Christian sources. A document from the Galician town of Celanova, for example, mentioned Jews selling silks and other textiles in 1184.[118] The reference to silk suggests that these Jewish merchants were either Andalusis or had commercial ties with the south. In most cases, however, the lack of differentiation in Latin documents between Andalusi Jews and members of the local Jewish community makes it difficult to determine the extent of the Andalusi Jewish presence in northern markets. Because of the hardships of Jewish life in the south under the

[115] Bernard: *Guglielmo Cassinese*, p. 38, #19. Obertus and William Ferrario: ASG Cart. 7, fols. 100–10, and elsewhere. Is the younger man the same William Ferrario who acted as a factor in two contracts to Cartagena in 1253 (ASG Cart. 18/II 65v, 66v)? Ogerius: Cumano, *Cartulario*, p. 266, #524.

[116] Krueger, "Genoese Trade with Northwest Africa," p. 394. Abulafia, on the other hand, considers *de Cartagenia* to be a true Spanish name (*The Two Italies*, p. 200).

[117] R.S. Lopez, "Concerning Surnames and Places of Origin," *Medievalia et humanistica* 8(1954), p. 14.

[118] A. Ballesteros y Baretta, *Historia de España y su influencia en la historia universal*. [Barcelona, 1920] II, p. 529; and I.F. Baer, *A History of the Jews in Christian Spain*. [Philadelphia, 1961] I, p. 84.

Almohad regime, a number of Jews – merchants and others – had moved north seeking freedom from persecution and better economic opportunities. Perhaps the silk merchants of Celanova were among their ranks. Thus, while Jewish commercial activity declined in al-Andalus, Jewish traders of Andalusi origin and otherwise came to play an important role in Christian Spanish markets during the late middle ages.

Muslims continued to operate in Andalusi trade into the early thirteenth century, in spite of the appearance of Christian competitors and after the demise of their Jewish compatriots. A Genoese contract from 1158 mentioned a merchant named Maraxi whose dealings with Denia and Mallorca suggest that he may have been a Muslim.[119] At about the same time, Idrīsī reported that Andalusis were trading with Salé and other Moroccan ports, bringing Andalusi oil in exchange for grain. Meanwhile, merchants from western Muslim lands, including al-Andalus, were seen in the markets of Alexandria by the Jewish traveler Benjamin of Tudela in about 1165.[120] Perhaps one of these Andalusis was the merchant-scholar Aḥmad b. Marwān who, according to his biographer Silafī, traveled to Alexandria, Isfahan, and Iraq at roughly this period.[121] Ibn al-ʿAbbār likewise provided information on five other merchant-scholars, all probably of Andalusi Arab heritage, who died between 1184 and 1245.[122] Shaqundī (writing between 1199 and 1212) also casually mentioned the presence of Muslim commercial shipping in Malaga.[123] Somewhat later, we learn in passing of yet another trader, the brother of a Murcian scholar Abū al-ʿAbbās, who traveled to the east on pilgrimage with his family in 1242.

[119] Giovanni Scriba, *Cartolare*, p. 260, #487. Abulafia has described this man as "perhaps a Saracen" (*The Two Italies*, p. 229).

[120] Idrīsī, *Opus geographicum*. III [Naples-Rome, 1972], p. 239; Benjamin of Tudela, "The Itinerary of Benjamin of Tudela," [trans. M.N. Adler] *Jewish Quarterly Review* 18(1906), p. 686. It is clear from the context of this latter passage that Benjamin is referring to non-Jewish merchants.

[121] Silafī, *Akhbār wa tarājim andalusiyya*. [ed. I. ʿAbbās, Beirut, 1963], p. 21, #5. It is possible that this merchant belongs to an earlier period, but since Silafī (d. 1180) does not provide a date for his death, he was probably a contemporary.

[122] Ibn al-ʿAbbar, *Takmila*; Three of these merchants had the name al-Anṣārī, but do not appear otherwise related. They came from Seville (d. 1184) [p. 249, #803]; Valencia (d. 1202) [p. 274, #864]; Baeza and Jaen (d. 1233) [p. 340, #993]; the other two merchants came from Valencia (d. 1225) [p. 650, #1810] and Malaga (d. 1245) [p. 519, #1456].

[123] This passage is preserved in Maqqarī, *Analectes sur l'histoire et la littérature des arabes d'Espagne*. [ed. R. Dozy, Leiden, 1855–60] II, p. 148.

Shipwrecked off Bône, only Abū al-ʿAbbās and his elder brother, the merchant, survived from the family. The brothers went to Tunisia, where the older one continued to work in commerce, while the younger opened a Quran school.[124]

Records of Andalusi Muslim traders are scarce after the middle of the thirteenth century. As will be discussed in the final chapter of this book, although some Muslims continued to trade in the ports of Nasrid Granada and (to a lesser extent) in the Crown of Aragon, they disappeared from the international trade of newly Christian Andalusia. Unlike Jewish merchants, it appears that Andalusi Muslims found it very difficult to reestablish their business under Christian rule. Instead, most Muslim traders either switched their interests to a more local trading sphere (such as coastal traffic between Granada and Valencia), or shifted their mercantile activities to Muslim ports in North Africa, the eastern Mediterranean, and the Indian Ocean. This exodus of Muslim merchants from Iberian trade occurred at the same time as other commercial developments in the peninsula, where not only did Muslims and Jews now face increased competition from Christian merchants, but Christian rulers also took a more active role in their kingdoms' economy than had their Muslim predecessors. We have already seen a case in which James I of Aragon promoted the rights of Catalan traders in Barcelona. This type of legislation encouraged certain groups of traders at the expense of others. In southern Castile (and even in Muslim Granada), Genoese merchants controlled most commercial activity with the aid of trading privileges granted to them by the Crown of Castile. In northern Castile a nascent Castilian merchant class came to dominate trade through Atlantic ports, while Catalans in the eastern peninsula were building a Mediterranean trading empire to rival that of the Italians.

With these changes in the Iberian merchant population in the thirteenth century, commerce in the peninsula began to shift away from an exclusively Mediterranean orientation toward the trading sphere of northern Europe and the Atlantic. Meanwhile, the southern Mediterranean east–west commercial routes, which had been so strong in the eleventh and twelfth centuries, began to disintegrate with the decline of the Muslim and Jewish

[124] G. Elshayyal, "The Cultural Relations between Alexandria and the Islamic West in al-Andalus and Morocco," *Madrid:MDI* 16(1971), p. 65.

mercantile network and the rise of Christian shipping routes along the northern shores. These trends combined to signal the creation of an entirely new axis for Iberian participation in Mediterranean and European trade. The realignment of the Iberian commercial network in the late middle ages, as Christian merchants gained control of trade in the peninsula, will be discussed in Chapter 9.

Chapter 5

MERCHANT BUSINESS AND ANDALUSI GOVERNMENT AUTHORITY

The medieval Mediterranean has been characterized as a zone of "free trade" because most international merchants were free to travel wherever habit, personal desire, commercial advantage, or a senior partner might direct them.[1] At the same time, however, merchant business in al-Andalus and elsewhere was circumscribed by the needs and regulations of regional government authority (*sulṭān*).[2] Once a merchant arrived in a particular port, he was likely to find himself enmeshed in a legal web of local regulations. His person and cargo would be subject to inspection and taxation; his movements, habitation, and conduct might be restricted; his transactions in the marketplace would be controlled. This chapter will examine the various points at which international merchant business was touched by local authority. These include the administration of ports and shipping, the collection of taxes and tolls, and the regulation of prices and goods.

Muslim rulers took a close interest in economic affairs, although it is unlikely that they viewed commerce as an abstract entity to be influenced or controlled. The motives behind government intervention in international trade ranged widely. Sometimes rulers were interested in protecting local food supplies, keeping an eye on foreigners, or preventing the export of certain goods (either items subject to government monopoly or potentially dangerous war materials). At other times, their actions were aimed at raising revenue for government and personal coffers, either through taxes or commercial speculation. Ibn

[1] S.D. Goitein described the Mediterranean as a "free-trade community" (*A Mediterranean Society*. [Berkeley, 1967–88] 1, p. 66).

[2] In Arabic, the term *sulṭān* (or *sulṭāniyya*) may be applied either to an abstract concept of secular government, or to the person of the ruler (usually in his role as the personification of abstract *sulṭān*). For more on the theory of *sulṭān*, see B. Lewis, *The Political Language of Islam*. [Chicago, 1988], pp. 51–2.

Khaldūn deplored the way some rulers dabbled in trade, often causing "harm to [their] subjects" in an effort to acquire profit above their legitimate income.[3]

Despite his censure, Ibn Khaldūn also recognized positive aspects to the relationship between government and commerce, noting that government constitutes "the greatest number of people who make expenditures, and their expenditure provides more of the substance of trade than that of any other group. When they stop spending, business slumps and commercial profits decline . . . the [ruling] dynasty is the greatest market, the mother and base of all trade."[4] This comment acknowledged the fact that rulers and members of their courts were the most important consumers of expensive luxury goods imported from abroad, but it also signified a more complex interaction. Local rulers, with the assistance of their bureaucratic entourage and Islamic law (*sharī'a*), influenced or controlled much of the economic activity within their domains. Because there was no clear line between secular and religious authority in an Islamic context, the administration of commercial affairs was handled jointly. Government administrators oversaw many aspects of local industries and agriculture, and they regulated port facilities, shipping, taxes, and the money supply. Islamic law meanwhile dictated the proper procedures for commerce, ruling on the correct forms for sales, contracts, forward buying, leases of ships and animals, and so forth. In a similar manner, the law intervened between persons in matters relevant to commercial loans and partnership agreements. In the case of commercial difficulty, damage, or dispute, Muslim jurists were well prepared to legislate a solution, and Islamic law books were filled with precedents of cases involving business relations (*mu'āmalāt*).

Official interest in Andalusi commerce is evident during all periods of Muslim rule in Spain, but there is better information for some periods than others. Umayyad rulers clearly took an interest in international trade and maritime affairs, and we know something about shipyards, port administration, and taxation under their rule. In contrast, Taifa rulers appear to have been

[3] Ibn Khaldūn, *The Muqaddimah*. [trans. F. Rosenthal, New York, 1958] II, p. 94.

[4] Ibn Khaldūn, *Muqaddimah*, II, p. 103 (punctuation has been slightly changed). Although Ibn Khaldūn was writing after the period under discussion, Dimashqī had earlier made similar observations in his *Kitāb al-'ashāra ilā maḥāsin al-tijāra*. [Cairo, 1318–1900], p. 41.

preoccupied with other concerns. There is little data on commercial or international interests in the eleventh century, with the notable exception of the ruler of Denia, Ibn Mujāhid (1044–75). Later, Almoravid and Almohad rulers were sufficiently concerned with international trade to arrange commercial treaties with Genoa and Pisa. The Almohads, in particular, seem to have monitored international trade more closely than did earlier dynasties. Foreign access to Almohad ports was strictly controlled, as shown in a Pisan–Almohad treaty drawn up in 1186 which permitted Pisan merchants to trade with four North African ports, but specifically forbad traffic to any Andalusi harbor except Almeria, where Pisan ships might stop only in an emergency for repairs but not for trade.[5] To some extent, Almohad rulers appear to have encouraged foreign traffic, but increasing tension between Christians and Muslims in the peninsula, with Almohad power under siege, resulted in an overall tightening of mercantile regulations in the late twelfth century.

PORTS AND PORT OFFICIALS

Much of an international merchant's business would have taken place in the Andalusi port where he arrived and whence he departed. Indeed, most international traders probably never ventured inland beyond these coastal cities, but instead sold their cargoes there or consigned them to local partners. Because of the concentration of commercial activity in ports, and because these cities were border zones, they tended to be subject to greater bureaucracy than their inland counterparts. Unlike inland towns which were governed by a regular governor (*wālī*), port cities were usually under the administration of a military governor (*qā'id*), as were towns along the Andalusi land frontier.[6] Likewise, the need to regulate and accommodate foreigners and their goods sojourning in port cities necessitated the creation of specialized facilities and administrative positions.

Although Andalusi sources do not reveal much about port facilities such as warehouses for goods or customs houses for the

[5] M. Amari, *I diplomi arabi del R. Archivio Fiorentino.* [Florence, 1863], p. 20.

[6] E. Lévi-Provençal, *Histoire de L'Espagne musulmane.* [Paris, 1950–3] III, p. 57; J. Bosch Vilá, "Algunas consideraciones sobre 'al-tagr' en al-Andalus y la división político-administrativa de la España musulmana," *Etudes d'orientalisme dédiées à la mémoire de Lévi-Provençal.* [Paris, 1962] I, p. 30.

collection of tolls, these were ubiquitous elsewhere in the Islamic world.[7] Merchants usually had to clear cargoes through the *diwān* (a customs and toll-collecting bureau), they may have had to store goods in a *makhzan* (warehouse), or stay at a *funduq* (hostelry).[8] The best information on Andalusi merchant activity comes from Seville and Almeria, and the administration of these cities was probably representative of structures elsewhere in Muslim Spain. Mercantile legislation would have been similar for any merchant arriving from abroad, although the activities of an Andalusi, returning to a home port, were probably less restricted than those of a visiting Egyptian, Genoese, or other foreigner.

On arrival, a merchant was subject to the authority of local administrators, of whom the most important was the chief *qāḍī* (judge) of the city. In the early twelfth century, Ibn ʿAbdūn described the duties of the chief qāḍī of Seville. These included the responsibility of keeping guard

> over the bank of the river [the Guadalquivir] which serves as the city's harbor for ships lest anything be sold there or any buildings built along it. This [is important] because this place is the source [of water] for the region, and the place whence depart the profitable commodities which merchants export. It is likewise a place of refuge for foreigners, and a site for the repair of ships. This place is not the property of any individual, but it belongs to the *sulṭān* only. It is incumbent upon the qāḍī to watch over [this region] with the greatest care, since it is a gathering place for merchants, travelers, and others . . .[9]

This statement makes clear that the region of the port differed from other sectors of the city. Not only was it the property of the *sulṭān*, as was frequently true of other public urban spaces (shops, markets, hostelries, and so on), but Ibn ʿAbdūn stressed that the harbor was the domain of merchants and foreigners.

[7] On Muslim ports generally, see S. Soucek, "Mīnā'," *Encyclopedia of Islam.* [2nd edn, Leiden 1960–] VII, pp. 66–72. On Egyptian ports, see C. Cahen, "Douanes et commerce dans les ports méditerranéens de l'Egypte médiévale d'après le 'Minhādj d'al-Makhzūmi'," *JESHO* 7(1964), pp. 217–314.

[8] A.E. Lieber, "Eastern Business Practices and Medieval European Commerce," *Economic History Review* 21(1968), p. 237. The word *diwān* had different meanings, but generally signified some type of governmental bureau. The Andalusi references to these institutions, particularly those closely connected with descriptions of markets or port facilities, probably intend a station for the collection of tolls.

[9] Ibn ʿAbdūn, *Risāla.* [ed. E. Lévi-Provençal, *Documents arabes inédits sur la vie sociale et économique en occident musulman au moyen âge: Trois traités hispaniques de ḥisba.* Cairo, 1955], p. 30.

Within the confines of the port, officials kept a close eye on these people and regulated their movement. Travelers could not come ashore until permitted, they must store their goods in certain places and stay in others. This arrangement was not simply restrictive, since it also benefited and protected strangers to the city. The harbor of Seville was, as Ibn 'Abdūn said, a "refuge" to foreigners, and the same was true in Almeria, where 'Udhrī (d. 1085) described the port as being an area "in which merchants feel safe about their goods, and to which people come from all regions."[10]

To assist them in their duties, chief qāḍīs maintained a staff of lower-ranking magistrates and associated urban officials who helped to maintain public order, oversee commerce, and deal with foreign merchants.[11] The best known of these officers was the market inspector (*muḥtasib* or *sāḥib al-sūq*), whose activities and responsibilities are preserved in *ḥisba* books (reference manuals written for his use). Theoretically, the *muḥtasib*'s task was to "promote good and prevent evil" in the Muslim community, and under this general rubric, his duties included overseeing the market place (where he should look out for "deceptions, swindles, and other [iniquities]"); supervising baths, hostelries, and public thoroughfares; and maintaining public decency and religious decorum.[12] Ibn 'Abdūn, a *muḥtasib* in twelfth-century

[10] 'Udhrī, "Nuṣūṣ 'an al-Andalus" [ed. A.A. al-'Ahwānī, *Tarḍī' al-akhbār wa tanwī' al-āthār*. Madrid, 1960], p. 86.

[11] These officials were ubiquitous in Muslim ports (see C. Cahen, "Douanes et commerce," pp. 271–2, on Egypt). Nevertheless, port officials were not a Muslim innovation in the peninsula, where officers called *thelonearii* had regulated commerce and assisted foreign merchants (*transmarini negotiatores*) in Visigothic times. See H. Pirenne, *Mohammed and Charlemagne*. [London, 1939 (reprinted New York, 1980)], p. 87.

[12] The reference to swindles is taken from Saqaṭī (an early thirteenth-century *muḥtasib* in Malaga), *Kitāb al-faqīh al-ajall al-'ālim al-'ārif al-awḥad* [*Un manuel hispanique de ḥisba*]. [eds. G.S. Colin and E. Lévi-Provençal, Paris, 1931], p. 13. Other Andalusi *ḥisba* texts include the *Risāla* of Ibn 'Abdūn of Seville (twelfth century), the *Risāla* of Ibn 'Abd al-Ra'ūf (tenth century), and the *Risāla* of Jarsīfī (thirteenth century). Jarsīfī may have been a Maghribi, but his text is very similar to Andalusi counterparts. These last three texts have been edited by Lévi-Provençal in his *Documents arabes*. On the profession of the *muḥtasib*, see R.P. Buckley, "The *Muḥtasib*," *Arabica* 39(1992), pp. 59–117. The *muḥtasib* in al-Andalus is described, at length, in P. Chalmeta, *El señor del zoco en España*. [Madrid, 1973]. This post is particularly interesting in an Andalusi context because it appears to have been transferred from al-Andalus into Christian Spain. The post of *zabazoque* (from *ṣāḥib al-sūq*) appeared in Leon by 1020; later we find references to the *almotacen* in Castile and the *mustasaf* in Aragon (see T. Glick, "Muhtasib and Mustasaf: A Case Study of Institutional Diffusion," *Viator* 2(1971), pp. 59–81).

Seville, was stringent in his watch over commerce in the city and insisted on the importance of keeping a moral eye on the harbor in order to prevent certain cargoes – including "any abominable thing such as wine" – from being loaded on shipboard.[13]

A *muḥtasib's* responsibilities also extended to the physical aspects of shipping and trade. The early thirteenth-century *muḥtasib* Saqaṭī indicated that his duties included the oversight of ships and their equipment in the port of Malaga. At the end of his manual he detailed various items (ropes, sails, and the like) that were necessary in order to equip a ship properly, together with materials (including nails and linen) required for ship-building.[14] A *muḥtasib* was likewise responsible for maritime safety, and should ensure that greedy boatmen did not overload their vessels, and thus endanger the lives of their passengers, nor make their passengers do the rowing.[15] In spite of these indications of the *muḥtasib*'s role in policing port facilities, this officer was not primarily responsible for the oversight of international trade or traders. In consequence, few international or long-distance commodities are mentioned in market handbooks. Instead, a *muḥtasib*'s principal concern was with the local population, not with foreigners, and his jurisdiction only extended to international trade where it touched upon the welfare of his flock.

While the *muḥtasib* saw to local people, other urban officers were concerned with the monitoring of foreign trade and traders. Their activities, however, are less well documented, and consequently more obscure, than those of the *muḥtasib*. There may have been a post parallel to the *muḥtasib*, whose holder was responsible for maritime administration and foreign trade. Perhaps Ibn ʿAbdūn was referring to this type of officer in his reference to an "overseer for the river" (*'amīn ʿalā al-wādī*) who was in charge of sailors.[16] No clear Andalusi references survive to such an officer, but later documentation from Aragon noted a cognate post, the *zalmedinos marítimos*, and Barcelona employed

[13] Ibn ʿAbdūn, *Risāla*, p. 29. In a similar moralistic vein, this author warned that sailors must be prevented from mixing with "women who have a reputation for immorality" (pp. 56–7).

[14] Saqaṭī, *Kitāb al-faqīh*, pp. 71–2.

[15] Ibn ʿAbdūn, *Risāla*, p. 29.

[16] Ibn ʿAbdūn, *Risāla*, p. 57.

both a *mustasaf* and *consules de mar* in the fourteenth century.[17] These *consules*, like the *mustasaf*, may have been derived from earlier Andalusi prototypes.

As far as foreign merchants were concerned, the most important local official was probably the "representative of the merchants" (*wakīl al-tujjār*), who occupied a rank somewhere between that of government officer and private partner. This personage was usually a merchant himself, and appointed by his colleagues to act as their agent, negotiator, and to liaise in matters concerning their relations with the government. He could also act as a legal representative, could arbitrate in disputes between merchants, or could provide secure storage for their goods. Although the *wakīl al-tujjār* does not specifically appear in Muslim Spanish texts, the concept of agency (*wakāla*) was well developed in Andalusi law.[18]

Other Andalusi data obliquely suggest the existence of various other officials involved in the oversight of trade. In the tenth century, Hasday b. Shaprūt supposedly remarked that, as a government official, he supervised foreign traders, "whose commerce and affairs cannot be conducted except through my hand and at my command."[19] This assertion suggests a centralization of control under the Umayyad regime. However, as with other spheres of Muslim administration, it is often difficult to distinguish a clear hierarchy within the bureaucratic network. Other posts having to do with mercantile business – agents, brokers, and the like – were frequently held by merchants, and their holders could function as intermediaries between merchants and the administration. A broker (*simsār*) might help a foreign merchant negotiate with the *diwān*, or might be employed privately to buy goods on commission.[20]

Relations between merchants and their agents were also subject to oversight. According to Saqaṭī, it was among the duties

[17] Saqaṭī, "El 'Kitāb fī ādāb al-ḥisba' (Libro de buen gobierno del zoco) de al-Saqaṭī" [trans. P. Chalmeta], *Al-Andalus* 32(1967), pp. 147–8.

[18] On the *wakīl al-tujjār* see Goitein, *Mediterranean Society*, 1, pp. 186–92; and A.L. Udovitch, "Merchants and *Amīrs*: Government and Trade in eleventh-century Egypt," *Asian and African Studies* 22(1988), p. 65.

[19] Y.F. Baer, *A History of the Jews in Christian Spain*. [Philadelphia, 1961], 1 pp. 29, 382. Baer notes that this letter may well be spurious.

[20] On the *simsār*, see C. Cahen, "Douanes et commerce," p. 239; and A.E. Lieber, "Eastern Business Practices," p. 237. Wansharīsī's *Mi'yār al-mu'rib*. [ed. M. Hajjī Rabat, 1981] includes several references to the *simsār* (see, for example, XIII, p. 122).

of the *muḥtasib* "to prevent merchants from staying either with an agent (*dallāl*) or with business associates (*jullās*)" lest these people take advantage of their foreign guests.[21] The eastern author Abū Faḍl al-Dimashqī advised similar precautions, warning that "a traveling merchant going to a place which he does not know should arrange for . . . a secure place [to stay] and other things, for fear of being taken in by tricksters."[22] In order to prevent such abuses, established hostelries (*funduqs*) became a prevalent feature of towns throughout the Islamic world.[23] An anonymous author reported that early thirteenth-century Cordoba contained as many as "sixteen hundred *funduqs* and *khāns*, the former being a place where merchants, travelers, single men, foreigners, and others may stay."[24] Somewhat earlier, Idrīsī had counted nine hundred and seventy *funduqs* in twelfth-century Almeria, while Maqqarī later tallied one thousand in the same city.[25]

Most Andalusi *funduqs* were of modest size and roughly built, one or two stories high, with a simple floor plan of small rooms around a central court. Merchants could stay in the guest rooms above, while their goods and animals were safely housed in the ground floor rooms around the courtyard. At least one Andalusi *funduq*, the fourteenth-century Corral del Carbón in Granada, still survives today. Its structure conforms to the basic plan of earlier Andalusi hostelries, though on a comparatively grand scale. The building is roughly thirty meters square, with a central courtyard and three floors, of which the two upper stories each contain about twenty small guest rooms opening on to galleries overlooking the central space. It appears that at least fifty merchants, if not many more, could have been housed in this *funduq* at the same time.[26]

Funduqs were subject to close scrutiny by the *muḥtasib*, and *ḥisba* manuals speak at length of their proper administration. It

[21] Saqaṭī, *Kitāb al-faqīh*, p. 60.

[22] Dimashqī, *Kitāb al-'ashāra*, p. 52.

[23] On Egyptian *funduqs*, see C. Cahen, "Douanes et commerce," pp. 237–8.

[24] H. Mones (ed.) "Waṣf al-jadīd li-Qurṭuba al-islamīyya," *Madrid:MDI* 13(1965–6), p. 170.

[25] Idrīsī, *Opus geographicum*. v, [Naples-Rome, 1975] p. 563; Maqqarī, *Analectes sur l'histoire et la littérature des arabes d'Espagne*. [ed. R. Dozy, Leiden, 1855–60], I, p. 102.

[26] For a detailed description of Andalusi hostelries and the Corral del Carbón in particular, see two articles by L. Torres Balbás: "Las alhóndigas hispanomusulmanas y el Corral del Carbón de Granada," *Al-Andalus* 11(1946), pp. 447–81; and "Alcaicerías," *Al-Andalus* 14(1949), pp. 431–55.

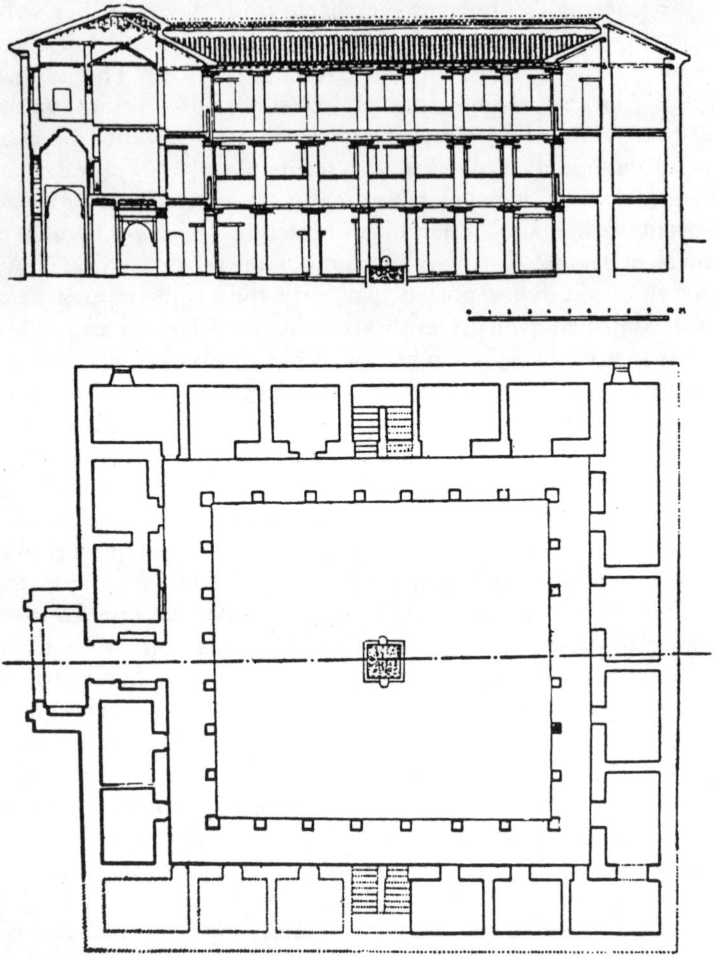

5 Plan and Elevation of the Corral del Carbón, a fourteenth-century *funduq* in Granada (L. Torres Balbás, *Al-Andalus* 11(1946) facing p. 464)

was important, for example, that the keeper of a *funduq* be male, lest the presence of a woman lead to fornication. Likewise, it was necessary to prevent loose women from wantonly unveiling their heads in front of *funduqs*, hoping to entice the residents.[27]

[27] Ibn ʿAbdūn, *Risāla*, pp. 49–51.

These legal strictures probably addressed a topic of real concern. Certainly, the loose living enjoyed in hostelries was a recurring image in popular literature, and even Ibn Ḥazm recounted the tale (tactfully set in Baghdad) of a man who fell madly in love with the poorly chaperoned daughter of a female innkeeper.[28] Foreign merchants were also subject to a night-time curfew, and if traders were found abroad after dark, Ibn ʿAbdūn instructed that they ought to be confined within a "*funduq* where they will be under the care of their fellow residents until morning."[29] A further moral duty of the *muḥtasib* required that he search out the Muslim occupants of *funduqs* to ensure their regular attendance at prayers.[30]

SHIPPING AND TRANSPORTATION

Not only did the Andalusi *sulṭān* control many aspects of port and market administration, but the presence of government was also felt in mercantile shipping. A ruler could also act as a merchant and ship-owner, leasing his vessel to individual merchants or groups of traders. Ibn ʿAbdūn made clear that it was not unusual to hire a boat "from the *sulṭān*.[31] On the other hand, the *sulṭān* might engage merchants or ship-owners to transport goods for the government, as shown in a *fatwa* collected by Wansharīsī that dealt with merchants carrying cargoes of food under government contract.[32] The *sulṭān* also had the power to impound merchant ships in Andalusi harbors or to prohibit them from sailing.

The titles of rulers frequently appear in conjunction with the names of particular ships, and Geniza letters are filled with references to the "ship of the *sulṭān*," the "ship of the *qāʾid*," the "ship of the *amīr*," and so forth.[33] Goitein has suggested that

[28] Ibn Ḥazm, *Ṭawq al-ḥamāma*. [Cairo, 1975], p. 138.

[29] Ibn ʿAbdūn, *Risāla*, p. 18. The author uses the phrase *taḥta ḍamān* ("under the care") but it has a stronger sense than the English in that the other merchants have pledged themselves, or guaranteed, to look after their erring fellow. Local people were probably also under curfew at night (Ibn Ḥazm, *Ṭawq al-ḥamāma*. p. 185).

[30] Ibn ʿAbd al-Raʾūf, *Risāla*. [ed. E. Lévi-Provençal, *Documents arabes*], p. 76.

[31] Ibn ʿAbdūn, *Risāla*, p. 31.

[32] Wansharīsī, *Miʿyār*, VIII, pp. 309–10. Food shipments were usually part of an administrative effort to amass a grain surplus for relief in time of famine.

[33] The wording (*markab al-sulṭān*) suggests that only one ship bore this title; otherwise the phrase would have been "one among the ruler's ships" (*markab min marākib al-sulṭān*).

references to government-owned vessels indicate that maritime travel was sometimes restricted to official ships. However, the abundance of contemporary references to privately owned ships makes this unlikely.[34] Nevertheless, the relative wealth of the *sulṭān*, a government's ability to commandeer shipping materials such as iron and timber, and a ruler's interest in commercial profit, all promoted official influence in maritime traffic.

Although the name of the ruler was not always specified in connection with a particular ship, it is often possible to make a good guess at his identity. Several rulers appear to have been from the Islamic west, indicating that Andalusi amirs and governors maintained commercial and naval fleets.[35] 'Alī ibn Mujāhid of Denia (1044–75), in particular, owned at least one commercial vessel, and his father, Mujāhid al-'Amirī (1012–44), had possessed a fleet that Ibn Ḥazm described as blockading the harbor at Almeria in the early eleventh century.[36] Two chroniclers report that Ibn Mujāhid dispatched a shipload of food to Egypt during a famine in the east, and the vessel returned to al-Andalus "filled with treasures and important gifts."[37] Although this does not appear, on the face of it, to have been a commercial voyage, frequent Geniza references to the "ship of Ibn Mujāhid" plying the route between Denia and Egypt during the 1040s–1060s, show that this ruler was certainly engaged in trade. For example, an account book of Nahray b. Nissīm for the year 1044–5 mentioned "a bale of flax, including all expenses, loaded on Mujāhid's boat."[38] This citation has no stated connection to al-Andalus, but a later reference to a boat of the same name (*markab Mujāhid*) arriving in Alexandria from Denia renders the

[34] S.D. Goitein, "La Tunisie du XIe siècle à la lumière de documents de la Geniza du Caire," *Etudes d'orientalisme dédiées à la memoire de Lévi-Provençal.* [Paris, 1962], p. 575.

[35] Many eastern rulers and viziers also owned fleets. In one Geniza letter (Bodl a2.20) the writer referred to "the ship of amir Nāṣir al-Dawla," who controlled Egypt from 1062 to 1073 (S.D. Goitein, *Letters of Medieval Jewish Traders.* [Princeton, 1973], p. 139). A century later, Usamah b. Munqidh dispatched his family from Egypt to Damietta on an official ship (*Kitāb al-'itibār.* [ed. H. Derenbourg, Paris, 1886–93]. 1.2, p. 25).

[36] Ibn Ḥazm, *Ṭawq al-ḥamāma.* p. 118. The fact that both father and son maintained a fleet is hardly surprising given that their Taifa kingdom encompassed Denia and the Balearics.

[37] Ibn al-Khaṭīb, *Kitāb al-'amāl al-'alām.* [ed. E. Lévi-Provençal, Beirut, 1956], pp. 221–2. A second account (and the source of this quotation) may be found in the anonymous fourteenth-century *Ḥulāl al-mawshīya.* [ed. I.S. Allouche, Rabat, 1936], p. 62.

[38] Bodl e98.64; trans. Goitein, *Letters*, p. 283. It is possible, given the date, that this boat belonged to the elder Mujāhid.

identification more secure.[39] During the late 1050s, or early 1060s, this boat appeared again in another letter to Nahray, where it was noted as sailing from Sicily to Egypt with a number of Andalusi Jews on board. In roughly the same period, we find a further mention of this ship sailing into Alexandria with another Andalusi vessel.[40]

In the same letter that cited these two Andalusi ships arriving in Egypt, the writer remarked that the "vessel of [the] am[ī]r [al]-An[d]alus" had just departed for the west, suggesting that other Andalusi rulers besides Ibn Mujāhid took an interest in commercial shipping.[41] Somewhat later, in 1083, another Geniza letter referred to the "boat of the *ḥājib*," whom Ashtor has identified as ʿImād al-Dawla Mundhir, the governor of Denia from 1081 to 1091.[42] In the following century, we find repeated references in the Geniza to both a *markab al-sulṭān* and a *markab al-qā'id*, with the two sometimes cited together in the same letter. In 1140, for example, Judah Ha-Levi journeyed to Alexandria from al-Andalus on the "new boat of the *sulṭān*," while other Jewish colleagues traveled on the *qā'id*'s ship. At about the same period, another letter reported that a number of merchants had recently arrived in Egypt from the west on these two vessels.[43] Goitein has identified the *sulṭān* in question as Yaḥyā b. al-ʿAzīz of Bougie (1124–52), and the *qā'id* as Muḥammad b. Maymūn of Almeria, commander of the Almoravid fleet during the 1130s.[44] The ship belonging to the Algerian ruler must have

[39] TS 8 J 20.2; This letter probably dates to the early 1060s.

[40] TS 13 J 19.20 and ENA 2805.26. In both cases, the ship was noted as belonging to Ibn Mujāhid, not merely Mujāhid. The other Andalusi ship mentioned in the latter document belonged to a certain Abū ʿAbd Allah [al-Andalusī]. This second boat appeared in other contemporary Geniza letters, many of which included the owner's *nisba*, proving an Andalusi connection (TS Box 28.37; Bodl c28.61; Bodl d66.15; probably also TS 8 J 20.2; TS 13 J 19.29; TS 13 J 17.3).

[41] ENA 2805.26; the text reconstruction is from an unpublished transcription by Goitein.

[42] TS 12.570; ed. E. Ashtor, "Documentos españoles de la Genizah," *Sefarad* 24(1964), p. 77.

[43] TS 13 J 15.16 and TS 12.290. Other letters also report the arrival of Judah Ha-Levi on this particular ship, see TS 10 J 10.23 and Goitein, *Mediterranean Society*. v, pp. 454–5.

[44] Goitein, *Mediterranean Society*, I, p. 310. It should be pointed out that these identifications are problematic, and Goitein elsewhere proposed different names ("La Tunisie," p. 575). The identity of the *qā'id* is considerably more secure than that of the *sulṭān*. References to a *markab al-sulṭān* are found in several letters from the mid eleventh century to the first half of the twelfth century. Among these are TS 12.226 (Egypt-Tripoli, ca. 1055); TS 24.77 (dated 1116; written in Alexandria by a passenger on this boat bound for al-Andalus); TS 8 J 18.2 and related TS 10 J 15.3 (here the boat is

frequently traveled the route between al-Andalus and the Mashriq, to judge from Geniza citations. However, it is less important to this discussion of Andalusi commerce than the ship of *qā'id* Maymūn, which appeared in several other Geniza documents in addition to those noted above. One letter, sent from Almeria ca. 1138, reported that the *markab al-qā'id ibn Maymūn* had just arrived from Alexandria, and a fragment written in Alexandria, ca. 1140, referred to the same ship.[45] Non-Geniza sources also describe the naval exploits of this Almerian governor.[46] We learn from Italian chroniclers that, although Pisa had reached a peace accord with Ibn Maymūn in 1133, the relations between Genoa and Almeria were less friendly. In February of 1137, a fleet of Genoese ships launched a successful attack on forty ships belonging to the *caito Maimono Almarie*.[47]

Whenever an Andalusi merchant hired a ship to carry him overseas, whether the vessel belonged to the government or to a private individual, the form of the lease was dictated by law. In a contract for hire, the lessor (*mukrin*) promised to transport the lessee(s) (*muktarin*) and his(their) goods on a particular voyage, carefully stating the route to be followed, items to be shipped, duration of the voyage, sum to be paid for the hire, and whether the ship was leased in whole or in part. The lessor himself often did not actually travel on the voyage – since in some cases he may have hired out several ships simultaneously – so each vessel was under the command of a captain (*rabb al-safīna*).[48] Every

noted as journeying to Almeria ca. 1135). Obviously, not all these references can refer to the same boat, or to the same *sulṭān* (who seems in this context to be a particular ruler). The citations from the 1130s and 1140s may indeed refer to the ruler of Bougie, and perhaps this is why Judah Ha-Levi was noted as traveling on the "new" ship of the *sulṭān*.

45 TS 13 J 14.21 and JTS Geniza Misc. 13.

46 N. Barbour, "The Influence of Sea Power on the History of Muslim Spain," *Madrid:MDI* 14(1967), p. 107.

47 1133: A. Schaube, *Handelsgeschichte der romanischen völker des Mittelmeergebiets bis zum ende der kreuzzüge.* [Munich-Berlin, 1906], p. 277. 1137: Caffaro, *Annali genovesi di Caffaro e de' suoi continuatori.* [ed. L.T. Belgrano, Genoa, 1890] 1, p. 29. The ships in question here were war ships, not merchant ships.

48 Information on the hire of ships may be found in law books, *fatwa* collections, and *wathā'iq* (contract) handbooks. Among the most useful sources on Andalusi and Maghribi shipping are the Ibn Abī Firās, *Kitāb akriyāt al-sufun.* [ed. M.A. Ṭahir] *Cahiers de Tunisie* 31(1983), pp. 7–52; Ibn Mughīth (d. 1067), *Muqni' fī 'ilm al-shurūṭ.* [Real Academia de la Historia, Madrid] Gayangos ms. 44; Fihrī al-Buntī (d. 1070),

stage of this contractual relationship, from the moment of hire until the arrival and unloading of the vessel at its final destination, was regulated. Among other things, a lessor had to choose whether the hire would be categorized as *ta'yīn* (in which all variables, including cargo, must be named in advance) or *maḍmūn* (a guaranteed hire, in which not all terms or items of cargo need be specified).[49] In the event that a boat went down *en route*, or was forced by the wind into the wrong port, or if the cargo were jettisoned in a storm, jurists were likewise ready to adjudicate the settlement of resulting disputes.

Local government also intervened in merchant activity through peremptory power over shipping. The hire of a ship, for instance, could be invalidated through the command of the *sulṭān*. According to Abū al-Ḥasan al-Jazīrī (d. 1189), a jurist from Algeciras, a hire contract was rendered void whenever adverse winds, fear of enemy attack, or "governmental detention" (*man' al-sulṭān*) kept a vessel in port "until the sailing season had passed."[50] Although there is no documentation of this actually happening in al-Andalus, there are comparable examples of detention of vessels and/or goods elsewhere. A Geniza text from the early twelfth century stated that an Andalusi ship in Alexandria had been "completely emptied on written order from the *sulṭān*."[51] Later, the Almohads kept a close eye on shipping moving through their ports. The notary Amalric of Marseille recorded in 1248 that a shipment of goods destined for Marseille had been detained in Ceuta by the Almohad governor Bencalas (Abū 'Alī b. Halas), a man who was originally a native of Valencia.[52]

Wathā'iq wa al-masā'il al-majmū'a. [Miguel Asín Institute, CSIC, Madrid] ms. 11; Jazīrī (d. 1189), *Maqṣud al-maḥmūd fī talkhīṣ al-'uqūd*. [Miguel Asín Institute, CSIC, Madrid] ms. 5. A reference from Ibn Mughīth, *Mugni'* (fol. 69v) suggests that a lessor might own more than one vessel. For a detailed discussion of ship hire in Mālikī law, see D. Santillana, *Instituzioni di diritto musulmano malichita con riguardo anche al sistema sciafita*. [Rome, 1938] II, pp. 259–85.

[49] Jurists debated the exact definition and distinction of these terms. See, for example, Ibn Rushd, *Fatāwā*. [ed. al-Talīlī, Beirut, 1407/1987], pp. 1247–9.

[50] Jazīrī, fol. 55r. Ibn Abī Firās' *Kitāb akriyāt al-sufun* also contains a question regarding invalidation of hire in the case of governmental detention (pp. 48–9).

[51] TS 13 J 27.9 (Bodl c50.19 relates to the same case); trans. Goitein, *Letters*, p. 237.

[52] L. Blancard (ed.), *Documents inédits sur le commerce de Marseille au moyen âge*. [Marseille, 1884–5] II, pp. 166–7, #729 (also p. 169, #732). On Valencian origins, see J. Caille, "Les marseillais à Ceuta au XIIIe siècle," *Mélanges d'histoire et d'archéologie de l'occident musulman; hommage à Georges Marçais*. [Algiers, 1957], p. 28.

Despite the prevalence of maritime commerce, the presence of the *sulṭān* was also evident in overland trade. The movement and business activities of traders arriving in Cordoba, Granada, or other inland markets were regulated, though not to the same degree as encountered in port cities. Tolls were levied along roads, at bridges, and city gates. Merchants were supposed to travel by known routes, and their contracts for hiring animals for transport were subject to legal rules. Most overland trade between Andalusi coastal cities and the interior, and between the inland towns themselves, was conducted along well-established itineraries. Not only did merchants need to know where they could expect to find facilities for housing themselves, their beasts, and their goods, but they had to work to some type of schedule for the benefit of their partners and customers. Moreover, contractual formulae for the hire of animals indicate that there was generally a stipulation requiring the lessee to outline the exact route which he intended to follow.[53] From the administrative point of view, established roads facilitated the collection of tolls. From the mercantile perspective, the greater safety and convenience of established routes made them worth the higher costs of government maintenance and oversight.[54]

TAXES AND TOLLS

Government taxation was an area in which the medieval merchant – like his modern counterpart – must have been keenly aware of the presence of the *sulṭān*. Tolls and tariffs were a ubiquitous feature of trade, whether local or international. A merchant encountered levies in many different places, not only when entering a port or crossing into a new administrative region, but also in the marketplace and at any other point where a toll could be conveniently collected.[55] Although Andalusi

[53] Pack animals were a crucial element in Andalusi overland trade since, as has been observed by R. Bulliet, wheeled vehicles were rare (*The Camel and the Wheel.* [Cambridge, Mass., 1975], pp. 230–1).

[54] Nuwayrī praised the security of Andalusi roads under Manṣūr, see *Historia de los musulmanes de España y Africa por en-Nuguirí.* [ed. M. Gaspar Remiro, Granada, 1917], p. 60.

[55] In Christian Spain there existed a special vocabulary for tolls, although in practice the terms were frequently used interchangeably. *Portaticum*, for example, was paid at a gate; *pontagium* at a bridge, *barcaje* at a river crossing, etc. See L. García de Valdeavellano, *El mercado en León y Castilla durante la edad media.* [2nd edn, Seville,

chroniclers and jurists described blanket taxation policies, for example under the Almoravids or Almohads, the widespread collection of trade tariffs shows that taxation was also a very local phenomenon. The central administration was not the only party interested in tax collection, despite efforts to attain this prerogative. Every regional governor, particularly those in port cities and along the *thughūr*, was ready to levy a percentage on goods traveling through his jurisdiction. This tendency may have been particularly prevalent during the Taifa period when, according to Ibn Ḥazm (writing in 1035), anyone who governed a city or controlled a certain road was accustomed to collect tribute and taxes on goods.[56] Ibn ʿAbdūn may have been responding to the same phenomenon when he recommended that fees paid on goods entering the gates of Seville ought to be officially fixed by the *muḥtasib* lest greedy gatekeepers charge excessive sums.[57] During periods of more centralized power, the extent of regional taxation was probably more closely controlled by government policy, and the right to collect local tolls was distributed as some form of tax-farm.[58]

Commercial tariffs were only one element in a larger system of Andalusi taxation. The bulk of government revenues were raised through taxes on land (*kharāj*), production and trade (*ʿushr*), poll taxes on Jews and Christians (*jizya*), and other levies. Expenditures from these monies included maintenance of the *sulṭan*'s army and navy, administrative costs, building projects, and – at least in the Taifa period – the payment of *paria* tribute to Christian Spanish rulers.[59] Figures from the Umayyad period suggest that during the reign of ʿAbd al-Raḥmān III (912–61) roughly 12 percent of revenues were derived from market taxes and other tolls, but there is no comparable later

1975], p. 151. The mass of different tolls noted in Andalusi sources is suggestive of a similar situation. Indeed, some Christian Spanish tolls derived from Andalusi models.

[56] Ibn Ḥazm, "Un códice inexplorado del cordobés Ibn Ḥazm" [ed. M. Asín Palacios] *Al-Andalus* 2(1934), p. 38.

[57] Ibn ʿAbdūn, *Risāla*, p. 33.

[58] There is no clear evidence of tax-farming *per se* in al-Andalus. However, comments such as those of Ibn ʿAbdūn and Ibn Ḥazm quoted above, and the extremely diffuse nature of tax collection, suggest that some kind of official distribution of rights to tax collection existed in return for a set fee.

[59] According to Ibn ʿIdhārī (*Bayān al-mughrib*. [ed. R. Dozy, (revised G.S. Colin and E. Lévi-Provençal) Leiden, 1951] II, pp. 231), Andalusi revenues (*jibāya*) under ʿAbd al-Raḥmān III were divided in three parts. One third went to support the army, one third to building campaigns, and one third to the treasury.

data.[60] Taxes fell under two theoretical categories: canonical (those expressly permitted by Muslim law) and non-canonical. Both categories were of concern to merchants, and here we may be able to see a distinction between official levies, which were universally found, and more idiosyncratic tolls that varied according to period and regime.

In theory, any merchant arriving in a Muslim port was required to pay a canonical tax, usually either *ʿushr* (literally "tenth") or *khums* ("fifth"), on his merchandise. As stated by one eighth-century legal scholar, Abū Yūsuf, taxes were calculated as a percentage of all goods valued at over one hundred dirhams, and varied with the religion and regional origin of the merchant carrying the goods. According to his rules, Muslims paid 2.5 percent, local non-Muslims (*dhimmis*) paid 5 percent, and non-Muslim foreigners (*ḥarbīs*) paid 10 percent. Later records show that in practice tax collection was very variable. By and large, rates were calculated according to the value of goods (with or without a minimum value), but percentages were flexible, and rates fluctuated according to the nature of the goods or the nationality of the merchant.[61]

Nevertheless, the *ʿushr*, usually with a basic rate of 10 percent, is mentioned again and again in medieval sources. Ibn Ḥawqal reported that Andalusi and European merchants arriving in the Maghrib in the mid tenth century were required to pay *ʿushr* upon reaching the North African coast.[62] In the following

[60] Maqqarī (*Analectes*, I, p. 130) cited Ibn Bashkuwāl (d. 1182) that under this caliph revenues reached 5,480,000 dinars, with an additional 765,000 dinars derived from market tolls and other taxes. These same figures are noted by Ibn ʿIdhārī (*Bayān*, II, pp. 231–2). Tax revenues may have been still higher than this assessment, for Ibn Ḥawqal reported taxes amounting to ca. 20,000,000 dinars levied in 951, "not counting that which comes to the treasury from commercial goods, crafts, and naval instruments" (Ibn Ḥawqal, *Kitāb ṣurat al-arḍ*. [ed. J.H. Kramers, Leiden, 1938], p. 112). Peninsular taxes on trade were nothing new, and M. Hendy has pointed out that the Visigoths (like the Romans before them) levied commercial taxes "although as usual the details and mechanisms remain difficult or obscure." ("From Public to Private: The Western Barbarian Coinages as a Mirror of Disintegration of late Roman State Structures," *Viator* 19(1988), p. 51).

[61] Abū Yūsuf, *Kitāb al-kharāj*. [Cairo, 1352/1933–4], pp. 132–3. Abū Yūsuf traced this system of taxation to an earlier Byzantine precedent (p. 135). See also M. Khadduri, *War and Peace in the Law of Islam*. [Baltimore, 1955], p. 226. C. Cahen provides extensive information on commercial taxes in Egypt, "Douanes et commerce," pp. 235, 242–57, 267–71.

[62] Ibn Ḥawqal, *Kitāb ṣurat al-arḍ*, p. 97. The *ʿushr* was not only a mercantile tax, but was also levied on agricultural produce. Under the caliph Ḥakam I (796–822), for example, Cordoba owed an *ʿushr* of 7,646 *mūdīs* of barley and 4,600 of wheat

century (ca. 1045), the Persian geographer Nāṣir-i Khusraw wrote that Andalusi, European, Byzantine, and Maghribi merchants all had to render a 10 percent toll "to the *sulṭān*" on arrival in Tripoli, Lebanon.[63] At about the same period, a Geniza merchant who sent a cargo of wool valued at thirty dinars from Alexandria to Almeria remarked in a letter to a colleague that the total freight charge came to six dinars. Three dinars (10 percent) had been paid in Egypt, and "the remaining three [again 10 percent] will be paid in Almeria after safe arrival."[64] Another Geniza letter, from ca. 1138, likewise reported customs dues owed on goods sent from Almeria to Fez.[65] Similarly, Italian merchants paid *ʿushr* in Islamic ports during the late twelfth and early thirteenth centuries. Shaqundī (writing 1119–1212) noted that *ʿushr* was collected from Christian merchants in Almeria, and earlier, in 1161, a Genoese trade treaty with the Almohads had specifically reduced the tolls paid by Genoese merchants in Almohad ports to 8 percent (which gave them an advantage over their Pisan rivals, who still owed 10 percent).[66]

Tolls and taxes of a non-canonical nature were ubiquitous, although they varied over time from place to place. These included transit taxes levied along routes (*marāṣid*) or at gates (*qabāla*), and transaction taxes when goods were sold or transferred (*maghāram*, *rusūm*, *iṭawa*, *mukūs*, etc.).[67] Ibn Khaldūn

annually; in the tenth century, the region of Elvira contributed 1,200 measures (*gisṭ*) of oil (J. Vallvé, "La agricultura en al-Andalus," *Al-Qantara* 3(1982), pp. 282, 286).

[63] Nāṣir-i Khusraw, *Nāser-e Khosrow's Book of Travels* [*Safarnāma*]. [trans. W. M. Thackston, Albany, 1986], p. 13.

[64] TS NS J 197; trans. Goitein, *Letters*, p. 236.

[65] Antonin 1105. See also TS 12.435, from about the same period, on tolls collected in Fez. In this latter letter, a merchant tried to pass off his goods as the property of a local merchant in order to avoid higher tariffs demanded on foreigners (Goitein, *Letters*, pp. 51–2).

[66] Shaqundī, *Risāla*. (in Maqqarī, *Analectes*, II, p. 148). On Italian tariffs, see H. C. Krueger, "Early Genoese Trade with Atlantic Morocco," *Medievalia et humanistica* 3(1945), p. 5. Other levies on Italian merchants could be much more burdensome. Schaube has cited Pisans paying up to 25 percent and 30 percent in Valencia, Denia, Almeria, and Malaga (Schaube, *Handelsgeschichte*, pp. 319, 323).

[67] Two useful studies on Andalusi and more general Muslim taxation, with particular reference to the variety on non-canonical levies are P. Chalmeta, "Facteurs de la formation des prix dans l'Islam médiéval," *Actes du premier congrès d'histoire et de la civilisation du Maghreb*. [Tunis, 1979] I, pp. 111–37; and M. Barceló, "Un estudio sobre la estructura fiscal y procedimientos contables del emirato omeya de Córdoba (138–

believed that non-canonical taxes were an inevitable feature of state development. As dynasties grew, he theorized, they adopted new luxuries and required more revenues. "Therefore, the ruler must invent new kinds of taxes. He levies them on commerce. He imposes taxes of a certain amount on prices realized in the markets and on various (imported) goods at the city gates."[68]

Muslim Spain was not exempt from this phenomenon. Indeed Ibn Khaldūn expressly cited the Andalusi Taifa kingdoms as representative of his model. Already in the mid-tenth century, when Ibn Ḥawqal visited al-Andalus, he had remarked on the existence of extra-legal tolls paid in markets and levied "on ships arriving and leaving" the country.[69] Shortly thereafter, we find further confirmation of these exactions in a letter from the Andalusi caliph Ḥakam II, supposedly written in 972 and preserved in Ibn Ḥayyān's *Muqtabis*. The letter criticized illicit levies and permitted only the canonical *zakāt*, *jizya*, and *ʿushr*.[70] Condemnation of earlier taxation became the repetitive slogan of each succeeding dynasty or ruler. After reputed Taifa tax abuses in the eleventh century, both Ibn Khaldūn and Ibn Abī Zarʿ portrayed Almoravid rule (1069–1147) as a golden age in which tolls and tariff exactions were restored to their legal limits.[71] In the same vein, the Almohads claimed similar innovations (reversing supposed Almoravid abuses) upon their arrival in the peninsula, although Ibn Ghālib particularly remarked on the weight of taxation in al-Andalus under their regime.[72]

The frequency of pronouncements against non-canonical taxes, as successive regimes claimed credit for their abolition, demonstrates their prevalence. The same is true of their appear-

300/755–912) y el califato (300–66/912–76)," *Acta medievalia* (1985), pp. 45–72. On similar taxes in Egypt, see also Maqrīzī, *Khiṭaṭ* [Bulaq, 1270/1853–4], pp. 103–5; and C. Cahen, "Douanes et commerce," pp. 223ff. Also, H. Rabie, *The Financial System of Egypt*. [London, 1972], pp. 80–106.

[68] Ibn Khaldūn, *Muqaddimah*, II, p. 92.

[69] Ibn Ḥawqal, *Kitāb ṣurat al-arḍ*, p. 108.

[70] Ibn Ḥayyān, *Muqtabis* VII, [ed. A. A. el-Hajji, Beirut, 1965] pp. 113–14. For a discussion of revenues from Andalusi market taxes in the tenth century, see P. Chalmeta, "An Approximate Picture of the Economy of al-Andalus," *The Legacy of Muslim Spain*. [ed. S. K. Jayyusi, Leiden, 1992], pp. 751–2.

[71] Ibn Abī Zarʿ, *Rawḍ al-qirṭās*. [trans. A. Huici Miranda, Valencia, 1964], pp. 326–7; Ibn Khaldūn, *Muqaddimah*, II, p. 92.

[72] A. Huici Miranda, *Historia política del imperio almohade*. [Tetuan, 1956–7], p. 215; Ibn Ghālib, "Naṣṣ andalusī jadīd" [ed. L.ʿAbd al-Badī], *Majalla ma'had al-makhṭūṭāt al-ʿarabiya* 1(1955), p. 281.

ance in law books, although jurists did not universally condemn the existence of these levies. Wansharīsī recorded a ruling from the jurist Abū ʿAbd Allah al-Saraqustī to the effect that all Muslims must render the *maghāram* so long as "they do not live on the frontiers and are [thus] prevented [from paying] by the enemy." The context of the question indicates that this particular tax was levied on goods at the point of sale.[73]

Overall, we have less data on tax collection and port facilities in al-Andalus than in other regions of the Islamic world. In Egypt, for example, Geniza documents and Muslim authors testify to a range of different government bureaux established in Egyptian ports to handle commercial affairs. In Fatimid Cairo, these included the *dār al-manak*, a center for the collection of tolls, and various "exchanges" – for flax and other commodities – that concentrated mercantile activity in particular regions of the city.[74] Although these Egyptian institutions do not appear in Andalusi texts, parallel forms of harbor administration and tax collection probably existed in Almeria, Seville, and other Andalusi cities. A few geographers hinted at the presence of such institutions, although they were not specifically described or named. Ibn Ḥawqal, for one, noted the existence of toll stations in Andalusi ports during the tenth century, and Idrīsī mentioned what appears to be a customs house in Lorca two centuries later.[75] Shaqundī likewise commented on the existence of *diwāns* for, or belonging to, Christian merchants in Almeria.[76]

Taxation on commerce tended to be a reciprocal gesture between regions and rulers. According to Abū Yūsuf, for instance, the earliest Islamic trade tariffs were imposed in response to similar Byzantine exactions.[77] Later, as we have already seen, Andalusis trading in the Maghrib or the Near East would have encountered taxes similar to those levied on merchants arriving in Muslim Spanish ports. The same was true of Andalusi traffic with Christian Spain and Europe, to the extent that certain Andalusi

[73] Wansharīsī, *Miʿyār*, v, p. 32.

[74] Udovitch, "Merchants and *Amīrs*," p. 59; Cahen, "Douanes et commerce," p. 237.

[75] Ibn Ḥawqal, *Kitāb ṣurat al-arḍ*, p. 108; Idrīsī, *Opus*, v, p. 560. The word in question here is *rahādira*, which R. Dozy and M.J. de Goeje gloss as "douane" in their translation of Idrīsī, *Description de l'Afrique et de l'Espagne*. [Leiden, 1866], pp. 239, 309.

[76] Shaqundī (in Maqqarī, *Analectes*, II, p. 148).

[77] Abū Yūsuf, *Kitāb al-kharāj*, p. 135.

tolls were directly adopted in Castile. The Arabic *qabāla*, for example, emerged as the Castilian *alcabala*.

Just as Christian Spanish merchants traveling in the south had to pay tolls to Andalusi rulers, so too did Andalusi merchants in the north (although northern tolls were not necessarily levied in response to Andalusi tariffs). In Jaca, Ramiro I of Aragon (1035–63) ordered that a toll be paid "by everybody coming and going, whether Christian or Saracen."[78] Town charters from Christian Spain frequently stated the proper tolls, and these tariff lists show the widespread nature of commercial taxes, whether levied on Christians or Muslims. In Alarilla, in the late twelfth century, one *murabiṭūn* was due on every "loaded beast coming from the land of the Moors." In Ocaña, in 1226, a set sum was charged on "everything which goes to the land of the Moors and comes from the land of the Moors," and in the *lezda* of Valencia, dated 1238, James I of Aragon ruled that one *bezantem* must be paid by every "saracen who comes [to the city] by sea or by land."[79] As with the differing rates of *ʿushr* in Muslim lands, it is probable that Christian and Muslim traders were not taxed equally in Christian Spain. In the *fuero* of Evora (1166), for instance, a Muslim trader dealing in rabbit pelts was required to pay double the fee levied on a Christian merchant in the same business.[80]

Foreign merchants and ships coming to Italian ports also paid a fee upon arrival. The 1143 *Registrum curiae archiepiscopalis*, from Genoa, recorded a charge of twenty-two and one half *solidi* (called a *decima*) on boats coming from the Levant, Alexandria, various North African ports, Almeria, and certain other regions.[81] Later, ca. 1160, Pisa would impose tolls on ships arriving from Malaga, Almeria, Denia, Valencia, Barcelona,

[78] J.M. Lacarra, "Un arancel de aduanas del siglo XI," *Actas del primer congreso internacional de pirenéistas*. [San Sebastián, 1950], p. 16.

[79] J.L. Martín, "Portazgos de Ocaña y Alarilla," *AHDE* 32(1962), p. 524, 526; *Fori antiqui valentia*. [ed. M. Dualde Serrano, Madrid-Valencia, 1950–67], p. 284 [CXLIV, 4]. It is possible that this levy applied to saracen slaves (i.e., merchandise), not free Muslim merchants.

[80] *Portugaliae monumenta historica: leges et consuetudines*. 1, [Lisbon, 1856], p. 393. Many other town charters from the later twelfth century (also in this collection) contained identical rulings (pp. 419, 427, 431, 488, 495, 513).

[81] L.T. Belgrano (ed.), "Il registro della curia arcivescovile di Genova," *ASLSP* 2 (1862), p. 9. A statute from the previous year, 1142 (included in C. Imperiale (ed.), *Codice diplomatico della repubblica di Genova*. [Rome, 1936–42] 1, p. 141) also recorded a charge levied on boats departing for *Yspania*.

and Mallorca.[82] The sources do not say whether these charges were levied on Italian or Andalusi vessels, but a 1228 reference from Marseille, noting that the *decima* was owed by saracens arriving in the city, shows that Muslim visitors were not unknown.[83]

PRICES AND AVAILABILITY OF GOODS

There still remains another sphere in which one might expect to find administrative intervention in mercantile affairs: the movement, availability, and price of commodities. In fact, this appears to have been an area of little if any official oversight, since Andalusi governments enforced only minimal controls over the flow of commodities between Muslim Spain and other regions of the Mediterranean. There is no evidence of restrictions or prohibition on the importation of particular items, although local rulers and religious authorities sometimes tried to control exports. Particularly after the arrival of the Almoravids and Almohads, rulers in al-Andalus and the Maghrib appear to have kept a close eye on international trade and regulated the export of war materials. Andalusi Muslim merchants were not allowed to sell arms or other prohibited items to Christians, and Ibn Rushd (d. 1126) went so far as to rule that any Muslim traders crossing out of Islamic lands ought to be searched to ensure that they were not carrying contraband.[84] This type of commercial restriction had clear parallels in Europe, where papal bans on commerce in wood, arms, ships, or other commodities with a possible military application had been a recurring theme at least since the Third Lateran

[82] F. Bonaini (ed.), *Statuti inediti della città di Pisa dal XII al XIV secolo*. [Florence, 1854–70] II, pp. 905–6.

[83] L. Méry and F. Guindon (eds.), *Histoire analytique et chronologique des actes et des délibérations du corps et du conseil de la municipalité de Marseille*. [Marseille, 1841] I, p. 334. This is not a reference to charges levied on Muslim slaves brought through Marseille. Benjamin of Tudela ("Itinerary," trans. M.N. Adler, *Jewish Quarterly Review* 16 (1904), p. 468) also remarked that he had seen merchants from Egypt and Palestine, presumably Muslims or Jews, in Montpellier in the 1160s.

[84] Ibn Rushd, *Kitāb al-muqaddimāt al-mumahhidāt*. [Cairo, 1325/1907] II, p. 287. A later Maghribi jurist, Ibn Juzayy (d. 1340) said that Muslims must not enter Christian lands, except to ransom another Muslim, and that borders should be blocked. He listed horses, weapons, iron, and copper among commodities which Muslims should not sell to Christians (*Qawānin al-aḥkām al-shar'īya*. [Beirut, 1968], p. 319). See also Wansharīsī, *Mi'yār*, V, pp. 213–14.

Council in 1179.[85] Overall, as will be discussed in chapter 9, later Christian kings took more interest in prohibiting traffic in war materials than did Andalusi rulers.

Prices, more than legal regulations, influenced the international movement of goods in the medieval Mediterranean. These prices largely "set themselves," achieving an acceptable level as merchants bargained with each other in the marketplace. The powerful forces of supply and demand are constantly evident in the pragmatic instructions exchanged between partners in Geniza letters, and in the more theoretical dictates of merchant handbooks. As Ibn Khaldūn later put it, if a merchant wished to make a profit, he should transport his goods "to another country, where they are more in demand than in his own . . . [because] when goods are few and rare, their prices go up." He defined commerce itself as "the buying of merchandise and goods, storing them, and waiting until fluctuation of the market brings about an increase in the prices."[86]

The most obvious causes for regional price variations were periods of local scarcity brought on by famine, drought, warfare, or other circumstances. Chroniclers often remark on unusually high prices for grains and other staples in lean years, or low prices in times of bounty. Nuwayrī, for example, reported that in 822 "there was a severe famine in al-Andalus" causing grain prices to rise dramatically.[87] International trade also generated its own high costs and risks. As well as the intangible hardships of travel itself, the dangers of transportation drove up prices since for every cargo lost at sea a merchant might, with reason, hope to recoup more from his remaining goods. Likewise, the

[85] As in the Muslim case, Christian bans on trade with "the enemy" were a long-standing phenomenon. Sawyer, for one, cited their existence in the Late Antique world ("Kings and Merchants," p. 142). However, their importance was brought to the fore by Alexander III at the Third Lateran Council, and trade prohibitions were supported by later popes, particularly Innocent III (who reiterated them at the Fourth Lateran in 1215) and Gregory IX, as well as by many secular Christian rulers.

[86] Ibn Khaldūn, *Muqaddimah*, II, pp. 337–8, 340. Despite the evident forces of supply and demand, it would be misleading to apply the modern concept of "market economy" – with its complicated mechanisms and controls – to medieval commerce. The model of a market self-regulated by supply and demand – by perfect competition between competing suppliers and competitive buyers – can only imperfectly apply to the medieval world, nor do we have the capability to test the extent of its applicability.

[87] Nuwayrī, *Historia de los musulmanes de España y Africa por en-Nuguarí*. [ed. and trans. M. Gaspar Remiro, Granada, 1917] I, p. 42.

hire of ships and beasts of burden, payment of taxes and tariffs on goods, and charges for labor, influenced the final price of an article.[88]

These factors, together with the tendency of chroniclers only to cite extraordinary prices, make it difficult to analyze prices or to determine a "normal" level. Even the detailed price lists exchanged between Geniza merchants indicate that they perceived prices as fluid, although in aggregate their calculations can now tell historians something of general trends in pricing. As Goitein has observed, "the study of prices . . . is like trying to solve an equation with four unknowns: the exact nature, type, and quality of the commodity traded; the identity of the weights, measures or other indications of quantity referred to; the value of the money paid; and, finally, the time, place, and specific circumstances of the transaction concerned."[89]

The intervention of government was merely one more variable in this unwieldy equation. There is no doubt that the *sulṭan* could influence prices through enjoining the *muḥtasib* to ensure fairness, through raising or lowering commercial taxes, through diplomatic agreements, through impounding particular cargoes, or by holding up certain ships. Local authorities were well aware of the forces of supply and demand, and enforced certain controls. Ibn ʿAbdūn, for instance, warned of the problems resulting from hoarding and ruled that known hoarders in Seville be allowed to buy no more than a certain amount of wheat at one time on the grounds that hoarding "causes prices and costs to rise, and brings harm to the Muslims."[90] *Ḥisba* books also record proper prices for foodstuffs, indicating both that there was a concept of a "fair price," and that the *sulṭan* had a role in regulating the costs of basic commodities. Unlike most luxury goods, supplies of grains and other staple foodstuffs fluctuated with the weather, although their demand remained constant. The government took an interest in controlling food supplies in order to avert famine, and official price regulations for staple goods probably reflected this intent rather than the workings of a more unified economic theory. Jurists were not unanimous in their views on the regulation of prices. In the second half of the tenth century, the Andalusi jurist Ibn ʿAbd al-

[88] Chalmeta, "Facteurs de la formation des prix," p. 111.
[89] Goitein, *Mediterranean Society*, 1, p. 217.
[90] Ibn ʿAbdūn, *Risāla*, p. 42.

Ra'ūf collected a number of legal opinions on the subject of price fixing, and concluded that it was permissible to have a set price for wheat, barley, honey, meat, and other staples, so long as these were sold by their importers, not by local merchants. Even so, other authors, including Yaḥyā b. 'Umar, cautioned that a *muḥtasib* could never force merchants to abide by a certain price.[91]

Evidence of price controls is less clear for luxury goods such as spices, textiles, metals, and the other important components of an international merchant's cargo. Geniza letters sometimes contain references to prices being "set" or "defined," both in al-Andalus and elsewhere, but it is not clear who was responsible for the setting. A letter written from Almeria in 1138 mentioned the price of an item being "set at one and one half *mithqāls* per pound (*raṭl*)," but this may have been a personal rather than an official determination.[92]

Local governments might also influence prices through their control of the mint and money supply, since, as observed in a fourteenth-century Andalusi manual on minting, "price is the primary factor [in any sale], and prices are based on gold and silver."[93] Two factors are in question here: the connection of prices with the quantity of coined money (in circulation and mint output) and with the quality of money (fineness of coinage, currency devaluation). Unfortunately, despite quite good data on Andalusi numismatics, the lack of information on either Andalusi prices or the Andalusi money supply at any given time prohibits any useful correlation between the two. Likewise, it is difficult to make a connection between particular coinage issues and price levels.

According to economic theory, one might expect to see higher prices in times of abundant money supply and lower prices in leaner times, but this is not necessarily supported by Andalusi data on prices. Ashtor has associated high Andalusi

[91] Ibn 'Abd al-Ra'ūf, *Risāla*, pp. 88–9; Yaḥyā b. 'Umar, *Kitāb aḥkām al-sūq*. [ed. M.A. Makkī] *Madrid:MDI* 4(1956), pp. 131–2. Chalmeta also remarked that a *muḥtasib* could control prices (*El señor del zoco*, p. 136). On price fixing, see also M.A. Khallāf, *Qurṭuba al-islāmiyya*. [Tunis, 1984], pp. 122–7.

[92] Bodl d74.41; The verb in question is *tahaddada*, which Goitein translates as "defined" in *Mediterranean Society* (1, pp. 218 and 453, n. 39) but as "you have fixed" in *Letters*, p. 263.

[93] Abū al-Hasan al-Hakīm, "Régimen de la casa de la moneda (al-dawha al-mushtabika fī dawābit dār al-sikka)" [ed. H. Mones], *Madrid:MDI* 6(1958), p. 156.

prices, relative to those of the Near East, with the greater abundance of Sudanese gold in Muslim Spain, but Andalusi prices were not consistently higher than those elsewhere.[94] With so many other potential variables, the proximity of Andalusi markets to gold routes did not automatically affect price levels. In the second half of the tenth century, for instance, Ibn Ḥawqal remarked that goods in al-Andalus "are sold very cheaply," and his report presumably described circumstances under the flourishing Umayyad economy after the reintroduction of gold currency by ʿAbd al-Raḥmān III.[95] In this case, Andalusi gold coinage was strong and abundant, but prices were low. After the Umayyad demise, inflation during the Taifa period has been credited to devaluation of currencies and unstable politics, in spite of the fact that mint output seems to have increased during the eleventh century.[96] In a similar contradictory vein, Ibn Abī Zarʿ (an Almoravid supporter) claimed that prices were low under this dynasty, despite Almoravid access to Sudanese gold and the dynasty's association with a popular and plentiful (though not particularly pure) gold coinage.[97] One explanation for problems in correlation may lie in the fact that rulers sometimes restricted the circulation of foreign currencies within their territories, thus limiting one variable in price fluctuation.

In spite of the many areas of government intervention in international commerce, it is unlikely that Andalusi rulers ever really looked at trade as an abstract entity deserving their attention. Instead, they were concerned with the individual components of commerce: ports, merchants, markets, hostelries, ships, goods, and especially taxes. Likewise, a medieval merchant in Muslim Spain would have experienced government influence in his daily business in terms of these individual aspects, not as overall control of his affairs. Even within the web of Andalusi government authority, an international trader was fairly free to trade where, when, whatever, and with whomever he wished.

[94] E. Ashtor, "Prix et salaires dans l'Espagne musulmane aux Xe et XIe siècles," *Annales:ESC* 20(1965) p. 667.

[95] Ibn Ḥawqal is quoted by Yāqūt, *Muʿjām al-buldān.* (*Jacut's Geographisches Worterbuch.*) [ed. F. Wüstenfeld, Leipzig, 1873] 1, pp. 375–8.

[96] M. Benaboud, "Tendances économiques dans al-Andalus durant la période des Etats Taifas," *Bulletin économique et social du Maroc* 151–2 (1983), p. 22. P. Spufford sees a similar phenomenon at work in European inflation during the late twelfth and early thirteenth centuries; "Le role de la monnaie dans la révolution commerciale du XIIIe siècle," *Etudes d'histoire monétaire, XIIe-XIXe siècles.* [ed. J. Day, Lille, 1984], p. 365.

[97] Ibn Abī Zarʿ, *Rawḍ al-qirṭās.* [trans. A. Huici Miranda, Valencia, 1964], pp. 326–7.

Chapter 6

COMMODITIES AND PATTERNS OF TRADE IN THE MEDIEVAL MEDITERRANEAN WORLD

PATTERNS OF COMMODITY PRODUCTION AND PROBLEMS OF INTERPRETATION

Commodities, even more than merchants, were the driving force behind commerce. An analysis of commodities traded to and from al-Andalus demonstrates the role of peninsular markets in the import, export, and exchange of goods in the Mediterranean. The next three chapters discuss the commodities of Iberian international trade, looking first at the composition, balance, and direction of trade in the medieval Mediterranean world, second at Andalusi exports during the Muslim period, and lastly at continuities and changes in the spectrum of Iberian exports after the early thirteenth century.

Information on commodities is found not only in the standard sources for economic data – books of geography, tariff lists, Geniza letters, and notarial records – but also in a number of more specialized works devoted to agriculture, industry, medicine, and pharmacology. Evidence from archeology and art also sheds light on items transferred from one region to another. Although these data cannot quantify the goods traded to and from Andalusi ports, they reveal categories of merchandise and elucidate more qualitative aspects of trade. Likewise, they suggest how political and economic changes in the wider medieval Mediterranean forced shifts in the peninsula's commercial production and exchange.

An analysis of the commodities in Andalusi trade also sheds light on broader questions. Economic historians have often been troubled by an apparent imbalance in medieval trade between the Islamic world and the Latin west, since there is better evidence for goods (textiles, spices, ceramics, paper, gems, and gold) entering Christian Europe from the *dār al-Islām* than for traffic in the opposite direction. Although it has been proposed that Europe sent slaves, furs, and raw metals to the Islamic east, there are few documentary examples of direct traffic between west and east. When the Iberian peninsula is added to this equation, however, and long-term changes in its trade are examined, the problem of balance becomes less perplexing. Because al-Andalus was an entrepôt for trade, and a distributor of goods both northward into Christian lands and eastward to the Islamic Mediterranean, the peninsula served as a fulcrum for trade and mediated the balance between east and west.

In the early middle ages, at least until the twelfth century, much of Mediterranean international trade was actually inter-Islamic, encompassing the Near East, the Maghrib, and Muslim Spain. The balance of trade presented little problem within this sphere, since al-Andalus imported goods from the Islamic east, but did not lack for exports of its own. However, European international trade was more limited, and some goods from the Islamic world came to northern markets by way of Muslim Spain. In the other direction, European goods entered the Islamic trading sphere through Andalusi channels. Andalusi markets provided a link between Europe and the Mediterranean system. This pattern is attested to by a number of authors in the ninth and tenth centuries, including Ibn Khurradādhbih, Ibn Ḥawqal, and Liutprand of Cremona, all of whom observed traffic in northern slaves to the Maghrib and eastern Mediterranean from al-Andalus.[1] Alongside his reference to slaves, Ibn Ḥawqal also mentioned Iberian ambergris, silk, and mercury, pointing to the fact that al-Andalus had its own goods to export to Europe and the Muslim world. While the Muslim Mediterranean trading axis existed, exports from Andalusi markets (whether originating in the peninsula or Europe) were sufficient to preserve ongoing trade between east and west.

Mediterranean trade became more diversified in the late middle ages as commercial patterns changed. By the late thirteenth century, when the sea was dominated by Christian shipping, any inequality in the balance of trade was reversed in favor of Europe. Not only were there changes in the commodities themselves, but their routes of traffic shifted northward as new

[1] Ibn Ḥawqal, *Kitāb ṣurat al-arḍ* [ed. J.H. Kramers, Leiden, 1938], p. 97; Ibn Khurradādhbih, *Kitāb al-masālik wa al-mamālik*. [ed. M.J. de Goeje, *BGA*, 2nd edn, VI, Leiden, 1967], pp. 153–5; Liutprand, *Antapodosis*. [in *Opera*, ed. J. Becker, *MGH* Scriptores in usum scholarum, Hanover-Leipzig, 1915] VI, 6, p. 156.

merchant groups undertook their transport. Italian and French mercantile activity tended to divert products away from Andalusi ports, so that goods from the eastern Mediterranean were increasingly carried to the western Mediterranean by way of Italian and Provençal cities, no longer via Almeria or Seville. Likewise, as European cities and population expanded, and new industries increased European purchasing power, tastes changed. Inevitably, as Lopez has observed, "the luxury of yesterday became the treat of today and the necessity of tomorrow."[2] With high demand at home, Italian merchants ceased to acquire spices from western Islamic markets in al-Andalus and North Africa, but went directly to Alexandria instead.

Political and demographic changes within the Iberian peninsula also affected patterns of exchange, so that, by the late thirteenth century, the spectrum of commodities in Iberian trade, the regions of production, and the directions of trade had altered from those of earlier times. After the conquest of Seville, Valencia, Cordoba, and other Andalusi cities, the new Christian inhabitants in the south often had different economic concerns, technical skills, and production interests than those of the Muslim population. In some conquered regions, Mudejar workers remained to preserve certain industries and transmit technical knowledge, but elsewhere the Muslim exodus destroyed previous patterns of production. At the same time, in northern regions never subject to Islam, new industries developed that had no Andalusi counterparts. In Granada too, commerce and industry were affected by external events despite the continuity of Muslim rule. In consequence, Iberian markets played a very different role in the distribution of commodities in the late middle ages. The peninsula was no longer an entrepôt for the redistribution of Islamic goods to Europe, or European goods to the Maghrib and Near East. Instead, many new industries and commodities developed in Castile and Aragon in response to changes within the peninsula and to new demand in northern Europe and the Christian Mediterranean world.

In the face of political fluctuations, Iberian climate and geography remained a more constant influence in shaping the region's commercial role. Al-Andalus was warmer and dryer than most

[2] R.S. Lopez, *The Commercial Revolution of the Middle Ages.* [New York, 1971], p. 91.

of Europe, yet cooler and wetter than much of the Islamic world. The advantages of its climate were recognized and exploited in medieval times, and remarked on by contemporary Muslim geographers. Indeed, it became almost a commonplace of the Arabic geographical genre to lavish praise on the natural productivity of al-Andalus, and to describe the peninsula as a garden.[3] Ibn Ghālib went so far as to compare the region to "China for its gems and mines [and] to India for its aromatics and fragrances."[4] When Granada was threatened with attack in 1125, a chronicler explained with less hyperbole that the invaders were attracted by the region's "advantages and fertility for wheat, barley and flax, and by its many silkworms, vines, olives, and fruits . . ."[5]

The variety of Andalusi production was enhanced by the fact that the southern peninsula encompassed several distinct ecological zones. The territory around Granada ranged from the snow-covered peaks of the Sierra Nevada to arid coastal plains, and supported an unusually wide range of products from silk to sugar. Along the Levant coast (Sharq al-Andalus) the land was widely given to irrigated garden agriculture (in Castilian, *huerta*), making the region famous for its fruits, vegetables, and rice. In the south-west, the Guadalquivir valley supported more agricultural land, less intensely irrigated, and especially known for olives and olive oil. Idrīsī remarked that near Seville one could walk for forty miles "in the shade of olive and fig trees."[6] These three regions (Granada, Sharq al-Andalus, and the Guadalquivir) are those most frequently noted by geographers for their economic production, but other areas – with arable river valleys, timber producing uplands, or rich lodes of mercury and copper – also appear in accounts of Andalusi natural advantages.

We should beware, however, of equating agrarian potential with international trade. In spite of its productivity, al-Andalus regularly imported agricultural goods, especially grain. Crops

[3] T. Glick discusses this phenomenon in *Islamic and Christian Spain*. [Princeton, 1979], pp. 53–6.

[4] Ibn Ghālib, "Naṣṣ andalusī jadīd qaṭʿia min kitāb farḥa al-anfūs li-Ibn Ghālib," [ed. L. ʿAbd al-Badī], *Majalla maʿhad al-makhtūṭāt al-ʿarabiyya* 1(1955), p. 281. Ḥimyarī cited a similar passage (*La Péninsule ibérique au moyen âge*. [ed. E. Lévi-Provençal, Leiden, 1938] Arabic text, p. 3); as did Maqqarī (E. Lévi-Provençal, "La vie économique de l'Espagne musulmane au Xe siècle," *Revue historique* 167(1931), p. 306).

[5] *Ḥulāl al-mawshīya*. [ed. I.S. Allouche, Rabat, 1936], p. 76.

[6] Idrīsī, *Opus geographicum*. v [Naples-Rome, 1975], p. 541.

grown in the peninsula were often not sufficient to meet local needs (certainly not in a bad year), let alone to generate a surplus for international trade. This was particularly true during the Nasrid period, when the Kingdom of Granada relied to a large extent on imported foodstuffs. The isolation of late medieval Granada intensified this pattern of trade, but imports to the peninsula were nothing new. In the 1150s, Idrīsī remarked that ships came "from al-Andalus to the region south of Salé (Morocco) to buy foodstuffs, [including] wheat, barley, beans, and chick peas."[7] At the end of the same century, the *Kitāb al-istibṣār* described Tenes as an area that produced cereals and foodstuffs for export to Muslim Spain and other parts of the Maghrib.[8]

Not all the Andalusi products that attracted the attention of geographers were commercially successful exports. Cotton provides one example of the need for attention to incongruities in evidence and for caution in the analysis of production and traffic. Arabic geographers noted the success of cotton cultivation and referred to international trade in the product, but their reports must be weighed against the lack of references to Andalusi cotton traffic in other sources. Rāzī reported that the region of Seville produced "a large quantity of cotton, which is exported to all regions and across the sea."[9] Later geographers routinely echoed Rāzī's words, with 'Udhrī claiming that "the soil of Seville is matchless, and it has the particular characteristic – not shared by any other region – of growing a wonderful cotton . . . [which] is available all over al-Andalus and taken as a commodity to Ifriqiya." Ibn Ghālib went further, saying that by the late twelfth century Sevillian cotton was "exported to all parts of the world."[10] Nevertheless, Andalusi cotton does not appear prominently in the Geniza, nor in Latin notarial contracts, nor are there many surviving examples of Andalusi cotton textiles. Although the consensus of geographers suggests that al-Andalus must have produced and exported some cotton, the

[7] Idrīsī, *Opus geographicum*. III [Naples-Rome, 1972], pp. 239–40.

[8] E. Fagnan (ed.), *L'Afrique septentrionale au XIIe siècle de notre ère; description extraite de 'Kitāb al-istibçār'*. [Constantine, 1900], p. 40.

[9] Rāzī, "La description de l'Espagne d'Aḥmad al-Rāzī" [ed. E. Lévi-Provençal], *Al-Andalus* 18 (1953), p. 93.

[10] 'Udhrī, "Nuṣūṣ 'an al-Andalus," *Tarḍī' al-akhbār wa tanwī' al-'athār*. [ed. A.A. al-Ahwānī, Madrid, 1960], p. 96; Ibn Ghālib, "Naṣṣ andalusī," p. 293. Later citations are found in Yāqūt, *Mu'jām al-buldān*. (*Jacut's Geographisches Worterbuch*.) [ed. F. Wüstenfeld, Leipzig, 1873] I, p. 275; and Ḥimyarī, *Péninsule*, p. 21.

lack of corroborating evidence points out both the difficulty of assessing the importance of cotton traffic and the potential for distortion in any one source.[11]

Other difficulties also arise in analyzing the commodities of Andalusi international trade. In many cases, for example, it is not possible to determine from physical evidence or textual references whether goods traveled from one place to another by commercial means. One may only assume commercial agency when a reference specifically mentions mercantile exchange, or when external evidence relating to routes, merchants, or other commodities supports the probability of commerce. Medieval sources (and thus modern economic historians) tend to concentrate on luxury goods rather than more mundane items, but the value of luxuries opens up the possibility of movement through theft, tribute, gift, and other non-commercial channels. In fact, goods of lesser value (such as ceramics, foodstuffs, or simple textiles) prove to be better indicators for trade. Different styles and varieties of these ordinary goods were produced in different regions, thus generating movement and demand, but their modest value and daily utility made it more likely that they were carried by merchants than by ambassadors or thieves.

Lopez has pointed out yet another way in which commercial data may be misleading. Among the pitfalls awaiting the economic historian, "We must be on our guard lest the often recurring mention of eastern goods in the west and western goods in the east induces us to magnify the intensity of commercial relations."[12] Reference to an item may indicate scarcity rather than abundance, and it is extremely difficult to make a

[11] For more on Andalusi cotton, see J.M. Millás Vallicrosa, "El cultivo del algodón en la España árabe," *BRAH* 139(1956), pp. 463–72; and L. Bolens, "The Use of Plants for Dyeing and Clothing: Cotton and Woad in al-Andalus," *The Legacy of Muslim Spain*. [ed. S.K. Jayyusi, Leiden, 1992], pp. 1004–7. On cotton trade in the medieval Mediterranean, see A. Watson, "The Rise and Spread of Old World Cotton," *Studies in Textile History in Memory of Harold B. Burnham*. [ed. V. Gervers, Toronto, 1977], p. 360; and the chapter on cotton in *Agricultural Innovation in the Early Islamic World*. [Cambridge, 1983], pp. 31–41. Also C.J. Lamm, *Cotton in Medieval Textiles of the Near East*. [Paris, 1937]. On Christian production, M. Mazzaoui, *The Cotton Industry of Medieval Italy*. [Cambridge, 1981]; D. Abulafia, "Catalan merchants and the Western Mediterranean, 1236–1300," *Viator* 16(1985), pp. 215–17; S. Epstein, *An Island for itself, Economic development and social change in late medieval Sicily*. [Cambridge, 1992], pp. 185–6.

[12] R.S. Lopez, "East and West in the Early Middle Ages: Economic Relations," *Relazioni del X Congresso internazionale di scienze storiche*. [Rome, 1955] III, p. 128.

quantitative judgment based on most medieval commercial information. Only in certain circumstances, as when Geniza records cite hundreds of bales of flax traveling westward from Egypt annually, may we reasonably conclude that an item was traded in substantial quantity. Nonetheless, the survival of even one solid reference proves that a commodity was traded, even if demand and quantity remain unknown. Although recurring mention cannot be used to assess quantity, repeated references may serve as a qualitative measure for trade. They may indicate, for example, that a particular commodity, or a certain regional variety, was considered more important or more desirable than another. Equally the appearance of an item in different contexts and sources (showing who carried it, who bought it, what they paid, where, when, and how it traveled) demonstrates the place of its trade within a wider economy.

The names of medieval commodities likewise deserve skeptical attention. Many items derived their names from the region in which they were produced, and these names can provide handy clues for tracking the movement of goods. Nevertheless, the tendency over time for regional names to become generic presents yet another snare for the unwary. It seems unlikely, for example, that the "Moorish peas" (*pisos Mauriscos*) grown on a Carolingian estate were any more an imported product than the French beans, Swiss chard, or Chinese cabbage that we cultivate in our own gardens.[13]

Andalusi leather goods and textiles seem to have been particularly prone to genericization. The prime example is cordoban, a tooled and gilded leather originally produced in Cordoba but later manufactured elsewhere in the peninsula and beyond. Cordoban became famous throughout Europe, and medieval references to leather of this type can be found as far away as Wales. Its wide use in the manufacture of shoes is linguistically demonstrated in the French *cordonnier* (shoemaker) and its English equivalent, *cordwainer*. The abundance of references to cordoban, often in a clearly commercial context, make it tempting to rank cordoban among the preeminent exports of al-Andalus. Nevertheless, a remark by John of Garland, writing in Paris ca. 1220, confirms the need for caution in attribution. John felt it necessary to explain that the word *cordevan* came "from Cordoba, a city in

[13] *Capitularia regum francorum*. [ed. A. Boretius, *MGH*, Leges II.1, Hanover, 1883], p. 90.

Spain, where [this type of leather] was first made."[14] His comment suggests that French leather-workers were producing cordoban by the early thirteenth century. More concretely, we know that by the late twelfth century a division of leather workers in Pisa devoted themselves to *ars pellariorum vel cordovaneriorum.*[15] At the same time, however, cordoban continued to be manufactured in the Iberian peninsula, as indicated by references to cordoban from Valladolid and Valencia in the 1230s and 1240s, and it remained an Iberian export through the thirteenth century.[16]

Andalusi textile nomenclature presents a rather different problem, since Andalusi fabrics often bore foreign names. This tendency to create imitation fabrics, textiles woven in one area in the style of those from another, was common throughout the Mediterranean world. Idrīsī stated without further comment that imitations of silk textiles from Jurjan and Isfahan (called *jurjānī* and *isbahānī*) were produced in Almeria.[17] Thus, the *jurjānī* silks which a twelfth-century father in Aden ordered from Cairo for his daughter's trousseau may almost as easily have come to Egypt from al-Andalus as from Jurjan itself (south-east of the Caspian Sea).[18] Another imitation, *'attābī*, a heavy silk taffeta which one twelfth-century Andalusi geographer described as striped in black and white like a zebra, was

[14] John's commentary reads *cordevan, alio modo cordubanum, a Corduba, civitate Hispaniae, ubi fiebat primo.* See A. Scheler (ed.), "Trois traités de lexicographie latine du XIIe au XIIIe siècle," *Jahrbuch für romanische und englische Literatur* 6(1865), p. 296.

[15] D. Herlihy, *Pisa in the Early Renaissance.* [New Haven, 1958], p. 138.

[16] Valladolid: *Documentos de la Iglesia colegial de Santa María la Mayor de Valladolid (siglo XIII, 1201–1280).* [ed. M. Mañueco Villalobos, Valladolid, 1920], p. 198. Valencia: A. García, "Contractes comercials vigatans de principis del segle XIII," *Ausa* (Vich) 43(1963), p. 329.

[17] Idrīsī, *Opus*, v, p. 562. For further discussion of imitations, see C. Partearroyo, "Almoravid and Almohad Textiles," *Al-Andalus: The Art of Islamic Spain.* [ed. J. Dodds, New York, 1992], pp. 105–6. The tradition of imitation continued in later Iberian textile nomenclature, as noted by J. Alfau de Solalinde, *Nomenclatura de los tejidos españoles del siglo XIII.* [Madrid, 1969], pp. 14–15. See also foreign fabric types listed by M. Martínez, *Los nombres de tejidos en castellano medieval.* [Granada, 1989], pp. 251, 294, 306, 450.

[18] West. College Frag. Cair. 9. See also, S.D. Goitein, *A Mediterranean Society.* [Berkeley, 1967–88] iv, p. 169. These *jurjānī* imitations may be related to textiles woven in imitation of fabrics from Dasht, a town very close to Jurjan. It has been suggested that the *dulcerias/duxerias/doxtouies* that appear in eleventh-century documents from Leon derived their name from *dashtī* textiles and were probably manufactured in Muslim Spain (C. Sánchez-Albornoz, *Estampas de la vida en León durante el siglo X.* [Madrid, 1934], p. 18).

originally produced in Baghdad but later made in other cities, including Almeria.[19] Geniza letters mentioned *ʿattābī* from al-Andalus, Ibn Saʿīd reported that it was exported from Minorca, and perhaps the *baghdādī* cloth which Ibn Ghālib cited in connection with Almeria was also this type of material.[20] Other Andalusi goods, including some types of ceramics and rugs, likewise imitated foreign designs.[21]

Imitations are interesting not only for themselves, but for what they reveal about Mediterranean trade. Isfahan and other eastern regions were renowned for their textiles, and these eastern fabrics must have been known and appreciated in the western Islamic world (hence the adoption of names like *isbahānī*). At least by the twelfth century, Andalusi weavers were producing their own versions of the style of Isfahan, both for local sale and export. The high productivity of the Andalusi silk industry allowed these imitations to be manufactured at a price and a quality that made them popular as far away as Egypt, where they may have been in direct competition with their prototypes. It is unclear, however, to what extent these textiles were designed to deceive consumers into believing they were buying another fabric, or to what extent their names had become commonly understood generic types. Idrīsī's uncomplicated comment on Almerian *jurjānīs* suggests the latter option as being the more likely. While it may be difficult today to determine exactly where a particular medieval fabric was woven, contemporary merchants and their customers probably knew whether they were dealing in *jurjānīs* from Jurjan or from Almeria.

Two further factors, prohibitions and monopolies, add complication to tracing the movement of commodities. Traffic in certain goods was at times subject to government, legal, or religious sanctions. Commodities with military potential, particu-

[19] Abū Ḥamid al-Gharnāṭī, "Le 'Tuḥfat al-albāb' de Abū Ḥāmid al-Andalusī al-Gharnāṭī" [ed. and trans. G. Ferrand], *Journal Asiatique* 207(1925), p. 110. The author described an animal which lived in Africa and had "black and white stripes like *ʿattābī* cloth." Ḥimyarī, *Péninsule*, p. 184.

[20] TS 13 J 21.12; Ibn Saʿīd in E. Fagnan (ed.), *Extraits inédits relatifs au Maghreb*. [Paris, 1924], p. 24; Ibn Ghālib, "Naṣṣ andalusī," pp. 283–4.

[21] Ceramic forms and designs were widely imitated around the Mediterranean world and beyond. On this phenomenon, see G.T. Scanlon, "Egypt and China: Trade and Imitation," *Islam and the Trade of Asia*. [ed. D.S. Richards, Philadelphia, 1970], pp. 81–95.

larly, rarely appear in commercial documents because of prohibitions on their traffic. Even the few references to arms traveling between al-Andalus and Christian regions are insubstantial. In 974, for example, Rāzī mentioned that the Andalusi caliphal army carried "Frankish iron lances," but it is impossible to tell whether these were lances in the Frankish style, lances of Frankish iron, lances made by Franks, or how they got to al-Andalus in the first place.[22] On the other hand, economic reality, the fame of Iberian weaponry in medieval times (even today, we still recognize the term "Toledo blade"), and the repeated prohibitions from both popes and qāḍīs, suggest that there was more to the arms trade than meets the researcher's eye in written sources.

Government monopolies also played a role in limiting mercantile access to goods and in determining the movement of commodities. Overall, the tendency of governments to monitor the production and use of certain goods seems to have been more common in the Muslim world and the Greek east than in the Latin west. It has been debated, particularly by Lopez, whether or not Islamic state monopolies over precious textiles, gold, and papyrus can explain the breaks in Mediterranean trade that Pirenne perceived following the Muslim conquests of the seventh century.[23] Much later, the imposition of state monopolies in Mamluk Egypt effectively destroyed the trading network of the Karimi merchants and re-routed spice traffic to the benefit of government coffers. Nevertheless, monopolies, like prohibitions, were not always effective (as in the case of futile Byzantine attempts to limit silk exports).

Andalusi monopolies first appeared in the Umayyad period, when tradition credits 'Abd al-Raḥmān II (822–52) with establishing monopolies over *ṭirāz*, coinage, and other items.[24] The grain trade may also have been under some degree of official administration in order to ensure regular supplies. Through holding a monopoly, a ruler could requisition all materials needed in the production of an item, supervise its manufacture, and oversee its distribution. The tenth century *Calendar of Cordoba*, for example, mentioned annual governmental requisitions of dyestuffs and

[22] Rāzī, *Anales palatinos del califa de Cordoba al-Ḥakam II.* [trans. E. García Gómez, Madrid, 1967], p. 240.

[23] R.S. Lopez, "Mohammed and Charlemagne: A Revision," *Speculum* 18(1943), pp. 14–38.

[24] E.,Lévi-Provençal, *Histoire de l'Espagne musulmane.* [Paris, 1950–3] I, pp. 256–7.

silk for the making of *ṭirāz*, a fabric embroidered with the name of the ruler in whose reign it was made, date and place of manufacture, and Quranic inscriptions.[25] At about the same time, Ibn Ḥawqal described a type of felt which was made in Muslim Spain specifically for the *sulṭān*.[26] Because it functioned as an emblem of state power, the production and export of *ṭirāz* were strictly regulated. Not only were the fibers and dyes used in its manufacture subject to annual state levies, but the quality of the product was overseen by a government appointed official, the *ṣāḥib al-ṭirāz*.[27] *Ṭirāz* was not a commodity as such (i.e., it could not be sold officially), and thus it was never cited among items traded to other regions of the Islamic world, although Andalusi rulers frequently sent pieces abroad as diplomatic gifts. In 993, for example, the caliph Hishām II sent gifts of *ṭirāz* to North Africa, and four years later, his chamberlain, Manṣūr, distributed 2,285 lengths of the material to allies in northern Spain.[28] There is no documentary evidence to show how strictly this monopoly was maintained under later rulers, although the production of *ṭirāz* certainly continued into the early thirteenth century.

Despite the official regulation of *ṭirāz*, Christian Spanish sources frequently mention this fabric and include it in tariff lists, a fact which suggests that – at least in the northern peninsula – *ṭirāz* was traded like any other luxury textile. These references to *ṭirāz* signal the need for caution in evaluating and explaining stray citations of apparently Andalusi goods in northern sources. Here is an item that clearly traveled, but probably not – at least in the first stage of its journey – through commercial exchange. When a sale document from Coimbra, made in 1090, mentioned "good pieces of Cordoban tiraz" (*tiraces bonos cordoueses*) these were undoubtedly of southern manufacture, but they probably came north as a gift, booty, or *paria* tribute, not

25 *Le Calendrier de Cordoue*. [ed. R. Dozy (new edn. C. Pellat), Leiden, 1961], pp. 90, 132.

26 Ibn Ḥawqal, *Kitāb ṣurat al-arḍ*, p. 114.

27 M. Lombard, *The Golden Age of Islam*. [Oxford, 1975], p. 82. See also A. Grohmann "Ṭirāz," (*Encyclopedia of Islam*. [1st edn., Leiden, 1913–42] IV.2, pp. 785–93) for further history and description of this type of textile.

28 Rāzī, *Anales palatinos*, p. 138; Maqqarī, *Analectes sur l'histoire et la littérature des arabes d'Espagne*. [ed. R. Dozy, Leiden, 1855–60] I, p. 271. For more on *ṭirāz* and other fabrics discussed in Rāzī's chronicle, see E. García Gomez, "Tejidos, ropas y tapicería en los *Anales de al-Hakam II* por 'Isā Rāzī," *Boletín de la Real Academia de la historia* 156(1970), pp. 43–53.

as a traded commodity.[29] Only later, at a secondary stage, were they sold in this transaction. It seems quite likely that *tiraz*, in Latin, could apply to any figured silk textile of Islamic manufacture, and did not carry the same official significance as the Arabic *ṭirāz*. Thus, the *pannos tirazes* donated to a Portuguese church in 994, the *almandra tiraze* mentioned in the 1053 Charter of Viariz, and the *tiraz sin oro* or *con oro* included in a 1207 Toledan tariff list, were all embroidered silks, but not necessarily *ṭirāz* proper.[30] Some may even have been woven in the northern peninsula, as indicated by a grant made by Alfonso V of Asturias-Leon (999–1028) to three Mozarab silk workers (*tiraceros*).[31]

MEDITERRANEAN COMMODITIES AND ANDALUSI IMPORTS

In his handbook for merchants, Abū Faḍl al-Dimashqī stressed the maxim that any "merchant who travels must, first and foremost, pay attention to the commodities he buys." He must be intimately aware of minute gradations in quality, freshness, purity, variety, price, availability, and other characteristics of these commodities. He must also study the more general nature of markets, and always look for commodities that will bring a profit. Above all, he "should not put his money into commodities that people do not use, because there is little demand for these [goods], and they sell slowly."[32] All this was excellent advice. A merchant needed considerable business acumen, savvy, and a very good memory in order to be successful in the medieval commercial world.

Most medieval merchants handled an enormous range of commodities, both expensive luxury goods and mundane everyday necessities, raw and manufactured, bulky and compact. Within each category, they sold not only the first-class products but also cheaper grades of the same item. Only rarely did merchants specialize, or restrict their trade to particular commodi-

29 *Portugaliae monumenta historica: diplomata et chartae*. I [Lisbon, 1867], p. 443, #744.

30 *Portugaliae monumenta historica*, p. 104, #168 and p. 234, #384. F. Hernández, "Las Cortes de Toledo de 1207," *Las Cortes de Castilla y León en la edad media*. [Valladolid, 1988], p. 241. This is only a small sample of Latin references to *ṭirāz*, for more see F. May, *Silk Textiles of Spain*. [New York, 1957], p. 4.

31 May, *Silk Textiles*, p. 5.

32 Dimashqī, *Kitāb al-'ashāra ilā maḥasin al-tijāra*. [Cairo, 1318/1900], pp. 51, 58.

6 Merchant weighing spices, thirteenth-century Castilian miniature from the *Cántigas de Santa María*, CV (courtesy of the Patrimonio Nacional, Madrid)

ties. Ibn ʿAwkal's extensive correspondence from the eleventh century contained references to eighty-three different types and classes of product. At roughly the same period, Dimashqī described sixty items of trade, and Francesco di Balduccio Pegolotti later included two hundred and eighty-eight commodities in his list of goods available in early fourteenth-century Florence.[33]

Medieval lists of commodities are not noteworthy for their strict organization, but Dimashqī categorized the items on his list according to basic type (gems, spices, foodstuffs, and so forth). This system has the obvious merit of clarity, and thus I adopt his principles here – though not his exact order or categories – to describe the genres of commodities widely traded in the medieval Mediterranean world. Except in special cases, these goods moved freely, and there is no evidence of restrictions on their traffic other than the economic limitations of the

[33] N.A. Stillman, "The Eleventh-Century Merchant House of Ibn ʿAwkal," *JESHO* 16(1973), p. 27; Dimashqī, *Kitāb al-'ashāra*, pp. 12–34; Pegolotti, *La pratica della mercatura.* [ed. A. Evans, Cambridge, Mass., 1936], pp. 293–7.

7 Merchants trading textiles and other goods (*Cántigas de Santa María*, CLXXII, courtesy of the Patrimonio Nacional, Madrid)

marketplace. The following discussion covers general categories of goods imported to Andalusi markets; Andalusi exports will be discussed in chapter 7.

Spices

The proverbial mainstay of medieval commerce, spices, constituted a huge generic category containing medicinal drugs, flavorings, aromatics, dye-stuffs, and mordants. Such items have become a truism of medieval international trade, since they fulfilled all the requirements of a merchant's ideal commodity: low weight, small volume, high demand, and limited geographical availability. The consequent value of pepper, cloves, indigo, or ambergris made it well worth the trouble of transporting them over great distances. Cinnamon, for example, regularly traveled from south-east Asia, where it was grown, to the markets of the western Mediterranean.[34] Adding to their value

[34] Arabic sources refer to several different types of cinnamon, including "common cinnamon" and "Chinese cinnamon" (see, for example, Kindī, *The Medical Formulary*

8 Merchant selling ceramics or goods in ceramic jars (*Cántigas de Santa María,* CVIII, courtesy of the Patrimonio Nacional, Madrid)

– or perhaps because of it – spices often served multiple purposes. Cloves are a case in point. They were employed to flavor foods, to cure certain ailments – including depression and toothache – and to perfume the air, breath, and clothing. Saffron, likewise, was both a cooking spice and widely used as a perfume and dyestuff. The same was true for cinnamon (used in treating stomach ailments as well as in flavoring), myrrh (both an aromatic and a medicine), and numerous other items.

The majority of spices were imports to al-Andalus, where they found a ready and stable market. In some cases, as with frankincense from south Arabia, an item might originate within the *dār al-Islām*, but many of the spices traded internationally came from India or the Far East. Sources indicate that spices of

or Aqrabadhin of al-Kindī. [trans. M. Levy, Madison, 1966], pp. 122, 206, 218 *et al.*). As P. Crone has pointed out in her *Meccan Trade and the Rise of Islam.* [Princeton, 1987], pp. 253–63, there were two varieties of medieval cinnamon, one that we would recognize today as cinnamon (the Indian or "Chinese" variety) and another spice of the same name from East Africa. See also N. Groom, *Frankincense and Myrrh.* [London, 1981] chapter 5.

9 Merchants buying bales of wool and loading them on a ship (*Cántigas de Santa María*, XXV, courtesy of the Patrimonio Nacional, Madrid)

all varieties were bought and sold in Andalusi markets. Saqaṭī included a long section on spices in his early thirteenth-century *ḥisba* manual, but he pointed out that it would be impossible to provide a complete inventory of items, since over three thousand varieties were available.[35] Andalusi cookery books provide data on the culinary use of spices, while medical handbooks show their medicinal properties.[36] Geniza letters also show eastern spices brought to al-Andalus, as when a ship arrived in Almeria, in 1138, bearing a cargo of pepper, brazilwood, lac, frankincense, and other exotic imports.[37] In another letter, from roughly the same period, we learn that the Egyptian merchant Halfōn b. Nethanel had sent gifts, including a parcel of cloves, to friends in Lucena.[38] This present suggests that cloves were more expensive in Muslim Spain, and perhaps harder to obtain than in Egypt. Nevertheless, references to cloves in other sources indicate that it would not have been impossible for Halfōn's friends to buy this article, for a price, in their own land.

A few medicinal drugs were derived from plants native to the Iberian peninsula, but most of the rarer items which a medieval physician might prescribe – frankincense, cinnamon, and so forth – were imported from the east. In many cases, their foreign origin was explicitly stated in recipes for cures, and botanical evidence roughly backs up their stated provenance. The Jewish Andalusi doctor Ibn Ezra (d. 1167), for example, recommended the application of Indian and Afghani myrobalans in cases for which a purge or laxative was required.[39] Other doctors prescribed Chinese cinnamon. Many drugs without a

[35] Saqaṭī, *Kitāb al-faqīh al-ajall al-ʿālim al-ʿārif al-awḥad* [*Un manuel hispanique de ḥisba*]. [eds. G.S. Colin and E. Lévi-Provençal, Paris, 1931], p. 43.

[36] See *Traducción española de un manuscrito anónimo del siglo XIII sobre la cocina hispano-magribī*. [trans. A. Huici Miranda, Madrid, 1966]; L. Bolens, *La cuisine andalouse, un art de vivre: XIe-XIIIe siècle*. [Paris, 1990]. Among medical treatises consulted for this study are S.K. Hamarneh and G. Sonnedecker, *A Pharmaceutical View of Abulcasis Alzahrāwī in Moorish Spain*. [Leiden, 1963]; Ibn Ezra, *Sefer Hanisyonot: The Book of Medical Experiences attributed to Abraham Ibn Ezra*. [ed. and trans. J.O. Leibowitz and S. Marcus, Jerusalem, 1984]; Ibn Buklārish, "El prólogo de *al-Kitāb al-mustaʿīnī* de Ibn Buklārish," [ed. A. Labarta, in *Estudios sobre historia de la ciencia árabe*. ed. J. Vernet, Barcelona, 1980], pp. 183–316; Kindī, *The Medical Formulary or Aqrābādhīn of al-Kindī*. [trans. M. Levy, Madison, 1966]; Moses b. Maimon, *Glossary of Drug Names*. [trans. F. Rosner, Philadelphia, 1979]; Ibn al-Bayṭār, *Traité des simples*. [trans. L. LeClerc] *Notices et extraits des manuscrits de la Bibliothèque Nationale* 26 (1883).

[37] TS 12.285.

[38] TS 8 J 18.2.

[39] Ibn Ezra, *Sefer Hanisyonot*, p. 147.

foreign name, such as the frankincense taken by the eleventh-century Andalusi scholar Ibn Ḥazm for a heart problem, must likewise have been imported.[40] References to imports also appear in other contexts, as when an early twelfth-century merchant wrote from Fez to Almeria to inquire at what price scammony, a plant native to Asia Minor which produced a cathartic resin, was selling in Almeria.[41] Somewhat later, Zuhrī reported that arsenic, which could be employed as both a medicine and a poison, was "imported to the land of al-Andalus" from Ifriqiya.[42]

Recipes and merchant letters make it clear that – like medicines – virtually all of the important condiments were imported rather than locally grown. A thirteenth-century Almohad cookery book described recipes for numerous dishes, many containing foreign ingredients – such as cinnamon, pepper, and camphor.[43] Pepper was particularly prominent among flavorings traded on the medieval international market. Many Geniza documents quote pepper prices and provide examples of shipments of pepper headed for Andalusi markets.

The range of aromatics demanded by Andalusi perfumers encompassed items of both eastern and western origin. Musk, camphor, aloes, ambergris, and saffron ranked as the five primary aromatic substances listed by medieval geographers and traded by medieval merchants. Other aromatics, including eastern products such as rose-water, sandalwood, spikenard, myrrh, and frankincense, were also widely traded, but never achieved the prominence of the preeminent five. From Masʿūdī in the tenth century to Maqqarī in the sixteenth, writers reported that the best musk, camphor, and aloes came from India, whereas the best ambergris and saffron were exported from al-Andalus.[44]

[40] Ibn Ḥazm, *Ṭawq al-ḥamāma*. [ed. T.A. Makkī, Cairo, 1975], p. 32. Medical handbooks do not list frankincense among remedies for palpitations of the heart (*khafqān al-qalb*) such as Ibn Ḥazm described. On frankincense, see Groom, *Frankincense and myrrh*; and G.W. van Beek, "Frankincense and Myrrh in Ancient South Arabia," *JAOS* 78 (1958), pp. 141–51.

[41] TS 12.435. Kindī recommended scammony in the treatment of fever and jaundice (*The Medical Formulary*, p. 126).

[42] Zuhrī, "Kitāb al-djaʿrāfiyya" [ed. M. Hadj-Sadok], *Bulletin des études orientales* 21 (1968) p. 199. Kindī cited arsenic as a cure for cankers and ulcers (*Medical Formulary*, pp. 50, 90, 98), and Rosner listed it as a "drastic purgative" in his notes to Moses b. Maimon's *Glossary*, p. 188.

[43] *Traducción española de un manuscrito anónimo*, p. 180 and *passim*.

[44] Masʿūdī, *Murūj al-dhahab* (*Les prairies d'or*). [ed. C. Barbier de Meynard, Paris, 1861],

Some authors disputed India's superiority in the quality of its aloes, claiming that there were aloes from the province of Murcia "which surpass Indian aloes in fragrance, perfume, and the quality of their scent."[45] Many other geographers, including Rāzī and Ḥimyarī, also compared al-Andalus favorably with India for its production of aromatics and fragrances.[46] Even Judah Ha-Levi referred fleetingly to the Andalusi perfume trade in his verses, addressed to the peninsula, "Your breeze, western shore, is perfumed. The scent of nard is on its wings . . .your origin is in the merchants' treasuries, surely not from the storehouse of the wind."[47] Other sources confirm the availability of local and imported aromatics in al-Andalus. During the tenth century, for example, an inventory taken of precious items belonging to ʿAbd al-Raḥmān III included ten pounds of Indian aloes (and two hundred pounds of other varieties), two hundred and twelve ounces of musk, three hundred ounces of camphor, and five hundred ounces of ambergris.[48]

The Andalusi dye-master also had a vested interest in the international spice trade. Medieval dyers had a wide range of colors to choose from, derived from many different sources, both local and foreign. Brilliant reds and purples could be produced from vegetable agents such as madder, safflower, and brazilwood, or extracted from mollusks (for an imperial purple) and beetles (for a brilliant crimson dye called *qirmiz*). Equally fine yellows came from saffron, turmeric, and mineral ochres; blues from indigo and woad; blacks and browns from gall nuts and walnuts. Al-Andalus was famous for its production and export of some of these substances, notably saffron and qirmiz, but Andalusi dyers turned to international trade for the reds and blues of imported lac, brazilwood, and indigo.

Despite Maqqarī's assertion that Sevillian qirmiz was "superior

p. 367; Maqqarī, *Analectes*, 1, p. 92. On Andalusi perfumery and cosmetics, see L. Bolens, "Les parfums et la beauté en Andalousie médiévale (XIe–XIIIe siècle)," in *Les soins de beauté. Actes du IIIe colloque international, Grasse (avril, 1985)*. [Nice, 1987], pp. 145–69.

45 L. Molina (ed.), *Descripción anónima de al-Andalus*. [Madrid, 1983] 1, p. 12; Qazwīnī, *Athār al-bilād wa akhbār al-ʿibār*. [Beirut, 1380/1960], p. 503, reports similar information on Andalusi aloes. The aloes in question were a variety of fragrant wood, not the bitter aloe which was used for medicinal purposes. See Crone, *Meccan Trade* (pp. 74–76, 267–9) for further discussion.

46 Rāzī, "Description de l'Espagne," p. 59; Ḥimyarī, *Péninsule*, p. 3.

47 *Jewish Poets of Spain, 900–1250*. [trans. D. Goldstein, London, 1965] p. 144.

48 Maqqarī, *Analectes*, 1, pp. 299–30.

to Indian lac (*lakk*),"[49] this latter substance (a resinous gum produced by trees in India and the Far East) was imported to the west and competed with qirmiz in Andalusi markets. Geniza documents indicate that lac was a staple Egyptian export to the western Mediterranean. Memos from the Egyptian trading house of Ibn 'Awkal cited transactions in lac during the early eleventh century, and two letters written in the following century between Jewish partners in Almeria and North Africa remarked on sales of lac.[50] Large quantities of brazilwood (*baqam*) were likewise shipped westward by the firm of Ibn 'Awkal. One correspondent, writing to Egypt in about 1000, described a dispute over a shipment of *baqam* to al-Andalus. The writer, based in Qayrawan, responded indignantly to an accusation that he had sent some jointly held brazilwood to al-Andalus with the intention of making a personal profit. He denied the charge, but the context shows that it was possible to reap high profits through shipping brazilwood to al-Andalus. Later in the same letter, the merchant reported that he would send another parcel of the dye "to al-Andalus [at a c]ommission, but on the condition that I will bear the responsibility (for its loss)."[51] Another missive written in the 1060s, again from Tunisia to Egypt, remarked that "brazilwood . . . sells slowly, unless one gets an Andalusi" merchant to buy it.[52] These Andalusis must have considered that the eagerness of their home market would justify this expenditure.

Medieval dyers owed the beauty and brilliancy of their best blues to indigo. Whereas contemporary painters, potters, and glaziers could turn to minerals – such as lapis lazuli – to extend their palate, the dye master was mainly dependent on indigo and, as a poor substitute, "garden indigo" (*nīl al-bustānī*), or woad. Indigo was imported to Muslim Spain, whereas woad was grown locally.[53] Ibn 'Awkal's correspondence detailed three

[49] Maqqarī, *Analectes*, I, p. 128. Lac was used not only as a dye, but also as a shellac and a medicine.

[50] Stillman, "The Eleventh-century Merchant House," p. 42; twelfth-century letters: TS 12.435 and TS 13 J 14.21.

[51] DK 13; translation based on Goitein, *Letters*, pp. 29–33.

[52] TS 16.163. See Goitein, *Letters*, p. 133. A later letter (TS. 20.162), ca. 1080, also mentioned a shipment of brazilwood to al-Andalus.

[53] According to agronomist Ibn al-'Awwām (twelfth century), woad (*nīl al-bustānī*) was grown in many regions of al-Andalus; his report has led to the mistaken impression that true indigo was cultivated in al-Andalus (Ibn al-'Awwām, *Le livre de l'agriculture*

basic types of indigo: the Persian, Palestinian, and Indian varieties.[54] However, a merchant writing from Egypt in the 1050s did not bother to identify a particular type, saying merely that he had sent half a bale of indigo "to the west and it continued until it arrived in al-Andalus. It was inspected there and no decay was found in it."[55] Another merchant, writing from Fez to Almeria in the twelfth century, asked his partner to "please take notice that indigo is much in demand here."[56] Presumably, the intended understanding was that if indigo was not selling so well in al-Andalus, his recipient should send some to Fez immediately.

Virtually no dye-stuff would work on its own. In order to produce or retain their color, dyes had to be used in combination with a mordant, a chemical agent which helped to bind the dye to the cloth. Many mordants were used, some rare and costly, others (like urine) inexpensive and readily available. The preeminent medieval mordant, alum (aluminum potassium sulphate), was an indispensable component of the medieval dye trade, and as such, probably more valuable than any other element of the industry. Alum was only found in certain regions, thus creating a significant international market for the mineral. The best alum was reputed to come from Egypt, Chad, and western Anatolia, but ceaseless demand for alum sometimes led to the mining and export of inferior varieties from Sicily, Spain, and north-west Africa. All of these sources had been known to the Roman

d'Ibn Awam. [trans. J.J. Clément-Mollet, Paris, 1866] II.1, p. 125); W. Heyd cited this source as a basis for his assertion that al-Andalus produced indigo, (*Histoire du commerce du Levant au moyen âge.* [Leipzig, 1885] II, p. 628). Nevertheless, other agricultural sources show that woad, but not indigo, was grown. The "sky blue dye" cited in the *Calendrier de Cordoue* (p. 132) was probably woad. See also Bolens, "Use of Plants for Dyeing and Clothing," pp. 1009–1010. Woad was likewise produced in and exported from Europe, particularly from southern France where it was commonly known as *pastel* (F. Borlandi, "Note per la storia della produzione e del commercio di una materia prima: il guado nel medio evo," *Studi in onore di Gino Luzzatto.* [Milan, 1950] I, pp. 297–326).

Some other sources of blues were also available in al-Andalus. A curious passage from the Egyptian historian 'Aynī (d. 1451), stated that there was a mine near Seville from which was extracted "a powder (cobalt?) which may be used in place of indigo for dyeing, and which is found only in this part of al-Andalus, from where it is exported for the use of dyers." See A. Zeki, "Mémoire sur les relations entre l'Egypte et l'Espagne," *Homenaje a Don Francisco Codera.* [Zaragoza, 1904], p. 464.

54 Stillman, "The Eleventh-century Merchant House," p. 38.

55 TS 12.226.

56 TS 12.435.

world, and recorded by Pliny, but it appears that the production of western Mediterranean mines dwindled during the Islamic period. Arabic geographers did not mention alum among Andalusi products or exports, nor did Geniza letters cite western sources of alum. Instead, they wrote of shipments of alum headed to the west.

Textiles

Raw fibers and woven cloth made up another major category of commodities in medieval Mediterranean commerce. "The best commerce is in textiles" wrote the pseudo-Jāḥiẓ in the ninth century, and his comment held true for Andalusi international trade through the late twelfth century.[57] Textiles ranked among the most highly organized and productive medieval industries in al-Andalus and elsewhere, and they provided the staple export of many areas.[58] There are records of thousands of bales of silk, wool, flax, and cotton, shipped across the Mediterranean in the medieval period. In al-Andalus, silk fabrics, as well as raw silk, made up the major portion of exported textiles, distantly followed by woven linens, cottons, woolens, and a peculiar fibre known as sea wool. Andalusi carpets and rugs were also widely traded.

Among textile imports, Andalusi textile ateliers received flax from Egypt and raw wool from the Maghrib. Although silk had a higher value, linen and flax were traded in greater volume. Geniza merchants often handled both silk and flax, carrying the former eastward from al-Andalus and Sicily and the latter westward from Egypt. Their letters indicate that hundreds – even thousands – of bales of Egyptian flax were shipped westward every year, with each bale weighing roughly six hundred

[57] Jāḥiẓ, *Tabaṣṣur al-tijāra*. [ed. H.H. 'Abd al-Wahhāb, Damascus, 1351/1932], p. 7.

[58] M. Lombard surveyed the Islamic textile industry, including production in al-Andalus, in *Les textiles dans le monde musulman*. [Paris, 1978]. R.B. Serjeant's article, "Material for a History of Islamic Textiles" [*Ars Islamica* 15(1951), pp. 29–61] lists Arabic sources on textiles. Several glossaries aid in the identification of textiles in the western Islamic world and Spain: R. Dozy, *Dictionnaire détaillé des noms des vêtements chez les arabes*. [Amsterdam, 1845]; M. Gual Camarena, *Vocabulario del comercio medieval*. [Tarragona, 1968]; J. Alfau de Solalinde, *Nomenclatura de los tejidos españoles del siglo XIII*. [Madrid, 1969]; M. Martínez, *Los nombres de tejidos en castellano medieval*. [Granada, 1989].

pounds.[59] Once in al-Andalus, Egyptian flax was transformed into woven linen, and the trading circle became complete when linen fabrics from Pechina and other regions returned as exports, according to Ibn Ḥawqal, "to Egypt, Mecca, Yemen, and elsewhere" in the tenth century.[60] This pattern persisted through the twelfth century, when a Genoese merchant contracted to carry ninety-four pounds of raw silk and ten bolts of Spanish linen to North Africa in 1161.[61]

Muslim Spain also imported raw wool, since unlike Roman Spain or later Christian Spain, the Andalusi economy never concentrated on wool production. Zuhrī remarked that al-Andalus obtained wools from Tlemcen, and Geniza letters referred to shipments of wool from Egypt to al-Andalus. In one letter, written in the late eleventh century, a merchant alluded to a cargo of wool, weighing five hundred pounds and costing a mere thirty dinars (compared to silk which could sell at thirty dinars for ten pounds in the 1050s), which he intended to send from Alexandria to Muslim Spain. However, his partner responded immediately to this letter, advising him not to dispatch "anything of the kind, for dyed purple [wool] is not worth a thing in al-Andalus."[62]

Foreign fabrics, as well as raw fibers, were also available in al-Andalus, though commercial citations are fewer. Ibn ʿAbd al-Raʾūf mentioned "cloth from Majās" (Morocco) in his late tenth-century *ḥisba* book, and a Jewish merchant in Tunisia wrote to his Egyptian partner, ca. 1020, to report that he had sent "the textiles in that consignment [received from Egypt] to al-Andalus."[63] It is also likely that a certain number of *jurjānīs*, *isbahānīs*, and other textiles bearing foreign names were genuine imports rather than Andalusi imitations.

59 Goitein, *Mediterranean Society*, I, p. 226.

60 Ibn Ḥawqal, *Kitāb ṣurat al-arḍ*, p. 114. Later Arab geographers, including Zuhrī ("Kitāb al-djaʿrāfiyya," pp. 188–9) and Yāqūt (*Muʿjām al-buldān*, I, p. 227), also mentioned exports of Andalusi linens to other regions of the Islamic world.

61 Giovanni Scriba, *Il Cartolare di Giovanni Scriba*. [eds. M. Chiaudano and M. Moresco, Rome, 1935] II, p. 4,#812.

62 TS NS J 197; TS Arabic Box 30.255. Both letters are translated in Goitein, *Letters*, pp. 233–6. On the price of silk, see TS 13 J 25.14 and *Mediterranean Society*, I, pp. 222–4.

63 Ibn ʿAbd al-Raʾūf, *Risāla*. in *Documents árabes inédits sur la vie sociale et économique en occident musulman au moyen âge: Trois traités hispaniques de ḥisba*. [ed. E. Lévi-Provençal, Cairo, 1955], p. 114; TS 8.12.

Foodstuffs

In contrast to spices and textiles, foodstuffs rarely appear as significant commodities in long-distance trade. Perhaps this was because, as Ibn Khaldūn remarked, "the prices of necessary foodstuffs . . . are low, and the prices for luxuries, such as seasonings . . . are high," but there was also the important fact that few foods traveled well in the days before refrigeration.[64] *Ḥisba* manuals indicate that even items sold locally were prone to imperfections resulting from decay, insect damage, damp or desiccation. These problems must have become much worse over the transit time of a long journey. However, the medieval grocer or merchant did have recourse to several techniques (drying, salting, smoking, crystallizing in sugar or honey, pickling in vinegar, or curing with spices) to prolong the usable life of commercial foodstuffs, making it possible to send certain foods the length of the Mediterranean without deleterious effect.[65]

Andalusi jurists concerned themselves with the problems arising from the transport of food, and their rulings show a clear differentiation between perishable and non-perishable goods. Abū al-Ḥasan al-Jazīrī (d. 1189), qāḍī of Algeciras, quoted the opinion of the ninth-century scholar Ibn Ḥabīb, in listing those foodstuffs which could be included for transport in a guaranteed (*ḍamān*) hire of a ship (i.e, a hire in which the cargo was not itemized in the contract). Among licit items were wheat, barley, millet, and other grains; beans, chick peas, lentils, and other dry legumes; dates, raisins, olives, olive oil, honey, clarified butter (*ghee*), vinegar, and salt. Perishable goods such as fruit juices, cheese, milk, all meats, butter, and fresh fruits were excluded.[66] When a source mentions a ship or a merchant carrying "food," without citing any specific type, the dictates of both legal precepts and mercantile common-sense indicate that this cargo probably consisted of non-perishable foods.[67] Certainly, in cases

[64] Ibn Khaldūn, *The Muqaddimah.* [trans. F. Rosenthal, New York, 1958] II, p. 276.

[65] Their value in food preservation increased the commercial value of sugar, spices, and salt.

[66] Jazīrī, *Maqṣud al-maḥmūd fī talkhīṣ al-ʿuqūd.* [Miguel Asín Institute, CSIC, Madrid] ms. 5, fol. 55v.

[67] The jurist Abū Imrān al-Fāsī (d. 1038–9) of Qayrawan was consulted concerning hire of a boat transporting food (*ṭaʿam*) to al-Andalus (Ibn Abī Firās, *Kitāb akriyāt al-sufun.* [ed. M.A. Tahir], *Cahiers de Tunisie* 31 (1983), p. 50).

where a source does identify the cargo, the goods found traveling over long distances almost always conform to Ibn Ḥabīb's guidelines.

Braudel has described an "eternal trinity" of foodstuffs, "wheat, olives, and vines," as a fundamental characteristic of Mediterranean climate and commerce, but this triad was not central to Andalusi trade.[68] Only olive oil ranked as a major international export, and its trade will be discussed in the next chapter. Raisins were also exported, but traffic in wine was virtually non-existent. The data on grain are more complicated.

Wheat, barley, millet, and rice, were staples of the medieval Mediterranean diet, and there is evidence of a regular low-level traffic in cereals. However, most documentation on grain shipments pertains to times of crisis, usually drought or famine, making it difficult to obtain a general view of this trade. Cereals were certainly grown in the Iberian peninsula, particularly durum wheat (Arabic *qamḥ* or *darmak*; Castilian *adárgama*) and sorghum (Arabic *dhura*; Castilian *aldora*), but it is not clear to what extent al-Andalus was self-sufficient in grain production.[69] According to Lévi-Provençal, al-Andalus produced sufficient grain to provide for its own needs, except in bad years, but not enough to export. Alternatively, Vernet proposed that there was a continuous import trade in grain from North Africa to al-Andalus from the ninth to the fourteenth century.[70] As early as the tenth century, at least, Ibn Ḥawqal wrote that Tabarca, near Oran, was "a commercial port to which Andalusis bring goods, and from which they take grain (*ghalāl*)."[71] In the twelfth century, Idrīsī and others confirmed these regular Andalusi

[68] F. Braudel, *The Mediterranean and the Mediterranean World in the Age of Philip II.* [New York, 1966] I, p. 236.

[69] The transfer of agricultural, botanical, and technical terms from Arabic to Castilian was extremely common. R. Dozy has compiled an entire dictionary of these linguistic loans in his *Glossaire des mots espagnols et portugais dérivés de l'arabe.* [Leiden, 1869]. For more on Andalusi wheat and grains, see T. Glick, *Islamic and Christian Spain*, pp. 80–3; J. Vallvé "La agricultura en al-Andalus," *Al-Qantara* 3(1982), pp. 275–81; and A. Watson, *Agricultural Innovation*, pp. 9–23. On internal Andalusi consumption and market, see J.D. Latham, "Some Observations on the Bread Trade in Muslim Malaga (ca. AD 1200)," *Journal of Semitic Studies* 29(1984), pp. 111–22.

[70] E. Lévi-Provençal, *L'Espagne musulmane au Xème siècle: Institutions et vie sociale.* [Paris, 1932] p. 162; R. Vernet, "Les relations céréalières entre le Maghreb et la péninsule ibérique," *Anuario de estudios medievales* 10(1980), p. 325.

[71] Ibn Ḥawqal, *Kitāb ṣurat al-arḍ*, p. 78. The word *ghalāl* generally means cereals or grains. However, it may also be applied to other crops, fruits, or general produce.

imports of Maghribi grain, and the *muḥtasib* Ibn ʿAbdūn wrote of ships at anchor in the harbor of Seville carrying cargoes of grain.[72]

There is some evidence that al-Andalus occasionally exported wheat, however, particularly during the tenth and eleventh centuries. In 936, according to Ibn Ḥayyān, ʿAbd al-Raḥmān III dispatched one thousand *mudīs* of wheat and barley to an ally in North Africa. If Ibn Ḥayyān was correct in his figures, this was a huge shipment by contemporary standards, equaling nearly three modern tons.[73] In the following century, ʿAlī b. Mujāhid, the ruler of Denia, dispatched a shipload of "food" (probably wheat) to famine-stricken Egypt. This was not a gesture of disinterested charity, for in the next sentence we learn that Ibn Mujāhid's ship returned to Denia loaded with money.[74] Two Geniza letters also mention Andalusi wheat. One, written ca. 1050, noted that a merchant had sold indigo in al-Andalus and purchased "Andalusi wheat," while another letter, written about ninety years later, mentioned a cargo of wheat shipped from Seville to Tripoli.[75]

Two points should be made here regarding Andalusi grain imports and exports. First, it may have been cheaper to transport grain to Andalusi coastal cities by sea, from North Africa, than to bring it overland from the interior. Thus, the existence of commerce might have little to do with the overall Iberian grain producing capacity. However, as a second point, references to grain imports appear to increase slightly by the twelfth century. This shift may be owing to a situation whereby, on the one hand, Almoravid and Almohad rule in both the Iberian peninsula and the Maghrib encouraged a unified grain trade, while at the same time the southward progress of the Christian reconquest removed the best Andalusi grain producing regions in the Duero

[72] Ibn ʿAbdūn, *Risāla*. in *Documents arabes inédits sur la vie sociale et économique en occident musulman au moyen âge*. [ed. E. Lévi-Provençal, Cairo, 1955], p. 47.

[73] Ibn Ḥayyān, *Muqtabas*. v, [eds. P. Chalmeta, F. Corriente, M. Subḥ, Madrid-Rabat, 1979] p. 389. The *mudī* was a large measure, weighing roughly 750 pounds (J. Vallvé, "Notas de metrología hispano-árabe II," *Al-Andalus* 42(1977), pp. 61–122 and "Notas de metrología hispano-árabe III," *Al-Qantara* 5(1984), pp. 162–67).

[74] Ibn al-Khaṭīb, *Kitāb al-ʿamāl al-ʿalām*. [ed. E. Lévi-Provençal, Beirut, 1956], pp. 221–2.

[75] TS 12.226 and TS 16.54. I have not seen the latter document, but Goitein referred to its contents in his personal notes (Geniza Laboratory, Princeton University, microfilm cards 00744 and 00765).

Valley from Muslim control. Certainly, by the second half of the thirteenth century, politics had forced Nasrid Granada to depend on North Africa for its grain supplies, and Ibn Saʿīd al-Gharnāṭī (d. 1286) mentioned ships arriving in al-Andalus with wheat from Tunis.[76]

Most of the other permissible foodstuffs listed by Abū al-Ḥasan al-Jazīrī only appear sporadically in sources on international commerce. Records mention salt, sugar, honey, and nuts, but trade in these items seems small-scale and probably restricted to the western Mediterranean. Salt from Muslim Spain (notably Ibiza) and the Maghrib was carried southward to barter for West African gold, while Moroccan and Granadan sweeteners rivaled each other for foreign trade.[77] Almonds, pistachios, and walnuts were brought to Andalusi markets from North Africa. In the eleventh century, Bakrī reported that the province of Qayrawan produced wonderful pistachios, which were distributed throughout the Maghrib, to Egypt, Sijilmasa, and al-Andalus. This information appears again a century later in the anonymous *Kitāb al-istibṣār*, and Zuhrī, likewise, cited exports of nuts from Morocco to "the Maghrib, al-Andalus, and *Rūm*."[78] A Geniza letter written in about 1040 shows an Andalusi merchant carrying shelled almonds from Sicily to Egypt, but these nuts were probably grown in North Africa rather than in the merchant's homeland.[79]

Metals and gems

Metals and gems constitute yet another category of commodities traded around the medieval Mediterranean. These were natural products, often valuable, and typically obtained through mining (with the exception of organic items such as coral, pearls, and ivory). Traffic in gemstones (diamonds, rubies, sapphires, and the like) was relatively simple, and followed a parallel course to that of other commodities of high value, rarity, and low volume.

76 Ibn Saʿīd, *Kitāb basṭ al-arḍ fī al-ṭūl al-ʿarḍ*. [ed. J. Vernet Gides, Tetuan, 1958], p. 76.

77 Arabic sources show Moroccan honey imported to al-Andalus by the twelfth century (Zuhrī, "Kitāb al-djaʿrāfiyya," p. 190 and Fagnan (ed.), *Kitāb al-istibṣār*, p. 183), although Saqaṭī remarked that Maghribi honey was more expensive in al-Andalus than the local variety (Saqaṭī, *Kitāb al-faqīh*, p. 13).

78 Bakrī, *Description de l'Afrique septentrionale*. [ed. M. de Slane, Paris, reprint 1965], p. 47; Fagnan (ed.), *Kitāb al-istibṣār*, p. 74; Zuhrī, "Kitāb al-djaʿrāfiyya," pp. 188–9.

79 TS Box 28.37.

Like many spices, most precious gems arrived in Mediterranean markets from India and/or the Far East. Abū Faḍl al-Dimashqī categorized gems among those slow-moving goods "which [ordinary] people do not use," yet even the limited demands of the very rich made it worthwhile for a merchant to carry a few gems in his cargo.[80] In contrast, minerals, such as marble, or non-precious metals, such as iron, lead, and tin, were bulky and extremely heavy – but probably in greater demand than gemstones. Most of these substances were mined within the Mediterranean world. The utility of these latter commodities for architecture, tombstones, weaponry, implements, and other purposes supported their trade. Traffic in precious metals (gold and silver) was more complicated, since these metals could be traded either in raw form, as gold dust and bullion, or as coins.

Because the sources of metals and gems tended to be geographically specific, trade in these commodities followed routes that changed little over the years. As a general rule, non-precious metals in Mediterranean trade traveled from west to east, while gems moved from east to west. In the eleventh century, for instance, Geniza records show copper, iron, lead, mercury, and tin carried eastward, while diamonds and rubies came west.[81] Substances of animal origin, though something of an anomaly in the larger category "gems," are also easy to trace. Coral was available in reefs off the coasts of the eastern Iberian peninsula and North Africa, but pearls, cowries, and ivory all traveled from east to west. Although some inferior pearls could be harvested along the Catalan coast, Andalusi merchants preferred the eastern variety, whether large or small.[82] In the early 1040s, for example, a Tunisian partner wrote to Nahray b. Nissīm in Egypt instructing that "if it happens that you are in the jewelry bazaar, and there are small pearls going cheaply . . . then buy as many as you think best, because the Andalusi [merchants] are seeking that type here." A few decades later, an unrelated letter sent from Alexandria to Old Cairo requested the recipient to keep an eye out for "the high quality pearls which are salable in al-Andalus."[83] In contrast to pearls, references to trade in cowries and ivory are sparse. One letter from an India trader in ʿAydhab

[80] Dimashqī, *Kitāb al-'ashāra*, p. 58.
[81] Goitein, *Mediterranean Society*, I, p. 154.
[82] On Catalan pearls see Bakrī, *Description*, p. 129.
[83] Bodl b3.20 and TS 12.373.

to his son in Alexandria, dated 1141, contained an inventory and instructions regarding a cargo of eastern goods sent to Egypt, and added, "as to the cowrie shells, if you think it best, send them [for sale] in al-Andalus."[84] A year or two earlier, ca. 1138, Halfōn b. Nethanel had received a letter from a colleague in Muslim Spain, which noted in the margin that somebody had "bought ivory at five dirhams [per ounce?]."[85] Ivory most likely entered the Mediterranean commercial sphere from East Africa by way of Red Sea traffic.[86] There is no question that the material was available in al-Andalus, as shown by the beautiful carved ivory boxes and other pieces preserved in modern museums.

The flow of gold and silver was related to mine locations, but high demand pressed even poor quality lodes into production and multiplied the routes of trade. Gold reached the Mediterranean world from several different regions, but the mines of the western Sudan (now the region of modern Senegal, Burkina Faso, southern Mali, and western Niger) provided by far the most famous and productive source. West African exports generated an overall north-westward flow of gold into the Maghrib, the Iberian peninsula, Europe, and the eastern Mediterranean. Particularly in the twelfth century, when the gold routes were largely controlled by the Almoravid and Almohad dynasties, Andalusi ports played an important role in the diffusion of raw gold and gold coinage to other Mediterranean regions. In contrast to the scarcity of gold-producing regions, silver was more widely available, particularly in the eastern Mediterranean. Regions of origin have been used to explain the flow of gold and silver in medieval Mediterranean trade, since precious metals (like other commodities) tend to move from areas of lesser value to those of greater value. Thus gold moved eastward by way of termini in the western Mediterranean, while silver moved westward.[87]

[84] BM Or5566 D6. Also, Goitein, *Letters*, pp. 197–201.

[85] TS 13 J 18.19.

[86] M. Horton, "The Swahili Corridor," *Scientific American* (Sept. 1987), pp. 86–7; and A. Cutler, *The Craft of Ivory: Sources, Techniques, and Uses in the Mediterranean World, AD 200–1400*. [Washington, DC, 1985], pp. 30–5.

[87] A. Watson, "Back to Gold – and Silver," *Economic History Review* 20(1967), pp. 1–34.

Ceramics

Evidence for the diffusion of medieval ceramics, whether through trade or other means, is distinct from that of other commodities owing to the important role that archeology and art history have played in their analysis. Because ceramics were so widely produced, art historians, particularly, have been active in tracing individual stylistic developments and, together with archeologists, in working up a chronology and typology of Mediterranean wares. In several respects, ceramics uniquely lend themselves to this type of investigation. First, they tend to be stylistically distinct by region; second, a geographical assignment made on the basis of style can often be cross-checked through chemical analysis of clay type;[88] third, ceramics survive well over time, and their physical preservation makes them useful in dating – or being themselves dated by – the milieu in which they are found. Added to these three, and of special concern for this study, is the fact that ceramics were easily and widely traded. Although a certain number of pieces may have moved through gift or other means, the large-scale diffusion of ceramics almost certainly indicates commercial traffic. By and large, dishes and jars were pretty and popular, but too cheap, utilitarian, and breakable to have been of much value for tribute, booty, or other payment. If they moved at all, they moved primarily through trade.

Al-Andalus produced and exported ceramics, as will be discussed in the following chapter, but imported ceramics also arrived from other areas of the Islamic world and beyond. Shards of what appear to be tenth-century Chinese pottery (Sung Dynasty, 960–1279), have been excavated in Cordoba and Almeria. Whether these ceramics had really come all the way from China or, as has also been suggested, they were Persian imitations, they had certainly traveled far from their kilns.[89] In a

[88] J. Hurst cited the fact that an Italian scholar, T. Mannoni, has classified several distinctive clay sources in the western Mediterranean that are identifiable by microscope or even by eye ("Spanish Pottery Imported into Medieval England," *Medieval Archeology* 21(1977), p. 72).

[89] J. Zozaya, "El comercio de al-Andalus con el Oriente: nuevos datos," *Boletín de la asociación española de orientalistas* 5(1969), pp. 197–9; J. Zozaya, "Cerámicas islámicas del Museo de Soria," *Boletín de la asociación española de orientalistas* 11(1975), pp. 143–4; D. Whitehouse, "Chinese Porcelain in Medieval Europe," *Medieval Archeology* 16(1972), p. 69.

less spectacular transfer, there is also considerable archeological evidence to show that Fatimid Egyptian and Maghribi ceramics were available in al-Andalus.[90] Westward traffic in ceramics is also documented, as in a Geniza letter that referred to a shipment of pottery [*mukhfiyāt*], probably of Maghribi origin, which an Egyptian merchant had sold in al-Andalus in about 1137.[91]

The five categories discussed above (spices, textiles, foodstuffs, metals and gems, and ceramics) cannot do justice to the range of commodities traded across the medieval Mediterranean world, but they give an idea of the variety of goods available to Andalusi traders and consumers. Merchants also trafficked in other types of commodities, including furs, leather, animals, slaves, and timber. These will be discussed in chapter 7, together with other major Andalusi exports, and in chapter 8, which examines the changes and continuities in Iberian trade after 1212.

[90] J. Zozaya, "Aperçu général sur la céramique espagnole" La *céramique médiévale en Méditerranée occidentale.* [Paris, 1980], pp. 273–4; M. Jenkins, "Medieval Maghribi Ceramics. A Reappraisal of the Pottery Production of the Western Regions of the Muslim world." [Ph.D. Dissertation, New York University, 1978], p. 130; G. Rosselló Bordoy, "Un ataifor norteafricano: un ensayo de interpretación iconográfica," *Sharq al-Andalus* 2(1985), p. 194.

[91] TS 13 J 27.17. Writing from al-Andalus to a partner in Egypt, the writer mentioned that he was sending "the price of the *mukhfiyāt*." I understand this to mean that this item had been brought to al-Andalus, and sold. These ceramics probably came from Ifriqiya, since Dozy cited other Maghribi instances of the word *mukhfiya* (*Supplément aux dictionaires arabes.* [Leiden, 1881] I, p. 387). Goitein, however, interpreted traffic in the other direction, and noted that *mukhfiyāt* was a western product (*Mediterranean Society*, I, p. 111).

Chapter 7

ANDALUSI EXPORTS BEFORE 1212

Just as Andalusi markets received goods from all over the Mediterranean world and beyond, Andalusi exports were equally widely disseminated. Poets in Baghdad wrote verses in praise of delicious Malagan figs, while French troubadours wove references to rich and costly Almerian silks into their lyrics. The spectrum of Andalusi exports encompassed a broad range of commodities. Some were rare luxury items (such as ambergris), while others were more common and utilitarian (olive oil and cumin); some were raw materials (floss silk, hides, and copper), others were created by highly skilled craftspeople (silk textiles, cordoban leather, and copper vessels); some were produced within the peninsula (timber and figs), while others were transferred from one place to another via Andalusi emporia (furs, gold, and slaves).

The nature and variety of these Andalusi exports remained stable throughout the period of Muslim rule. Goods that had been exported during the Umayyad period generally continued to be exported under Taifa and Berber rule, indicating that internal politics had little effect on Andalusi production. Certain exports only came to prominence in the post-Umayyad period, however, and styles varied over time. In contrast to these centuries of relative continuity in production, the period of Christian conquests from 1212 to 1248 marked a dramatic turning point for Iberian trade. This chapter will survey the major Andalusi exports before this economic and political watershed, looking first at indigenous Andalusi exports, then at goods passing through Andalusi markets in transit to more distant destinations.

COMMODITIES OF ANDALUSI PRODUCTION AND EXPORT

Spices

Despite references to Andalusi cumin and caraway, the peninsula exported no culinary spices to match the value or volume of eastern imports such as pepper or cinnamon. The same was true for aromatics, with the exception of ambergris, a waxy grey secretion from the sperm whale which was employed both in medieval cooking and perfumery. Almost every medieval geographer describing al-Andalus marveled at the ambergris found along the peninsula's western Atlantic coast, claiming that the quality of this substance was "not found elsewhere in the inhabited world." Santarem was a source of "extremely good ambergris in great quantities," and the coast of Lisbon was rich in "the same wonderful ambergris as that of India."[1] Not every critic agreed with this comparison, yet Andalusi ambergris predominated in Mediterranean markets and commanded a substantial price that increased as the product traveled eastward. In the tenth century, Masʿūdī remarked that an ounce of western ambergris fetched one third of a dinar in Cordoba, but an ounce of the same "in Baghdad and likewise in Egypt [went for] ten dinars, [even though] this ambergris is of inferior quality."[2] In defense of western ambergris, Bakrī claimed that the ambergris of Sidonia was the best in the world, and a single dirham's worth was equal to several times that amount of the imported variety.[3] Ambergris does not appear frequently in the Geniza corpus, but one letter mentioned the transfer of a parcel of the

[1] L. Molina (ed. and trans.), *Una Descripción anónima de al-Andalus.* [Madrid, 1983] I, p. 13; *Ḥudūd al-ʿālam: "The Regions of the World", A Persian Geography.* [ed. V. Minorsky, London 1970], p. 156; Yāqūt, *Muʿjam al-buldān.* (*Jacut's Geographisches Worterbuch.*) [ed. F. Wüstenfeld, Leipzig, 1873], I, pp. 274, 343. There are also similar comments in Iṣṭakhrī, *Kitāb al-masālik wa al-mamālik.* [ed. M.J. de Goeje, *BGA*, 2nd edn, I, Leiden, 1967], p. 42, and Rāzī, "La 'Description de l'Espagne' d'Aḥmad al-Rāzī" [ed. E. Lévi-Provençal], *Al-Andalus* 18(1953), p. 91.

[2] Masʿūdī, *Murūj al-dhahab* [*Les praires d'or*]. [ed. C. Barbier de Meynard, Paris, 1861], p. 366.

[3] Bakrī, *Masālik wa al-mamālik.* [ed. A.A. al-Ḥajjī, Beirut, 1968], pp. 125,127; also Molina, *Descripción anónima*, I, p. 13.

perfume from Fez to Egypt ca. 1110.[4]

A similar competitive situation between eastern and western products prevailed in the Mediterranean dye industry, where dyers might choose eastern indigo and brazilwood, or western qirmiz and saffron. Qirmiz was the primary dye-stuff produced in and exported from Muslim Spain, and ʿUdhrī claimed that "the crimson of Seville is better than the Indian variety."[5] Qirmiz came from a beetle (*coccum ilicis*) native to the Iberian peninsula, southern Europe, North Africa, and Greece, which could be dried, crushed, and mixed with water to extract its color. The dye-stuff was called *granum* in Latin because the dry product usually came in the form of granules. The value of qirmiz derived from its ability to produce a variety of colors according to the mordant used with it; its range extending from a bright scarlet to violet or yellow. This versatility made it popular, but its fame was based on the wonderful crimson "which no [other] red can surpass."[6] The color took best when applied to textiles of animal origin, such as silk and wool, since, as Ibn al-Bayṭār observed, linen, cotton, and other vegetable fibers did not hold the dye so well.[7]

According to Bakrī, "the best qirmiz is Andalusi qirmiz, and most of it comes from the regions of Seville, Niebla, Sidonia, and Valencia. From al-Andalus, it is exported to foreign lands."[8] Its trade in the western Mediterranean is attested to by the Geniza, as in a letter from the middle of the eleventh century requesting a shipment of qirmiz from al-Andalus to Tunisia, whence it may have been traded to Egypt. Andalusi qirmiz certainly reached the eastern Mediterranean, as indicated by another letter written to Egypt by a woman in Jerusalem in the 1050s, ordering five pounds of *Shadhūna* qirmiz (from Sidonia).[9] Andalusi qirmiz was also traded to Europe, perhaps as early as

4 Bodl d66.52.

5 ʿUdhrī, "Nuṣūṣ ʿan al-Andalus," *Tarḍīʿ al-akhbār wa tanwīʿal-'āthār.* [ed. A.A. al-Ahwānī, Madrid, 1960], p. 96. The Iberian Peninsula exported qirmiz long before the Arab period, and Pliny commented on its production near Merida (*Natural History.* [ed. H. Rackham, Cambridge, Mass., 1983] Book IX, lxv, p. 258).

6 Maqqarī, *Analectes sur l'histoire et la littérature des arabes d'Espagne.* [ed. R. Dozy, Leiden, 1855–60] I, p. 123.

7 M. Lombard, *Les textiles dans le monde musulman du VIIe au XIIe siècle.* [Paris, 1978], p. 119; Ibn al-Bayṭār, "Traité des simples" [trans. L. LeClerc], *Notices et extraits des manuscrits de la Bibliothéque Nationale* 26(1883), p. 74.

8 Bakrī, *Masālik*, p. 127.

9 ULC Or1080 J 77; TS 13 J 6.22.

the Carolingian period when Notker cited "purple dye-stuffs from Spain."[10] Andalusi qirmiz, mainly from Valencia and Murcia, was available in Christian Spain by the twelfth century, when it appears in tariff lists from the Ebro region.[11] A later reference to *zafri de grana* in a 1207 tariff list from Toledo shows that the dye was used in Castile for a yellow as well as a red colorant.[12] Genoese contracts also mentioned Andalusi crimson. One notary mentioned a shipment of *grane de Ispania* destined for sale in Lucca in 1192, and another parcel of unspecified crimson in the same year.[13]

Saffron was another prominent Andalusi export, although once again some authors considered it inferior to eastern varieties. Unlike qirmiz, saffron was not widely produced in the Iberian peninsula before the Arab period, but Andalusi geographers and agronomists refer to its extensive cultivation and export by the tenth century. Rāzī, for one, claimed that Valencia "produced enough to supply all of al-Andalus, and merchants carry it to other regions of the world."[14] In the following century, Toledan saffron was "found all over the country and exported abroad" as was that of Seville and Guadalajara, while Shaqundī, Yāqūt, and other later writers noted that the saffron of Baeza was "exported over land and sea" as "the best variety, appreciated and recognized throughout the Maghrib."[15] Andalusi saffron probably also found its way into European markets by way of Genoa, for Giovanni Scriba wrote out a contract for the transport of saffron

[10] Notker the Stammerer, *De Carlo Magno*. [ed. P. Jaffé, *Monumenta carolina*, IV, *Bibliotheca rerum germanicarum*, Berlin, 1867], p. 677. Notker's reference to *ferrugine Hibera* may have been loosely borrowed from Virgil, in which case it bears no relation to ninth-century trade (see L. Thorpe, *Two Lives of Charlemagne*. [London, 1969], p. 196, n. 89).

[11] M. Gual Camarena, "Peaje fluvial del Ebro (siglo XII)," *Estudios de la edad media de la Corona de Aragón* 8(1967), p. 184.

[12] F.J. Hernández, "Las Cortes de Toledo de 1207," *Las Cortes de Castilla y León en la edad media*. [Valladolid, 1988], pp. 240,254.

[13] *Guglielmo Cassinese [1190–1192]*. [eds. M. Hall, H.C. Krueger, R.L. Reynolds, Turin, 1938] II, p. 235,#1700. D. Abulafia suggests that the second reference to *carrico grani* (II, p. 223,#1668) also referred to Spanish crimson (D. Abulafia, *The Two Italies: Economic Relations between the Norman Kingdom of Sicily and the Northern Communes*. [Cambridge, 1977], p. 200).

[14] Rāzī, "Description," p. 72. Also, *Le Calendrier de Cordoue*. [ed. R. Dozy, new edn. C. Pellat, Leiden, 1961], pp. 172–3.

[15] Bakrī, *Masālik*, p. 88; 'Udhrī, "Nuṣūṣ," p. 96; Idrīsī, *Opus geographicum*. v, [Naples-Rome, 1975] p. 553; Shaqundī, in Maqqarī, *Analectes*, II, p. 146; Yāqūt, *Mu'jam*, I, p. 773.

and coral (both very likely of Andalusi origin) from Genoa to Alexandria in 1156.[16]

Textiles

Although spices were the proverbial mainstay of general Mediterranean trade, textiles and textile fibers were far more important to the Andalusi economy. Silk predominated, although flax, wool, and cotton also commanded a small share of trade. Silk worms, and the knowledge of their care and use, probably reached the Iberian peninsula in the eighth century, having arrived in the Mediterranean world from China, by way of Sassanian Persia and Byzantium. The regions of Mediterranean silk cultivation may be roughly traced along a line somewhat below 40° north latitude (just south of Naples, Madrid, and Istanbul), particularly in mountainous regions, including the Andalusi Sierra Nevada, where mulberry trees flourished.[17]

Three factors were generally necessary for the success of the silk industry. First, the mulberry trees on which to feed the silk worms; second, the human technical skills required to handle the silk; and third, sufficient numbers of people involved in the business to maintain viable levels of production. These requirements limited the silk industry geographically and rendered it susceptible to climatic and demographic fluctuations, but it thrived in al-Andalus for most of the Muslim period. Silk was already produced in the peninsula during the eighth and ninth centuries, but the industry reached its height under Taifa, Almoravid, and Almohad rule.[18] Idrīsī counted as many as three thousand farms raising silk worms in the mountains around Jaen in the middle of the twelfth century, and Shaqundī labeled this region "Jaen of the silk" because so many people, both in the city and countryside, were involved in the silk trade.[19] We

[16] Giovanni Scriba, *Cartolare di Giovanni Scriba.* [eds. M. Chiaudano, M. Moresco, Rome, 1935] I, p. 56, 105. For a brief discussion of the later medieval saffron trade in Europe, see L. Bardenhewer, *Der Safranhandel im Mittelalter.* [Bonn, 1914].

[17] Lombard, *Textiles*, p. 79; Some mulberries, and thus silk worms, also grew further north, but did not do so well.

[18] E. Morral i Romeu and A. Segura i Mas, *La seda en España: Leyenda, poder, y realidad.* [Barcelona, 1991], p. 62. See also section devoted to Andalusi textile manufacture in J. Vallvé, "La industria en al-Andalus," *Al-Qantara* 1(1980), pp. 225–36.

[19] Idrīsī, *Opus*, v, p. 568; Shaqundī, in Maqqarī, *Analectes*, II, p. 146.

know most about the silk industry in Almeria, where Idrīsī reported eight hundred workshops devoted to the production of silks and brocaded fabrics adorned with stripes and other patterns.[20] Zuhrī also lavished praise on this city's textile industry, reporting that "nothing is hidden from any of the craftspeople here . . . in Almeria, every type of elegant furnishing is manufactured, and everything is perfectly made. All the people here, men and women, work with their hands; the most frequent craft of women is spinning, which brings silk to its high price, and the most frequent craft among men is weaving." Later writers echoed these reports.[21] The high numbers cited by Idrīsī suggest that silk production was a cottage industry, both at the level of cultivation and later textile manufacture. Many people would have been involved, and even children were useful because their small fingers were better at unwinding the delicate filaments from the silk cocoons.[22] Because mulberries did well at high altitudes where snow often blocked mountain passes during the winter, the silk trade was seasonal. Most of the silk yield came to port cities between June and September, coinciding with summer shipping schedules.[23] In order to facilitate this exchange, merchants would frequently contract in advance for silk, as shown in a sample contract provided by the jurist Fihrī, for an advance sale of spun silk.[24]

Medieval Arabic authors refer to numerous varieties of raw silk or silk thread, with gradations dependent both on the original quality of the silk and on the care with which the delicate fibre was handled. Among the most common commercial categories for raw silk, were *ibrīsim* (high quality raw silk), *ḥarīr* (raw silk thread), *khazz* (lower quality floss silk), *lasīn* (waste silk), *iltiqāṭ* (thread woven from waste silk, literally 'pick-

[20] Idrīsī, *Opus*, v, p. 562.

[21] Zuhrī, "Kitāb al-dja'rāfiyya" [ed. M. Hadj-Sadok], *Bulletin des études orientales* 21(1968), pp. 205–6. See also Yāqūt, *Mu'jam*, iv, p. 517; and later citations in Ḥimyarī, *La Péninsule ibérique au moyen âge d'après le "Kitāb ar-rawḍ al-mi'ṭār fī habar al-akhtār*. [ed. and trans. E. Lévi-Provençal, Leiden, 1938], p. 184, and Maqqarī, *Analectes*, i, p. 102.

[22] In order to obtain the silk fibre, the cocoon was briefly immersed in boiling water to loosen the filaments, then an individual thread could be gently unwound to produce the highest quality silk. If the cocoon were damaged or the fibers tangled, the broken filaments could be spun together to create a lower quality thread.

[23] R. Arié, *La España musulmana*. [Barcelona, 1982], p. 250.

[24] Fihrī, *Watha'iq wa al-masā'il al-majmū'a min kutub al-fuqahā*. [Miguel Asín Institute, CSIC, Madrid, ms. 11], fol. 18v.

ups' or 'scraps'). Woven textiles were also specified by type, with names such as *dibāj, siqlāṭūn, washī,* and *'attābī.*[25]

The Geniza corpus abounds in documents relating to sales of Andalusi raw silk in the central and eastern Mediterranean during the eleventh and twelfth centuries. One commercial order sent from Egypt to Tunisia in the mid-eleventh century asked that the recipient buy some "*lasīn* silk from Isma'īl al-Andalusī, or fine Andalusi pick-ups," and a young Nahray b. Nissīm may have made a similar request in the 1040s, since a partner in Ifriqiya told him to expect "a parcel containing . . . [among other things] twelve pounds, less one third, of Andalusi silk pick-ups."[26] Later letters, from the 1060s–1070s, mentioned Andalusi ships and merchants arriving in Alexandria with silk that had come directly from al-Andalus without a Tunisian intermediary.[27] This pattern continued into the twelfth century, when an Egyptian factor was entrusted with gold for the express purpose of purchasing Andalusi silk (ca. 1110). Another letter, written in 1138, concerned eastern merchants arriving in Almeria bringing lac, frankincense, and brazilwood to trade for Andalusi silk.[28] On the Egyptian end, we find local merchants fretting over the price and availability of Andalusi silk. A Geniza merchant writing from Alexandria in 1119 lamented that

As to silk, when the Andalusi ship arrived, all business was at a standstill; no one sold and no one bought. Afterwards, small quantities were traded at the price of 21–22 (dinars) per ten (pounds). Later on, when no other ships came, there was a demand for silk, but those who had it held back from selling. . .not a single ship has arrived from the west, and no news about ships has come through; in addition, the winds are unfavorable, they are neither east nor west winds. This very day people have offered 23 dinars for [ten pounds of] coarse silk, but no one wanted to sell. Everyone is refraining from selling until the situation clears up.[29]

This letter may be compared with a number of similar docu-

[25] For more on silk varieties, see S.D. Goitein, *A Mediterranean Society.* [Berkeley, 1967–88] IV, pp. 167–69.

[26] TS 12.389; Bodl b3.19.

[27] ENA NS 2.13; TS 10 J 16.17.

[28] Bodl d66.52; TS 12.285.

[29] TS 13 J 22.30; translation (with minor changes) from Goitein, *Mediterranean Society,* I, p. 303.

ments relating to the fluctuations in the silk market, and the cited prices are relatively low. By comparison, another Egyptian letter, probably from the 1060s, stated that ten pounds of Andalusi *khazz* silk were going for 25–6 dinars, whereas an 1140 price list from Alexandria listed *khazz* at 36–9 (dinars), probably for a ten pound quantity.[30] Andalusi raw silk also found a market in Christian lands, as shown in the twelfth-century *Fuero* of Cuenca, for example, which stated tolls to be paid on a *libra serici* (almost certainly imported from al-Andalus).[31] Early thirteenth-century records from Montpellier showed similar duties due on each *libra de seda Yspanie* entering the city, while a contemporary Genoese contract (dated 1225) referred to one hundred and eighty and one half pounds of Spanish silk (*sete de Yspania*).[32]

Andalusi woven textiles and items of clothing were widely disseminated throughout the Islamic world from as early as the ninth century, when the Jewish Rādhānite merchants carried western brocades to other regions of the Mediterranean.[33] A century later, Ibn Ḥawqal extolled the "precious garments of linen, cotton, and silk" that were available in Umayyad Cordoba, and reported that Andalusi silks were sent to Egypt and even as far as Khurasan.[34] His contemporary, Muqaddasī, noted that many wonderful and specialized fabrics originated in al-Andalus, while Rāzī (writing at about the same time) claimed that Zaragoza produced precious textiles that were famous throughout the world.[35] In the middle of the next century, a commercial order sent from Tunisia to al-Andalus in the 1050s requested (among other things) fifty mantles, ten pairs of stockings, and "two cloaks of sea wool . . . faced with green and red

[30] ENA NS 2.13; TS 10 J 10.23.

[31] Hernández, "Cortes de Toledo," p. 250.

[32] A. Germain (ed.), *Liber instrumentorum memorialium. Cartulaire des Guillems de Montpellier.* [Montpellier, 1884–6], p. 438; ASG, Cart.16/II, fol. 23v.

[33] Ibn Khurradādhbih, *Kitāb al-masālik wa al-mamālik.* [ed. M.J. de Goeje, *BGA*, 2nd edn, VI, Leiden, 1967], p. 153.

[34] Ibn Ḥawqal, *Kitāb ṣurat al-arḍ.* [ed. J.H. Kramers, Leiden, 1938], pp. 110,113,114.

[35] Muqaddasī, *Description de l'occident musulman.* [ed. C. Pellat, Paris, 1950], p. 48; Rāzī, "Description," p. 78. For more on Andalusi woven silks, see F. May, *Silk Textiles of Spain.* [New York, 1957], pp. 1–55, and the text and bibliography in C. Partearroyo, "Almoravid and Almohad Textiles," *Al-Andalus: The Art of Islamic Spain.* [ed. J.D. Dodds, New York, 1992], pp. 105–13.

silk."[36] A similar list, written about ten years later, mentioned a purchase of eighty-five "Andalusi cloaks."[37] Late in the same century, a coppersmith in Egypt was recorded as having "a new Spanish robe, a raw [unfulled] Spanish robe" and ten other "Spanish raw robes" in his possession, either for his own use or for resale.[38] Another letter from Egypt, probably from about this period, mentioned the purchase of garments from Mallorca.[39] In the twelfth century, Idrīsī produced a long list of luxurious silks and brocades exported from Almeria, and Shaqundī (writing 1199–1212) reported that "Valencian brocade was exported to all regions of the Maghrib."[40] Andalusi silks may also have penetrated markets even further east by the twelfth century, since Zuhrī claimed that India imported "costly whole garments of silk brocade" from the land of al-Andalus.[41] In confirmation of this claim, two Geniza letters from the same period mentioned textiles made in, or in the style of, Manara (near Seville), traded between Aden and India.[42]

Andalusi fabrics also made their way into the Christian world through trade and other means. References to "Spanish" textiles (probably of Andalusi manufacture, since Christian Spain was not producing many luxury fabrics in this period) already appear in European Latin sources during the early ninth century, when Louis the Pious presented precious fabrics, including a Spanish

[36] ULC Or1080 J.77; also Goitein, *Mediterranean Society*, IV, pp. 181–2. Sea wool (*ṣūf al-baḥr*) occasionally appeared in geographers' inventories and merchants' letters. It was a fine and pliant fibre produced by mollusks, although medieval geographers were frequently confused regarding its exact source. Sometimes it was mistaken for sable or seal fur, at others merely described as the product of a mysterious sea animal. Iṣṭakhrī, for example, wrote of a marine creature that emerged once a year from the sea near Santarem, and rubbed itself on the rocks leaving behind a soft, golden, silky substance which could be woven into garments. These garments, he continued, were only exported in limited quantities, since their production was under government control, and they could cost up to one thousand dinars (Iṣṭakhrī, *Masālik wa al-mamālik*, p. 42). Andalusi production is also attested by the fact that the regent Manṣūr dispatched twenty-one pieces of sea wool as diplomatic gifts in the late tenth century (Maqqarī, *Analectes*, I, p. 271).

[37] TS 24.40.

[38] ENA 1822.46; trans. Goitein, *Mediterranean Society*, IV, p. 339. Goitein generally used the term "Spanish" to translate "Andalusi."

[39] TS 13 J 19.1.

[40] Maqqarī, *Analectes*, II, p. 149.

[41] Zuhrī, "Kitāb al-dja'rāfiyya," p. 276.

[42] ULC Or1080 J 95; TS 24.66. These *fuwat manārī* may, of course, be eastern imitations of Andalusi textiles.

coverlet (*stragulum hispanicum*), to the Abbey of St. Wandrille ca. 823. His son, Charles the Bald, received a variety of textiles (*diversi generis pannis*) as a gift from Cordoba in 865.[43] Likewise, fourteen pieces of Spanish cloth woven with silver thread (*vela cum argento spanisca*) were cited among the ecclesiastical donations of Pope Gregory IV (827–44), while a number of other *vela de spanisco* were presented to different churches during the pontificate of Leo IV (847–55).[44]

References to Andalusi textiles in Christian lands are infrequent in texts from the tenth and eleventh centuries. Perhaps Andalusi ateliers in this period were more devoted to the production of royal *ṭirāz* and fabrics intended for export to the *dār al-Islām*. Nevertheless, a few Andalusi textiles appear in charters from Amalfi and Naples dating to the early eleventh century, and they are also found in Christian Spanish records from this period, including references to *genabes mauriscos* in documents from Leon.[45] By the end of the century, inhabitants of the northern peninsula enjoyed Muslim textiles both of Andalusi and eastern manufacture, since Andalusi markets provided a convenient channel of access to goods from all over the Islamic world. Thus, the "very splendid fabrics of silk worked with gold" (*muy ricos pannos de seda labrados en oro*) that adorned the Cid in the late eleventh century may have been Andalusi products, but the *buenos çendales d'Andria* (Alexandria) that he wore in a ceremonial procession were probably eastern imports that had come to Castile through Andalusi commercial channels.[46]

In contrast to this paucity of references from before the twelfth century, Christian sources document an explosion of interest in Andalusi textiles after ca. 1100. This wealth of data may reflect an increased output from Andalusi ateliers under Almoravid and

[43] *Gesta sanctorum patrum Fontanellis coenobii*. XIII.4 [eds. F. Lohier and J. Laporte, Rouen-Paris, 1936], p. 102. *Annales Bertiniani*. [ed. G. Waitz, *MGH* Scriptores in usum scholarum, Hanover, 1883], p. 80.

[44] *Liber pontificalis*. II [ed. L. Duchesne, Paris, 1955], pp. 75, 107, 122, 128.

[45] Two Spanish *pallia* appeared on a list of items belonging to a monastery (probably in Amalfi) in 1019 (L.A. Muratori, *Antiquitates italicae medii aevi sive dissertationes*. [Rome, 1741], p. 770). Two years later, *duas flectas spaniscas* were mentioned in a Naples charter (ed. B. Capasso, *Monumenta ad neapolitani ducatus historiam pertinentia*. [Naples, 1881–92] II.1, p. 252, #402). On Leonese examples, see C. Sánchez-Albornoz, *Estampas de la vida en León durante el siglo X*. [Madrid, 1934], p. 19; also "El precio de la vida en el reino de Astur-Leonés hace mil años," *Logos* 3(1944), p. 232.

[46] (Alfonso X), *Primera crónica general de España*. [ed. R. Menéndez Pidal, Madrid, 1906 (reprint 1977)], p. 616; *Cantar de mío Cid*. [ed. R. Menéndez Pidal, trans. W.S. Merwin, New York, 1975], pp. 180–1.

Almohad rule, as well as contemporary European commercial expansion and new consumption of luxury goods. French romances from this period are filled with references to precious Andalusi fabrics woven in Almeria (*pailes d'Aumarie, cendals d'Aumarie, mantel d'Aumarie*, and *soie d'Aumarie*), together with *drap de Mulce* (Murcia) and *siglatons d'Espagne*.[47] These literary allusions are supported in other sources, showing that Christian listeners and consumers were perfectly familiar with Andalusi textiles. In 1190, for instance, the English traveler Roger of Hoveden mentioned *pannos de serico de Almaria* sent to the Crown of Aragon from the Balearics, and he explained as he passed Almeria that this was the city in which "the noble and fine silk called *sericum de Almaria* is produced."[48] There is also physical evidence of Almerian textiles in twelfth-century Europe, since a chasuble associated with Thomas Becket, now preserved in the Cathedral of Fermo, bears an Arabic inscription to the effect that it was woven in Almeria in 510 AH/1116 AD.[49] Genoese notarial contracts also show that Andalusi textiles were available in Italian markets. Giovanni Scriba wrote a contract for shipment of ten pieces (bolts?) of "Spanish" cloth (*tela Yspanie*) in 1161, and a later contract, written out by Oberto Scriba in 1186, noted six textiles from Granada (*panni de Granata*), four

[47] Among French romances citing Andalusi textiles see Richard the Pilgrim, *Chanson d'Antioche, composée au XIIe siècle par Richard le pèlerin*. [ed. L. de Sainte-Aulaire, Paris, 1862] "étoffes d'Almerie" (p. 16); *Aye d'Avignon. Chanson de Geste*. (late twelfth century) [eds. F. Guessard and P. Meyer, Paris, 1861] "paile vermeill d'amoravine" (p. 7), "porpre d'Aumarie" (p. 29); Bertrand de Bar-sur-Aube (fl. ca. 1220), *Girart de Vienne*. [ed. W. van Emden, Paris, 1977] "tirez et pailes et soie d'Aumarie" (p. 113), "soie d'Aumarie" (p. 200), "paile d'Aumarie" (p. 207), "soie d'Aumarie" (p. 273); Lambert Li Tort, *Li Romans d'Alixandre*. [ed. H. Michelant, Stuttgart, 1846] "siglatons d'Espagne ... pales d'Aumarie" (p. 4), "soie d'Aumarie" (p. 119), "pale de soie d'Aumarie" (p. 532); *Raoul de Cambrai. Chanson de Geste*. [eds. P. Meyer and A. Longnon, Paris, 1882] "mantel d'Aumarie" and "soie d'Aumarie" (p. 277). Similar references from a number of unpublished manuscripts have been collected by F.X. Michel, *Recherches sur le commerce, la fabrication et l'usage des étoffes de soie, d'or et d'argent, et autres tissus précieux en occident, principalement en France, pendant le moyen âge*. [Paris, 1852–4] I, pp. 232–3, 258, 285–6, 294–5.

[48] Roger of Hoveden, *Chronica*. [ed. W. Stubbs, London, 1868–71] III, pp. 48, 51. Stubbs noted that Roger may have taken the reference to *pannos de serico* from the work of so-called Benedict of Peterborough and added *de Almaria*.

[49] F. Gabrieli and U. Scerrato (eds.), *Gli arabi in Italia, Cultura, contatti e tradizioni*. [Milan, 1979], facing p. 481. Scerrato did not elaborate on the association with Becket, nor did he report on how this textile reached Fermo. Perhaps this chasuble came to Becket among royal gifts of *pannos sericos* mentioned in an 1170 letter to the archbishop from Cardinal Theodwin (*Recueil des historiens des Gaules et de la France*. XVI [Paris, 1878], p. 445E).

green and two brown.[50] Other contracts, from 1200, 1224, and 1238 mentioned *cendates* (or *cendal*), a variety of fine silk cloth.[51]

While other regions of Europe were discovering the delights of Andalusi fabrics, Christian Spain continued to enjoy imports of luxury and everyday textiles from the Muslim south during the twelfth and thirteenth centuries. Tolls were collected along the Ebro River on a number of apparently southern items, including *alquiceles* (capes or cloaks) and *albernochs* (a type of hooded cloak).[52] The 1162 *fuero* for the town of Mos set a toll on "robes coming from the land of the Moors."[53] In a more domestic setting, Mozarabic wills from twelfth-century Toledo mentioned Andalusi articles of clothing, and Valencian fustians appear in an inventory of household effects from Zaragoza in the mid-twelfth century.[54] In 1207, the Cortes of Toledo set tariffs on *cendal* imported from Murcia.[55] In addition to these documentary references, examples of surviving fabrics found in the royal tombs at the monastery of Santa Maria la Real de las Huelgas in Burgos, and elsewhere in Christian Spain, testify to the diffusion of Almoravid, Almohad, and Nasrid fabrics in the northern peninsula.[56]

Woven and knotted carpets, made of silk or wool, constituted another significant Andalusi textile export. Like ceramics, these items were produced throughout the Mediterranean world, but their utility and beauty and the variety of their regional styles fueled international trade. Ibn Ḥawqal praised the woolen carpets made in al-Andalus in the tenth century, and an inventory of goods belonging to ʿAbd al-Raḥmān III included silken rugs together with "thirty carpets (*bisāṭ*) of pure wool, of many different colors and types, each one of which was twenty cubits

[50] Giovanni Scriba, *Cartolare*, II, p. 4, #812; *Oberto Scriba de Mercato [1186]*. [ed. M. Chaiudano, Genoa, 1940], p. 98, #263.

[51] ASG Cart.4, fol.171r; Cart.16/II, fol.14v; Cart.11, fols.185r-186v.

[52] Gual Camarena, "Peaje," p. 167.

[53] *Portugaliae monumenta historica: leges et consuetudines*. [Lisbon, 1856] I, p. 391.

[54] A. González Palencia, *Los mozárabes de Toledo en los siglos XII y XIII*. [Madrid, 1926–8] III, pp. 381, 391–2; J.M. Lacarra, *Documentos para el estudio de la reconquista y repoblación del Valle del Ebro*. [Zaragoza, 1946–52], p. 651, #280. It is possible that this latter fabric was from the Flemish center of Valenciennes rather than Valencia.

[55] Hernández, "Cortes de Toledo," p. 241.

[56] M. Gómez-Moreno, *El Panteón real de las Huelgas de Burgos*. [Madrid, 1946]; C. Herrero Carretero, *Museo de telas medievales: Monasterio de Santa María la Real de Huelgas*. [Madrid, 1988]; J. Dodds (ed.), *Al-Andalus: The Art of Islamic Spain*. pp. 105–13, 224–30, 318–41.

(*dhirā'*) in length."[57] Andalusi rugs may already have been made and exported earlier, as suggested in a satirical comment by the Baghdadi author Azdī (ninth century), mocking the lack of "carpets from al-Andalus and Cordoba" in Isfahan.[58] In the next century, 'Udhrī remarked the "marvelous workshops for bedding and carpets" located in Tudmir.[59] Andalusi carpets also turn up in Geniza documents, confirming the praise lavished by geographers. One letter, written ca. 1050, mentioned an Andalusi rug shipped from Tunisia to Egypt, and a commercial order from the same period (also containing the order for the mantles, stockings, and cloaks of sea wool noted above) requested that "two fine runners, newly made, each twenty-four cubits long; four fine white prayer carpets; two dark blue; two green; and two red ones" be sent from al-Andalus. A similar order, sent from Egypt in 1143, requested "an Andalusi runner . . . a small runner, a prayer carpet, and a piece of runner."[60] The export of Andalusi rugs to Egypt in the twelfth century is likewise attested to by Maqrīzī, who described Andalusi carpets at the Fatimid court in 1124.[61] Andalusi rugs also traveled northward to Christian Spain, as shown in a late twelfth-century Mozarab will from Toledo, which listed woolen and silken rugs among the possessions of the deceased.[62]

Foodstuffs

Al-Andalus was famous for its production and export of foodstuffs, notably olive oil and dried fruits, leading the late twelfth-century Andalusi traveler Ibn Jubayr to assert that "concerning foods, fruits, and other good things . . . al-Andalus was especially favored above all other regions" excepting only the Hijaz.[63] Ibn Jubayr was not alone in his admiration, since many other sources

[57] Ibn Ḥawqal, *Kitāb ṣurat al-arḍ*, p. 114; Maqqarī, *Analectes*, I, p. 230.

[58] Abū al-Muṭahhar al-Azdī, *Abulķāsim ein bagdāder Sittenbild*. [ed. A. Mez, Heidelberg, 1902], p. 36.

[59] 'Udhrī, "Nuṣūṣ," p. 9.

[60] TS NS J 128; ULC Or1080 J 77; TS NS J 27. On all three, see Goitein, *Mediterranean Society*, IV, p. 126. Mats, as well as rugs and carpets were exported from al-Andalus, and another commercial order, sent from Fez to Almeria in 1141, requested a shipment of mats from al-Andalus (TS 13 J 21.12).

[61] Maqrīzī, *Mawā'iz wa al-i'tibār bi-dhikr al-khiṭaṭ wa al-'athār*. [Bulaq, 1270/1853–4] I, p. 474. (Passage dated to 518AH/1124–25AD on p. 472).

[62] A. González Palencia, *Los mozárabes de Toledo*, III, pp. 449–50.

[63] Ibn Jubayr, *The Travels of Ibn Jubair*. [trans. R.J.C. Broadhurst, London, 1952], p. 117.

likewise remark on the abundance of Andalusi olive and fruit trees.

Olive oil was a major export from the Iberian peninsula under Roman, Muslim, and Christian rule, and continues to be exported from Spain today. The economic importance of the crop, and the development of extensive olive cultivation in al-Andalus, is demonstrated by the fact that Castilian and Portuguese, unlike other European languages, derive their word for olive oil (*aceite/azeite*) from the Arabic *zayt*, whereas French, Italian, Catalan, English, and even German employ derivatives of the Latin *oleum*.

Arabic geographers and historians were unanimous in their praise of Andalusi olive oil, particularly the oil exported from Seville. The production of this region was so abundant that, during the tenth century, Rāzī claimed that "if Seville could not export its olive oil, it would have so much that it would be impossible to store it, and it would all go to waste."[64] Production and export remained high throughout the Taifa period, when 'Udhrī described the region around Seville as entirely "planted with ancient olive trees . . . the city is blessed (*mubārak*) by their productiveness, for their condition is invariable and not subject to imperfections. [The oil] is exported throughout the land, far and wide . . . and the highest grade pressings are sent to the most distant areas and travel by sea to the east."[65] At roughly the same time, letters written by merchants associated with the trading firm of Ibn 'Awkal also show sales of western olive oil – either from al-Andalus or Ifriqiya – in Egypt.[66] These indications of traffic in Andalusi oil in the eastern Mediterranean disprove the idea, held by some, that Andalusi oil was only traded as far as Morocco under the Umayyad and Taifa regimes.[67]

Evidence for widespread trade in oil increases by the twelfth century, when Idrīsī confirmed that "the people [of Seville] are wealthy and the major portion of their commerce is in olive oil, which is exported from there to the farthest points of the east and west by land and sea. All of the oil comes from [the region]

[64] Rāzī, "Description," p. 93.

[65] 'Udhrī, "Nuṣūṣ," p. 95.

[66] N. Stillman, "The Eleventh-Century Merchant House of Ibn 'Awkal (A Geniza Study)," *JESHO* 16 (1973), p. 66.

[67] See, for example, the maps provided by M. Lombard, *The Golden Age of Islam*. [Oxford, 1975], p. 166.

of Sharaf, and this Sharaf is forty miles distant [from Seville]." Idrīsī also noted that Sevillian merchants brought olive oil by sea to Salé, on the western coast of Morocco, to trade for grain.[68] Following Idrīsī's data, Zuhrī described the productivity of Sharaf in the late twelfth century, and listed "the lands of *Rūm*, the Maghrib, Ifriqiya, Misr, and Alexandria" among those places receiving Sevillian oil. It was even possible, he added, that "a small quantity reaches Yemen."[69] Shaqundī (writing 1199–1212) likewise reported that Seville exported its oil to Alexandria, and this information was supported by a statement of Maimonides (d. 1204) that boats loaded with oil traveled down the Guadalquivir from Seville to the sea, and from there "they frequently went to Alexandria."[70] Christian Spain also received Andalusi oil, and Castilian tariff lists, including an early thirteenth-century *portazgo* from Ocaña, listed duties on "oil which comes from the land of the Moors."[71]

Just as olives could be preserved for long-distance travel through pressing or pickling, fruits could be conserved by drying, sugaring, or cooking into jams. Figs were the best-known Andalusi fruit export, particularly during the Nasrid period when Ibn Baṭṭūṭa described how Malaga figs were "dried in the sun, and packed in reed baskets" for transport.[72] Although citruses were grown in the Iberian peninsula in medieval times, they had not yet attained the international status that the Valencia orange, for example, enjoys today.[73] As with olives, geographers repeatedly cited the marvels of Andalusi fruit production. Ibn Ḥawqal described Seville as a city "with many assets, especially its fruits, vines, and figs," and Zaragoza was later "known throughout the four regions of the world" for "the quality and abundance of its fruits."[74]

According to one Andalusi agronomist, Abū al-Khayr al-

[68] Idrīsī, *Opus*, v, p. 541, and *Opus*, III, [Naples-Rome, 1972] p. 239.

[69] Zuhrī, "Kitāb al-dja'rāfiyya," p. 218.

[70] Shaqundī, in Maqqarī, *Analectes*, II, p. 143; Moses b. Maimon, *Responsa*. [ed. J. Blau, Jerusalem, 1957–61] II, p. 576.

[71] J.L. Martín, "Portazgos de Ocaña y Alarilla," *AHDE* 32 (1962), p. 523.

[72] Ibn Baṭṭūṭa, *The Travels of Ibn Baṭṭūṭa, A.D. 1325–1354*. III [trans. H.A.R. Gibb, Cambridge, 1971], p. 547.

[73] Medieval citruses included lemons, limes, citrons, and sour ("Seville") oranges, but they were not yet an item of international commerce. See A. Watson, *Agricultural Innovation in the Early Islamic World*. [Cambridge, 1983], pp. 42–50.

[74] Ibn Ḥawqal, *Kitāb ṣurat al-arḍ*, p. 115; Ibn al-Shabbāṭ, "Un fragmento de la obra de Ibn al-Sabbāṭ (s. XIII) sobre al-Andalus" [trans. E. de Santiago Simón], *Cuadernos de historia del Islam* 1973, p. 62.

Ishbīlī, the Doñegal fig originally came to the peninsula from Byzantium in the ninth century.[75] However, the peninsula may have produced figs even before this, since an inventory from the French Abbey of Corbie, dated 716, listed one hundred pounds of figs alongside two other likely Iberian exports: cordoban leather and cumin.[76] Figs certainly flourished in al-Andalus by the reign of ʿAbd al-Raḥmān III, who was said to have ordered the shipment of three hundred *qafīz* of figs to North Africa in 936.[77] In the next century, the *Fuero* of Sepulveda (1076) listed a charge levied on *figos troxiere de tierra de moros*.[78] The commercial export of figs is best known from the twelfth century and after, when both Malaga and Seville were renowned for their fig production. Idrīsī and other authors praised the figs of Malaga, while Saqaṭī, the market inspector for this city in the early thirteenth century, described a commercial transaction involving figs from Seville that were "of an extraordinary size and deep black color."[79] At about the same time, Shaqundī claimed that Malagan figs were "sold as far away as Baghdad as something precious and rare."[80] Later, the jurist Ibn Salmūn discussed the hire of a boat to carry one hundred bushels of figs from Seville to Ceuta, and the legal complications arising when the ship was blown off course to Salé. Although Ibn Salmūn wrote in the fourteenth century, the case must have dated from a period prior to the Christian reconquest of Seville, and presumably – in light of its interest to a Muslim judge – pertained to Muslim merchants transporting figs between al-Andalus and the Maghrib.[81]

Al-Andalus also produced grapes, raisins, and wine, although the international export of these items is not well documented

[75] D. Wasserstein, "Byzantium and al-Andalus," *Mediterranean Historical Journal* 2(1987), p. 85.

[76] L. Levillain, *Examen critique des chartes mérovingiennes et carolingiennes de l'abbaye de Corbie.* [Paris, 1902], pp. 235–6. It is also possible that these figs were grown in southern France.

[77] Ibn Ḥayyān, *Muqtabas*, v, [eds. P. Chalmeta, F. Corriente, M. Subḥ, Madrid-Rabat, 1979] p. 389. If J. Vallvé is correct in estimating a *qafīz* at roughly 54–64 pounds, this was an enormous cargo ("Notas de metrología hispano-árabe, II: Medidas de capacidad," *Al-Andalus* 42(1977), pp. 89–94; "Notas de metrología hispano-árabe, III: Pesos y monedas," *Al-Qantara* 5(1984), p. 167).

[78] *Los Fueros de Sepúlveda.* [ed. E. Saez, Segovia, 1953], p. 138.

[79] Idrīsī, *Opus*, v, p. 570; Saqaṭī, *Kitāb al-faqīh al-ajall al-ʿālim al-ʿārif al-awḥad* (*Un manuel hispanique de ḥisba*). [eds. G.S. Colin and E. Lévi-Provençal, Paris, 1931], p. 17.

[80] Maqqarī, *Analectes*, II, p. 148.

[81] Ibn Salmūn, *Kitāb al-ʿaqd al-munaẓẓam bi al-ḥukkām*. Escorial, ms. 1077, fol. 120r.

before the thirteenth century. Due to Islamic restrictions on alcohol, the scarcity of references to the export or open consumption of Andalusi wines is not surprising, although their existence is nonetheless clear. During the eleventh century, the Jewish poet and statesman Samuel b. Naghrīla wrote in praise of wine: "red in appearance, sweet to the taste, vintage of Spain yet renowned in the east" indicating that, even in this period, the wines of Malaga, Jerez, and other Andalusi regions were already widely appreciated – at least by non-Muslims.[82] Wine consumption may, as Goitein has suggested, have been more strictly regulated in Muslim Spain than in the east.[83] Jurists and *muḥtasibs* frequently reiterated bans on alcohol – although their very number suggests that these rules were honored in the breach – and restrictions probably intensified under the Almoravid and Almohad regimes. In the twelfth century, Ibn ʿAbdūn specifically warned that sailors in the port of Seville should not be allowed to buy wine from Christian merchants, and that if "this comes to the attention of an officer (*'amīn*) he should discipline the sailor."[84] If wine was a commodity of international trade, perhaps sailors and others on board ship were particularly given to drinking. Certainly, several works by the Almerian poet Ibn Safar, roughly a contemporary of Ibn ʿAbdūn, describe raucous drinking parties on shipboard.[85]

Metals and Minerals

The Iberian peninsula was rich in metals, and Arabic geographers repeatedly noted the availability of gold, silver, lead, copper, iron, mercury, zinc, and other substances in Andalusi soils.[86]

[82] *The Jewish Poets of Spain.* [trans. D. Goldstein, London, 1965], p. 47. On Jewish wine-making in al-Andalus, see N. Roth, "Some aspects of Muslim-Jewish Relations in Spain," *Estudios en homenaje a D. Claudio Sánchez-Albornoz.* [Buenos Aires, 1983] II, pp. 206–12.

[83] Goitein, *Mediterranean Society*, I, p. 122.

[84] Ibn ʿAbdūn, *Risāla*, in *Documents arabes inédits sur la vie sociale et économique en occident musulman au moyen âge: Trois traités hispaniques de ḥisba.* [ed. E. Lévi-Provençal, Cairo, 1955], p. 57.

[85] Ibn Saʿīd al-Gharnāṭī, *Rāyāt al-mubarrizīn wa ghāyāb al-mumayyizīn.* [ed. A.M. al-Qādī, Cairo, 1393/1973], p. 107. Also on wine, see L. Bolens, "La viticulture d'après les traités d'agronomie andalous (XIe-XIIe siècles)," *L'Andalousie du quotidien au sacré (XIe-XIIIe siècles).* [Aldershot, 1991] article V, pp. 1–7.

[86] Geographers citing Andalusi metals include Rāzī, "Description," p. 62; *Ḥudūd al-ʿālam*, p. 154; and Ibn Ḥawqal, *Kitāb ṣurat al-arḍ*, p. 114.

Not all of these were sufficiently plentiful to warrant export, although a number of Andalusi metals and minerals (notably copper, mercury, tin, and marble) made their way to other Mediterranean regions.

According to the eastern author Abū Faḍl al-Dimashqī, the best variety of copper was "that which is cast in al-Andalus, in terms of its receptivity to being worked."[87] Geniza documents show many varieties of copper exported from al-Andalus, including "burnished" copper, "hammered" copper, "cast" copper, "broken" copper, and "elastic" copper.[88] Perhaps it was this last variety, which one letter mentioned as sent from Almeria to Fez in the early twelfth century, that had earlier caught Dimashqī's attention. Other Geniza writers from the same period also referred to copper – one noted a cargo sent from Almeria to Tlemcen ca. 1138, while another wrote from Alexandria to Old Cairo in the 1140s: "I would like to know the price of Andalusi copper ingots, because I have some, and if there is a market for them, I will send them."[89] Some Andalusi copper exports were in the form of raw metal, while others were of worked copper. Idrīsī particularly praised the copper implements manufactured in Almeria, and his opinion is confirmed by the fact that the Geniza is filled with references to Andalusi copperwares.[90] Egyptian trousseau inventories, for example, sometimes listed Andalusi copper lamps or basins of Andalusi copper among the possessions of a new bride.[91] Andalusi copper also traveled northward into Christian Spain, and twelfth-century Ebro tariff lists cited fees levied on shipments of copper, probably coming from the regions of Riotinto and Aljustrel, still under Muslim control.[92]

After copper, mercury and its derivative, mercuric sulphide (cinnabar) were the most noted Andalusi metallic exports. Among other uses, mercury was important in the refining of

[87] Dimashqī, *Kitāb al-'ashāra ilā maḥāsin al-tijāra.* [Cairo, 1318/1900], p. 28.

[88] S.D. Goitein, "Judeo-Arabic Letters from Spain (early 12th century)," *Orientalia Hispanica; Studies in Honor of F.M. Pareja.* [Leiden, 1974], p. 349. The translations are Goitein's. The last reference, to "elastic" copper, comes from TS 12.435. J. Vallvé has suggested that some references to copper may actually intend bronze ("La industria en al-Andalus," p. 216).

[89] Bodl d74.41; TS Arabic Box 40.113.

[90] Idrīsī, *Opus*, v, p. 562.

[91] TS J 1.29; Firkovitch II, 1700.

[92] Gual Camarena, "Peaje," p. 182.

gold, while cinnabar produced a vermillion pigment employed in dyes, inks, and paints. References to the export of Andalusi mercury are earlier than those for copper, with Mas'ūdī describing Andalusi mercury "exported to the entire Islamic and non-Islamic world" by the middle of the twelfth century.[93] One Andalusi mine, north of Cordoba at Almaden (from the Arabic *al-ma'dan*, "mine"), was particularly famous for its mercury and cinnabar, which were dug from shafts of up to two hundred and fifty fathoms (*qāma*) – according to Idrīsī – by a work force of over one thousand miners. The products of this mine were exported "to all regions of the world."[94] Idrīsī may have exaggerated his figures, but the importance of Almaden at this period is attested to by its capture and exploitation by the Christians in the mid twelfth century, followed by its recapture by the Almohads, who held it into the next century.[95] Geniza documents also mention mercury and cinnabar among Andalusi exports during the eleventh and twelfth centuries. In one instance, a court record from Denia, ca. 1083, described the settlement of a dispute over cinnabar sent from al-Andalus to Ifriqiya in the care of an agent. A century later, and further afield, a price list from Aden quoted rates for mercury and cinnabar along with those for other Andalusi goods.[96]

"Perhaps," wrote a merchant from Egypt to Sicily in the mid eleventh century, "you could buy me some tin." Since tin was another Andalusi export, it is likely that this request referred to a product of Muslim Spain, particularly since the writer specified that the item be bought from an Andalusi merchant, and continued with instructions to buy Andalusi silk.[97] Likewise, Goitein has associated a reference to tin in the accounts of Nahray b. Nissīm, from the 1060s, with traffic in Andalusi tin to Egypt.[98]

Other metals and minerals, including zinc, sulphur, and anti-

[93] Mas'ūdī, *Murūj*, p. 367.

[94] Idrīsī, *Opus*, v, p. 581. Idrīsī was probably indicating length, not depth. Other Andalusi mines exporting mercury and cinnabar were cited by Dimashqī, *Kitāb al-'ashāra*, p. 29; Ibn Ghālib, "Naṣṣ andalusī jadīd qaṭ'ia min kitāb farḥa al-anfūs li-Ibn Ghālib" [ed. L. 'Abd al-Badī], *Majalla ma'had al-makhṭūṭāt al-'arabiya* 1(1955), p. 289; Zuhrī, "Kitāb al-dja'rāfiyya," p. 220; and Yāqūt, *Mu'jam*, I, p. 733.

[95] J. O'Callaghan, *A History of Medieval Spain*. [Ithaca, 1975], p. 299.

[96] TS 12.570; Mosseri L12. In this latter list, dated 1198, the mercury and cinnabar are not specified as Andalusi, but follow after goods from Madrid and Shalwadh (S.D. Goitein, *Letters of Medieval Jewish Traders*. [Princeton, 1973], p. 215, notes 14–17).

[97] TS 12.389.

[98] TS Arabic Box 30.215; Goitein, *Letters*, pp. 290–5.

mony, were also exported from al-Andalus – though apparently on a small scale to judge by the paucity of references. Geographers tended to cite these items only within larger lists of Andalusi products, although Zuhrī added that red sulphur, mined near Murcia, was exported as far as Iraq, Yemen, Syria, and India.[99] Antimony came in two forms, *kuḥl* (or kohl) and *ithmid*, the former being more frequently traded. These were used for cosmetic and medicinal purposes, often in collyriums, as well as in other chemical compounds.[100] Bakrī stated that kohl was carried from Tortosa "to all lands" in the eleventh century, while Zuhrī later reported both the export of kohl from Cartagena to the Near East and traffic in *ithmid* from the region of Granada to North Africa.[101] Somewhat after Zuhrī's report, a late twelfth-century price list from distant Aden quoted kohl from the Andalusi village of Shalwadh selling at "17 [dinars] per sack."[102] Somewhat earlier, ca. 1137, a merchant in al-Andalus wrote to inform his wife in Egypt that he was sending "six baskets of kohl" to her. Some of this may have been intended for her own use, but the quantity suggests commercial intent.[103]

Andalusi marble was also traded abroad, and Maqqarī, among others, noted the quality of Iberian marble and the admiration which it inspired in the Near East.[104] Because marble has distinctive colors and characteristics depending on where it was quarried, an international trade developed in this bulky and heavy material. Almeria was known for its white marble, as well as for its style of marble cutting, and four stelae found in the West African town of Gao have been attributed to Almerian ateliers. All four date to the first decades of the twelfth century, when the Almoravids ruled in both the Iberian peninsula and North Africa, and when Gao was an important way-station along the gold route from the Sudan. If marble did move southward through trade – more likely in a period when traffic was facilitated by the extensive

[99] Zuhrī, "Kitāb al-dja'rāfiyya," pp. 208, 276.

[100] L. Bolens, "Henné et koḥl: Le corps peint du rituel nuptial chez les hispano-arabes du moyen âge," *Razo* 7(1987), pp. 63–79.

[101] Bakrī, *Masālik*, pp. 129–30; Zuhrī, "Kitāb al-dja'rāfiyya," p. 211.

[102] Mosseri L12. See also Goitein, *Letters*, pp. 212–16. Yāqūt confirmed that Shalwadh produced kohl (*Mu'jam*, III, p. 316).

[103] TS 13 J 27.17. Goitein translated *kuḥl* in this passage as "collyrium." See "Glimpses from the Cairo Geniza on Naval Warfare," *Studi orientalistici in onore di Giorgio Levi della Vida*. [Rome, 1956], I, pp. 404–5.

[104] Maqqarī, *Nafḥ al-ṭīb min ghuṣn al-Andalus al-raṭīb*. [Cairo, 1949] I, pp. 187–8.

rule of a single dynasty – it may have come in exchange for gold.[105]

Coral from the Maghribi and Andalusi coasts was also a source of wealth for the western Mediterranean, although some reports of its trade seem exaggerated. In the ninth century, Ibn Khurradādhbih listed coral among commodities carried eastward by the Rādhānite merchants. Bakrī (writing in the 1060s) reported that coral was "taken out of the sea around al-Andalus" and – amazingly – "in the province of Almeria [alone], about eighty *qintārs* [roughly 8,000 pounds] were collected in less than a month." Also unconvincing is the information from the late twelfth-century *Kitāb al-istibṣār* that western coral was "sold at high price in India and China" (both places where the Andalusi product would have competed with local varieties).[106]

Ceramics

Evidence for trade in Andalusi ceramics comes both from documents and existing examples, although it is not always easy to reconcile the two.[107] Idrīsī, for instance, reported that the region around Calatayud manufactured golden ceramic wares that were "exported to all regions," and two *wathā'iq* handbooks from the mid eleventh century likewise described contracts for the sale of gilded ceramics. These written reports suggest that Muslim potters in the peninsula were producing some type of lustreware during the eleventh and twelfth centuries, but no samples of their work survive. This lack of material evidence has sparked debate and cast doubt on the location and chronology of Andalusi lustreware production.[108]

[105] On the Gao stelae, see J. Sauvaget, "Les épitaphes royales de Gao," *Al-Andalus* 14(1949), pp. 123–41; M. Vire, "Notes sur trois épitaphes royales de Gao," *Bulletin de l'Institut français d'Afrique du Nord* 20(1958), pp. 368–76; R. Mauny, "Découverte à Gao," pp. 514–6. On the Almeria style, L. Torres Balbás, "Cementerios hispanomusulmanes," *Al-Andalus* 22(1957), pp. 180–1.

[106] Ibn Khurradādhbih, *Kitāb al-masālik*, p. 92; Bakrī, *Masālik*, p. 129; E. Fagnan (ed.), *Kitāb al-istibṣār* [Constantine, 1900], p. 29.

[107] G. Rosselló Bordoy provides a brief analysis and up-to-date bibliography on Andalusi ceramics, "The Ceramics of al-Andalus," in *Al-Andalus: The Art of Islamic Spain*. [ed. J. Dodds], pp. 97–103. See also J. Zozaya's overview of Andalusi ceramic types in "Aperçu général sur la céramique espagnole," in *La céramique médiévale en Méditerranée occidentale*. [Paris, 1980], pp. 265–96; M. González Martí, *Cerámica del levante español, siglos medievales*. [Barcelona, 1944]; and F.C. Lister and R.H. Lister, *Andalusian Ceramics in Spain and New Spain*. [Tucson, 1987].

[108] Idrīsī, *Opus*, v, p. 554; the term in question is *al-ghaḍḍārr al-mudhahhab*. R. Dozy and M.J. de Goeje translate *ghaḍḍār* as "poterie" (Idrīsī, *Description de l'Afrique et de*

In other contexts, archeological finds and extant ceramics add supportive detail to the sketchy documentary picture of commerce in Andalusi ceramics. Three Arab shipwrecks found off the coast of Provence have yielded shards of a type similar to tenth-century Andalusi ceramics.[109] Likewise, pottery glazed in a style distinctive of the eleventh-century Taifa kingdom of Denia occur in sufficient quantities all over eastern Spain to suggest commercial distribution.[110] Further afield, bits of Andalusi ceramics dating to the Fatimid period have been excavated in Cairo, and early twelfth-century shards of Cordoban enameled pottery were found in the West African region of Gao.[111] Evidence from Italy, also, shows that Andalusi ceramic jars and tablewares, dating from the eleventh to thirteenth centuries, were imported "on a significant scale."[112]

The most striking object lesson in the diffusion of medieval ceramics comes from Pisa and other Italian towns, where small pieces of glazed ceramic, or whole dishes, were used in architectural decoration between the eleventh and fifteenth centuries. These ceramics, collectively called *bacini*, produced a colorful

l'Espagne. [Leiden, 1866], p. 354). The term designates a very fine, porcelain-like ware. See also Goitein, *Mediterranean Society*, 1, p. 111. The proper vocalization and translation of *mudhahhab* have been disputed; the term could mean "gilded" or possibly just "exported" (see Ibn al-Khaṭīb, "El 'Parangón entre Malaga y Salé' de Ibn al-Khaṭīb" [trans. E. García Gómez], *Al-Andalus* 2(1934), p. 187). A. Lane "is doubtful whether El-Edrisi's statement should be trusted" ("Early Hispano-Moresque Pottery: A Reconsideration," *Burlington Magazine* 88(1946), p. 246).

References from the *wathā'iq*: Ibn Mughīth, *Mugni' fī 'ilm al-shurūt*. [Real Academia de la Historia, Madrid, Gayangos, ms. 44] probably fols. 36ff. (I have been unable to check this reference in the manuscript); and Fihrī, *Wathā'iq wa al-masā'il*. [Miguel Asín Institute, CSIC. Madrid, ms. 11], fol. 24r. Mention of gilded pottery by these authors was remarked by M. Gómez Moreno, "La loza dorada primitiva de Málaga," *Al-Andalus* 5(1940), p. 385. Since then, Gómez Moreno's information has been repeated, more or less verbatim, by later art historians. See, for example, A.W. Frothingham, *Lustreware of Spain* [New York, 1951], p. 12; L.M. Llubía Munné, *Cerámica medieval española*. [Barcelona, 1967], p. 56; M. Jenkins, "Medieval Maghribi Ceramics" [Ph.D. Dissertation, New York University, 1978], p. 185.

[109] G. Vindry, "Présentation de l'épave arabe de Batéguier (Baie de Cannes, Provence orientale)," *La céramique médiévale en Méditerranée occidentale*. [Paris, 1980], p. 225.

[110] J.A. Gisbert, "La ciudad de Denia y la producción de cerámicas vidriadas con decoración estampillada," *Sharq al-Andalus* 2(1985), pp. 161, 166.

[111] A. Lane, *Early Islamic Pottery*. [London, 1947], pp. 20–1; R. Mauny, "Découverte à Gao d'un fragment de poterie émaillée du moyen âge musulman," *Hespéris* 39(1952), pp. 514–16.

[112] D. Whitehouse, "Medieval pottery in Italy: The present state of research," *La céramique médiévale en Méditerranée occidentale*, p. 72. See also I. Cabona *et al.*, "Contributi dell'archeologia medievale ligure alle conoscenze dei prodotti ceramici nel Mediterraneo occidentale," *La céramique médiévale en Méditerranée occidentale*, pp. 117–18.

jewel-like effect when affixed to the exterior walls of churches and other buildings. In all, something over 1,700 *bacini*, from ceramics originating in Egypt, North Africa, Sicily, Italy, Byzantium, and Spain, have been counted in northern Italian buildings. In Pisa, particularly, both ceramic and architectural style allow precise dating of individual *bacini*, and recent scholarly analysis of these imported items has yielded valuable information on the movement of ceramics between Italy and other regions of the Mediterranean.[113]

At least a dozen Pisan churches built between ca. 1063 and ca. 1175 contain *bacini* thought to be of Andalusi origin, and later buildings incorporated increasing numbers of Spanish ceramics. Many of these *bacini* are lustred, or glazed with a characteristically Andalusi technique called *cuerda seca* creating designs using glazed patches set off by unglazed lines. Although art historians often disagree regarding the exact provenance of ceramic types, particularly in cases where certain styles were adopted from one region to another, mineralogical analysis has proven that some of these *bacini* were manufactured from Iberian clay, probably dug in the region of Malaga.[114] In view of the fact that geographers mentioned Malagan "gilded" lustreware, and that lustre shards have been found in Malaga itself, it is almost certain that this city supported a trade in lustred ceramics by the twelfth century, some of which made their way to Pisa.[115]

Leather and paper

The high reputation of Iberian leatherwork was already established by the eighth century, and has continued into the modern

[113] In Pisa, eighty-seven buildings and building complexes are known to have been decorated with *bacini*. See H. Blake, "The Bacini of North Italy," *La céramique médiévale en Méditerranée occidentale*, p. 93 (and other articles on *bacini* in the same collection). Two scholars, G. Berti and L. Tongiorgi, have devoted themselves to the study of Pisan *bacini*, and have together produced the most extensive and definitive studies of these dishes. Their work is compiled in their book *I bacini ceramici medievali delle chiese di Pisa.* [Rome, 1981], as well as in their numerous shorter monographs and articles (among which see particularly *Ceramiche importate dalla Spagna nell'area pisana dal XII al XV secolo.* [Florence, 1985] and *Arte islamica in Italia: i bacini delle chiese pisane.* [Rome, 1983]). The importance of the *bacini* as evidence for Mediterranean commerce has already been noted by D. Abulafia, "The Pisan *Bacini* and the Medieval Mediterranean Economy: A Historian's Viewpoint," *Papers in Italian Archeology* 5(1985), pp. 287–302.

[114] Cabona, "Contributi," p. 120.

[115] This theory was first proposed by Gómez Moreno in 1940 ("La loza dorada," p.

period. Cordoban leather was renowned for its tough yet supple quality, rendering it ideal for shoes, chairs, bags, harnesses, etc. The leather was usually made from goat hide, dyed a brilliant red (through treatment with alum and qirmiz), then cut and tooled (often in gold) with surface designs. In spite of the caveats of the previous chapter concerning the nomenclature and true origins of cordoban, it is clear that considerable quantities of this leather must have been produced and exported from the peninsula. However, although cordoban was widely distributed in Europe, there is almost no evidence of its distribution within the *dār al-Islām*.[116]

This eurocentric pattern of distribution was less true for another type of worked leather, *guadameci*, which is more frequently mentioned in Arabic sources. However, this leather was so similar to cordoban that the two were frequently confused and the names used interchangeably. Although *guadameci* derived its name from the Maghribi town of Ghadames, it became as much associated with al-Andalus as with North Africa. Unlike cordoban, it tended to be manufactured of cow hide, gilded and polychromed, and its brilliant colors and ornamentation suited it for decorative purposes.[117] It seems likely that a ruling of Ibn Sahl, concerned with the purchase of "leather adorned with spun gold" in eleventh-century Cordoba, referred to *guadameci* (or possibly cordoban).[118]

Latin references to cordoban are found as early as the eighth

394). Although it has been disputed since then, and scholars have questioned Gómez Moreno's far-reaching conclusions, most recent evidence tends to support the general theory of Malagan exports. See also, Lane "Early Hispano-Moresque Pottery," p. 249; Frothingham, *Lustreware*, p. 11; M. Jenkins, "Medieval Maghribi Ceramics," pp. 178–9; D. Whitehouse, "La collezione pisana e la produzioni ceramiche dei paesi circummediterranei nei secoli XI–XV," *Bollettino storico pisano* [Collana storica, 25, Pisa, 1983], p. 34.

116 Cordoban may have been exported to the Islamic world (not necessarily under this name), although Arabic geographers do not specifically mention worked leather among Andalusi exports. One Geniza letter from about 1050 (ULC Or1080 J 77) contains a commercial order for Andalusi goods, including something designated as *qurṭubī*. Goitein (*Mediterranean Society*, IV, p. 169) has interpreted this as some type of silk textile, since the items preceding it are fabrics. However, since the items immediately following it are shoes, it is possible that this mention of *qurṭubī* actually refers to cordoban leather.

117 For more on these two products, see J. Ferrandis Torres, *Cordobanes y guadamecíes; Catálogo ilustrado de la exposición. Sociedad de amigos de arte.* [Madrid, 1955] and C. Davillier, *Notes sur les cuirs de Cordoue, guadamaciles d'Espagne, etc.* [Paris, 1878].

118 Ibn Sahl, *Aḥkām al-kubrā*. General Library, Rabat, ms. 838Q, fol. 138.

century, when a diploma granted by the Merovingian king Chilperic II to the Abbey of Corbie in 716 mentioned "ten skins of cordoban leather."[119] Since it seems unlikely that the cordoban leather industry could have established an international market in the five years since the Arab invasion of the peninsula in 711, we must presume that Cordoba (and perhaps other regions) were already manufacturing this product in Visigothic times. At the end of the eighth century, or early ninth century, the poet Theodulfus mentioned the transport to Arles of "leather bearing the name of Cordoba," some of which was white, some red.[120] Not long after this, in 833, a document relating to the Abbey of St. Wandrille cited an annual expenditure for the purchase of cordoban leather (*cordebisos*).[121] Clearly, cordoban was available in Carolingian France, although if the number of references reflects supply, trade decreased during the tenth century.

As with many other Andalusi exports, cordoban and *guadameci* begin to appear more frequently in Latin and vernacular Christian texts during the eleventh and twelfth centuries. The *Cantar de mío Cid*, for example, contains passages which show these Andalusi leathers as imports to eleventh-century Castile. When the Cid went south into exile, two Jews from whom he had borrowed money requested that he bring them "a skin of crimson leather, Moorish, and highly prized."[122] Perhaps they made this request in the hopes of avoiding the tariff duties which might have been incurred had they, as merchants, transported these goods from the south themselves. *Portazgo* documents from Castilian and Aragonese towns routinely cited leather products among items subject to such levies. The *Fuero* of Sepulveda (1076) set a toll of one *dinero* for a dozen cordobans brought into the town, and two *dineros* for the same quantity of *quadamecis*.[123] In the middle of the next century, the *Fuero* of Molina set a toll of one *maravedi* on each batch of cordoban or

[119] Levillain, *Examen critique*, pp. 235–6. Pirenne cited this donation in his *Mohammed and Charlemagne*. [London, 1939] (p. 90) as an example of flourishing Merovingian trade.

[120] Theodulfus, *Versus contra iudices*. [ed. E. Dümmler, *MGH* Poetae latini medii aevi 1.2, Berlin, 1881], p. 500.

[121] *Gesta abbatum fontanellensium*. [ed. G.H. Pertz, *MGH* Scriptores II (in folio), Hanover, 1829], p. 300. This reference is appended to the main text, and is not included in more recent editions.

[122] *Cantar de mío Cid*, pp. 50–1.

[123] *Los Fueros de Sepúlveda*. [ed. E. Saez, Segovia, 1953], pp. 137, 142.

guadameci, while a similar document from Estella, dated 1164, charged two *denariis* per dozen *cordoanorum* or *godmecinorum*. Likewise in 1207 we find a charge of one *morabedi* set on *cuero de godameci* brought to Toledo.[124]

At roughly the same period, tariff lists from Narbonne, Marseille, and other southern French towns also included cordoban among taxable commodities, and numerous Italian notarial records cited sales of this leather.[125] A contract from Savona, dated 1180, mentioned a shipment of six pieces of cordoban to Genoa, while a Genoese contract drawn up in August 1197 acknowledged the receipt of ten cordoban pieces, valued at £11.10d. A later Genoese document, from 1213, recognized a debt of £13.12d. owed for *corduanum*.[126] While it is doubtful that every one of these literary and notarial references concerned genuine Iberian cordoban, we may assume that the popularity of cordoban leather did not diminish either its production in the peninsula or its value as an export.

Andalusi leather was not used merely for shoes, clothing, harness, and furniture, beautiful tooled and gilded leathers were also worked into book bindings. And between the bindings, we find another important Andalusi commodity: paper. Both books and paper were noted among Andalusi exports, although trade in paper is better attested since it was in higher demand. Books appealed to only a limited market, and Abū Faḍl al-Dimashqī specifically warned against a merchant investing in "philosophi-

[124] *Fuero de Molina de Aragón.* [ed. M. Sancho Izquierdo, Madrid, 1916], pp. 66–7 (this is a thirteenth-century Romance version of a Latin original dating 1152–6); *Fuero de Estella.* [ed. J.M. Lacarra] *AHDE* 4(1927), p. 439; Hernández, "Cortes de Toledo," p. 241.

[125] Narbonne (1153): G. Mouvnès (ed.), *Inventaire des archives communales. Ville de Narbonne.* [Narbonne, 1871], p. 4; Marseille (1228): L. Méry and F. Guindon (eds.), *Histoire analytique et chronologique des actes et des délibérations du corps et du conseil de la municipalité de Marseille depuis le Xe siècle jusqu'au nos jours.* [Marseille, 1841] I, pp. 347–8; Other Provençal references (thirteenth century): B. Guérard (ed.), *Cartulaire de l'abbaye de Saint-Victor de Marseilles.* [Paris, 1857], pp. LXXIII–C, LXXVI.

[126] Savona: Cumano, *Cartulario di Arnaldo Cumano e Giovanni di Donato (Savona, 1178–1188).* [ed. L. Balletto, Rome, 1978], p. 336. Genoa (1197): *ASG* Cart. 56, fol.184v. (1213): *Lanfranco (1206–1226).* [eds. H.C. Krueger and R.L. Reynolds, Genoa, 1952] II, p. 59. Other notarial references to cordoban: *ASG* Div. 102, fol.58r (1197); *Lanfranco*, I, p. 396 (1210), II, pp. 147–8 (1216), II, p. 349, (1226); *ASG* Cart 5, 110r (1213), 232r (1216); *ASG* Cart 26/II, 88r (1248); *ASG* Cart 29, 2r (1253), 15v (1253). Notarial records from Marseille also record transactions in cordoban dating 1233–48 (L. Blancard, (ed.), *Documents inédits sur le commerce de Marseille au moyen âge.* [Marseille, 1884–5] I, #43, 47, 100; II, #14, 117, 129, 149, 788, 791, 796, 800–4).

cal books [since these] are bought only by wise men and scholars, most of whom are poor, and whose numbers are few."[127] Paper, on the other hand, was widely used, not merely in books but for a myriad of other purposes. The Geniza corpus, with its wealth of books, letters, legal documents, marriage contracts, laundry lists, price inventories, and other items, mostly written on paper, admirably illustrates this point.

The best known Andalusi paper was made in Jativa, thus called *shatibī* in Arabic sources, but other regions also produced the heavy, smooth, glazed paper which was characteristic of al-Andalus.[128] Papers were manufactured of flax or rags, and it was among the duties of the *muḥtasib* to ensure that papers were properly made. Ibn 'Abdūn, for instance, instructed that paper makers "finish the paper a little," while Jarsīfī advised that paper should be smooth, without dents, pure, glazed, and uniform in size.[129] The geographer Muqaddasī described paper making in al-Andalus in the tenth century, and Peter the Venerable mentioned Jewish books made with rag paper in his *Tractatus contra judaeos*. Peter had probably observed this paper during his travels in the peninsula in 1142, a few years before writing this work.[130] Even today the superiority of medieval Andalusi paper remains apparent, causing Goitein to remark that a letter from Granada, dated 1130, was written on the best paper "ever seen by me in the Geniza. It is almost entirely white, strong, and pleasantly smooth."[131] No wonder this Andalusi export was in wide demand.

[127] Dimashqī, *Kitāb al-'ashāra*, p. 58.

[128] E. Lévi-Provençal, *L'Espagne musulmane au Xème siècle*. [Paris, 1932], p. 185; R. Arié, *España musulmana*, p. 250.

[129] Ibn 'Abdūn, *Risāla*, p. 48; Jarsīfī, *Risāla* (also in *Documents arabes*. [ed. Lévi-Provençal]), p. 124. There is considerable debate as to whether or not Andalusi paper was manufactured in a paper mill. If, as has been argued, mills were employed in Aragon as early as 1193, this would be the oldest known reference to the process. On paper production and paper mills, see O. Valls i Subirà, "El paper al al-Andalus i a la Corona d'Aragó," *Second International Congress of Studies on Cultures of the Western Mediterranean*. [Barcelona, 1978], pp. 441–8; and criticism of Valls by R.I. Burns, "The Paper Revolution in Europe: Crusader Valencia's Paper Industry," *Pacific History Review* 50(1981), pp. 1–30, and *Society and Documentation in Crusader Valencia*. [Princeton, 1985], pp. 151–5. Also, at a more general level, G. Schaefer, "The Development of Paper Making," *Ciba Review* 6(1947–9), pp. 2641–49; and A.Y. al-Hassan and D.R. Hill, *Islamic Technology*. [Cambridge, 1986], pp. 190–6.

[130] Muqaddasī, *Aḥsan al-taqāsīm fī ma'rifat al-aqālīm*. [ed. M.J. de Goeje, *BGA*, Leiden, 2nd edn, III, Leiden, 1967], p. 239; Peter the Venerable, *Adversus iudeorum inveteratam duritiem*. [ed. Y. Friedman, Corpus Christianorum: Continuatio Medievalis, 58, Turnhout, 1985], p. 130.

[131] Goitein, *Mediterranean Society*. V, p. 288. This is in reference to ULC Add.3340.

Geniza merchants not only wrote on Andalusi paper and traded it, they also gave it as gifts. Their letters often mention small parcels of Andalusi paper sent between partners, usually in quantities of one dozen to three dozen sheets.[132] However, in one example, from ca. 1125, we learn that Judah Ha-Levi dispatched five hundred sheets of Toledan paper to his friend Halfōn b. Nethanel in Egypt. The size of the parcel, and the content of Ha-Levi's cover letter, have led Goitein to conclude that this shipment represented a commercial enterprise, not merely a friendly gift.[133] Tariff lists also cited tolls collected on Andalusi and Maghribi paper in towns along the Ebro River in the late twelfth century, demonstrating that paper was moving from Muslim to Christian regions in this period.[134] It is quite possible, along the same lines, that a shipment of paper recorded in Genoa in 1163 originally came from al-Andalus.[135]

Timber

Al-Andalus was famous for its pine forests and timber, particularly those along the Levant coast, in the Balearics, and in the Algarve. Timber from Andalusi forests was widely exported as one of the most important commodities supplied by al-Andalus to other areas of the Islamic Mediterranean world. The wood was used as a building material, for fuel and charcoal, for artisanry, but above all for ship-building.

In the 1150s, Idrīsī wrote of Tortosa:

> there are markets, buildings, ateliers and an industry for building large ships from the timber of the [surrounding] hills. This pine wood is unlike any other, in terms of its length and toughness. It is taken to make masts and yards [for ships] . . . this pine timber has no equal in the known world for excellence of reputation, strength, and length. It is transported to all regions of the world, far and near . . .[136]

South of Tortosa, the mountains around Cuenca also produced "many pine trees, [whose] wood was cut, then thrown into the

[132] Goitein, *Mediterranean Society*, v, p. 457.

[133] ENA 40; Goitein, *Letters*, p. 20 and *Mediterranean Society*, v, p. 457 [x, D, n. 187].

[134] Burns, "Paper Revolution," p. 24.

[135] Giovanni Scriba, *Historia patria monumenta VI: Chartae*. [Turin, 1853], II, p. 900, #1345. Genoese notaries were writing on paper by the middle of the twelfth century.

[136] Idrīsī, *Opus*, v, p. 555, and *Opus* VII [Naples-Rome, 1977], p. 734.

water [of the Jucar river, which] carried it to Denia and Valencia on the sea." Because the Jucar actually flowed to a spot south of Valencia, Idrīsī felt the need to explain that, at the river mouth, the timber was "loaded on boats, and taken to Denia, where it was used in the construction of large ships and small boats."[137] In south-western al-Andalus, Silves was also surrounded by forests, producing "large quantities of wood, which is exported from there in all directions," and "all the lands around [Alcacer do Sal] are covered in pine trees, from which they construct many ships."[138]

Only a few regions around the Mediterranean basin were capable of supporting forests of this kind, and the scarcity of timber gave it a "tyranny over trade routes."[139] Even where the climate was suitable for forests, Mediterranean trees were fragile and arid conditions slowed their growth. Many regions of the southern Mediterranean – in essence much of the Islamic Mediterranean – were either naturally unforested, or had been deforested before the medieval period. Only some cooler hilly regions in al-Andalus, Morocco, northern Syria, Lebanon, Crete, and Sicily were able to provide timber for Muslim shipyards and other ateliers.[140] Andalusi timber traveled abroad as raw lumber, but fully built ships were also exported – as shown in a Geniza letter, written from Tunisia ca. 1040, which remarked that "the new Andalusi ships . . . were bought by the merchants and loaded" for passage to Egypt.[141] As will be demonstrated in the following chapter, the scarcity of Mediterranean timber and its necessity for ship-building turned forested regions into strategic targets for conquest. The Christian acquisition of Iberian timber resources in the twelfth and thirteenth centuries would help to tip the balance of naval power in the Mediterranean.

137 Idrīsī, *Opus*, v, p. 560.

138 Idrīsī, *Opus*, v, p. 543.

139 T. Glick, *Islamic and Christian Spain in the Early Middle Ages.* [Princeton, 1979], p. 107.

140 On Mediterranean forests and trade in timber see R. Meiggs, *Trees and Timber in the Ancient Mediterranean World.* [Oxford, 1982]; C. Higounet, "Les fôrets de l'Europe occidentale du Ve au XIe siècles," *Settimane di studio del Centro italiano di studi sull'alto medioevo.* XIII [Spoleto, 1966], pp. 343–98; M. Lombard, "Un problème de cartographié: le bois dans la Méditerranée musulmane (VIIe-XIe siècles)," *Annales:ESC* 14(1959), pp. 234–54 (this article is particularly useful for its maps); M. Lombard, "Arsenaux et bois de marine dans la Méditerranée musulmane (VIIe-XIe siècle)," *Le navire et l'économie maritime du moyen âge au XVIIIe siècle principalement en Méditerranée.* [ed. M. Mollat, Paris, 1958], pp. 53–106.

141 Bodl a2.17.

AL-ANDALUS AS A TRANSFER ZONE: FURS, GOLD, AND SLAVES

Goods redistributed through Andalusi markets may also be considered, to some degree, Andalusi exports. The three case studies discussed here – furs, gold, and slaves – did not originate in Muslim Spain, yet the peninsula and its merchants played an important role in making these commodities available to buyers elsewhere. Transit trade was more subject to the fluctuations of politics and war than was trade in locally produced commodities. Traffic in furs, gold, or slaves was lucrative, but their commerce tended to be less stable over the years than comparable commerce in figs, textiles, olive oil, or other classic Andalusi exports.

Furs

The best furs came to the medieval Mediterranean world, including al-Andalus, from northern Europe, Scandinavia, Russia, and Central Asia. The Andalusi caliph ʿAbd al-Raḥmān III, for example, owned eastern sable pelts imported from Khurasan.[142] Nevertheless, Arab geographers are consistent in their references to furs from Muslim Spain, a phenomenon that Lévi-Provençal has attributed to the fact that the Iberian peninsula is cooler than most other regions of the Islamic world.[143] Iṣṭakhrī, Muqaddasī, and the *Ḥudūd al-ʿālam* all reported that sable pelts were exported from al-Andalus in the tenth century, and Ibn Khurradādhbih wrote of marten and other furs carried from west to east.[144] Either these furs came from animals native to the peninsula, or, as seems more likely in the case of sable, they were imported to al-Andalus from further north, and then exported to other Islamic regions. Already in the tenth century, Masʿūdī attempted to sort out this confusion, explaining that furs from northern Europe often came "into the Maghrib [from the north], which leads to the belief that they come from

[142] Maqqarī, *Analectes*, I, 230. On the early medieval fur trade in northern Europe, see P.H. Sawyer, "Kings and Merchants," in *Early Medieval Kingship*. [eds. P.H. Sawyer and I.N. Wood, Leeds, 1977], p. 149.

[143] Lévi-Provençal, *L'Espagne musulmane au Xème siècle*, p. 184.

[144] Iṣṭakhrī, *Masālik*, p. 45; Muqaddasī, *Aḥsan al-taqāsīm*, p. 50; *Ḥudūd al-ʿālam*, p. 520–3 (this work also lists lizard skins as an Andalusi export, p. 155); Ibn Khurradādhbih, *Kitāb al-masālik*, p. 153

al-Andalus and the bordering Frankish and Slavic regions."[145]

The Andalusi role as a transit zone for northern furs seems to have been limited to the early medieval period, since references to this trade decline after the tenth century. Perhaps contacts with fur-producing regions in northern Europe declined after the Umayyad and Carolingian period. In place of transit trade, al-Andalus began to export local furs, particularly rabbit skins. This commerce was noted by Maqqarī, who described "an animal smaller than an *arnab*" (here probably a hare) called a *qunaliya* (cognate with the Italian *coniglio*), of which the "pelts are worn and used by the people of al-Andalus, both Muslim and Christian, and [which] is not found in Berber lands except for those that are exported from [al-Andalus] to Ceuta."[146] Although Maqqarī was writing at a later period, sources show that traffic in rabbit skins was already well established by the 1100s. Zuhrī mentioned that rabbit pelts (*julūd al-qunaliyāt*) were sent from al-Andalus to Daylam (south of the Caspian Sea) in the late twelfth century, and contemporary Latin sources indicate their export to Christian lands. For example, the *Fuero* of Centocellas, dated 1194, charged a toll of five *solidi* for a Christian [transporting] a load of rabbit skins, and one *murabiṭūn* for a Muslim carrying the same cargo.[147] Other Castilian tariff lists from the period 1166–1200 cited similar fees.[148] Andalusi rabbit pelts also made their way further abroad, as demonstrated in a contract noting *cuniculorum de Spania* in Genoa in 1206.[149]

Gold

During the twelfth century, ports in al-Andalus and the western Maghrib became centers for the diffusion of gold to other Mediterranean regions, particularly Europe. Most gold came to al-Andalus (in the form of dust or ingots) from the western Sudan, by way of North Africa. Once in Muslim Spain, gold

145 Mas'ūdī, *Kitāb al-tanbīh wa al-ishrāf*. [ed. M.J. de Goeje, *BGA* 2nd edn, VIII, Leiden, 1967], p. 63

146 Maqqarī, *Analectes*, I, p. 122 (1949 edition, I, p. 184).

147 L. García de Valdeavellano, *El mercado en León y Castilla durante la edad media*. [2nd edn, Seville, 1975], p. 162.

148 M. Gual Camarena, "Tarifas hispano-lusas de portazgo, peaje, lezda, y hospedaje (siglos XI y XII)," *Anuario de estudios medievales* 9(1974–9), pp. 370–1.

149 *Giovanni de Guiberto*. [eds. M. Hall, H.C. Krueger, R.L. Reynolds, Turin, 1940] II, p. 389.

was processed through Andalusi mints, and the movement of the resulting specie is traceable through both physical and documentary evidence.

Scholars disagree concerning the origins of the gold trade between the Sudan and the Mediterranean world. Although Andalusi markets did not enter the picture until the central middle ages, most evidence suggests that the Sudanese gold trade was well established by the sixth century AD. Indeed, the prospect of increased access to Maghribi gold routes may have been an incentive spurring Arab expansion westward in the following century.[150] Many medieval writers mentioned traffic in Sudanese gold, and almost all geographical works in Arabic include passages citing the Kingdom of Ghana (now much of Senegal, Mali, Burkina Faso, and Niger) as a source for gold.[151] The gold mined here was of a quite high standard, averaging 92 percent purity, and supplies were vast.[152] In his book on metals and gems, *Kitāb al-jawharatain*, the tenth-century author

[150] T.F. Garrard. "Myth and Metrology: The Early Trans-Saharan Gold Trade," *Journal of African History* 23(1982), p. 450. This motivation seems less likely if one accepts M. Lombard's theories concerning the release of hoarded gold into circulation after the Arab conquests. This release, he argued, yielded up large quantities of gold, and provided fuel to the early Islamic economy. See Lombard, *Les métaux dans l'ancien monde du Ve au XIe siècle.* [Paris, 1974], pp. 195–201. In return for gold, salt was probably the primary commodity traded southward from the Mediterranean to West Africa. On the exchange for salt, see M. Malowist, "Quelques observations sur le commerce de l'or dans le Soudan occidental au moyen âge," *Annales: ESC* 5–6(1970), p. 1636; J. Devisse, "La question d'Awdaghust," *Tegdaoust I; Recherches sur Aoudaghost.* [Paris, 1970], p. 141; J. Devisse, "Routes de commerce et échanges en Afrique occidentale en relation avec la Méditerranée: Un essai sur le commerce africain médiéval du XIe au XVIe siècle," *Revue d'histoire économique et sociale* 50(1972), p. 51.

[151] A case has also been made for the inclusion of East Africa under the general term "the Sudan." M. Horton argued that the purity of Fatimid dinars (96 percent) leads to the conclusion that the gold in these coins was mined not in West Africa but on the Indian Ocean coast (Horton, "The Swahili Corridor," *Scientific American* (Sept. 1987), p. 86). Alternatively, others have attributed the high quality of Fatimid gold to careful refining.

[152] The natural purity of Sudanese gold allowed it to be minted with little or no refining. Nevertheless, refined gold from other sources could produce coinage of considerably higher standard (up to 99 percent pure). Thus, despite the great popularity of Sudanese gold, it actually produced an inferior coin. Analysis of Andalusi and Maghribi coins has been done by A. Ehrenkreutz, measuring the specific gravity of different coin types ("Studies in the Monetary History of the Near East in the Middle Ages," *JESHO* 6(1963), pp. 243–77), and R.A. Messier, using neutron activation analysis to measure the radioactivity of individual elements in coins ("The Almoravids: West African Gold and the Gold Currency of the Mediterranean Basin," *JESHO* 17(1974), pp. 31–47).

Hamdānī claimed that "the most productive gold mine in the world is the mine of Ghānah in the country of the Maghrib."[153] By the twelfth century, Idrīsī described the structure of the Sudanese gold trade at North African termini, where "most of the gold is bought by inhabitants of Ouargla, and by those of the western Maghrib; they bring this gold to minting houses in their countries, where it is struck into dinars and exchanged in commerce for merchandise."[154] But not all gold would have been immediately minted, as shown by a roughly contemporary Geniza letter in which the writer reported that an associate had sent him "a bar of gold from Fez . . . [with instructions] to sell the gold in Almeria."[155] Geniza letters frequently mention sums of gold sent from west to east in return for eastern goods shipped westward. In the case where a purse containing a specified sum is cited, it seems clear that money was sent in cash.[156] However, the practice of sending sealed bags of coinage, marked according to their weight rather than the number of coins they contained, indicates that metallic content was often more important than face value.

The transit trade, and control of the routes linking the North African ports with southern gold fields, was generally in the hands of Berber middlemen. No direct transactions took place between the Sudan and Mediterranean merchants until the late middle ages. Gold traveled north by several different routes: during the ninth century, an eastern route ran from Gao to Ouargla to Qayrawan to the Near East, while a western route went through Awdaghost to Sijilmasa to Tahert, Tlemcen, and al-Andalus. A third, more westerly route, coming via Aghmat and ending in Fez, developed in the twelfth century.[157] The bar of gold mentioned above, which was traded from Fez to Almeria

[153] D.M. Dunlop, "Sources of Gold and Silver in Islam according to al-Hamdānī," *Studia islamica* 8(1957), p. 39. Other Arab authors mentioning Sudanese gold include Yāqūt, Bakrī, Ibn Ḥawqal, Idrīsī, Masʿūdī, *et al.*

[154] Idrīsī, *Opus*, 1, [Naples-Rome, 1970] pp. 24–5.

[155] Bodl d66.52; trans. Goitein, *Letters*, p. 50.

[156] Goitein points this out with particular reference to TS 8.12, written from Tunisia to Egypt (*Letters*, p. 83), but the practice was widespread.

[157] Both M. Brett, "Ifrīqiya as a Market for Saharan Trade from the 10th to the 12th C. AD," *Journal of African History* 10(1969), p. 350 and T. Lewicki, "L'état nord-africain de Tahert et ses relations avec le Soudan occidental à la fin du VIIIe et au IXe siècle," *Cahiers d'études africaines* 8(1962), p. 519 provide maps of these trade routes.

by a Jewish merchant ca. 1110, probably traveled northward by this latter route.

Because these three south–north routes were controlled by different tribes at different times, Mediterranean access to gold was dependent on a shifting network of alliances between Berber tribes and northern states. Thus, it is not surprising to find a new westerly route, channeling gold to the western Maghrib and Muslim Spain, developing under the Almoravids and Almohads, when these two successive dynasties ruled most of the western Islamic world. With North African gold routes under Almoravid and Almohad control, more gold came to and through Andalusi markets and mints. Ibn Rushd distinguished between "Almoravid gold" and "eastern gold" (*dhahab al-mashriqiyya*), indicating that both were available in the peninsula.[158] More striking evidence for the importance of Sudanese gold in al-Andalus during the Almoravid period comes from the unprecedented influence of the Almoravid dinar (*murabiṭūn*). Although Andalusi rulers had minted gold since the first half of the tenth century, the *murabiṭūn* and its imitations circulated widely through the Islamic west, Christian Spain, and southern Europe. These Almoravid coins were destined to become one of the most utilized and copied currencies in the medieval western Mediterranean.

The Almoravids minted dinars in the Maghrib from 1068, and the first known Andalusi *murabiṭūn* was struck in Seville (the Almoravid capital) in 1096. Other Andalusi mints were soon established, many in eastern cities, perhaps in response to increasing Italian commercial contacts with Almeria, Denia, and Valencia.[159] The relatively large number of Almoravid mints, particularly in contrast to those existing later under the Almohads, suggests a high quantity of coins produced. Nevertheless, Almoravid Andalusi dinars tended to be of a lower weight (4.05 grams or less) and lower standard of fineness (91.5 percent) than

[158] Ibn Rushd, *Fatāwā Ibn Rushd.* [ed. al-Talīlī, Beirut, 1407/1987], p. 571.

[159] Devisse has estimated that 57 percent of Almoravid Andalusi dinars struck between 1097 and 1136 were minted in eastern al-Andalus. He likewise points out that in the early years of Almoravid rule in al-Andalus, the dynasty's numismatic efforts concentrated on the peninsula: 63 percent of existing gold coins minted in the years 1097–1106 were struck in Andalusi mints, 60 percent from the period between 1107 and 1126. After this point, the representation of Andalusi mints diminishes, both in numbers and output. By 1136–45, Andalusi coins, struck in only four mints, represented 30 percent of known Almoravid output, although overall production had increased during these years (Devisse, "Routes de commerce," pp. 65–6).

contemporary coins elsewhere.[160] Because the standard of many Almoravid coins was close to that of Sudanese gold (of seventy Andalusi *murabiṭūns* examined by Messier, at least half had a gold to copper ratio similar to that of Sudanese gold), the Almoravids probably derived a considerable quantity of the gold for their mints from West Africa.[161]

In spite of the relatively low standard of Almoravid gold (or perhaps because of it), *murabiṭūns* achieved wide acceptance and circulation. As a rule, coins of poorer quality tend to drive those of higher quality out of the market, but this is not sufficient explanation for the fame of the *murabiṭūn*. Certainly they were minted in great quantity, and it is possible that the Almoravids enforced the exclusive use of the *murabiṭūn* within their empire. More likely, however, is the fact that the *murabiṭūn* arrived in the Mediterranean world just at the right moment to take advantage of the "commercial revolution" in Europe, when Christian rulers and merchants became more eager than ever for gold. References to *murabiṭūns* begin to appear in Italian documents by the middle of the eleventh century, indicating a widespread familiarity with the currency whether or not actual examples reached Italian markets. Under the sway of this *pax morabetina*, before direct routes were established between European and Maghribi ports, Andalusi markets provided a convenient point of distribution for the popular Almoravid dinars.[162] Soon, as already remarked in chapter 2, Christian Spanish markets not only used genuine *murabiṭūns* but Christian rulers began to mint their own imitations (perhaps reusing gold from melted-down originals).

Slaves

Slaves were the third major commodity redistributed through Andalusi markets. As early as the ninth century, Muslim and

[160] R. A. Messier, "Muslim Exploitation of West African Gold during the Period of the Fatimid Caliphate." [Ph.D. Dissertation, University of Michigan, 1972], pp. 107–9. Individual Almoravid mintings could vary considerably from these averages, with gold contents ranging between 76.2 percent and 96.2 percent, which suggests minimal standardization or control of the minting process.

[161] Messier, "Muslim Exploitation," pp. 117–18. One quarter of the coins examined, however, show a finer standard which led Messier to postulate the use of Iberian mines as a secondary source of gold for Almoravid mints.

[162] The term *pax morabetina* is from D. Abulafia, "Asia, Africa, and the Trade of Medieval Europe," [*Cambridge Economic History of Europe*. 2nd edn, Cambridge, 1987], p. 467.

Jewish merchants brought slaves into al-Andalus from eastern Europe and Christian Spain, and then re-exported them to other regions of the Islamic world. Ibn Khurradādhbih remarked that the Rādhānite merchants sold Andalusi slave girls, and his contemporary, Ibn al-Faqīh, listed slave girls among Andalusi exports to the Maghrib.[163] These women may well have been natives of the northern peninsula, as in a case recorded by the ninth-century jurist Ibn Saʿīd, in which Jewish merchants sold a number of Galician women in Merida.[164] Male slaves, including a Basque musician at the court of ʿAbd al-Raḥmān II (822–52), were also brought into al-Andalus from the north of Spain.[165]

Bishop Agobard of Lyons wrote (ca. 826) of two young men abducted from Arles and Lyons by Jewish slavers, with at least one of the pair sent as a slave to Cordoba. Agobard went on to claim that instances of Jewish slaving were common, and insisted that "it should not be permitted for Jews to sell Christians to Spain," particularly since the Jews sometimes "do things [too] horrible to write about."[166] The context of Agobard's complaint makes it difficult to judge the accuracy of his information. It is significant that he is the only ninth-century writer to object to the taking of Christian captives within Carolingian realms. Other contemporary sources show Jews operating as slave traders in France, but they do not suggest that these merchants enslaved local Christians.[167] Because Agobard was himself a Mozarab, it is likely that he was particularly sensitive to the existence of Christian enslavement in al-Andalus. His complaints may, in fact, reflect an Iberian phenomenon – the enslavement

[163] Ibn Khurradādhbih, *Kitāb al-masālik*, pp. 153–5; Ibn al-Faqīh, *Kitāb al-buldān*. [ed. M.J. de Goeje, *BGA*, 2nd edn., v, Leiden, 1967] p. 252.

[164] J. Ribera y Tarrago, *Disertaciones y opúsculos*. [Madrid, 1928] I, pp. 24–5.

[165] J. Vernet, "El Valle del Ebro como nexo entre orient y occidente," *BRABLB* 23(1950), p. 258.

[166] Agobard, *Epistolae*. [ed. E. Dümmler, *MGH*, Epistolae v, Berlin, 1899], pp. 183, 185. Most readers have taken these horrible deeds to mean castration, but it is also possible that Jewish traders were circumcising, not castrating, their slaves.

[167] A charter of Louis the Pious (814–40) granted to an Iberian Jew, Abraham of Zaragoza, permitted the latter to traffic in foreign slaves (*mancipia peregrina*) within Louis' kingdom. Another document concerning two Jews, David and Joseph of Lyons, and dated before 825, granted similar rights to trade in foreign slaves (*Formulae merowingici et karolini aevi*. [ed. C. Zeumer, *MGH* Leges v (in quarto), Hanover, 1886], p. 325, #52; p. 310, #31). At about the same time, a rabbinic source cited the arrival of Jewish merchants bringing with them "slaves and young eunuchs" (S. Assaf, *Gaonic Responsa from Geniza mss.* [Jerusalem, 1928], p. 38–9).

of Basques and Galicians – which he transplanted to France.[168]

Information from the tenth century, however, lends more credibility to Agobard's assertions. Ibn Ḥawqal (writing in the 970s) reported that "among the most famous exports [from al-Andalus to other Muslim lands] are comely slaves, both male and female, from Frankish (*Ifranja*) and Galician regions."[169] According to Iṣṭakhrī, likewise, "white slaves and costly slave girls" came from al-Andalus to other regions of the *dār al-Islām*, but he was surely exaggerating their price when he added that "slave girls and slaves without skill, depending on their appearance, can be had for one thousand dinars or more."[170] Liutprand of Cremona described trade in eunuchs between Verdun and Muslim Spain in the same century, confirming the general pattern of traffic through Andalusi emporia.[171]

Ibn Ḥawqal also noted another type of slave, the *ṣaqāliba* (generally translated as Slavic eunuchs), who came through Andalusi markets for transport abroad. According to this report, "all Slavic eunuchs on earth come from al-Andalus, because they are castrated in that region and the operation is performed by Jewish merchants."[172] Muqaddasī, writing at about the same

[168] My thanks to David Nirenberg for his ideas on this subject.

[169] Ibn Ḥawqal, *Kitāb ṣurat al-arḍ*, p. 110. In Arabic, Galician might apply to anyone from the northwestern Peninsula – Leon, Galicia, Asturias, even Portugal.

[170] Iṣṭakhrī, *Masālik*, p. 45.

[171] Liutprand, *Antapodosis*. [in *Opera*, ed. J. Becker, *MGH* Scriptores in usum scholarum, Hanover-Leipzig, 1915], p. 156. No Arabic sources cite Verdun as a source of eunuchs coming to al-Andalus. Some scholars have taken this information as confirmation of Agobard's earlier assertions, but it seems unlikely that these eunuchs were either of local origin or Christian, since these are facts which Liutprand would surely have mentioned. There is also disagreement over how slaves would have been brought to al-Andalus from Verdun. A. Lewis opted for an entirely overland route, while C. Verlinden suggested a sea route departing from Arles (Lewis, *Naval Power and Trade*. [Princeton, 1951], p. 180; Verlinden, *L'esclavage dans l'Europe médiévale*. [Bruges, 1955] I, p. 223–4). Also on the early slave trade and Verdun, see Verlinden, "Les Radaniya et Verdun," *Estudios en homenaje a D. Claudio Sánchez Albornoz*. [Buenos Aires, 1983], II, pp. 105–32.

[172] Ibn Ḥawqal, *Kitāb ṣurat al-arḍ*, p. 110. The *ṣaqāliba* were perhaps the best-known slave population in al-Andalus, and their identity has been a matter for debate. Although many scholars have assumed that the term was generic, D. Ayalon has argued that all the ṣaqāliba were ethnic Slavs, imported both to Muslim Spain and the eastern Islamic world. D. Ayalon, "On the Eunuchs in Islam," *Jerusalem Studies in Arabic and Islam* [Jerusalem, 1979] I, pp. 67–124. The link between the name ṣaqāliba and Slav (as well as romance derivatives, *esclave*, etc.) has been generally supported in modern scholarship. See C. Verlinden, "L'origine de sclavus-esclave," *Bulletin Du Cange: Archivum latinitatis medii aevi* 17(1942), pp. 97–128; and R. Kahane and H. Kahane, "Notes on the linguistic history of *Sclavus*," *Studi in onore di Ettore Lo Gatto e Giovanni Maver*. [Rome, 1962], pp. 345–60. Also on trade in Slavs

time, provided similar information to the effect that Jews in "a town behind Pechina" produced *ṣaqāliba* to be sent from al-Andalus to Egypt.[173] However, not all northern captives were handled by Jews, since an eleventh-century Muslim writer noted that both Jewish and Muslim slavers in the regions along the Andalusi *thughūr* castrated slaves for foreign export.[174]

Chroniclers mention thousands of Slavic slaves at the Umayyad court in the ninth and tenth centuries, when tensions on the eastern borders of the Carolingian Empire could have fed the supply of *ṣaqāliba* to Europe and Muslim Spain.[175] The great popularity of the *ṣaqāliba* in al-Andalus and elsewhere in the Muslim world may have been based on the fact that the distant origins of these slaves tended to promote their loyalty in military and domestic duties. By the eleventh century, in contrast, references to Slavic slaves virtually disappear. Indeed, by this period, many of these former slaves had risen from servitude to join ruling elites in the Taifa states. There are several plausible explanations for this shift. First, the decline of Slavic slavery in the eleventh century may have been owing to the eastward expansion of Europe and the increasing christianization of Slavic lands. Second, perhaps the demise of the centralized Umayyad state, whose rulers had at one time employed thousands of the *ṣaqāliba*, reduced the demand for a large and loyal corps of Slavic slaves. Meanwhile, Islamic rulers in the Near East began to turn to slave sources on their own eastern and northern borders. Lastly, Brett has put forward the possibility that the arrival of the Almoravids and Almohads created new markets for, and new channels of access to, black slaves in al-Andalus and North Africa, replacing the demand for whites.[176]

Muslim Spanish markets and merchants continued to deal in

during the tenth century, see Verlinden, "La traite des esclaves. Un grand commerce international au Xe siècle," *Etudes de civilisation médiévale. Mélanges offerts à E.R. Labande*. [Poitiers, 1974], pp. 721–30; and A.M. 'Abbadī, *Los esclavos en España. (al-Ṣaqāliba fī Isbāniyā.)* [Madrid, 1953]. For a map of traffic in Slavs, see Lombard, *The Golden Age*, p. 197.

[173] Muqaddasī, *Description*, pp. 242–3.

[174] Maqqarī, *Analectes*, I, p. 92. Maqqarī attributed this information to Ibrāhīm b. al-Qāsim al-Qarawī (or al-Qayrawānī) who died in 1026 (C. Brockelmann, *Geschichte der arabischen Litteratur*. Supplement I [Leiden, 1937–42], p. 252).

[175] Lévi-Provençal has cited figures ranging from 3,750 to 13,750 *ṣaqāliba* in tenth-century Cordoba (*Histoire*, II, p. 126). However, this information is derived from a much later author, Ibn 'Idhārī (d. 1320).

[176] M. Brett, 'Ifrīqiya as a Market for Saharan Trade,' p. 360

slaves through the twelfth century, when slaves in Andalusi markets increasingly came from Christian territories in northern Spain, where warfare and border raids provided a steady supply of captives. Given the ethnic diversity of the Andalusi population, this trend could sometimes cause confusion, as is shown in comical anecdotes related by the early thirteenth-century jurist Saqaṭī. He tells of how a buyer from out of town arrived in Cordoba and purchased a Christian slave girl whom, he was assured, had been recently acquired from the frontier regions. This was demonstrated by the fact that she only spoke a northern language. Because she had been recently imported, he paid an exorbitant price, after which he bought beautiful clothes for her and prepared to take her home. However, at this point she revealed – in fluent Arabic – that she was actually a free Muslim woman, and threatened to take him before a judge unless he did as she instructed. "If you fear [losing] your money," she counseled, "take me to Almeria, where you can increase what you originally paid [because] Almeria is a terminus for ships and a center for merchants and travelers." The implication, here, was that foreign merchants would pay a higher price to buy a slave for export to other regions of the Islamic world. When the duped buyer tried to complain to the original seller, the latter claimed to have left the business. Finding himself trapped, the man heeded his slave's advice, allowed her to keep her new finery, took her to Almeria, and sold her at a profit – presumably handing over a certain amount of this money to her.[177]

So long as buyers remained susceptible to blackmail, a deception of this nature might have continued repeatedly until a watchful market inspector put a stop to it, or the region was conquered by the Christians. Indeed, Saqaṭī's tale could not have been written much later, since Christian armies reached Cordoba in 1236 and effectively ended Muslim traffic in northern Christian slaves in that city. In place of this former traffic through markets in Cordoba and other conquered Andalusi cities, a new trade developed to sell Muslim slaves to Christian buyers. This shift represents only one aspect of the realignment of Iberian markets in the thirteenth century. As Muslim territories came into Christian hands, local economies, industries, and exports under-

[177] Saqaṭī, *Kitāb al-faqīh*, pp. 54–5. This retelling is an amalgam of two very similar stories related by Saqaṭī.

went profound change as they were reoriented to suit new needs and circumstances. These changes, and continuities, will be discussed in the following chapter.

Chapter 8

CONTINUITIES AND CHANGES IN IBERIAN EXPORTS AFTER 1212

In 1436, the *Libelle of Englyshe Polycye* listed the *commodytees of Spayne* (i.e., Castile) with the following verses:

> Knowe welle all men that profites in certayne
> Commodytes called commynge oute of Spayne
> And marchandy, who so wyll wete what that is,
> Bene fygues, raysyns, wyne . . .
> And lycorys, Syvyle oyle and also grayne,
> Whyte Castell sope and wax is not in vayne,
> Iren, wolle . . .
> Saffron, quiksilver; wheche Spaynes marchandy
> Is into Flaundres shypped full craftylye
> Unto Bruges as to here staple fayre.[1]

This poetical list was not merely an exercise in literary fancy, since these commodities appear repeatedly in other late medieval documents from England, France, and the Low Countries. Flemish tariff lists and English chancery rolls mention Spanish (usually Castilian) wool, Granadan figs, and olive oil from Seville, while Chaucer's pilgrims weave references to Iberian wine and qirmiz into their tales.

There is much that is familiar in this fifteenth-century catalogue of Iberian exports, but there are also significant additions and omissions in comparison with the range of earlier Andalusi exports. Even a rough sampling of documentation reveals marked changes from the Muslim to the Christian period in the nature and variety of Iberian products. It is not possible here to examine in detail the trade between the Iberian peninsula, the Mediterranean, and Europe in the late middle ages, nor does this chapter pretend to cover the vast array of sources and secondary

[1] *The Libelle of Englyshe Polycye. A Poem on the Use of Sea-Power, 1436.* [ed. G. Warner, Oxford, 1926], p. 4. A similar list of commodities exported from Portugal appears on p. 7.

works pertinent to this subject. Instead, it aims to highlight examples of continuity and change in the spectrum of Iberian exports from 1250 to 1500 in order to demonstrate the impact of the Christian conquest, with the consequent changes in Iberian industries and economic structure, on international trade through the peninsula.

Deciphering the chronology of change is not perplexing, since both common sense and documentation point to the period between 1212 and 1248 as a watershed. The Christian acquisition of Muslim territories clearly had a profound effect on local commodities produced for export, while at the same time, changes in production and demand elsewhere in the western Mediterranean and northern Europe influenced all Iberian commercial organization and output. Castilian and Aragonese political relations abroad affected patterns of trade, as did events outside the peninsula. The Hundred Years War, together with trade disputes between England, France, and Flanders, and the development of northern textile industries, all held ramifications for sales of Spanish goods abroad. Without elaborating further here on the intricacies of European diplomacy and politics, the very fact that they had such an influence demonstrates the degree to which Iberian trade had shifted from a Muslim to a Christian orientation by the middle of the thirteenth century.

Political and linguistic divisions between (and even within) Christian Iberian kingdoms also represented a change from prior patterns of Andalusi rule. Although it would be wrong to envision al-Andalus as a homogenous society, it had been bound together as a single political unit under Umayyad, Almoravid, and Almohad rule (despite the disruptions of civil wars or ethnic and religious factionalism). In contrast, the peninsula in the thirteenth century was divided between the vast realms of Castile-Leon and Aragon-Catalonia, along with the smaller kingdoms of Navarre and Portugal – not to mention Nasrid Granada. Despite their mutual commitment to the Christianization of the peninsula, Christian rulers had little in common, and were often diametrically opposed in their ambitions, political interests, and diplomatic alliances.

Political changes and divisions within the peninsula brought economic changes in their wake. Not only did the Iberian merchant population change by the early 1200s, but in many places the local economy was forced to adjust as agricultural, industrial, and market structures accommodated new political and demographic conditions. Yet the fundamental nature of the land did not change, and its productive capacity remained the same, so long as farming techniques, crops, and irrigation could be maintained. Thus, in some regions, Andalusi exports survived virtually unchanged as the country moved from Muslim to Christian rule. In others, however, earlier patterns of agriculture, manufacturing, and trade disintegrated after the Christian arrival, making way for the development of new Castilian and Aragonese exports to meet the demands of emerging European markets. Even in the north of the peninsula, new industries emerged in regions untouched by Muslim rule.

In Nasrid Granada, that corner of al-Andalus to remain under Muslim rule until 1492, thirteenth-century events also altered patterns of international trade. Although the region still exported many of the same products that had made Almeria, Malaga, and other southern cities famous in the eleventh and twelfth centuries, the output of new foreign industries began to compete with Granadan goods. This competition put Granada in doubly straitened circumstances, since the region no longer had the benefit of the larger Andalusi economy that had once allowed it to export luxuries abroad while obtaining many basic staples through trade with other regions of Muslim Spain. Instead, Granada was now forced to look to North Africa and elsewhere for wheat and other necessities, and to reach an accommodation with its northern Christian neighbors. Although Granada could produce food, as Ibn Khaldūn pointed out, labor was very expensive.[2] Thus, even in the face of external competition, the Nasrid kingdom still produced the silk and fruits that were so well suited to its climate, and relied on staples imported from abroad.

Many Iberian goods (particularly olive oil and figs) continued to be exported from the same southern and eastern regions that had produced them earlier, whether those regions were newly Christian or still Muslim. In other instances, the region of manufacture expanded – as was the case with cordoban leather. What is striking, however, is that the items that continued to be produced into the thirteenth century were no longer sold to the same markets as had received them previously. By and large, Muslim

[2] Ibn Khaldūn, *The Muqaddimah*, [trans. F. Rosenthal, New York, 1958] II, pp. 278–9.

buyers in the Near East and North Africa now turned to other sources, leaving the majority of Iberian exports to go for sale in Christian lands. References to Iberian products vanished from (or diminished in) Arabic texts, only to appear almost simultaneously in European records. Thus, by the second half of the thirteenth century, the Malaga figs that had once been so esteemed in Baghdad were being enjoyed in Bruges, and Iberian qirmiz was sold in England rather than Egypt.

In addition to these continuities, Christian Spanish kingdoms also began to export a number of commodities that had been unimportant (although not always unknown) to Andalusi international trade. These new exports included alum, iron, wine, Muslim slaves, and – most famously – merino wool. Many of these items were produced in northern Castile and exported from the newly developing network of ports (Santander, Castro Urdiales, and others) on the Bay of Biscay. The majority of these new exports were raw goods, carried abroad to provide working materials for European industries. Although the peninsula did continue to export a good number of manufactured items (including ceramics, paper, and textiles) the balance of production had changed to favor raw materials.

In addition to these continuities and new exports, there is also a third category of goods, namely those former Andalusi exports that had largely disappeared from records by the early thirteenth century. Either their production and export had ceased, their traffic had sufficiently declined to go unrecorded, or prohibitions on their trade forced merchants to avoid documentation of ongoing commerce. For various reasons these disappearances were no longer viable commodities, their routes had changed, or they were not competitive in the Christian commercial world to which the peninsula was now an aspiring southern adjunct. As examples of these three options, Christian slaves were no longer a permissible export from a newly Christian country, Sudanese gold no longer came through the peninsula after the destruction of Almohad power since Mediterranean merchants could now obtain it directly from North African ports, and Iberian timber was not so valuable in European markets as it had been in the wood-poor regions of the Near East and North Africa (where Christian religious scruples now prohibited its sale). Discontinuities in the slave, gold, and timber trades will be discussed at the end of the chapter to show how prohibitions on trade, government policy, and the new northern orientation of the peninsula in the late middle ages destroyed the earlier Andalusi role as a western transfer zone between the Christian and Muslim commercial worlds. In place of this role, ports in Andalusia and Granada now served as way-stations for goods passing through the Straits of Gibraltar between the Christian commercial zones of the Mediterranean and the Atlantic.

CONTINUITIES IN EXPORTS

Olive oil

The mention of *Syvyle oyle* in the *Libelle of Englyshe Polycye* demonstrates that olive oil continued to be an important Sevillian export long after the Christian capture of this city by Ferdinand III of Castile in 1248. Indeed, the *Primera crónica general* seems to echo the praises of earlier Arab authors in its description of the excellence and wide distribution of oil from the region of Sharaf.[3] Even before the Castilian conquest of the city, the oil trade was already largely in the hands of the Genoese, as shown by a charter granted to Genoa by Ferdinand III in which he allowed Genoese merchants to continue carrying Sevillian oil "to other regions of the world," as had been their custom "during the time that the city was held by the Saracens."[4] It is not clear when this Genoese trade originated, particularly since no early notarial contracts mention Sevillian olive oil. However, some oil may have been carried by Italians as early as the 1160s, by which date both Genoa and Pisa probably maintained trading houses in Seville. Later records show that although the Genoese (or at least Genoese ships) continued to play a dominant role in traffic in Andalusian olive oil to the Mediterranean and northern Europe, other Italian and Aragonese merchants also handled some of this trade.[5]

[3] (Alfonso X), *Primera crónica general de España*. [ed. R. Menéndez-Pidal, Madrid, 1906 (reprint 1977)] II, p. 769.

[4] Caffaro, *Annali genovesi di Caffaro e de suoi continuatori*. [ed. L.T. Belgrano, Genoa, 1890] III, pp. 183–84. These privileges were renewed in 1251 (C. Verlinden, "Italian Influence in Iberian Colonization," *Hispanic American Historical Review* 33(1953), p. 201).

[5] J.A. Sesma Muñoz, "El comercio de exportación de trigo, aceite y lana desde Zaragoza a mediados del siglo XV," *Aragón en la edad media*. [Zaragoza, 1977], pp. 209–18.

In the fourteenth century, the Muslim geographer Ḥimyarı praised the oil of Seville, claiming that this "olive oil ranks among the best olive oil; there is a high yield when [the olives] are pressed, and [the oil] does not become [rancid], even over long periods, and [thus] it is exported from [the peninsula] by land and sea to the farthest regions."[6] Ḥimyarī's comments indicate the continued availability of Iberian olive oil in the *dār al-Islām*, although it probably arrived there on Christian ships. Both Genoese and Venetian merchants carried olive oil from Andalusia to Egypt in the fifteenth century.[7] Sevillian oil was also sold in Christian Mediterranean markets by the first half of the fourteenth century, when Pegolotti recorded details of its measurement and cost in comparison with other varieties of oil. Contemporary Genoese traders likewise supplied Sevillian oil to Chios.[8]

As with several other Iberian products, despite its high quality Spanish oil always faced competition in the Mediterranean world. This was less true in northern European markets, however, where olive oil was much in demand for the textile and dye industries, as well as being a primary ingredient in soap (including the newly popular *whyte Castell sope*). A Bruges tariff list from the second half of the thirteenth century listed olive oil among the exports from the region of Seville, and oil appeared again on a 1355 list of Spanish imports to Bruges.[9] Likewise, records from English ports show considerable traffic in Sevillian and Portuguese olive oil during the fourteenth and fifteenth centuries. In 1309, for example, two Portuguese ships arrived in

[6] Ḥimyarī, *La Péninsule ibérique au moyen âge*. [ed. E. Lévi-Provençal, Leiden, 1938], p. 101. Qazwīnī provided similar information in his *Athār al-bilād wa akhbār al-ʿibār*. [Beirut, 1380/1960], p. 497. ʿUmarī, Badr al-Dīn al-Aynī, and Ibn Baṭṭūṭa were among other authors who mentioned Andalusi oil exports to the Maghrib and Egypt in the late middle ages. On their reports, see R. Arié, *España musulmana*. [Barcelona, 1982], p. 223; and A. Zeki, "Mémoire sur les relations entre l'Egypte et l'Espagne pendant l'occupation musulmane," *Homenaje a Don Francisco Codera*. [Zaragoza, 1904], p. 464.

[7] E. Ashtor, *The Levant Trade in the Later Middle Ages*. [Princeton, 1973], pp. 230,267.

[8] Francesco Balducci Pegolotti, *La pratica della mercatura*. [ed. A. Evans, Cambridge, Mass., 1936], pp. 270–1; E. Otte, "El comercio exterior andaluz a fines de la edad media," *Actas del II Coloquio de historia medieval andaluza: Hacienda y comercio. Sevilla, 8–10 de Abril, 1981*. [Seville, 1982], pp. 194–5. Otte discusses trade in Andalusian oil, pp. 194–205.

[9] J. Finot, *Etude historique sur les relations commerciales entre la Flandre et l'Espagne au moyen âge*. [Paris, 1899], p. 303; L. Gilliodts-van-Severen, *Cartulaire de l'ancien consulat d'Espagne à Bruges*. [Bruges, 1901] 1, p. 15.

Southampton carrying oil, and a safe-conduct was issued to a Spanish ship in Bristol carrying oil, wine, and iron in 1434.[10] Later in the fifteenth century (1475–80), a Genoese merchant in London complained that he had brought a cargo of *oyles* and other merchandise from Spain for sale in London or Southampton, but the master of the ship had taken the goods to Bristol instead.[11] A few years after this, in 1490, a London merchant made a contract to deliver nine barrels of *good Civill oyle*, with the promise that this would be shipped on the *Anne* of Hampton in the next voyage *whiche the sayde ship wyth Godis grace shall make to the porte of Saint Lucard Baramed in the ryver of Syvill.*[12]

Spices and mercury

Qirmiz was likewise continuously exported from old and newly Christian regions of the peninsula and found its way to markets in both northern and southern Europe. A Spanish ship attacked by pirates off Sandwich in 1228 was reported to have carried one hundred pounds of qirmiz (*grein*) in its cargo, while qirmiz from Castile, Andalusia, and Portugal was available in Bruges at roughly the same period.[13] The transport of Iberian dye-stuffs to Bruges is hardly surprising, since textile centers in the Low Countries provided a ready market for colorants. Indeed, when another cargo of qirmiz arrived in Sandwich in 1337 (under less dramatic circumstances than the shipment of 1228) and did not sell well, the Spanish merchant who carried it sought permission to take it to Brabant or Hainault in hopes of a better market.[14] Spanish merchants were certainly bringing *greynen* to Bruges in 1355, although they were required to pay relatively high tariffs on this cargo.[15] Iberian qirmiz continued to be available in the late fourteenth and fifteenth centuries when it was featured in a variety of English documents, both chancery and literary. In the

[10] L.F. Salzman, *English Trade in the Middle Ages.* [Oxford, 1931], p. 412; E.M. Carus-Wilson (ed.), *Overseas Trade of Bristol in the later Middle Ages.* [Bristol, 1937], p. 63.

[11] Carus-Wilson, *Overseas Trade*, p. 149.

[12] Arnold, R. *The Customs of London, otherwise called Arnold's Chronicle.* [London, 1811], p. 110. See also W.R. Childs, *Anglo-Castilian Trade in the Later Middle Ages.* [Manchester, 1978], pp. 45, 109–11.

[13] *Calendar of Close Rolls.* (CCR) [London, 1896–1938] (1227–31), p. 89; Finot, *Etude*, p. 303.

[14] CCR (1333–7), p. 644.

[15] Gilliodts-van-Severen, *Cartulaire*, p. 15.

latter context, a character in the *Canterbury Tales* (ca. 1367) referred casually to "*grain* of Portingale," while in the fifteenth century *grayne* (also *greyne* and *grene*) appeared in the *Libelle of Englyshe Polycye*'s list of Spanish and Portuguese exports and in the *Customs of London.*[16] In 1445, two Venetian galleys arrived in London carrying, among other things, *grana hispánica pro pannos.*[17]

In the Mediterranean, Genoese notarial contracts continued to refer to Iberian qirmiz, including a 1253 record for the sale of *grana de Yspania,* demonstrating continuity of commerce from the previous century.[18] This ongoing traffic with Genoa is confirmed in a 1265 document from Montpellier, in which James I of Aragon ruled on Italian trade and use of this dyestuff.[19] Pegolotti later listed *grana di Spagna* along with six other varieties of qirmiz traded by merchants in Florence, and references from the Datini archives (1383–1411) mentioned qirmiz from Murcia and Valencia (although qirmiz from Provence was deemed somewhat superior).[20]

Iberian saffron and cumin are also found in Christian records from the thirteenth and fourteenth centuries. Both were cited as Spanish exports in the thirteenth-century Bruges list, the former from Aragon and the latter from Castile, but only cumin appeared in the Bruges list of 1355.[21] Pegolotti listed both as Iberian exports.[22] In England, Spanish saffron may have met with competition from locally grown crocuses, but cumin was certainly imported. A complaint made in 1294 concerned a cargo, including "thirty sacks of cumin," said to belong to Spanish merchants in Sandwich, while another record from the same town, dated 1305, mentioned another shipment of Spanish cumin.[23]

[16] G. Chaucer, "The Nun's Priest's Tale," *Chaucer's Poetry.* [ed. E.T. Donaldson, New York, 1958], line 639, p. 514; *Libelle of Englyshe Polycye,* pp. 4, 7; Arnold, *Customs of London,* p. 235. See also Childs, *Anglo-Castilian Trade,* p. 106.

[17] E. Ferreira Priegue, "El papel de Galicia en la redistribución de productos andaluces visto a traves de los archivos ingleses," *Actas del II Coloquio de historia medieval andaluza: Hacienda y comercio. Sevilla, 8–10 de abril, 1981.* [Seville, 1982], p. 243.

[18] ASG Cart. 18/1, fol. 84v.

[19] M.G. Fagniez (ed.), *Documents relatifs a l'histoire de l'industrie et du commerce en France.* [Paris, 1898] I, pp. 261–62.

[20] Pegolotti, *Pratica,* p. 297; F. Melis, *I trasporti e le comunicazioni nel medioevo.* [Florence, 1984], pp. 56–9.

[21] Finot, *Etude,* p. 303; Gilliodts-van-Severen, *Cartulaire,* p. 15.

[22] Pegolotti, *Pratica,* pp. 294, 376.

[23] C.C.R. (1288–96) p. 365; Salzman, *English Trade,* p. 414; Childs, *Anglo-Castilian Trade,* p. 124.

The *quiksilver* mentioned by the *Libelle of Englyshe Polycye* ranked as yet another continuity, since the mines at Almaden, north of Cordoba, were exploited under Christian rule as they had been in earlier centuries. Mercury was traded through Seville to markets in the Mediterranean, England, and Flanders during the thirteenth and fourteenth centuries.[24] By the fifteenth century, a royal grant from the Crown of Castile ceded a monopoly on the mercury trade to Genoese merchants.[25]

Leather and furs

Cordoban, together with other types of worked leather and hides, also continued to be an important Iberian export during and after the thirteenth century. Some leather may have been traded to the *dār al-Islām*, since both Qazwīnī (d. 1283) and Ibn al-Khaṭīb (d. 1374) mentioned exports of Iberian leather.[26] As before, cordoban was in demand in Christian markets where non-Iberian imitations were also often available. In spite of this competition, however, it is clear that both manufacture and commerce of Spanish leathers flourished. Castilian and Aragonese tariff lists had earlier differentiated between red and white cordobans, but the significance of the distinction seems to have increased by the thirteenth century. When tolls were set on cargoes traveling along the Ebro River during the reign of Alfonso II (1162–96), including twenty *solidi* levied on *cordovans blanchs o vermels*, the charge was the same for both varieties. By 1238, in contrast, tariffs in Valencia were set at six *deniers* per dozen for white cordoban, double this amount for red.[27] Since

[24] F. Pérez Embid, "Navigation et commerce dans le port de Séville au bas moyen âge," *Le moyen âge* 75 (1969), p. 489; Finot, *Etude*, p. 303; Gilliodts-van-Severen, *Cartulaire*, p. 15; Salzman, *English Trade*, p. 411; Childs, *Anglo-Castilian Trade*, pp. 119–20.

[25] J. Heers, "Les hommes d'affaires italiens en Espagne au moyen âge: Le marché monétaire." *Fremde Kaufleute auf der iberischen Halbinsel*. [ed. H. Kellenbenz, Cologne-Vienna, 1970], p. 75.

[26] Qazwīnī, *Athār*, p. 555; Ibn al-Khaṭīb, *Mufākharāt Mālaqa wa Salā*. [ed. A.M. al-'Abbādī, Alexandria, 1958], p. 59.

[27] M. Gual Camarena, "Peaje fluvial del Ebro (siglo XII)," *Estudios de la edad media de la Corona de Aragón* 8 (1967), p. 167; *Fori antiqui valentiae*. [ed. M. Dualde Serrano, Madrid-Valencia, 1950–67], pp. 282–3. For Valencia, see also similar documents from the 1240s collected by M.D. Sendra Cendra, *Aranceles aduaneros de la Corona de Aragón (siglo XIII)*. [Valencia, 1966], pp. 22–3, 29, 38.

higher tariffs often signal more expensive, scarcer, or imported goods, this discrepancy may arise from the fact that white cordobans were locally manufactured, in what was now Aragonese territory, while the red variety still came from the Islamic – or recently Christian and Castilian – south. By 1240, at least, a mercantile contract from Vich cited "Valencian" cordobans, and by the following century Valencia had become famous for its production of white leather.[28] Pegolotti referred to the sale of white cordoban from Valencia and Barcelona in southern French ports in the early fourteenth century, and noted the availability of unidentified cordoban in Venice.[29]

Cordoban was also esteemed in northern Europe, as indicated by its mention by John of Garland in Paris, ca. 1220, and the appearance of cordoban and *cordovan vermeil* in a tariff list from Paris (dating between 1272 and 1297).[30] Likewise, a thirteenth-century French fable described two dandies dressed in "soft shoes of cordoban leather and good trousers from Bruges."[31] Although these references do not explicitly state an Iberian provenance, it is quite possible that the cordoban for these shoes came from the peninsula to France by way of Bruges – the source of the trousers. Cordoban from Castile, Leon, and Navarre was certainly available in Flanders by the middle of the thirteenth century.[32] Further afield, the Welsh *Mabinogion* contains a reference to shoes made of gilded cordoban, indicating that this type of leather was familiar as far away as western Britain.[33] Cordoban was undoubtedly available in southern

[28] A. García, "Contractes comercials vigatans de principis del segle XIII," *Ausa* (Vich) 43 (1963), p. 329; Gual Camarena, "Peaje," p. 182.

[29] Pegolotti, *Pratica*, pp. 225, 141. Other types of Iberian leather traded in the Mediterranean also appear in Pegolotti (*Pratica*, pp. 124, 270) and in the Datini archives (Melis, *I trasporti*, pp. 54–6).

[30] A. Scheler (ed.), "Trois traités de lexicographie latine du XIIe au XIIIe siècle," *Jahrbuch für romanische und englische Literatur* 6 (1865), p. 296; D. D'Arcq, "Tarif de marchandises qui se vendaient à Paris à la fin du XIIIe siècle," *Revue archéologique* 9 (1852), p. 227.

[31] A. de Montaiglon (ed.), *Recueil général et complet des fabliaux des XIIIe et XIVe siècles*. [Paris, 1872] 1, p. 1. This passage has been cited by R. van Uytven, "Cloth in medieval literature of Western Europe," *Cloth and Clothing in Medieval Europe: Essays in Memory of Prof. E.M. Carus-Wilson*. [London, 1983], p. 155.

[32] Finot, *Etude*, pp. 302–3. Cordoban was also sold in Bruges in 1355 (Gilliodts-van-Severen, *Cartulaire*, p. 15).

[33] *Math vab Mathonwy*. [edition, translation, and commentary by W.J. Gruffydd, Cardiff, 1928], p. 20. The Welsh *cordwal* is cognate with English *cordwain* and other variations on cordoban. The text, from the *Red Book of Hergest*, dates to ca. 1400 (*The Mabinogion*. [trans. J. Gantz, London, 1976], p. 29).

England by 1228, when the document describing the Spanish ship attacked by pirates near Sandwich listed an astonishing variety of leather goods carried in its cargo. The unfortunate vessel carried not only a large quantity of cordoban (some badly damaged by sea-water – a perennial mercantile danger), but also rabbit skins, cat skins, lamb skins, kid skins, and many other pelts.[34] Much later, the *Libelle of Englyshe Polycye* cited *cordeweyne* among exports from Portugal (though not, it seems, from Castile).[35]

References abound to other types of Spanish leather and hides sold in Europe in the fourteenth and fifteenth centuries, but only rabbit skins persist as another hold-over from earlier Muslim traffic. Rabbit skins had been noted as an Andalusi export by Zuhrī in the twelfth century, when they also appeared in contemporary Castilian and Aragonese *portazgos*. By the mid thirteenth century, they turn up in records of Iberian trade to England and the Low Countries. Not only were they carried to Sandwich in 1228, but rabbit skins came to London, where Castilian and Galician merchants delivered a shipment of six thousand *pellium cuniculorum* in 1237, and to Bruges from Navarre in the middle of the thirteenth century.[36] From time to time, monarchs in Castile attempted to limit the export of Iberian goods, and these prohibitions were extended to include rabbit skins by the late thirteenth century.[37] The motivation behind restrictions on these apparently innocuous goods is not clear, but these prohibitions cannot have carried lasting weight since traffic in rabbit skins continued in the fourteenth century. In 1337, for example, Spanish merchants carried "fifty bales of hare skins and of rabbit skins" to Sandwich, and *coninen* figured among Spanish goods brought to Bruges in 1355.[38] At roughly the same period, Pegolotti cited rabbit skins for sale (presumably to foreign traders) in Mallorca and Seville.[39]

[34] C.C.R. (1227–31), p. 89. The Close Rolls and Fine Rolls (C.F.R.) are filled with reference to hides shipped from Spain. See, for example, C.C.R. (1333–7), p. 644; C.F.R. (1337–47), p. 5; C.C.R. (1337–9), p. 85. See also Salzman, *English Trade*, pp. 414–15, and Childs, *Anglo-Castilian Trade*, pp. 136–7.

[35] *Libelle of Englyshe Polycye*, p. 7.

[36] C.C.R. (1227–31) p. 89; C.C.R. (1234–7) p. 479; Finot, *Etude*, pp. 302–3.

[37] J. O'Callaghan, *The Cortes of Castile-León, 1188–1350*. [Philadelphia, 1989], pp. 189–90.

[38] CCR (1337–9), pp. 85–6; Gilliodts-van-Severen, *Cartulaire*, p. 16. On the English fur trade and introduction of rabbits to England, see E.M. Veale, *The English Fur Trade in the Later Middle Ages*. [Oxford, 1966], especially pp. 209–14.

[39] Pegolotti, *Pratica*, pp. 124, 270.

Dried fruits

Revenues from the export of figs and other fruits were crucial to the economy of Nasrid Granada in the fourteenth century. "Oh fig," wrote one Malagan poet in acknowledgment of this important source of income, "You have sustained the life of Malaga, and because of you boats arrive to [this city]."[40] The figs of Malaga maintained their superior reputation as a delicacy, both in Muslim and Christian markets, and profits from this trade became increasingly valuable as traffic in Granadan silk faltered. The geographer 'Umarī (d. 1348) wrote that Malagan figs were carried to all the countries neighboring al-Andalus, and Ḥimyarī claimed that they were "carried to Egypt, Syria, Iraq, and even, perhaps, as far as India, for they are the best and sweetest fig." Ibn Baṭṭūṭa and Maqqarī likewise mentioned the export of figs from Malaga to all regions of the west and east, extending as far as China.[41] Andalusi grapes, famous for the size and meatiness of their raisins, were also exported. The *marabalī* grape, from Marabella, and the *munakabbī*, from Almuñecar, were particularly esteemed, as was fruit from Elche, Malaga, and other Granadan regions.[42] Ibn Baṭṭūta saw "raisins sold in the markets [of Malaga]," and Qazwīnī reported that the grapes exported from Niebla had no equal in the world.[43]

Figs and other dried fruits were one of the few regular and ongoing exports from Muslim Granada to Europe, despite the fact that other Iberian regions (including Seville, Cordoba, Catalonia, and Mallorca) had started to export fruits by the middle of the thirteenth century.[44] Christian merchants were already dealing in Iberian figs in the twelfth century, when Genoese notaries recorded shipments of figs (*fegie*) carried by Genoese merchants (though only as far as Ceuta) in 1162 and 1179.[45] Not long after this, the Arab author Shaqundī (writing

[40] Ibn Baṭṭūṭa, *Tuḥfa al-naẓar fī gharā'ib al-amṣār.* [Cairo, 1934], p. 291.

[41] 'Umarī, *Masālik al-abṣār.* [trans. M. Gaudefroy-Demombynes, Paris, 1927], pp. 240–1; Ḥimyarī, *Péninsule*, p. 178; Ibn Baṭṭūṭa, *Tuḥfa*, p. 291; Maqqarī, *Analectes sur l'histoire et la littérature des arabes d'Espagne.* [ed. R. Dozy, Leiden, 1855–60] I, p. 95.

[42] J. Vallvé, "La agricultura en al-Andalus," *Al-Qantara* 3(1982), pp. 289–90.

[43] Ibn Baṭṭūṭa, *Tuḥfa*, p. 291; Qazwīnī, *Athār*, p. 555.

[44] Finot, *Etude*, p. 303; Pegolotti, *Pratica*, p. 123.

[45] H.C. Krueger, "The Commercial Relations between Genoa and North-West Africa in the Twelfth Century." [Ph.D. dissertation, University of Wisconsin, 1931], p. 121.

1199–1212) reported that "[both] Muslims and Christians export [figs from Malaga] in such large quantities that they cannot be counted."[46] By the late fourteenth century, the Genoese family of Spinola had negotiated with Nasrid rulers to obtain a virtual monopoly over exports of dried fruit from Granadan ports.[47]

Some dried fruits from Granada were sold within the peninsula, as demonstrated in a 1252 tariff list from Tortosa that specified a toll of three *denarios* per basket of figs from Malaga or Alicante, and the same for a large basket (*sporta grossa*) of figs from Denia.[48] Cargoes of figs, raisins, and almonds also arrived in northern European ports, brought on Iberian and Italian ships.[49] Domingo Gunsalves, a merchant from Lisbon, carried fifty sacks of almonds and one hundred and nineteen *frails* of figs to Sandwich in 1299. Ten years previously, merchants on a Spanish ship in Portsmouth had sold a quantity of raisins, dates, pomegranates, lemons, and oranges, to an emissary of Queen Eleanor of Castile, who may have been longing for the sweet tastes of her homeland.[50] English records likewise show the arrival of two more Iberian ships bearing cargoes of figs and raisins early in the next century.[51] Needless to say, the English were not the only northern consumers with a craving for Iberian figs. In 1350, at least forty Spanish ships (many with cargoes of dried fruit) arrived in Bruges, where tariffs were levied on *rosinen* and *fighen*.[52] Later, a record from 1395 mentioned English merchants shipping figs and raisins to Normandy

[46] Maqqarī, *Analectes*, II, p. 148.

[47] J. Heers, "Le royaume de Grenade et la politique marchande de Gênes en occident (XVe siècle)," *Le moyen âge* 63(1957), p. 108; Otte, "Comercio exterior," p. 223; E.J. López de Coca Castañer, "Comercio exterior del reino de Granada," *Actas del II Coloquio de historia medieval andaluza. Hacienda y comercio. Sevilla, 8–10 de Abril, 1981*. [Seville, 1982], p. 344.

[48] Sendra Cendra, *Aranceles*, p. 61.

[49] F. Melis, "The Nationality of Sea-Borne Trade between England and the Mediterranean around 1400," *Journal of European Economic History* 4(1975), p. 376.

[50] Salzman, *English Trade*, pp. 412–13.

[51] Salzman noted Portuguese ships bringing dried fruits to Southampton in 1309 (*English Trade*, p. 412); Patent Rolls (C.P.R.) (1334–8) [London, 1895] contain a complaint that 300 *couples* of figs and grapes were stolen from a Spanish ship in Sandwich in 1337 (p. 443). Also on figs, see Childs, *Anglo-Castilian Trade*, p. 125.

[52] F. Rörig, *The Medieval Town*. [Berkeley, 1967], p. 81; Gilliodts-van-Severen, *Cartulaire*, p. 15.

from the Algarve.[53] Back in Britain, traffic in Iberian fruit continued through the fifteenth century, as shown by a legal dispute that arose between two merchants in Bristol over a cargo of *certeyn Tonnes of ffrute called ffyges and resans* brought from southern Castile in the 1470s.[54]

Ceramics

Evidence from the Pisan *bacini*, perhaps the best laboratory for examining the distribution of ceramics around the medieval Mediterranean world, shows that Iberian ceramic production and export continued from the Muslim into the Christian period. Within the peninsula, Lister and Lister have remarked that "the extant transition period pottery in Andalusia . . . [also] confirms an unbroken craft continuity, despite the political upheaval." According to their observations, ceramics continued to be produced in Cordoba and other southern cities in very much the same styles as before, while Nasrid Granada and Andalusia maintained ceramic exports during the thirteenth and fourteenth centuries. In contrast, ceramic production in northern Castile remained undeveloped.[55] The situation was different in the Crown of Aragon, at least in the Balearics, where Rosselló Bordoy has noted an "absolute rupture" in the Muslim ceramic tradition following the Christian conquest.[56]

Data from the *bacini* and elsewhere suggest that the diversity of Iberian ceramics diminished in the late middle ages, although new forms and glazing techniques were developed at this period. Most striking in this regard is the appearance of *maiolica*, a variety of lustreware that became popular in the fourteenth and fifteenth centuries. According to some scholars, *maiolica* derived its name from Malaga, although it has been more commonly associated with Mallorca, and was – in any case – widely imitated.[57] Malaga had long been famous for its pottery (as well as its figs), and ceramics from this region appear to have main-

[53] C.C.R. (1392–6), p. 324.

[54] Carus-Wilson, *Overseas Trade*, pp. 147–8.

[55] F.C. Lister and R.H. Lister, *Andalusian Ceramics in Spain and New Spain*. [Tucson, 1987], p. 72.

[56] G. Rosselló Bordoy, "Mallorca: Comercio y cerámica a lo largo de los siglos X al XIV," *II Coloquio internacional de cerámica medieval en el Mediterraneo occidental, Toledo, 1981*. [Madrid, 1986], p. 199.

[57] U. Scerrato, *Gli arabi in Italia*. [Milan, 1979], p. 441.

tained their reputation into the fifteenth century. The city's wares were traded to both Muslim and Christian markets, as indicated by the fact that several late medieval Muslim authors referred to these ceramics, and Malagan pots show up in Provençal texts during the late thirteenth century.[58] Iberian pottery also made its way to England, where a number of dishes, saucers, and jars were purchased off a Spanish ship in 1289, and a shipment of dishes and pitchers *de Malyk* came to Southampton early in the next century. A later source noted "jars of *Malik*" available in London in 1462.[59]

THE DECLINE OF ANDALUSI SILK

References to Andalusi silk and silk textiles, for so long the preeminent exports of Muslim Spain, decline after the early thirteenth century. Although silk was still produced in Nasrid Granada, where the slopes of the Alpujarras continued to support mulberry trees, Andalusi silk no longer dominated western Mediterranean markets as it had in the eleventh and twelfth centuries. Some Granadan silk was still traded to the *dār al-Islām*, and Maqrīzī noted pieces of Andalusi *siqlāṭūn* in thirteenth-century Cairo.[60] Ibn Saʿīd (d. 1286) likewise claimed that Malaga, Murcia, and Almeria all produced a "gilded brocade that amazes people in the east with the beauty of its workmanship," but his comment may have been taken from an earlier source.[61] From the viewpoint of Christian demand, it is noteworthy that Pegolotti's exhaustive catalogue of Mediterranean commodities included no mention of Spanish silk, although the author cited many other regional varieties, mainly from the Near East and Anatolia. In contrast, the Datini archives contain references to *seta spagnola*, suggesting that at least some raw silk from the peninsula arrived in Venice, Lucca, and other textile centers

[58] Ḥimyarī, *Péninsule*, p. 163; Qalqashandī, *Ṣubḥ al-ʿashā fī kitābāt al-inshā'*. [trans. L. Seco de Lucena, Valencia, 1975], p. 26; Ibn Baṭṭūṭa, *Tuḥfa*, p. 291; Maqqarī, *Analectes*, I, p. 96, 123. See also B. Martínez Caviró, *La loza dorada*. [Madrid, 1983]. For Provençal references, see M. Jenkins, "Medieval Maghribī Ceramics." [Ph.D. Dissertation, New York University, 1978], p. 183.

[59] Salzman, *English Trade*, pp. 415–16. Salzman dates the Southampton record to 1304. It is also cited by A. Lane ("Early Hispano-Moresque Pottery: A Reconsideration," *Burlington Magazine* 88(1946), p. 249), who dates it to 1303.

[60] Maqrīzī, *Khiṭaṭ*. [Bulaq, 1270/1853] I, p. 427.

[61] Maqqarī, *Analectes*, I, p. 123.

during the fourteenth and fifteenth centuries.[62] Genoa probably provided the most important Italian market for Nasrid silk in the late middle ages, since Genoese merchants were firmly entrenched in Granadan trade and could ensure a supply to meet the needs of Genoese weavers. Andalusi silk also arrived in other parts of Europe, but references are rare after the middle of the thirteenth century in comparison with data from the century before. French poets no longer sang of *soie d'Aumarie* as had their twelfth-century counterparts. Granadan silk does appear in the thirteenth-century Bruges tariff list, where it is remarkable as the only Nasrid product not also cited as an export from some other region of the peninsula.[63] Some silk also came to Bruges from Granada in the following century, with a cargo arriving in the port of Swin in 1350.[64] Andalusi silk textiles were still available in Christian Spain too, as demonstrated by their presence in the royal tombs at Santa Maria la Real de los Huelgas in Burgos.

With the exception of these Castilian examples and the Andalusi brocades noted in Arabic sources, most late medieval references to Granadan silk pertain to the raw fiber. Overall, the data indicate first that Andalusi silk no longer enjoyed the prestige and economic dominance, either in Europe or in the Mediterranean, that it had once commanded. Second, they suggest that the volume of exports of Granadan silk had declined, and third, they show a shift from mixed traffic in both raw and woven silk to a concentration on the raw material.

Changes in the Andalusi silk industry and exports are striking, but not inexplicable, since the sources and demands for silk in the Mediterranean and Europe were changing by the early thirteenth century. Competition was one important factor in the decline of Andalusi silk. Christian Mediterranean regions – particularly southern Italy and Sicily – had begun to produce their own silk as early as the tenth century, but the Italian industry expanded in the twelfth and thirteenth centuries to meet the needs of local silk weavers.[65] Christian Spanish regions were also producing silk by the twelfth century, but their output was

[62] Melis, *I trasporti*, pp. 58–9, 149, 171.

[63] Finot, *Etude*, p. 303.

[64] Rörig, *The Medieval Town*, p. 81.

[65] R.S. Lopez, "China Silk in Europe in the Yuan Period," *JAOS* 72(1952), p. 72; M. Lombard, *The Golden Age of Islam*. [Oxford, 1975], p. 184.

not competitive until the fifteenth century.[66] In the eastern Mediterranean, Latin treaties with Byzantium in the twelfth century increased western access to Byzantine silk, and Latin merchants controlled trade routes through Byzantium for much of the thirteenth century. At the same time, the rise of the Mongols, and their maintenance of the *pax mongolica*, opened the famous silk road and allowed western traders to obtain silk from China and from centers of production in the Islamic world. A similar pattern is seen in Muslim lands, where merchants no longer looked to the Islamic west for silk because they could obtain it either from China or closer to home.

Other fibers and textiles also came to compete with Andalusi raw silk and brocades in the late middle ages. By the fourteenth century, even Muslim markets in the eastern Mediterranean preferred to import non-silk textiles from Europe over silks from the Islamic west. The new northward orientation of Iberian commerce in the thirteenth century is signaled by the quantity of fabrics from the Low Countries, France, and Italy that began to be imported to the peninsula. Whereas al-Andalus had once exported Muslim silks to Europe, now Iberian consumers were eager for Flemish and Italian woolens and linens. In 1234, James I of Aragon granted special privileges to local cloth merchants in a document that cited textiles from England and France, but not from the Muslim south. Six years later, his *leuda* conceded to Valencia listed fabrics woven in Ghent, Ypres, Rheims, Narbonne, Montpellier, Milan, Barcelona, and other European cities, with only one brief mention of *tela hispanie*.[67] Fabrics from northern European cities were also widely available in Castilian markets by the second half of the thirteenth century.[68] Since most of these European fabrics were not made from silk, their production had a double impact on the Iberian silk industry. Not only did demand for these textiles compete with demand

[66] E. Morral i Romeu and A. Segura i Mas, *La seda en España: Leyenda, poder, y realidad.* [Barcelona, 1991], pp. 62–7. Mulberry trees and silk weaving were also recorded in Catalonia in the eleventh and twelfth centuries (F. May, *Silk Textiles of Spain, 8th-15th century.* [New York, 1957], pp. 10–11) and in Toledo in 1192 (A. González Palencia, *Los mozárabes de Toledo en los siglos XII y XIII.* [Madrid, 1926] I, p. 171).

[67] (James I), *Documentos de Jaime I de Aragón.* [ed. A. Huici Miranda, Valencia, 1976]; Sendra Cendra, *Aranceles*, pp. 30–1. See also *Fori antiqui valentiae*, CXLIV.14, p. 286.

[68] The *Córtes de Jerez de 1268*, for example, set prices for commodities, including a sizeable array of textiles from towns in the Low Countries (*Cortes de los antiguos reinos de León y Castilla.* [Madrid, 1861] I, pp. 65–74).

for Andalusi woven silks, but northern weaving ateliers wanted raw wool, flax, and cotton more than raw silk.

By the late middle ages, the main centers of textile production and trade had shifted from Andalusi markets to the northern peninsula. At the same time, the majority of textiles available in Iberian markets were made of wool and fibers other than silk.[69] An analysis of references to textiles in fifteenth-century Castilian documents indicates the direction of changes in production and trade from the Muslim to the Christian period. Out of one hundred and four Castilian names for textiles, forty-four referred to woolens, thirty-three to silks, seven to linens, and twenty to other fabrics. The list includes textiles woven both in Castile and elsewhere, and tells something of the diversity of fabrics though not absolute quantities. Linguistic analysis indicates that just over half the silks were Arabic fabric types, probably holdovers from the Muslim period (and perhaps still woven in mudejar ateliers), while most woolens and other textiles bore Romance names.[70] Iberian Christians, it seems, preferred to work with wool.

Demographic changes in the peninsula adversely affected the Iberian silk industry. As new Christian populations took root in southern regions they brought their own economic interests and technical capabilities. In many cases, these settlers did not, or could not, adopt the lifestyles or businesses of previous inhabitants, leading to the decline of some industries and the development of others.[71] Also, because successful silk production and weaving relied on a large skilled workforce, the industry in

[69] The development and structure of the northern textile industry have already garnered considerable scholarly attention and need not be described at length here. On the Castilian textile industry, see P. Iradiel Murugarren, *Evolución de la industria textil castellana en los siglos XIII-XVI*. [Salamanca, 1974]. On Catalan and Aragonese production, see M. Gual Camarena, "Origenes y expansión de la industria lanera catalana en la edad media," *Atti della seconda settimana di studio, Istituto F. Datini*. [Florence, 1976], pp. 511–23 (and other articles in this collection); M. Riu, "The Woollen Industry in Catalonia in the Later Middle Ages," *Cloth and Clothing in Medieval Europe. Essays in Memory of Professor E.M. Carus-Wilson*. [London, 1983], pp. 205–29; E. Ashtor, "Catalan Cloth on the Late Medieval Mediterranean Markets," *Journal of European Economic History* 17(1988), pp. 227–57; and Sesma Muñoz, "El comercio de exportación," pp. 219–24.

[70] Of the thirty-three silks, seventeen have names deriving from Arabic, while sixteen have Romance names. Of the woolens, in contrast, five have Arabic names and thirty-nine are Romance. The names have been collected by M. Martínez, *Los nombres de tejidos en castellano medieval*. [Granada, 1989].

[71] T. Ruiz, "Expansion et changement: la conquête de Séville et la société castillane (1248–1350)," *Annales: ESC* 34(1979), p. 551.

Granada was disrupted not only by Muslim immigration to Nasrid lands in the wake of Christian victories, but also by contemporary Muslim emigration from the peninsula.

NEW IBERIAN EXPORTS

As the decline in the Andalusi silk trade makes clear, the quantity of data for the continuity of certain Iberian exports, albeit to new northern European markets, should not obscure the very real changes that were taking place simultaneously in the range of Iberian commodities. By the fourteenth century, a number of items that had been virtually unknown to Andalusi traders had become staple exports from Christian Spanish kingdoms. It is almost impossible to overestimate the importance of these goods, particularly wool, to the Iberian economy in the late middle ages.

Wool

There was a lag of nearly one hundred years between the decay of the Andalusi silk industry and the full-fledged development of international trade in Iberian wool. Whereas Andalusi silk had ceased to be a major export by the early thirteenth century, the wool industry only began to take hold in the peninsula in the second half of that century. Already by 1253, however, the main routes (*cañadas*) for the flocks had been established, and the official incorporation of the "Honorable Council of the Mesta of the Shepherds of Castile" by Alfonso X in 1273 probably confirmed earlier royal grants (now lost).[72] Small quantities of Iberian wool were imported to England by the 1260s, and a Bruges ordinance of 1304 also noted sales of Spanish wool.[73] By

[72] J. Klein, *The Mesta: A Study in Spanish Economic History*. [Cambridge, Mass., 1920], p. 12; J. Hillgarth, *The Spanish Kingdoms*. [Oxford, 1976], pp. 288–9; R. Pastor de Togneri, "La lana en Castilla y León antes de la organización de la Mesta," *Atti della prima settimana di Studio, Istituto F. Datini*. [Florence, 1974], pp. 253–69. For a more recent analysis of the Mesta, see J. Bishko, "Sesenta años después: *La Mesta* de Julius Klein a la luz de la investigación subsiguente," *Historia, Instituciones, Documentos* [Seville] 8(1981), pp. 9–57.

[73] Childs, *Anglo-Castilian Trade*, p. 106; Gilliodts-van-Severen, *Cartulaire*, p. 7. Spanish wool may even have arrived in England in the twelfth century, since Henry II saw fit to prohibit this commerce in 1172 (M. Carlé, "Mercaderes en Castilla (1252–1512)," *Cuadernos de historia de España* 21–2(1954), p. 275).

the middle of the fourteenth century, exports of Iberian wool were well established and the wool trade would dominate the peninsula's commerce for the next two hundred years.

Sheep had been raised in the peninsula since ancient times. The wool produced in and exported from Roman Baetica had a widespread reputation, but the long smooth staple of Roman and Andalusi wools differed from the short crimped merino wool that later became the standard Castilian export. Merino sheep may have been brought to the peninsula during the thirteenth century, but the word *merino* does not actually appear in Spanish texts until the early fifteenth century. The name probably derives from the Banū Marīn, a Maghribi dynasty succeeding the Almohads in the late twelfth century. However, it is not clear whether the sheep were brought to al-Andalus in the Muslim period, whether they were imported by later Christian rulers, or whether (as Lopez believed) they were introduced from North Africa to the peninsula in the fourteenth century by Genoese intermediaries who were hoping to establish a reliable Iberian source of wool to supply Italian looms.[74] Whichever was the case, the Castilian wool industry developed slowly, as sheep were imported from North Africa and local herds reproduced. Nevertheless, it has been estimated that by 1467 the Castilian sheep population had reached 2,700,000 head, double what it was in the thirteenth century.[75]

The renaissance of Iberian wool production marked a dramatic reorientation of the peninsula's economy, since a textile industry and trade based on sheep, and on the long seasonal migrations of shepherds, was very different from the small, sedentary, family-based operations characteristic of silk cultivation. The reintroduction, growth, and success of the wool trade in the Iberian peninsula may be attributed to several interrelated causes. First, the fact that the climate and terrain of Castile were well suited to migratory sheep herding, particularly in a period when military campaigns had disrupted agriculture in the central peninsula. Second, conquests and territorial expansion in the thirteenth century thinned and redistributed the Castilian and Aragonese populations, as did the plague in the next century. Third,

[74] Klein, *Mesta*, p. 4; M. Lombard, *Les textiles dans le monde musulman du VIIe au XIIe siècle*. [Paris, 1978], p. 26; R.S. Lopez, "The Origin of the Merino Sheep," *Joshua Starr Memorial Volume*. [New York, 1953]), p. 163.

[75] J. O'Callaghan, *A History of Medieval Spain*. [Ithaca, 1975], p. 617.

foreign demand fostered traffic, and burgeoning textile industries in Flanders, France, and Italy provided a ready market for Spanish wool. Although Iberian wool was usually deemed inferior to higher quality varieties from England, it was in demand for rougher textiles and – in times of economic difficulty or political discord – it replaced English wool in European markets.[76]

Iron

Before the full-blown development of the Iberian wool industry, Castilian iron competed with wool as the peninsula's most important new export. Iron had always been available in the peninsula, but it was neither exploited nor exported before the late twelfth century. The growth of iron technology and use in Europe during the central middle ages – with the metal's increased military, naval, and agricultural applications – generated a new demand for iron at just the time when the peninsula was beginning to emerge as a commercial entity in the northern European trading sphere. Weapons, fittings for ships, horseshoes, the blades of heavy ploughs, and other implements all required large quantities of iron, and Castilian mines and merchants met these needs.

Arab geographers had written about iron mines in the peninsula – in Saltes, Guadix, Huesca, and elsewhere – and remarked that, because of its naval uses, iron working was "an industry [common to] ports where ships put in," although as Ḥimyarī warned, "this is a strenuous industry, which weakens local

[76] For a general survey of the medieval wool trade, see E. Carus-Wilson, "The Woollen Industry," *Cambridge Economic History of Europe*. [Cambridge, 1952 (and 2nd edn 1987)], and collection edited by M. Spallanzani, *Produzione commercio e consumo dei panni di lana [nei secoli XII-XVIII]. Atti della seconda settimana di studio, Istituto F. Datini*. [Florence, 1976]. On Iberian wool and wool traffic, see earlier references (particularly Iradiel Murugarren, *Evolución*); C.R. Phillips, "The Spanish Wool Trade, 1500–1780," *Journal of Economic History* 42(1982), pp. 775–95; and C.R. Phillips, "Spanish Merchants and the Wool Trade in the 16th Century," *Sixteenth Century Journal* 14(1983), pp. 259–82. I am most grateful to T. Ruiz for permission to read a draft of chapter 8 from his *Crisis and Continuity: Land and Town in Late Medieval Castile* [Philadelphia, 1994]. I am likewise indebted to W.D. Phillips and C.R. Phillips for advice on wool traffic and for permission to read a draft of chapter 2 from their forthcoming volume *Spain's Golden Fleece*.

people."[77] However, there is almost no data on Andalusi exports of iron, a silence that may indicate either a lack of trade, perhaps owing to slow growth in iron technology, or an unwillingness to document traffic in potential war materials. When Zuhrī mentioned exports of black iron used to manufacture "instruments of war" in the late twelfth century, it is significant that he was describing Barcelona (by then long in Christian hands).[78] Castilian harbors on the Bay of Biscay, as well as Catalan ports, emerged as centers for iron export in the thirteenth century, and this industry would dominate their business until the rise of the wool trade. Throughout the late thirteenth, fourteenth, and fifteenth centuries, Iberian iron was shipped northward to ports in England and Flanders, where its arrival is abundantly attested in a variety of documents.[79]

Wine

Although the prohibitions of judges and the praises of poets reveal that wine was widely available in al-Andalus, it was never acknowledged as either a commodity or an export. This ceased to be the case under Christian rule, when Iberian wines (both from Andalusia and northern regions) were openly produced and introduced into Mediterranean and northern European markets. As with many other Iberian goods, however, Spanish wines met with serious competition from counterparts produced elsewhere in Europe. Iberian wines arriving in England, for

[77] Ḥimyarī, *Péninsule*, p. 110. On medieval Islamic ironworking, see A.Y. Hassan, "Iron and Steel Technology in mediaeval Arabic Sources," *Journal for the History of Arabic Science* 2(1978), pp. 31–43.

[78] Zuhrī, "Kitāb al-dja'rāfiyya" [ed. M. Hadj-Sadok], *Bulletin des études orientales* 21(1968), p. 203.

[79] On Iberian iron coming to Flanders, see Finot, *Etude*, p. 303 and Rörig, *The Medieval Town*, p. 81. For traffic to England, there is a comprehensive discussion in Childs, *Anglo-Castilian Trade*, pp. 112–19; also Salzman, *English Trade*, pp. 408–10, 414; Carus-Wilson, *Overseas Trade*, p. 63; T. Ruiz, "Castilian Merchants in England, 1248–1350," in *Order and Innovation in the Middle Ages: Essays in Honor of Joseph R. Strayer*. [Princeton, 1976], pp. 181–82; C.C.R. (1288–96), p. 365, (1346–9), p. 213; C.P.R. (1307–13) pp. 246–7, (1340–3), p. 364; Arnold, *The Customs of London*, p. 190. On the Mediterranean, see R. Sprandel, "Le commerce du fer en Méditerranée orientale au moyen âge," *Sociétés et compagnies de commerce en orient et dans l'Océan indien*. [Paris,1970] pp. 387–92. Also on Iberian iron: T. Glick, *Islamic and Christian Spain*. [Princeton, 1979], p. 134; T. Ruiz, "Burgos y el comercio castellano en la baja edad media," *La ciudad de Burgos. Actas del congreso de historia de Burgos*. [Madrid, 1985], p. 48; and J. Hillgarth, *The Spanish Kingdoms*, p. 40.

example, were never considered to be in a class with their French competitors – and in consequence these sweet heady spirits were often cheaper than the finer vintages of Bordeaux. Chaucer's Pardoner, for one, slyly derided the practice of adulterating good French wines with stronger and less expensive *win of Spaine*.[80] This is not to say that Iberian wines were all of one type, however, since when a ship arrived in Bristol in 1474, the Galician merchants on board had cargoes of both sweet and dry wines – the former probably from Andalusia, the latter perhaps from the Rioja.[81]

Spanish wines were available in England by 1228, when a shipment of wines and other merchandise came to Grimsby, and wines figured in the cargo of the unfortunate Spanish vessel attacked near Sandwich in the same year.[82] Small quantities of Spanish wine continued to arrive in English ports during the next century, but always in competition with wines from Gascony. Iberian wines only gained a significant foothold in the English market after 1453, when the French capture of Bordeaux reduced (but did not discontinue) imports of Gascon wine.[83] Spanish and Portuguese wines also made their way to markets in the Low Countries and Italy during the thirteenth and fourteenth centuries.[84]

Alum

Alum, like wine, was produced in the peninsula during the Arab period, but international trade only developed under Christian rule. Although many of the Iberian regions that produced alum had been under Muslim control, alum traffic is not mentioned in Arabic sources before the thirteenth century when Ibn al-Shabbāṭ referred briefly to Andalusi alum.[85] Because this mordant was a

[80] Chaucer, "The Pardoner's Tale," line 237, p. 415.
[81] Ferreira Priegue, "El papel de Galicia," p. 246.
[82] C.C.R. (1227–31), pp. 71, 89.
[83] C.C.R. (1346–49), p. 213 provides an example of Spanish wine imported to Southampton in 1347. Documents collected by E. Carus-Wilson show Iberian wine coming to Bristol in 1434 (*Overseas Trade of Bristol*, p. 63). On the wine trade see also M. James, *Studies in the Medieval Wine Trade*. [Oxford, 1971], pp. 29,84; Salzman, *English Trade*, p. 401; and Childs, *Anglo-Castilian Trade*, pp. 126–36.
[84] Finot, *Etude*, p. 303; Pegolotti, *Pratica*, p. 125.
[85] Ibn al-Shabbāṭ, "Un fragmento de la obra de Ibn al-Sabbāṭ (s.XIII) sobre al-Andalus" [trans. E. de Santiago Simón], *Cuadernos de historia del Islam* (1973), pp. 23–4.

crucial element in both the textile and leather industries, even supplies from second-rate mines (a category that included Iberian alum) could find a market when better sources faltered. Superior alum was available in Asia Minor, where its trade was alternately monopolized by the Venetians and the Genoese, and new sources of good alum were later discovered in the fifteenth century at Tolfa, in the Papal States, but these supplies were not always available or affordable. Despite the inferiority of Iberian alum, therefore, its traffic was fueled by the ever-increasing needs of European industries.

Latin sources mention traffic in Castilian alum in the western Mediterranean from the middle of the twelfth century, when a 1153 list of tolls from Narbonne cited *alum de Castelha*, and *alumine de Castilia* appeared in contemporary Genoese contracts.[86] In the next century, Genoese notaries cited Castilian alum (as did those who wrote contracts in Pisa, Narbonne, and Marseille), and Pegolotti later included *allume di Castiglio* in his vast inventory of commercial goods.[87] Alum from Castile and Mallorca also made its way to cities in northern Europe – including Bruges, Sandwich, and Southampton – during the thirteenth and fourteenth centuries.[88]

Other commodities

Honey, sugar, salt, grain, and other commodities likewise figured as Iberian exports at this period, although they too faced competition from other areas of production. As with alum, most had been available in al-Andalus before the thirteenth century, but only developed as exports within the later Christian commercial sphere. By the fourteenth century, considerable quantities of honey arrived in English and Flemish ports, carried by Spanish and Portuguese ships, and sugar from Nasrid Malaga was sold in

[86] M.G. Mouynès, *Inventaire des archives communales. Ville de Narbonne.* [Narbonne, 1871], p. 4; Giovanni Scriba, *Cartolare di Giovanni Scriba.* [eds. M. Chiaudano and M. Moresco, Rome, 1935] I, p. 101, #193; II, pp. 203–5, #1212.

[87] ASG Div. 102, 5v (1179); ASG Cart. 5, 60r (1213); D. Herlihy, *Pisa in the Early Renaissance.* [New Haven, 1958], p. 31; Mouynès, *Inventaire*, II, cxxix, p. 207; L. Blancard (ed.), *Documents inédits sur le commerce de Marseille au moyen âge.* [Marseille, 1884–5] II, p. 11 (1248); Pegolotti, *Pratica*, p. 293.

[88] Finot, *Etude*, p. 304; Gilliodts-van-Severen, *Cartulaire*, p. 16; Salzman, *English Trade*, p. 411; Childs, *Anglo-Castilian Trade*, pp. 108–9; Ferreira Priegue, "El papel de Galicia," p. 245.

Bruges ca. 1300.[89] Later, the Datini archives documented traffic in Malagan sugar in western Mediterranean markets.[90] Christian Spain was also exporting sugar by the early fourteenth century, after its cultivation had been introduced in the Algarve and elsewhere, but sugar exports from the peninsula declined in the next century due to competition from sugar produced in the Canary Islands.[91] Christian Iberia likewise exported a certain amount of salt (both rock salt and sea salt) to markets in the Mediterranean and Europe, along with wax, soap, tallow, rice, and other goods.[92] Grain traffic was more complex, and varied in times of shortage and plenty. Although the northern peninsula was a major producer of grain, both Andalusia and Granada (like al-Andalus in earlier centuries) were more likely to find themselves with a shortfall than a surplus.

DISCONTINUITIES AND PROHIBITIONS

Not all Iberian exports in the late middle ages were continuities or new appearances. A number of earlier exports disappeared from trade by the middle of the thirteenth century, while traffic in others declined in the face of more stringent government

[89] C.C.R. (1333–7), p. 644, (1337–9), p. 85; C.F.R. (1337–47), p. 5; C.P.R. ((1350–4), pp. 396–7, 441–2 (this last record indicates that the honey was intended for shipment to Bruges, where earlier tariff lists [Finot, *Etude*, p. 303] also indicate trade in Spanish honey to Flanders); see also Salzman, *English Trade*, p. 411, Childs, *Anglo-Castilian Trade*, pp. 124–5. Sugar in Bruges: C. Verlinden, "From the Mediterranean to the Atlantic: Aspects of an Economic Shift," *Journal of European Economic History* 1(1972), pp. 636–9. The late fifteenth-century Arnold's *Customs of London* also mentions sugar from Portugal (p. 234).

[90] Melis, *I trasporti*, p. 58.

[91] A. MacKay, *Spain in the Middle Ages, From Frontier to Empire, 1000–1500*. [London, 1977], p. 172; Gual Camerena, "Peaje," p. 187.

[92] On the salt trade, see M. Mollat, ed., *Le rôle du sel dans l'histoire*. [Paris, 1968] (especially articles by V. Rau and J. Heers); J.-C. Hocquet, *Le sel et la fortune de Venise*. (vol. II, *Voiliers et commerce en Méditerranée, 1200–1650*.) [Lille, 1979]; A.R. Bridbury, *England and the Salt Trade in the Later Middle Ages*. [Oxford, 1955]; M. Gual Camarena, "Para un mapa de la sal hispana en la edad media," *Homenaje a Jaime Vicens Vives*. [Barcelona, 1965–7] I, pp. 483–97; and A. Malpica Cuello, "Regimen fiscal y actividad económica de las salinas del reino de Granada," *Actas del II Coloquio de historia medieval andaluza: Hacienda y comercio. Sevilla, 8–10 de Abril, 1981*. [Seville, 1982], pp. 393–403.

On wax, tallow and soap: Pegolotti, *Pratica*, p. 293; Finot, *Etude*, p. 303; Gilliodts-van-Severen, *Cartulaire*, p. 15; C.C.R. (1288–96), p. 365; Arnold, *Customs of London*, p. 235; Childs, *Anglo-Castilian Trade*, pp. 111, 141; Salzman, *English Trade*, pp. 410–11. On rice: Pegolotti, *Pratica*, p. 296; Finot, *Etude*, pp. 303–4; Melis, *I trasporti*, pp. 54, 67; Salzman, *English Trade*, p. 411.

regulation. As noted at the start of the chapter, some discontinuities can be explained by the changing commercial role of the peninsula in the wider Mediterranean world. Once Andalusi markets no longer functioned as emporia on the western frontier of the Islamic world, many merchants went elsewhere for their purchases. By the late thirteenth century, the Genoese obtained gold from Maghribi ports, and Egyptian slave traders looked to Central Asia for supplies. At the same time, the legislation of Christian Spanish rulers often reflects more attention to their kingdoms' exports than was shown by their Andalusi predecessors. Trade in certain goods was prohibited not merely for religious and military reasons, but also on the grounds that it removed valuable resources from the kingdom.

Slaves

Christian slaves bound for Muslim lands were no longer a permissible export from newly Christian markets in the peninsula, but their place was taken by Muslims sent for sale in southern Europe. This switch reflects the ongoing reality of slavery throughout the medieval Mediterranean world, both Christian and Muslim. In the past, al-Andalus had distributed Christian and pagan slaves to other regions of the Islamic world. By the middle of the thirteenth century, however, large numbers of Muslim slaves began to appear for sale in Christian cities – sometimes in the same city where they had once been free residents. Although there had been saracen slaves in Christian Spain and Europe throughout the eleventh and twelfth centuries, the enslavement of Muslims in the thirteenth century can often be directly linked to Christian victories in Islamic lands.

This trend emerges with particular clarity in the Iberian context, although perhaps the best evidence for the export of Andalusi Muslims comes from documentation of slave sales in southern French and Italian port cities. Notarial documents usually state that a particular slave was a Muslim, calling them either a Saracen (*sarracenus/a*) or a Moor (*maurus/a*), or else recently enslaved Muslims may be identified by their Muslim names. Most contracts also cited a slave's city or region of origin, and noted their sex. Genoese notarial records, in particular, yield an important group of slave sales contracted in that city, in the thirteenth century. Not all of these sales relate to

Andalusi slaves, but the Spanish contracts are especially interesting since there appears to be a correlation between Christian military victories and the dates of these sales. It is surely not a coincidence, for example, that following the conquest of Valencia by James I of Aragon in 1238, Genoese notaries recorded many sales of Valencian Muslim slaves in 1239.[93]

Iberian urban records also provide evidence on the sale of Muslim slaves in the late twelfth and thirteenth centuries. The 1166 *Fuero* of Evora, for example, quoted a charge of one *solidus* levied on merchants for every "Moor whom they sell in the market," a phrase reiterated in many other charters of the period.[94] Muslim slaves were certainly an important export from the Crown of Aragon under James I (1213–76), when their trade was subject to government licence and regulation.[95] As with earlier tariff lists, charters to Aragonese and Catalan cities (including the 1238 *lezda* of Valencia) stated duties to be collected on Muslim slaves sold in the city.[96] Catalan notarial contracts also testify to slave trading, with one merchant sending a female slave to be sold in Sicily in 1238, and another sending six slaves to Crusader Palestine in 1252.[97]

The sale of Andalusi Muslims in the Christian Mediterranean appears to have diminished by the late thirteenth century, as Iberian society achieved a new status-quo and merchants turned to other sources for slaves. Nevertheless, the early revenues derived from the enslavement and export of local Muslims must have provided an invaluable new asset both to recently Christian Spanish cities and to the merchants who brought trade to their markets.

[93] See my article "Muslim Spain and Mediterranean Slavery: The Medieval Slave Trade as an Aspect of Muslim–Christian Relations." *Christendom and its Discontents* [ed. S. Waugh, Berkeley, forthcoming].

[94] *Portugaliae monumenta historica: leges et consuetudines.* [Lisbon, 1856] 1, p. 393 (also pp. 407, 412, 416, 419, 427, 431, 475, 488, 495, 496, 513). On Castilian and Catalan references, see C. Verlinden, "L'origine de sclavus-esclave," *Bulletin Du Cange: Archivum latinitatis medii aevi* 17(1942), pp. 116–7.

[95] R. Burns, *Islam under the Crusaders: Colonial Survival in the thirteenth century Kingdom of Valencia* [Princeton, 1973], p. 111.

[96] *Fori antiqui valentiae*, p. 287.

[97] J. Madurell and A. García, *Comandes comerciales barcelonesas de la baja edad media.* [Barcelona, 1973], pp. 151–4 (documents 2 and 5).

Horses

The export of horses from the peninsula was more strictly regulated than the export of human beings. During the late middle ages, Christian rulers were concerned lest these valuable military assets fall into enemy hands – whether Muslim or Christian. Andalusi rulers, in contrast, had showed little concern over traffic in horses, perhaps because animals had never been an important export from their lands.[98] International trade in horses across the Iberian frontier may have been easier in an earlier period, before the Christian conquest of Toledo and the launching of crusades to Palestine increased Christian–Muslim hostilities. The *Fuero* of Sepulveda (1076), for example, had included a tariff – but not a ban – on horses and other riding animals carried to Muslim lands.[99] But starting in the thirteenth century, Christian Spanish kings regularly reiterated bans on the export of horses from their kingdoms, sometimes basing these restrictions on external factors (lest horses come into enemy hands), sometimes on internal needs (horses were needed at home for the king's own armies and personal use).[100]

As with all such prohibitions, however, their existence in itself suggests trade, and exceptions and loopholes were common. In the Toledo Cortes of 1207, for instance, Alfonso VIII of Castile at first prohibited the traffic of horses, mules, donkeys, and similar animals to Muslim lands, then allowed their trade so long as it did not include war horses or saddle mares (*cavallo o egua con albarda*).[101] Documents from Valencia, dating to 1238 and 1243, are even more matter of fact, and list charges to be levied on "horses [and] mules . . . that enter Saracen lands for

[98] The *equos et mulos hispanos* sent by Charlemagne to Persia may have been animals actually brought from the Iberian peninsula, or merely a breed associated with Spain (Notker the Stammerer, *De Carolo Magno*. [ed. P. Jaffé, *Monumenta carolina*, IV, *Bibliotheca rerum germanicarum*, Berlin, 1867], p. 677).

[99] *Los Fueros de Sepúlveda*. [ed. E. Saez, Segovia, 1953], p. 223.

[100] Castilian prohibitions on traffic in horses were reiterated in Jerez (1268), Burgos (1338), Valladolid (1351), and elsewhere (*Cortes de los antiguos reinos de León y Castilla*. [Madrid, 1861] I, pp. 71, 450; II, p. 25). See also the discussion of *cosas vedadas* in J. O'Callaghan, *The Cortes of Castile-León*, pp. 189–91. Contemporary Muslim jurists also prohibited the sale of horses (and other military items) to Christians. See Ibn Juzayy (d. 1340), *Qawānin al-aḥkām*. [Beirut, 1968], p. 319.

[101] Hernández, "Cortes de Toledo," pp. 234–5; 245.

commercial purpose."[102] Later, in 1345, the Cortes of Burgos allowed some war horses (*cavallos*) to be carried out of the kingdom (except to Muslim lands) in return for a customs fee paid to the crown.[103] In the end, whether or not local rulers had approved their export, Iberian horses found their way to foreign buyers, and into northern European commercial records, throughout the late middle ages.[104]

Timber

Alongside their bans on traffic in animals, Iberian monarchs often attempted to control traffic in timber. Once again, it was generally the military potential of the item that caused concern, although there could also be other motives behind restrictions on trade. At the Cortes of Valladolid in 1351, Peter I of Castile explained that the export of wood was unacceptable for two reasons: first, it denuded the kingdom's hills and second, if local timber went to build ships for foreign monarchs then it would not be available for the king's own navy.[105] To some extent, royal prohibitions reflected papal bans on Christian timber traffic to Muslim lands. In 1237, for example, Gregory IX ruled that Catalan merchants from Tarragona must not sell timber for ships (*lignamina galearum*) to Muslims in the Balearics. Other similar pronouncements were made by later popes, although not always aimed specifically at Catalonia.[106]

Changes in the Iberian timber trade profoundly affected the course of mercantile and naval development in the western

[102] *Fori antiqui valentiae*, CXLIV.4, p. 284; (James I), *Documentos*, II, pp. 167–70. See also, R.I. Burns, "Renegades, Adventurers, and Sharp Businessmen: The 13th century Spaniards in the Cause of Islam," *Catholic Historical Review* 58 (1972), p. 363. It is possible that *terram sarracenorum* referred to North Africa.

[103] *Cortes de los antiguos reinos de León y Castilla*. I, p. 487.

[104] Childs, *Anglo-Castilian Trade*, pp. 120–2; Ruiz, "Castilian merchants," pp. 181–2; Y. Renouard, "Un sujet de recherches: L'exportation des chevaux de la péninsule ibérique en France et en Angleterre au moyen âge," *Homenaje a Jaime Vicens Vives*. [Barcelona, 1965] I, pp. 571–7.

[105] *Cortes de los antiguos reinos de León y Castilla*, II, pp. 22–3. The king conceded that merchants in Galicia and Asturias might continue trafficking in timber according to their usual custom.

[106] (Gregory IX), *Les régistres de Grégoire* IX. [ed. L. Auvray, Paris, 1896–1919] II, p. 554, #3491. See also *Corpus iuris canonici*. [ed. E. Friedberg, Leipzig, 1879–81] II, 5.6.6 p. 774; and *Regesta pontificum romanorum*. [ed. A. Potthast, Berlin, 1874–5], p. 1653, no. 20522. These prohibitions, and other papal restrictions on trade with Muslims, are discussed by J. Muldoon, *Popes, Lawyers, and Infidels*. [Philadelphia, 1979], pp. 52–4.

Mediterranean during the late middle ages. Before the thirteenth century, al-Andalus had had plenty of timber both for its own needs and for export to other regions of the Islamic world. Because the Iberian peninsula had provided so much timber to shipyards in North Africa and even to the eastern Mediterranean, the Christian capture of Andalusi forests in Catalonia during the twelfth century, and in the Balearics and Algarve early in the next century, had a significant impact on the relative strength of Christian and Muslim shipping. Indeed, some Christian campaigns (such as the combined Catalan, Pisan, and Genoese assaults on Tortosa in 1092 and 1147) had specifically targeted forested regions. With timber at their command, rulers in Christian Spain could expand their navies at will, with wood to spare for building up the new Catalan and Castilian merchant fleets. On the other hand, if profits came before prohibitions, rulers and merchants might sell off local timber to Muslim and non-Muslim buyers (a scenario suggested by repeated bans). In any event, Muslim loss of access to Iberian timber after the Christian acquisition of Andalusi forests intensified the imbalance of naval power in the late medieval Mediterranean.

Royal prohibitions on the export of certain commodities in the late middle ages mark a change not only in the specifics of Iberian international trade, but also in the official attitude toward trade. Andalusi rulers had rarely interfered with mercantile cargoes, except in so far as they represented a source of government revenue, although some goods (such as wine and Muslim slaves) were routinely banned by religious authorities. Christian rulers, on the other hand, exhibited a more coherent appreciation of their kingdom's economy as a whole, as well as continuing to keep an eye on opportunities for profit. There are several possible explanations for this shift in attitude, including the growing emphasis on national frontiers and perception of "the state" in this period, together with the new Iberian northward orientation. Prohibitions on the exchange of particular commodities were not merely an attempt to keep war materials from falling into Muslim (or any other hostile) hands. Together with privileges granted to local merchant groups, these prohibitions may also represent (often misguided and ineffectual) royal attempts to control commerce within the realm and to create legislative distinctions between one Christian kingdom and another.

Taken together, late medieval data on changes and continuities in Iberian exports, and royal intervention in trade, show the peninsula emerging as a southern satellite within the commercial and political universe of northern Europe. It still remained part of the Mediterranean economic world, but Iberian markets and exports no longer played, nor could play, the same role as their earlier Andalusi counterparts.

Chapter 9

SPAIN, NORTHERN EUROPE, AND THE MEDITERRANEAN IN THE LATE MIDDLE AGES

Changes in Iberian exports and in the markets that received them indicate profound shifts in the structure of the Iberian economy and its role in late medieval international commerce. Following the data on new commodities, this final chapter will discuss Iberian ports and their merchant populations in the late middle ages, placing these cities and merchants in the context of newly emerging patterns of international trade and political interests in the Mediterranean, the Atlantic, and the Indian Ocean.

ATLANTIC AND MEDITERRANEAN TRADE

Christian Spanish victories in the thirteenth century, and the consequent opening of the Straits of Gibraltar to Christian shipping, altered the structure of European and Mediterranean trade and changed the function of the peninsula within these commercial spheres. After the Muslim east–west trading axis in the Mediterranean had disappeared, a Christian north–south system developed to link markets in the Mediterranean and Europe. It is easy to see the emergence of the Atlantic trading world as a catalyst for the realignment of peninsular trade. The ports of Portugal and northern Castile were nurtured by the new trading opportunities in northern Europe, eventually making Castile "a better guide to the Atlantic, which dominated her entire economic life, than to the Mediterranean on which she turned her back."[1] Southern ports in Andalusia and Granada likewise shifted to encompass their new role as way-stations for sea traffic between northern and southern Europe. All in all, the opening of the Atlantic (with its implications for Iberian trade with the New World in later centuries) is a compelling demon-

[1] F. Braudel, *The Mediterranean and the Mediterranean world in the Age of Philip II.* [New York, 1966] 1, p. 294.

stration of the European and Christian orientation of Iberian life after the middle of the thirteenth century.

But the Mediterranean still retained considerable influence in Iberian international affairs and trade. The peninsula had always been an integral part of the Mediterranean world, and it continued to be so in the late middle ages. Changes in Mediterranean trade were equally powerful, although perhaps less dramatic, and they show another aspect of the same shifts that were occurring in the Atlantic. Mediterranean trade also took on a European and Christian orientation as commercial power switched from the southern to the northern shores of the sea. Two related trends were at work in the wake of Christian territorial expansion. First, western Christian merchants, mainly based in north-western ports, gained control of most of Mediterranean trade, including traffic to Granada, the Maghrib, the Near East, and Byzantium. Second, Muslim merchants, mainly based in Egypt, reoriented their maritime commercial interests away from the Mediterranean to the Red Sea and Indian Ocean. Europe had become a powerful market, both as a producer and a consumer, and it now stretched southward to encompass the Mediterranean within its commercial sphere. Mamluk Egypt also remained a center for international commerce through the fifteenth century, but it increasingly turned to the south and east, not west (with the exception of some overland trade across North Africa). Alexandria (no longer al-Andalus) became the frontier market between the Muslim and Christian trading spheres. To paraphrase Braudel on Castile, Egypt had also turned its back on the Mediterranean in order to concentrate on a new maritime sphere.

Routes across the Mediterranean altered their orientation as this sea became part of the European commercial orbit. In the eleventh and twelfth centuries, the most important route for maritime trade had followed the Maghribi coast, linking al-Andalus and Egypt and passing through the crucial hub of Tunisia-Sicily. By the thirteenth century, in contrast, this southern route fell into disuse in favor of more northerly coastal routes, including those along the eastern Iberian coast and those that took advantage of Mediterranean islands now in Christian hands.[2] During the thirteenth and fourteenth centuries, mer-

[2] These changes in routes have been described by J.H. Pryor, *Geography, Technology, and War*. (Cambridge, 1988).

chants from Genoa, Marseille, and Catalonia traded with Muslim ports (including Malaga, Ceuta, Bougie, Tunis, and Alexandria), but their itineraries were different from those followed by Geniza merchants two centuries before. Rather than following a roughly linear route between east and west, European merchants now plotted triangular itineraries. After the late twelfth century, it was common to find Christian vessels traveling from southern Europe to ports in the Near East and Spain in one trip. In 1464, for example, a Genoese boat was hired for an itinerary starting in Genoa and going to Alexandria, Tripoli, Jerba, Tunis, and Malaga.[3] Alternately, merchants might limit their voyages to the western Mediterranean basin, as did a Catalan vessel that made stops in Tunis, Sardinia, Mallorca, Almeria, and Malaga in 1327–8.[4]

With the reorientation of Mediterranean traffic through Christian ports, spices and other eastern commodities began to travel directly from the Near East to Italy, southern France, and Catalonia on Christian ships. Pepper, cinnamon, ginger, and other imports were redistributed from these Christian cities to secondary markets, including Granada. The role of al-Andalus as an entrepôt and distribution point for eastern goods had given way in the face of Christian mercantile competition. By the thirteenth century, Genoese notaries recorded shipments of spices arriving in Genoa directly from Alexandria, and wrote contracts for the re-export of these items to northern Europe, Granada, or the Maghrib. The same pattern is also seen elsewhere, as when, in 1248, the notary Amalric of Marseille wrote forty-four *commenda* contracts for the transshipment of eastern goods coming through Marseille, many of them headed to ports in North Africa.[5]

THE NEW ROLE OF IBERIAN PORTS

In tandem with these developments in Mediterranean and Atlantic

[3] J. Heers, "Le royaume de Grenade et la politique marchande de Gênes en occident (XVe siècle)," *Le moyen âge* 63(1957), p. 105.

[4] C.E. Dufourcq, "Les communications entre les royaumes chrétiens ibériques et les pays de l'occident musulman, dans les derniers siècles du moyen âge," *Les communications dans la péninsule ibérique au moyen âge* (*Actes du Colloque de Pau, 28–29 mars 1980*). [Paris, 1981], p. 32.

[5] J.H. Pryor, *Business Contracts of Medieval Provence; Selected "Notulae" from the Cartulary of Giraud Amalric of Marseilles, 1248*. [Toronto, 1981], p. 77.

trade routes, Iberian port cities fell into three distinct groups by the late thirteenth century: those in northern Castile and Portugal, those in Andalusia and Granada, and those in the Crown of Aragon. Although all three regions were now controlled by Christian trade and shipping, each had its own commercial interests, merchant populations, and geographical specialization. This is in contrast to the earlier period, when all Andalusi ports had focused on the Mediterranean and catered to roughly the same mixture of merchants. Except in the Taifa period, Andalusi ports had been under the same political regime and although rulers, merchants, and geography tended to favor certain ports over others (creating a hierarchy in size, economic activity, and harbor amenities), foreign traders could expect to experience roughly comparable regulations and taxes in any one. Christian Spanish ports and international maritime trade were virtually non-existent at this time – with the noteworthy exception of Barcelona.

Under Christian rule, however, political distinctions and economic rivalries between Iberian kingdoms and their merchants outweighed any similarities. Eastern ports in Aragon-Catalonia (the most important being Barcelona and Valencia) looked toward the Mediterranean and grew rapidly in the thirteenth and fourteenth centuries. Encouraged by their rulers' political aspirations in Sicily and elsewhere in the Mediterranean, Catalan and Aragonese merchants sought to rival the commercial power of Genoese and Venetian traders. At the same time, northern Castilian merchants from Burgos and ports along the Cantabrian, Asturian, and Galician coasts, together with merchants from Portugal, began to take advantage of economic opportunities in the Bay of Biscay and northern Europe. Gradually, these traders came to control much of the traffic from the Iberian peninsula to England and Flanders. The commercial situation in the southern peninsula was likewise distinct, and here the ports of Muslim Granada and newly Christian Andalusia had more in common with each other than with those in Aragon-Catalonia or northern Castile. Unlike their northern counterparts, southern Iberian ports lacked the independence insured by a local merchant population controlling their traffic. Instead, they became way-stations for foreign commerce.

Seville provides a good example of this trend. Although this city remained an important Iberian port, its commercial role had changed by the second half of the thirteenth century and new merchant groups dominated its markets. The *Primera crónica general de España* described Seville after its conquest by Ferdinand III of Castile in 1248 in terms that, while reminiscent of earlier Arabic descriptions, show a different mercantile presence in the port after the Christian conquest. According to the chronicle, Seville was a city to which

> ships come up the river every day from the sea, including *naves*, galleys, and many other sea-going vessels. They stop under the [city] walls, and bring in all kinds of merchandise from all over the world: from Tangiers, Ceuta, Tunis, Bougie, Alexandria, Genoa, Portugal, England, Pisa, Lombardy, Bordeaux, Bayonne, Sicily, Gascony, Catalonia, Aragon, other parts of France, and many other regions of the sea, both Christian and Muslim . . .

"Why should this be the case?" continues the text, and answers that it is because of the wonderful qualities of Sevillian olive oil.[6] The region had exported oil for centuries, but it went to new markets after Seville became a port of call for merchant ships traveling back and forth between the Mediterranean and the Atlantic. During the eleventh and twelfth centuries, Muslim and Jewish merchant ships had traveled through the Straits bringing goods from the central and eastern Mediterranean, then traveling back eastward with Iberian and northern products. By the late thirteenth century, however, Seville had become part of a more extensive maritime network linking England and Gascony with Catalonia, Sicily, Tunis, and Alexandria. Christian control of Seville and the Iberian coastline west of the Straits of Gibraltar made it possible for Christian fleets to travel back and forth through the straits in relative safety. Perhaps as early as 1278, merchant ships began to make regular runs between Mediterranean ports and destinations in northern Europe, bypassing the overland routes through France that had once dominated north–south trade in Europe.[7]

[6] (Alfonso X), *Primera crónica general de España.* [ed. R. Menéndez Pidal, Madrid, 1906 (reprint 1977)] II, p. 769. C.E. Dufourcq has noted that there may be some exaggerations in this account ("La question de Ceuta au XIIIe siècle," *Hespéris* 42(1955), p. 72), and it may better reflect conditions during the reign of Alfonso X, who commissioned the work, than of his father. It may likewise consciously paraphrase earlier descriptions of Seville.

[7] F. Pérez Embid noted Genoese voyages to Bruges from 1278; "Navigation et commerce dans le port de Séville au bas moyen âge," *Le moyen âge* 75(1969), p. 487. The question of the date of earliest regular passage through the straits has been discussed by R.S. Lopez, "Majorcans and Genoese on the North Sea Route in the 13th century," *Revue belge de philologie et d'histoire* 29(1951), pp. 1163–79.

The opening of this maritime route not only held consequences for the interior markets of France, particularly the already declining region of Champagne with its famous fairs, but it also altered the role of southern Iberian harbors and markets. In earlier centuries, Andalusi ports had served the multiple functions of import, export, and distribution of commodities. From the tenth to the early thirteenth centuries, a commercial network stretched from Cairo to Cordoba, and Andalusi markets were trading hubs at the western edge of the Muslim Mediterranean system. Located on the frontier, Iberian markets redistributed goods between the Christian and Islamic commercial spheres. Eastern goods were bought for local consumption or acquired for redistribution to markets in the northern peninsula, southern France, and Italy, and Iberian products (together with Sudanese gold and some northern items) were sold to merchants traveling eastward to Tunisia, Sicily, Egypt, and beyond.

Once Andalusi ports became the southern tip of a Christian European trading system, their function shifted to providing some commodities and – more importantly – serving as a point of passage and exchange between the Mediterranean and the Atlantic. Foreign Christian merchants dominated southern Iberian ports in both Andalusia and Granada, using them as sites for the sale and acquisition of goods *en route*. Italian or Catalan traders heading westward put into ports along the Granadan or Andalusian coast to buy olive oil or dried fruits on their way to Southampton or Bruges. Alternatively, they stopped in Seville to pick up iron or other northern goods destined for final sale in North Africa and other parts of the Mediterranean. On the Atlantic side of the straits, Cantabrian ships came south to Seville bringing northern commodities bound for the Mediterranean, intending to pick up a cargo of local products, or of eastern spices and Italian textiles, for transport northward to England or Flanders.[8]

The economy of Granada, like that of Christian Andalusia,

[8] Much has been written on late medieval Sevillian economy and trade. See, among others, A. Ballesteros y Beretta, *Sevilla en el siglo XIII.* [Seville, 1913]; R. Carande, *Sevilla, fortaleza y mercado.* [Seville, 1972]; and F. Pérez Embid, "Navigation et commerce," pp. 263–89, 479–502 (also bibliography, p. 266).

was oriented towards export trade and transshipment. Again like Andalusia, Granadan trade was controlled by foreigners, particularly the Genoese. Because the region's exports were very specialized, Granadan consumers became largely dependent on foreign imports for both the luxuries and necessities of life. The economic relationship between Granada and Christian Spanish kingdoms in the late middle ages also marked a change from the Umayyad, Almoravid, and Almohad periods. Nasrid rulers paid tribute to northern states, and whereas merchants and commercial ideas had once flowed northward, Granada was now on the receiving end. Granada's newly-dependent economic status is evident in the linguistic transfer of the *faniqa*, an Andalusi dry measure adopted in Christian Spain as the *hanega* (or *fanega*) in the middle of the twelfth century, just as it was dropping from use in al-Andalus. The measure was unused in the Muslim south until it reappeared as the *haniga* (a term apparently borrowed from the Castilian) in Nasrid Granada.[9]

Shifting patterns of trade, and especially the greater importance of traffic through the Straits of Gibraltar, are demonstrated by the new roles of Malaga and Almeria. Almeria had once been the premier Andalusi port, but Malaga took precedence by the fourteenth century. The Nasrid historian Ibn al-Khaṭīb (d. 1374) described Malaga as "a pilgrimage spot for merchants," who stopped in the city to pick up Granadan fruits and sugar and to sell a wide variety of imported goods.[10] As in previous centuries, Malaga continued to function as a holding port for ships preparing to make the westward passage through the straits, and as a stopping point for vessels traveling back and forth to Seville from the Mediterranean. Dufourcq has cited three ships from the Crown of Aragon that stopped in Malaga on their way from Barcelona to Seville in 1279, and many fourteenth-century vessels from Mallorca, Valencia, and Barcelona put into its

[9] J. Vallvé Bermejo, "Notas de metrología hispano-árabe II: Medidas de capacidad," *Al-Andalus* 42(1977), p. 101. On Granadan trade, see E.J. López de Coca Castañer, "Comercio exterior del reino de Granada," *Actas del II Coloquio de historia medieval andaluza. Hacienda y comercio. Sevilla, 8–10 de Abril, 1981.* [Seville, 1982], pp. 335–77; and in the same volume, C. Torres Delgado, "El reino nazari de Granada (1232–1492). Aspectos socio-económicos y fiscales", pp. 297–334.

[10] Ibn al-Khaṭīb, *Mufākharāt Mālaqa wa Salā.* [ed. A.M. al-'Abbadī, Alexandria, 1958], p. 59.

harbor *en route* to Seville, Cadiz, Galicia, and northern Europe.[11] Malaga was also a stopping point on voyages between southern Europe and North Africa. Genoese notarial records show that ships headed for the Maghrib paused in Malaga to collect information on market conditions across the sea. With this information in hand, Genoese merchants could decide whether to direct their journey to Ceuta, Bougie, Tunis, or elsewhere.[12] The Genoese continued to stop in Malaga in the fifteenth century, and the importance of their trade is shown by a large fortified Genoese compound in the city.[13]

Almeria also remained an important port under Nasrid rule, when both Abū al-Fidā (d. 1331) and ʿUmarī (d. 1349) noted it as a center for commerce and ship-building, and Ibn al-Khaṭīb called the city "a place of merchants" remarking that its harbor could accommodate large boats.[14] Nevertheless, Almeria served a different function in the late middle ages than it had in earlier times. With better access to the Mediterranean, Almeria had been the primary port of arrival (the "key," as one geographer put it) to Andalusi markets. During the eleventh and twelfth centuries, most Mediterranean merchant ships journeying to al-Andalus had Almeria as their destination. By the fourteenth century, in contrast, Almeria had lost traffic to Malaga. Catalan merchants still found it convenient for its access to Granadan markets, but other traders used it merely as a stopping point in longer itineraries.

THE NEW STRUCTURE OF MERCHANT POWER

The merchant groups trading in the peninsula changed with Christian political expansion and the reorientation of commercial routes. Thus, although Seville, for example, remained in direct

[11] C.E. Dufourcq, "Les communications," pp. 30–9. Despite the frequency of stops in Malaga, J. Hinojosa Montalvo cited trips between Valencia and Seville made without intermediate stops ("Las relaciones comerciales entre Valencia y Andalucía durante la baja edad media," *Actas del II Coloquio de historia medieval andaluza: Hacienda y comercio (Sevilla, 8–10 de abril, 1981)*. [Seville, 1982], p. 256.

[12] ASG Cart. 29, fol.164r (dated July, 1253), E.H. Byrne (ed.), *Genoese Shipping in the Twelfth and Thirteenth centuries*. [Cambridge, Mass., 1930], p. 36.

[13] F. Guillen Robles, *Málaga musulmana*. [Malaga, 1880], p. 524.

[14] Abū al-Fidā, *Geographie d'Aboulféda*. [ed. M. Reinaud and M. de Slane, Paris, 1840–8], p. 177; ʿUmarī, *Masālik al-abṣār fī mamālik al-amṣār*. [trans. M. Gaudefroy-Demombynes, *L'Afrique moins l'Egypte*. Paris, 1927], p. 239; Ibn al-Khaṭīb, *Miʿyār al-ikhtiyār*. [ed. M.K. Chabana, Rabat, 1397/1977], p. 100.

contact with ports in the Muslim world, the merchants who linked it with Alexandria, Tunis, and Bougie were now mainly Catalans, Provençals, Genoese, and other Italians – no longer Andalusi Muslims or the Egyptian-based Jewish merchants of the Geniza. Peninsular trade, in ports along every coast, was now almost exclusively in the hands of Christian traders, with only a few Muslims and Jews continuing to do business in the Crown of Aragon and Nasrid Granada.

Christians

Christian merchants working in the peninsula were a diverse group, as is shown in their different business interests and spheres of operation. These merchants reflected the sharp political and economic divisions which marked the peninsula by the late thirteenth century.

Traffic through Barcelona, Tortosa, Valencia, and other ports in the Crown of Aragon was largely in the hands of local merchants whose commercial interests centered on the Mediterranean. The power of this merchant bloc was reinforced by legislation that favored local traders. In 1227, for example, James I decreed that no foreign ships be allowed to carry cargo out of Barcelona to Egypt, Syria, or Ceuta if there were a Catalan ship willing to make the trip.[15] In years that followed, protectionism was more evident in the Crown of Aragon than elsewhere in the peninsula, exhibiting the close link between Aragonese politics, territorial expansion, and commercial aspirations in the Mediterranean. Even in the fifteenth century, when Aragonese trade was in decline, Alfonso V tried to encourage commerce by ordering (in 1419) that all goods coming from Mallorca and Catalonia must be carried on local ships.[16] Legal measures did not, in fact, keep all foreign merchants out of Aragonese trade. Pisans, Genoese, and Provençals traded in Barcelona and the Balearics in the late thirteenth and fourteenth centuries, and the Datini archives (dating 1383–1411) indicate considerable Florentine activity in the Crown of Aragon.[17]

[15] J.N. Hillgarth, *The Spanish Kingdoms, 1250–1516*. [Oxford, 1976] I, p. 291.

[16] J. O'Callaghan, *A History of Medieval Spain*. [Ithaca, 1975], p. 623.

[17] See J. Heers, "Les relations commerciales entre Gênes et le royaume d'Aragon vers le milieu du XVe siècle," *IV Congreso de Historia de la Corona de Aragón. Actas y Comunicaciones*. [Barcelona, 1970] II, pp. 1–14.

Traders from ports in the Crown of Aragon were primarily concerned with trade to Granada, North Africa, Egypt, Sicily, and Byzantium – all regions where they competed for trade with Italian and Provençal merchants. Nevertheless, a Catalan merchant colony was established in Alexandria by 1264, and Catalan traders held virtual control of traffic through this city in the fourteenth century.[18] At the other end of the Mediterranean, there were Catalan *funduqs* in Bougie and Tunis in the thirteenth century, and in Almeria and Malaga by the early 1300s.[19] Traders from Barcelona and Mallorca also did business in England and Flanders in the fourteenth century, although the bulk of northern trade was handled by Castilians and Italians.[20] Catalan trade diminished in the fifteenth century as local merchants lost ground to the Genoese and withdrew their interests from Alexandria, Tunis, and other ports where they had once thrived. This commercial decline has been variously attributed to particularly high mortality from the plague in the Crown of Aragon, failure of Catalan banks, depletion of gold and silver reserves, and greater investments in land than in maritime ventures. The only region of the Crown of Aragon that continued to prosper through the fifteenth century was Valencia, where a re-born silk industry and close commercial links to Granada preserved trade.[21]

Trade through southern Iberian ports in Muslim Granada and Christian Andalusia was largely controlled by foreign traders, most notably the Genoese. When Alfonso X of Castile put a Genoese admiral, Hugo Vento, in control of the kingdom's navy in 1264, his action reinforced Genoese dominance (though not, as is sometimes stated, hegemony) in southern Castile. Genoa also obtained trading privileges in Granada, negotiating treaties with the Nasrids to allow Genoese merchants to export dried fruits and to continue their long-standing traffic with Malaga and Almeria. Other Italian merchants – including Vene-

[18] O'Callaghan, *A History of Medieval Spain*, p. 482.

[19] C.E. Dufourcq, *L'Espagne catalane et le Maghrib aux XIIIe et XIVe siècle*. [Paris, 1966], pp. 99–101, and "Les communications," p. 40.

[20] Dufourcq noted the establishment of a regular route between Barcelona and Flanders in 1369, and cited Mallorcan traders arriving in England and Flanders in 1301, 1323, 1340, 1350, and 1372 ("Les communications," p. 31).

[21] O'Callaghan, *A History of Medieval Spain*, p. 623.

tians, Milanese, Pisans, Lombards, Savonese, and Florentines – also traded in the southern peninsula during the fourteenth and fifteenth centuries, as did merchants from northern Castile, Catalonia, Marseille, and England. Pegolotti noted special tax exemptions granted to Italians trading in Seville, and fifteenth-century Sevillian tariff lists also show a broad range of merchants doing business in that city.[22]

The situation was very different along the Atlantic coasts of the peninsula, where merchants from Portugal and northern Castile vied for control of traffic across the Bay of Biscay. Meanwhile, Portuguese merchants were also venturing southward along the west African coast. Traders from northern Castile came to dominate traffic between the peninsula and northern Europe in the thirteenth century with the assistance of favorable political alliances. The names of Castilian merchants and ship-owners (often called merely "Spaniards" in northern documents) began to appear in records from Bristol, Southampton, London, Bruges, Arras, and elsewhere early in the century. Other southern merchants, including Catalans, Genoese, and Venetians, also brought Iberian goods to northern cities in the late middle ages, but they faced competition from Castilians. Cordial relations existed between England and Castile during the reign of Alfonso X (1252–84), following the marriage of his sister Eleanor to Edward I of England in 1254, but became strained when Sancho IV (1284–95) broke with his father's policies and allied with France.[23] Castilian and Portuguese merchants had also established colonies in the Low Countries by the late thirteenth century,

[22] Pegolotti, *La pratica della mercatura.* [ed. A. Evans, Cambridge, Mass., 1936], p. 271; M.A. Ladero Quesada, "Almojarifazgo sevillano y comercio exterior de Andalucía en el siglo XV," *Anuario de historia económica y social* 2(1969), pp. 92–3; M.A. Ladero Quesada, "Las aduanas de Castilla en el siglo XV," *Revue internationale d'histoire de la banque* 7(1973), p. 102. Also on Italian traders, see F. Melis, *Mercaderes italianos en España [siglos XIV–XVI*). [Seville, 1976]; R. Carande, "El puerto de Málaga y la lana de Menorca en la edad media (dos estudios de F. Melis)," *Moneda y crédito* 64(1958), pp. 14, 17; B. Gari, "El reino de Granada y la política comercial genovesa en la península ibérica en la segunda mitad del siglo XIII," *Relaciones exteriores del reino de Granada. IV Coloquio de historia medieval andaluza.* [Almeria, 1988], pp. 287–96; and Pérez Embid, "Navigation," pp. 274–75. Savonese merchants trading in Almeria in 1345 were noted by Dufourcq ("Les communications," p. 32), and in the fifteenth century by Heers ("Le royaume de Grenade," p. 105). Dufourcq cited Venetians in Malaga in 1324 and 1332 ("Les communications," p. 31).

[23] T.H. Lloyd, *Alien Merchants in England in the High Middle Ages.* [New York, 1982], p. 159.

after Count Guy of Flanders extended privileges to Spanish (i.e., Castilian) merchants trading in his domains in 1280. Similar privileges were extended again in 1294, for a set period, at the request of Edward I.[24] Commerce became more regular in the fourteenth century, although the vicissitudes of internal Iberian politics and the Hundred Years War (1337–1453) further complicated patterns of friendship – and commerce – between Castile, Aragon, England, France, and Flanders.

The commercial fluctuations engendered by war and diplomacy are illustrated by the actions of Edward III of England (1327–77), who imposed an embargo on English wool shipments to Flanders at the start of the Hundred Years War, a move that led Flemish weavers to rely more heavily on imports of Iberian wool.[25] In 1345, Edward granted safe-conduct to foreign merchants, including Castilians, bringing goods to Bruges. These promises must have carried weight, since at least forty Spanish ships arrived in the port of Swin, near Bruges, in 1350.[26] Edward (then an ally of Peter I of Castile) made a further treaty with the *hermandad de las marismas* in 1351, promising protection of their merchant ships in any of his ports.[27] These cordial relations between England and Castile were ruptured when Henry II succeeded his brother to the throne of Castile in 1369, followed by a Castilian alliance with France and an agreement to provide ships for the French navy. The Anglo-Castilian friendship would not be repaired until the reigns of Ferdinand and Isabella at the end of the following century, and commercial relations remained precarious. Castilian and French merchants were forbidden to trade in Flanders in 1371, only to find this ruling overturned by Duke Philip of Burgundy in 1384.[28] In contrast to their Castilian neighbors, the Portuguese remained on amicable commercial terms with England.

[24] L. Gilliodts-van Severen, L. *Cartulaire de l'ancien consulat d'Espagne à Bruges*. [Bruges, 1901] 1, pp. 7–8; M. Carlé, "Mercaderes en Castilla (1252–1512)," *Cuadernos de historia de España* 21–2(1954), p. 275. See also H. Laurent, *Un grand commerce d'exportation au moyen âge: la draperie des Pays-Bas en France et dans les pays méditerranéens (XIIe–XVe siècle)*. [Liège-Paris, 1935], pp. 106–7.

[25] O'Callaghan, *A History of Medieval Spain*, pp. 616–17.

[26] Gilliodts-van Severen, *Cartulaire*, p. 12; F. Rörig, *The Medieval Town*. [Berkeley, 1967], p. 81.

[27] O'Callaghan, *A History of Medieval Spain*, p. 482.

[28] Gilliodts-van Severen, *Cartulaire*, p. 18. For a detailed analysis of politics and trade between Castile and England in this period, consult W.R. Childs, *Anglo-Castilian Trade in the Later Middle Ages*. [Manchester, 1978].

Iberian traders continued to trade in the north in the fifteenth century, and established close ties with Hanseatic ports. In Flanders also, a guild of Castilian merchants (primarily traders from Burgos) was organized in Bruges in 1441, and Philip the Good of Burgundy granted recognition to Basque merchants in that city ten years later.[29]

Merchant ships from northern Castile and Portugal also traveled south, and their trips to Seville and Cadiz forged an important link in the chain of commercial transfer between the Atlantic and the Mediterranean. Traders from Santander, for example, would arrive in Andalusia carrying textiles from Flanders, wool from England (despite the growing Iberian wool industry), and iron from northern Castile. In Seville, they sold these goods to acquire spices from the eastern Mediterranean, Italian textiles, and local olive oil, all of which they intended to carry northward on their return trip. Northern merchants rarely ventured eastward beyond the Straits of Gibraltar since Mediterranean ports were already crowded with Genoese, Pisan, Venetian, Catalan, and Provençal merchants. Early in the fifteenth century, Genoese–Catalan rivalries provided a brief window of opportunity for Basque and Portuguese traders to do business in the Mediterranean, but the Genoese succeeded in pushing them back westward by the end of the century.

Muslims and Jews

Muslim and Jewish traders did not disappear from Iberian trade in the late middle ages, but in most areas (especially Andalusia) their numbers – and their economic influence – were greatly reduced. Some non-Christian traders continued to do business in the kingdom of Granada, while mudejar and Jewish merchants also traded in the Crown of Aragon, although their commercial activities lacked the independence of earlier centuries. Because the north-western Mediterranean was now a domain of Christian political, commercial, and naval hegemony, non-Christian traders were forced to do business according to Christian rules. Muslim and Jewish travelers were likewise obliged to seek passage on Christian ships, even though Muslim authorities might object to this mode of transport. The latter trend was

[29] O'Callaghan, *A History of Medieval Spain*, pp. 621–22.

already clear by the late twelfth century, when Ibn Jubayr and Benjamin of Tudela traveled on Christian boats between al-Andalus and the eastern Mediterranean, and became more pronounced over time. When a party of Tunisian merchants wished to trade in Granada in 1327, they boarded a Catalan vessel in Tunis, and went by way of Sardinia and Mallorca on their way to Almeria and Malaga. Another Catalan ship, owned by a Christian from Barcelona, carried a mudejar, merchant to Egypt in 1333 (because trade with Mamluk lands was forbidden in this period, this merchant is known through the pardon issued by Peter IV of Aragon in 1339).[30] In the next century, at least two Muslim traders from Granada voyaged to Tunis on a Genoese boat; in 1443 a Genoese boat arrived in Rhodes with passengers from Tunisia and merchandise from Granada, and another Genoese vessel carried an Egyptian trader from Oran to Malaga.[31]

Aside from this data on the transportation of Granadan Muslim traders, there is little evidence of their business in the late middle ages. In contrast, the activities of mudejar traders are better documented owing to records in Christian archives. A recent study of the mudejars of Valencia has identified two hundred and seventy-three Muslims trading between Valencia and Granada in the fifteenth century. All these traders were natives of Valencia, except for two Granadan silk merchants – one of whom traveled home on a Venetian boat in 1465.[32]

A number of Jewish merchants also continued to trade in the Crown of Aragon, in Granada, and in Andalusia (though not in northern Castile). Jewish merchants traveled between ports around the western Mediterranean, but they did not venture into Atlantic trade. Jewish merchants appear in contracts from Marseille in the middle of the thirteenth century, some carrying goods to Mallorca and the Maghrib.[33] Jews also traded between

[30] Dufourcq, "Les communications," p. 32; E. Ashtor, *The Levant Trade in the Later Middle Ages.* [Princeton, 1983], p. 51.

[31] Heers, "Le royaume de Grenade," p. 104. López de Coca Castañer, "Comercio," p. 351.

[32] M. Ruzafa García, "Las relaciones económicas entre los mudejares valencianos y el reino de Granada en el siglo XV," *Relaciones exteriores del Reino de Granada. IV Coloquio de historia medieval andaluza.* [Almeria, 1988], p. 349.

[33] Pryor concluded from these data that "Jews still participated strongly in commerce [at this period] . . . but they were certainly no longer the economic force they had once been." (Pryor, *Business Contracts*, pp. 86–87).

Valencia and Andalusia through the fourteenth and fifteenth centuries, and records from Malaga show that Genoese traders often dealt with Jewish merchants in this port.[34] Aragonese Jews even did business as far east as Egypt, as we know from legal censures on their activities. In 1312, two Jews from Barcelona were fined (though later pardoned) for transporting prohibited merchandise (grain, iron, and wood) to Alexandria on a Christian ship, and similar cases were recorded in 1305 and 1307. Fines were likewise levied on Jews trading between Barcelona and Egypt in the 1340s.[35]

Ports and markets in the northern peninsula were entirely the domain of Christian commerce in the late middle ages, and Muslims and Jews had never traded in these regions. In the eastern and southern peninsula, Muslim and Jewish trade diminished in the face of Christian political domination and commercial competition. This shift is in line with the contemporary realignment of trade throughout the Mediterranean world, and the polarization of commerce around centers in Europe and Egypt. With the Mediterranean a largely Christian lake, Jewish merchants were no longer useful as commercial go-betweens and they concentrated their activities within either the Christian or Muslim commercial spheres. Meanwhile, Muslim merchants (who had never traded willingly in Christian lands) largely confined their trade to markets within the *dār al-Islām* and further east.

As Egyptian trade turned toward the Red Sea and Indian Ocean, a new group of merchants, called the Karimis, took hold of international trade in the Muslim world.[36] Although it is doubtful whether their collective name signified any corporate identity, the term Karimi was applied from the late twelfth

[34] Hinojosa Montalvo, "Las relaciones comerciales," p. 252; Heers, "Le royaume de Grenade," p. 103.

[35] J. Regné, *History of the Jews in Aragon. Regesta and Documents 1213–1327*. [Jerusalem, 1978] no. 2975, p. 550; no. 2840, p. 526; no. 2878, p. 531–2; Ashtor, *Levant Trade*, p. 51.

[36] There is a considerable bibliography on the Karimis, including articles by G. Wiet, "Les marchands d'epices sous les sultans Mamlouks," *Cahiers d'histoire égytienne* 7(1955), pp. 81–147; and W.J. Fischel, "The Spice Trade in Mamluk Egypt," *JESHO* 1(1958), pp. 157–74. For a brief overview, see D. Abulafia, "Asia, Africa, and the Trade of Medieval Europe," *Cambridge Economic History of Europe*. [2nd edn, Cambridge, 1987] II, pp. 437–43.

century to a number of powerful Muslim merchants who controlled Red Sea traffic in spices and other eastern goods coming to Egyptian markets. The appearance of this merchant group in Egypt by the thirteenth century, replacing the earlier Jewish merchant population of the Geniza but showing little interest in Mediterranean affairs, indicates the changing orientation of Egyptian life and trade in the late middle ages. Mamluk rulers supported the Karimis and promoted their interests in return for the payment of taxes, loans, and other services to the government. Later, a new policy under Barsbay (1422–37) instituted tighter government controls, established monopolies over many goods, and effectively put an end to Karimi business.

As Muslim commercial interests were directed eastward on trade in the Indian Ocean, Alexandria became the new economic and conceptual border between two worlds. When Ibn Saʿīd al-Gharnāṭī (1208–86) arrived in Egypt as an Andalusi refugee, he was well aware that the Muslim world had changed during his lifetime. "I was overcome by desolation," he wrote, "as I remembered those happy familiar places in al-Andalus from which my life is now [forever] separated."[37] Although tiny Granada remained in Muslim hands, al-Andalus had slipped away from the sphere of eastern Islamic commerce and – except for a lingering nostalgia – from their concern.

LATE MEDIEVAL IBERIA AND THE WORLD COMMERCIAL SYSTEM

From the thirteenth to the fifteenth centuries, the markets of Christian Spain and Muslim Granada served an important – yet peripheral – role within European commerce. The peninsula was now incorporated within the northern trading sphere, but its traffic with the north was unbalanced. In spite of the efforts of Iberian rulers to legislate economic policy, peninsular trade remained largely subject to external markets and interests. Commerce, particularly in Andalusia and Granada, was dependent on foreign demand and business in southern Iberian ports was controlled by foreign merchants.

Christian Iberian monarchs appear to have been more concerned to regulate international trade than had their Andalusi

[37] Maqqarī, *Analectes sur l'histoire et la littérature des arabes d'Espagne*. [ed. R. Dozy, Leiden, 1855–60] I, p. 647.

predecessors. Some Christian legislation was motivated by political and diplomatic needs, but other rulings addressed mercantile demands or promoted royal interests. These Iberian efforts were in line with perceptions of legal and royal power taking shape throughout Europe, and the nascent idea that it was possible to influence regional economies. Rulers in Castile, Aragon, and Portugal issued laws concerning the goods that could or could not be traded (*cosas vedadas*), what taxes must be paid, which merchants would be allowed to carry goods, where these traders could conduct their business, and to whom they could sell their wares. Shipyards and maritime traffic were likewise subject to royal oversight. Many of these concerns had been expressed in earlier Muslim legislation, yet to a lesser degree. For example, we do not find long lists of prohibited exports appearing in Andalusi *fatwas* or *ḥisba* manuals, nor was there ever more than token effort taken to prevent traffic between al-Andalus and Christian regions (unlike later papal and royal restrictions on European trade with Mamluk Egypt). Overall, Muslim rulers in al-Andalus had been more concerned to profit from international commerce than to restrict it. In contrast, their Christian successors were interested in regulating the movement of merchants and commodities, but generally participated less directly in trade and commercial shipping.

This greater awareness of and interest in the possibility of economic regulation seems to have hindered, rather than aided, the success of Iberian (and particularly Castilian) international trade. Extensive catalogues of items that could not be carried out of the kingdom (usually including horses, arms, iron, wood, and grain – and sometimes extending to cover virtually every possible item of local export) did more to promote than to rectify Iberian economic dependence. The same may be said of prohibitions on imports, since these did not show a coherent policy in support of local industries. In 1286, for instance, Sancho IV ordered that wine from Navarre not be imported into Castile. In 1303, Ferdinand IV prohibited the sale of Portuguese wines in Seville, and later rulers followed suit with similar laws.[38] These rulings may have promoted the Castilian wine industry, but, at the same time, almost no effort was made to regulate the vast influx of foreign textiles (with their far greater

[38] Carlé, "Mercaderes," p. 309.

potential to inhibit local industries) into peninsular markets. Even legislation that favored local traders over foreigners, or that required merchants to export local goods of equal value to those they had imported into the kingdom, seem to have been ineffective.[39] John I of Portugal (a monarch who took an unusually close interest in commercial investments) perhaps understood the futility of such policies when he reversed them in 1386, granting privileges to foreign merchants and removing limits on imports.[40]

On a wider scale, papal prohibitions on commerce with Muslim lands (which were reiterated in secular legislation) also stifled Iberian participation in Mediterranean trade and concentrated interests on its unbalanced trade with Europe. Trade in war materials to enemy lands (whether Muslim or not) had been banned in the thirteenth century, but papal rulings in the 1320s and 1330s categorically forbad any Christian commercial contact with Mamluk ports. Such bans were ultimately unenforceable (and soon degenerated into a system whereby trading nations could buy a license to trade with Muslims) but contemporary maritime regulations in Genoa, Venice, and Aragon all reflected at least token compliance with papal demands.[41] Aragonese complicity demonstrates the new alliance of peninsular political and economic affairs with those of Christian Europe, in contrast with the more *laissez faire* Andalusi participation in the Mediterranean trading world of two centuries before.

By the middle of the thirteenth century, the Iberian peninsula had become – and would remain – part of Europe. As with the first two hundred years of Muslim rule in al-Andalus, the first centuries of integration into the northern Christian milieu were awkward and unbalanced, particularly from the economic perspective. While the kingdoms of the peninsula were recovering from the changes following the Reconquest, and were preserving an uneasy peace across the Granadan frontier, they could only assert themselves slowly as powers to be reckoned with in the European world. After the gradual reorganization and realignment of Iberian industries, however, the peninsula's economy

[39] Rulings of this type have been described by Pérez Embid, "Navigation," pp. 481–2; Ladero Quesada, "Las aduanas de Castilla," pp. 85–7; and Hillgarth, *The Spanish Kingdoms*, pp. 291–92.

[40] O'Callaghan, *A History of Medieval Spain*, p. 621.

[41] Ashtor, *Levant Trade*, pp. 44–7.

gained strength in the fourteenth century when massive exports of Iberian wool to Europe became the mainstay of commerce. But even as the peninsula achieved some degree of economic parity, its role in world affairs altered again. The Castilian-Aragonese crossing of the Atlantic and Portuguese circumnavigation of Africa at the end of the fifteenth century (not to mention the final conquest of Nasrid Granada and the appearance of an Ottoman empire in former Byzantine and Mamluk territories) permanently changed the relationship between Europe, the Mediterranean, and the Atlantic. At the end of the middle ages, geography once again placed the peninsula in the vanguard of a shift in world alignment. This time, however, it could take better economic and political advantage of the change.

BIBLIOGRAPHY

PRIMARY SOURCES

UNPUBLISHED

Archivo di Stato, Genoa (ASG); Cartularies 1, 2, 3/II, 4, 5, 7, 11, 15, 16/II, 17, 18/I, 18/II, 20/I, 20/II, 21/I, 24, 25, 26/I, 26/II, 29, 34, 56, 143, Diversorum 102.

al-Fihrī al-Buntī, Abū Muḥammad ʿAbd Allah. *Wathā'iq wa al-masā'il al-majmūʿa min kutub al-fuqahā*. Miguel Asín Institute, CSIC, Madrid, ms. 11.

Ibn Mughīth, Abū Jaʿfar Muḥammad. *Muqniʿ fī ʿilm al-shurūṭ*. Real Academia de la Historia, Madrid, Gayangos Collection ms. 44.

Ibn Sahl, Abū Asbagh ʿIsā. *Aḥkām al-kubrā*. General Library, Rabat, ms. 838Q

Aḥkām al-kubrā. General Library, Rabat, ms. 370Q

Aḥkām al-kubrā. General Library, Rabat, ms. 3398D

Ibn Salmūn, Abū al-Qāsim ʿAbd Allah. *Kitāb al-ʿaqd al-munaẓẓam bi al-ḥukkām*. Escorial Library, ms. 1077.

al-Jazīrī, Abū al-Ḥasan ʿAlī b. Yaḥyā al-Sinhajī. *Maqṣud al-maḥmūd fī talkhīṣ al-ʿuqūd*. Miguel Asín Institute, CSIC, Madrid, ms. 5.

al-Shāṭibī, Abū Muḥammad b. Hārūn b. Aḥmad. *Ṭurar al-mawḍuʿa ʿalā al-wathā'iq al-majmūʿa*. Biblioteca Nacional, Madrid, ms. 21573.

Unpublished Geniza documents were consulted through photocopies and microfilms held in the S.D. Goitein Geniza Research Laboratory at Princeton University. Where available, Goitein's transcriptions, India Book notes, subject notes, and other documents were also consulted.

PUBLISHED

ʿAbd Allah al-Zīrī. *The Tibyān: Memoirs of ʿAbd Allah b. Buluggīn, last Zirid Emir of Granada*. English trans. A.T. Tibi, Leiden, 1986.

Abraham ben Daud. *Sefer ha-qabbalah* (*The Book of Tradition*). English trans. Gershon D. Cohen, Philadelphia, 1967.

Abū al-Fidā. *Geographie d'Aboulféda*. ed. and French trans. M. Reinaud and M. de Slane, Paris, 1840 and 1848.

Abū al-Ḥasan al-Ḥakīm, ʿAlī b. Yūsuf. "Régimen de la casa de la moneda (al-dawḥa al-mushtabika fī ḍawābiṭ dār al-sikka)," ed. H. Mones, *Madrid-:MDI* 6(1958), pp. 63–204.

Abū al-Muṭahhar al-Azdī, Muḥammad b. Aḥmad. *Abulḳāsim ein bagdāder Sittenbild*. ed. A. Mez, Heidelberg, 1902.

Abū Ḥamid al-Gharnāṭī. *Abu Ḥamid el Granadino y su relación de viaje por tierras eurasiáticas*. ed. and Spanish trans. C.E. Dubler, Madrid, 1953.

"Le 'Tuḥfat al-albāb' de Abū Ḥāmid al-Andalusī al-Gharnāṭī," ed. and French trans. G. Ferrand, *Journal Asiatique* 207 (1925), pp. 1–304.

Abū Yūsuf, Ya'qūb b. Ibrāhīm. *Kitāb al-kharāj*. Cairo, 1352/1933–34.

Agobard, *Epistolae*. ed. E. Dümmler, *MGH*, Epistolae, v, Berlin, 1899.

Alfasi, Isaac ben Jacob. *She'elot u-teshuvot*. Bilgoraj, 1935 (reprint Jerusalem, 1973).

(Alfonso X) *Primera crónica general de España*. ed. R. Menéndez Pidal (*Nueva biblioteca de autores españoles*. v), Madrid, 1906 (reprint Madrid, 1977).

Amari, Michele, ed. *I diplomi arabi del R. Archivio Fiorentino*. Florence, 1863.

"Nuovi ricordi arabici su la storia di Genova," *ASLSP* 5(1867).

Annales Bertiniani. ed. G. Waitz, *MGH*, Scriptores in usum scholarum, Hanover, 1883.

Annales Petaviani. ed. G.H. Pertz, *MGH*, Scriptores (in folio), I, Hanover, 1826.

Annales pisani. ed. Michele Lupo Gentile, *Rerum italicarum scriptores*, VI, pt. 2, Bologna, 1930.

Arberry, A.J., ed. and English trans. *Arabic Poetry: A Primer for Students*. Cambridge, 1965.

Arnold, Richard. *The Customs of London, otherwise called Arnold's Chronicle*. London, 1811.

Ashtor, Eliyahu, ed. and Spanish trans. "Documentos españoles de la Genizah," *Sefarad* 24(1964), pp.41–80.

Assaf, Simha, ed. *Gaonica: Gaonic Responsa and Fragments from Halachic Literature*. Jerusalem, 1933.

Gaonic Responsa from Geniza mss. Jerusalem, 1928.

"Letters from Kairwan and Alexandria to R. Joseph ibn Ukal," *J.N. Epstein Jubilee Volume*. Jerusalem, 1950. pp. 177–90.

Mekorot u-mehkarim [*Texts and Studies in Jewish History*]. Jerusalem, 1946.

Sifran shel rishonim. Jerusalem, 1935.

Aye d'Avignon. Chanson de geste. eds. F. Guessard and P. Meyer, Paris, 1861.

al-Bakrī, Abū 'Ubayd 'Abd Allah. *Kitāb al-masālik wa al-mamālik*. ed. and French trans. M. de Slane, *Description de l'Afrique septentrionale par Abou-Obeid-el-Bakri*. Paris, 1911–13. (reprint Paris, 1965); ed. A.A. al-Ḥajjī. *Jughrafiyat al-Andalus wa 'Urubba*. Beirut, 1968; Spanish trans. E. Vidal Beltran, *Geografia de España*. Zaragoza, 1982.

Belgrano, Luigi T., ed. "Documenti e genealogia dei pessagno genovesi ammiragli del portogallo," *ASLSP* 15(1881), pp. 245–95.

"Il registro della curia arcivescovile di Genova," *ASLSP* 2(1862).

"Il secondo registro della curia arcivescovile di Genova," *ASLSP* 18(1887).

Benjamin of Tudela. "The Itinerary of Benjamin of Tudela," English trans. M.N. Adler, *Jewish Quarterly Review* 16 (1904), pp. 453ff, 715ff; 17(1905), pp. 123ff, 286ff, 514ff, 762ff; 18(1906), pp. 84ff, 664ff.

Bibliography

Bertrand de Bar-sur-Aube. *Girart de Vienne par Bertrand-sur-Aube*. (ed. W. van Emden), Paris, 1977.

Blancard, Louis, ed. *Documents inédits sur le commerce de Marseille au moyen âge*. 2 vols., Marseille, 1884–5.

Bonaini, Francesco, ed. *Statuti inediti della città di Pisa dal XII al XIV secolo*. 3 vols., Florence, 1854–70.

Bonvillano (1198). eds. J.E. Eierman, H.C. Krueger, R.L. Reynolds, Turin, 1939.

Buzurg b. Shahriyar. *The Book of the Wonders of India*. ed. and English trans. G.S.P. Freeman-Grenville, London, 1981.

Caffaro, *Annali genovesi di Caffaro e de' suoi continuatori*. ed. L.T. Belgrano, 5 vols., Genoa, 1890–1929.

Calendar of Close Rolls, 1227–1399. London, 1896–1938.

Calendar of Fine Rolls, 1272–1509. London, 1911–62.

Calendar of Patent Rolls, 1216–1399. London, 1891–1913.

Le Calendrier de Cordoue. ed. R. Dozy, new edn and French trans. Charles Pellat, Leiden, 1961.

Cantar de mío Cid. ed. R. Menéndez Pidal, English trans. W.S. Merwin, New York, 1975.

Capasso, Bartolomeo, ed. *Monumenta ad neapolitani ducatus historiam pertinentia*. 2 vols., Naples, 1881–92.

Capitularia Regum Francorum. eds. A. Boretius and V. Krause, *MGH*, Leges (in quarto), II.1–2, Hanover, 1883–97.

Capmany y de Monpalau, Antonio de, ed. *Memorias históricas sobre la marina, comercio y artes de la antigua ciudad de Barcelona*. (new edn), 3 vols., Barcelona, 1961–63.

Carmi, T., ed. and English trans. *The Penguin Book of Hebrew Verse*. London, 1981.

Cartolari notarili genovesi. Inventario. Archivio di Stato di Genova, 2 vols., Rome, 1956–61.

Carus-Wilson, E.M., ed. *Overseas Trade of Bristol in the Later Middle Ages*. Bristol, 1937.

Chau Ju-Kua. *Chau Ju-Kua: His Work on Chinese and Arabic Trade*. English trans. F. Hirth and W. Rockhill, St. Petersberg, 1911.

Chaucer, Geoffrey. *Chaucer's Poetry. An Anthology for the Modern Reader*. ed. E.T. Donaldson, 2nd edn, New York, 1958.

Chronicle of the Reigns of Henry II and Richard I (AD 1169–1192). ed. W. Stubbs, II, London, 1867.

Chronicon Moissiacense. ed. G.H. Pertz, *MGH*, Scriptores (in folio), I, Hanover, 1826.

Una crónica anónima de 'Abd al-Raḥmān III al-Nāṣir. ed. and Spanish trans. E. Lévi-Provençal and E. García Gómez, Madrid-Granada, 1950.

Colección de fueros y cartas-pueblas de España por la Real Academia de la historia: catálogo. Madrid, 1852.

Cortes de los antiguos reinos de León y Castilla. ed. Real Academia de la historia, 5 vols., Madrid, 1861–1903.

Cumano, Arnold. *Il Cartulario di Arnaldo Cumano e Giovanni di Donato (Savona, 1178–1188)*. ed. Laura Balleto, Rome, 1978.

Cuoq, Joseph M., ed. and French trans. *Recueil des sources arabes concernant l'Afrique occidentale du VIIIe au XVIe siècle*. Paris, 1975.

al-Ḍabbī, Aḥmad b. Yaḥyā. *Kitāb bughyat al-multamis fī ta'rīkh rijāl ahl al-Andalus*. eds. F. Codera and J. Ribera, *BAH*, III, Madrid, 1885.

D'Arcq, D., ed. "Tarif de marchandises qui se vendaient à Paris à la fin du XIIIe siècle," *Revue archéologique* 9(1852), pp. 213–28.

al-Dimashqī, Abū al-Faḍl Ja'far. *Kitāb al-'ashāra ilā maḥāsin al-tijāra*. Cairo, 1318/1900.

al-Dimashqī, Shams al-Dīn. *Cosmographie de Chams ed Din Abou Abdallah Muhammed ed-Dimichqui*. ed. M.A.F. Mehren, St. Petersberg, 1899.

Fagnan, E., ed. *L'Afrique septentrionale au XIIe siècle de notre ère: description extraite de 'Kitāb al-istibçār'*. Constantine, 1900.

Extraits inédits relatifs au Maghreb. Paris, 1924.

Fagniez, Gustave, ed. *Documents relatifs à l'histoire de l'industrie et du commerce en France*. Paris, 1898.

Ferretto, Arturo, ed. "Codice diplomatico delle relazioni fra la Liguria la Toscana e la Lunigana al tempi di Dante (1264–1321)," *ASLSP* 31(1901).

Florez, Enrique, ed. *España sagrada. Teatro geografico-histórico de la iglesia de España*. x, Madrid, 1753.

Font Ruiz, J. M. *Cartas de población y franquicia de Cataluña*. Madrid, 1969–83.

Fori antiqui valentiae. ed. M. Dualde Serrano, Madrid-Valencia, 1950–67.

Formulae merowingici et karolini aevi. ed. C. Zeumer, *MGH*, Leges (in quarto), v, Hanover 1886.

Friedberg, Emil, ed. *Corpus iuris canonici*. 2 vols., Leipzig, 1879–81.

Fuero de Cuenca. Spanish trans. A. Valmaña Vicente, Cuenca, 1978.

Fuero de Estella. ed. J.M. Lacarra, *AHDE* 4(1927) pp. 404–51.

Fuero de Molina de Aragón. ed. M. Sancho Izquierdo, Madrid, 1916

Los Fueros de Sepúlveda. ed. E. Saez, Segovia, 1953

Germain, A, ed. *Liber instrumentorum memorialium. Cartulaire des Guillems de Montpellier*. Montpellier, 1884–6.

Gesta abbatum fontanellensium. ed. G.H. Pertz, *MGH*, Scriptores (in folio), II, Hanover, 1829. 2nd edn S. Löwenfeld, *MGH*, Scriptores in usum scholarum, Hanover, 1886.

Gesta sanctorum patrum Fontanellis coenobii. eds. F. Lohier and J. Laporte, Rouen-Paris, 1936.

Gil, Moshe, ed. *Palestine during the First Muslim Period*. [Hebrew] 3 vols., Tel Aviv, 1983.

Gilliodts-van-Severen, L., ed. *Cartulaire de l'ancien consulat d'Espagne à Bruges*. I, Bruges, 1901.

Giovanni Scriba, *Il Cartolare di Giovanni Scriba*. eds. M. Chiaudano and M. Moresco, 2 vols., Rome, 1935. Also in *Historia patria monumenta VI: Chartae*. II, Turin, 1853.

Giovanni di Guiberto (1200–1211). eds. M. Hall, H.C. Krueger, R.L. Reynolds, 2 vols, Turin, 1940.

Goitein, S.D., ed. and English trans. *Letters of Medieval Jewish Traders*. Princeton, 1973.
González, Julio, ed. *El reino de Castilla en la época de Alfonso VIII*. Madrid, 1960.
González, Tomás, ed. *Colección de privilegios, franquezas, exenciones, y fueros, concedidos a varios pueblos y corporaciones de la Corona de Castilla, copiados de orden de S.M. de los registros del Real archivo de Simancas*. IV, Madrid, 1833.
(Gregory IX). *Les régistres de Grégoire IX*. ed. L. Auvray, 3 vols., Paris, 1896–1919.
Gregory of Tours. *Historia Francorum*. eds. W. Arndt and B. Krusch, *MGH*, Scriptores rerum Merovingicarum, I.I, Hanover, 1884.
Guérard, B., ed. *Cartulaire de l'abbaye de Saint Victor de Marseilles*. Paris, 1857.
Guglielmo Cassinese (1190–1192). eds. M. Hall, H.C. Krueger, R.L. Reynolds, 2 vols., Turin, 1938.
Le guide du pèlerin de Saint Jacques de Compostelle. ed. J. Vielliard, 2nd edn, Mâcon, 1950.
Harkavy, A.E., ed. *Teshuvot ha-geonim*. Berlin, 1887 (reprint Jerusalem, 1966).
Herman of Tournai. "Epistola de corpore S. Vincentii diaconi," *Analecta bollandiana* 2 (1883), pp.243–6.
Hernández Sánchez, Francisco J., ed. *Los cartularios de Toledo: Catálogo documental*. Madrid, 1985.
"Las Cortes de Toledo de 1207," *Las Cortes de Castilla y León en la edad media*. Valladolid, 1988, pp.221–63.
al-Ḥimyarī, Muḥammad b. ʿAbd Allah. *La Péninsule ibérique au moyen âge d'après le "Kitāb ar-rawḍ al-miʿṭār fī habar al-akhtār."* ed. and French trans. E. Lévi-Provençal, Leiden, 1938.
Hirschberg, H.Z., ed. "ʿAl gezeirut hameihadim vesakhar huhu," *I.F. Baer Jubilee Volume*. Jerusalem, 1961, pp.134–53.
Hirschfeld, H., ed. "Some Judeo-Arabic Legal Documents," *Jewish Quarterly Review* 16 (1925–6), pp.279–86.
Ḥudūd al-ʿālam: "The Regions of the World," A Persian Geography. English trans. V. Minorsky, Gibb Memorial Series, ns XI, London, 1970.
Ḥulāl al-mawshiyya. ed. I.S. Allouche, Rabat, 1936. Spanish trans. A. Huici Miranda, *"Al-Ḥulāl al-mawsiyya": crónica árabe de las dinastías Almorávide, Almohade, y Benimerín*. Tetuan, 1952.
(James I) *Documentos de Jaime I de Aragón*. ed. A. Huici Miranda, Valencia, 1976:
John of Gorze. *Vita*. ed. G.H. Pertz, *MGH*, Scriptores (in folio), IV, Hanover, 1841.
Ibn al-ʿAbbār, Abū ʿAbd Allah. *Kitāb al-takmila li-kitāb al-ṣila*. ed. F. Codera, *BAH*, V, Madrid, 1886.
Ibn ʿAbd al-Raʾūf. *Risāla*. See Lévi-Provençal, *Documents arabes*. French trans. R. Arié, "Traduction annotée et commentée des traités de ḥisba d'Ibn ʿAbd al-Raʾūf et de ʿUmar al-Garsīfī," *Hespéris-Tamuda* 1(1960), pp.5–37, 199–210, 349–84.
Ibn ʿAbdūn, Muḥammad b. Aḥmad. *Risāla fī al-qaḍāʾ wa al-ḥisba*. See Lévi-

Provençal, *Documents arabes*. Spanish trans. E. Lévi-Provençal and E. Garc·: Gómez, *Sevilla a comienzos del siglo XII; el tratado de Ibn 'Abdūn*. Madrid, 1948.

Ibn Abī Zar', 'Alī b. 'Abd Allah. *Rawḍ al-qirṭās*. Spanish trans. A. Huici Miranda, 2nd edn, Valencia, 1964.

Ibn Abī Firās, Abū al-Qāsim Khalaf. "Kitāb akriyat al-sufun wa al-nizā' bayna ahliha," ed. M.A. Tahir, *Cahiers de Tunisie* 31 (1983), pp.7–52.

Ibn al-'Arabī, *Sufis of Andalusia. The Rūḥ al-quds and al-Durrat al-fākhirah of Ibn 'Arabī*. English trans. R.W.J. Austin, Berkeley, 1977.

Ibn 'Aṣim, Abū Bakr Muḥammad b. Muḥammad. *Traité de droit musulmane; La Tohfat d'Ebn Acem*. ed. and French trans. O. Houdas and F. Martel, Algiers, 1882.

Ibn al-Athīr, Abū al-Ḥasan 'Alī. *Kāmil fī al-ta'rīkh*. ed. C.J. Tornberg, Leiden, 1851–76. Partial French trans. E. Fagnan, *Annales du Maghreb et de l'Espagne*. Algiers, 1898.

Ibn al-'Awwām, Yaḥyā b. Muḥammad. *Le livre de l'agriculture d'Ibn Awam*. French trans. J.J. Clémont-Mollet, 3 vols., Paris, 1866.

Ibn Bashkuwāl, Abū al-Qāsim Khalaf. *Kitāb al-ṣila fī ta'rīkh al-immat al-Andalus*. ed. F. Codera, *BAH*, 2 vols., Madrid, 1882–3; Also edited, 2 vols., Cairo, 1955.

Ibn Baṣṣāl, Muḥammad b. Ibrāhim. *Kitāb al-filāḥa*. ed. J.M. Millás Vallicrosa, Tetuan, 1955.

Ibn Bassām, Abū al-Ḥasan 'Alī. *Dhakhīra fī maḥāsin ahl al-jazīra*. 8 vols., Cairo, 1358/1939–1364/1945.

Ibn Baṭṭūṭa, Muḥammad b. 'Abd Allah. *Tuḥfa al-naẓār fī gharā'ib al-amṣār*. eds. A. al-'Awāmarī and M. al-Mawlī, Cairo, 1934.

Voyages III: Inde, extrême-orient, Espagne, et Soudan. French trans. C. Defremery and B.R. Sanguinetti, Paris, 1858.

The Travels of Ibn Baṭṭūṭa, A.D. 1325–1354. English trans. H.A.R. Gibb, III, Cambridge, 1971.

Ibn al-Bayṭār, 'Abd Allah b. Aḥmad, "Traité des simples par Ibn el-Beither," French trans. L. LeClerc, *Notices et extraits des manuscrits de la Bibliothèque Nationale*. Paris, 23 (1877), 25 (1881), 26 (1883).

Ibn Buklārish, Yūnus b. Isḥāq. "El prólogo de 'al-Kitāb al-musta'īnī' de Ibn Buklārish," ed. and Spanish trans. A. Labarta, *Estudios sobre historia de la ciencia árabe*. (ed. J. Vernet), Barcelona, 1980, pp.183–316.

Ibn Ezra, Abraham. *"Sefer Hanisyonot": The Book of Medical Experiences attributed to Abraham Ibn Ezra*. eds. and English trans. J.O. Liebowitz and S. Marcus, Jerusalem, 1984.

Ibn al-Faqīh al-Hamadhānī, Aḥmad b. Muḥammad. *Kitāb al-buldān*. ed. M.J. de Goeje, *BGA*, 2nd edn, v, Leiden, 1967. French trans. H. Massé, *Abrégé du livre des pays*. Damascus, 1973.

Ibn al-Faraḍī, 'Abd Allah. *Kitāb ta'rīkh 'ulama' al-Andalus*. ed. F. Codera, *BAH*, 2 vols., Madrid, 1890.

Ibn Ghālib, Muḥammad b. Ayyūb. "Naṣṣ andalusī jadīd qaṭ'ia min kitāb farḥa al-anfūs li-Ibn Ghālib," ed. L. 'Abd al-Badī, *Majalla ma'had al-makhṭūṭāt al-'arabiya* 1 (1955), pp.272–310.

"Una descripción de España de Ibn Ghālib," Spanish trans. J. Vallvé Bermejo, *Anuario de filología* 1 (1975), pp.369–84.

Ibn Ḥawqal, Abū al-Qāsim. *Kitāb ṣurat al-arḍ*. ed. J.H. Kramers, Leiden, 1938. French trans. J.H. Kramers and G. Wiet, *Configuracion de la terre*. Paris, 1964.

Ibn Ḥayyān, Ḥayyān b. Khalaf. *Muqtabis*. (vol. II) ed. M.'A. al-Makkī, Beirut, 1973.

Kitāb al-muqtabis min ta'rīkh rijāl al-Andalus. (vol. III) ed. M. Antuña, Paris, 1937.

Muqtabas. (vol. v) eds. P. Chalmeta, F. Corriente, M. Subḥ, Madrid-Rabat, 1979; Spanish trans. M.J. Viguera, F. Corriente, *Crónica del califa 'Abdarraḥmān III an-Nāṣir entre los años 912 y 942*. Zaragoza, 1981.

Muqtabis. (vol: VIII) ed. 'A.'A. al-Ḥajjī, Beirut, 1965.

Ibn Ḥazm, 'Alī b. Aḥmad. "Un códice inexplorado del cordobés Ibn Hazm," ed. M. Asín Palacios, *Al-Andalus* 2(1934), pp.1–56.

Maḥallī. Cairo, 1347/1928–9.

Ṭawq al-ḥamāma. ed. T.A. Makkī, Cairo, 1975. English trans. A.J. Arberry, *The Ring of the Dove*. London, 1953.

Ibn 'Idhārī al-Marrākushī, Abū al-'Abbās. *Bayān al-mughrib*. (vol. II) ed. R. Dozy, Leiden, 1849. New edn, G.S. Colin and E. Lévi-Provençal, Leiden, 1951.

Bayān al-mughrib. (vol. III) ed. E. Lévi-Provençal, Paris, 1930.

Ibn Jubayr, Muḥammad b. Aḥmad. *Riḥla*. English trans. R.J.C. Broadhurst, *The Travels of Ibn Jubair*. London, 1952.

Ibn Juzayy, Muḥammad b. Aḥmad. *Qawānin al-aḥkam al-shar'īya wa al-masā'il al-furū' al-fiqhiya*. ed. A.A. Sayyid al-Ahl, Beirut, 1968.

Ibn Khaldūn, 'Abd al-Raḥmān b. Muḥammad. *The Muqaddimah*. English trans. F. Rosenthal, 3 vols., New York, 1958.

Ibn al-Khaṭīb, Lisān al-Dīn. *Kitāb al-'amāl al-'alām*. ed. E. Lévi-Provençal, Beirut, 1956.

Mi'yār al-ikhtiyār. ed. M.K. Chabana, Rabat, 1397/1977.

Mufākharāt Mālaqa wa Salā. ed. A.M. al-'Abbādī, Alexandria, 1958.

"El 'Parangón entre Malaga y Salé' de Ibn al-Khaṭīb," Spanish trans. E. García Gómez, *Al-Andalus* 2(1934), pp. 183–96.

Ibn Khurradādhbih, 'Ubayd Allah. *Kitāb al-masālik wa al-mamālik*. ed. M.J. de Goeje, *BGA*, 2nd edn, VI, Leiden, 1967.

Ibn Māsawaih. "Ibn Māsawaih and his Treatise on Simple Aromatic Substances," ed. and English trans. M. Levey, *Journal of the History of Medicine* 16(1961), pp. 394–410.

Ibn Paquda, Bahya ben Joseph. *The Book of Direction to the Duties of the Heart*. English trans. M. Mansoor, London, 1973.

Ibn Rushd, Muḥammad b. Aḥmad. *Fatāwā Ibn Rushd*. ed. Ibn al-Tāhir al-Talīlī, Beirut, 1407/1987.

Kitāb al-muqaddimāt al-mumahhidāt. Cairo, 1325/1907.

Ibn Rustah, Aḥmad b. 'Umar. *'Alaq al-nafīsah*. ed. M.J. de Goeje, *BGA*, 2nd edn, VII, Leiden, 1967.

Ibn Sahl, Abū al-Asbagh ʿIsā. "Les 'nawāzil' d'Ibn Sahl; section relative a l'iḥtisāb," ed. Thami el-Azemmouri, *Hespéris Tamuda* 14(1972–4), pp. 7–107.

Thalāth wathā'iq fī muḥāraba al-'ahwā' wa al-bidaʿ fī al-Andalus. ed. M. ʿAbd al-Wahhāb Khallāf, Cairo, 1981.

Wathā'iq fī shu'ūn al-ḥisba fī al-Andalus. ed. M. ʿAbd al-Wahhāb Khallāf, Cairo, 1985.

Wathā'iq fī shu'ūn al-ʿumrān fī al-Andalus: al-masājid wa al-dūr. ed. M. ʿAbd al-Wahhāb Khallāf, Cairo, 1983.

Ibn Saʿīd al-Gharnāṭī, *Kitāb basṭ al-arḍ fī al-ṭūl wa al-ʿarḍ.* ed. J. Vernet Gides, Tetuan, 1958.

Rāyāt al-mubarrizīn wa ghāyāb al-mumayyizīn. ed. A.M. al-Qādī, Cairo, 1393/1973. English trans. A.J. Arberry, *Moorish Poetry: A Translation of 'The Pennants'; an Anthology compiled in 1243 by the Andalusian Ibn Saʿīd.* Cambridge, 1953.

Ibn Salmūn, ʿAbd Allah. "Algunos capítulos del formulario notarial de Abensalmun de Granada," ed. P.J. López Ortiz, *AHDE* 4(1924), pp. 319–75.

Ibn Sammāk al-ʿAmalī, Muḥammad. "Al-zahrāt al-manthūra fī nakt al-akhbār al-ma'thūra," ed. M.A. Makkī, *Madrid:MDI* 20(1979–80), pp. 5–76; 21(1981–2), pp. 5–79.

Ibn al-Shabbāṭ, Muḥammad b. ʿAlī. "Un fragmento de la obra de Ibn al-Sabbāṭ (s. XIII) sobre al-Andalus," Spanish trans. E. de Santiago Simón, *Cuadernos de historia del Islam.* Granada, 1973.

Ibn al-Zubayr, Abū Jaʿfar Aḥmad. *Kitāb ṣilat al-ṣilah.* ed. E. Lévi-Provençal, Rabat, 1938.

al-Idrīsī, Muḥammad b. Muḥammad. *Opus geographicum (Kitāb al-nuzhat al-mushtāq fī al-ikhtirāq al-'afāq).* 9 vols. Rome-Naples, 1970–84.

Description de l'Afrique et de l'Espagne. ed. and French trans. R. Dozy and M.J. de Goeje, Leiden, 1866.

Geografia de España. Spanish trans. E. Saavedra, Madrid, 1881.

Imperiale di Sant'Angelo, Cesare, ed. *Codice diplomatico della repubblica di Genova.* 3 vols., Rome, 1936–42.

Isḥāq b. al-Ḥusayn. "Il compendio geografico arabo di Isḥāq ibn al-Ḥusayn," ed. and Italian trans. A. Codazzo and C.A. Nallino, *Rendiconti della R. accademia nazionale dei Lincei* (Rome) 6th series, 5(1929).

al-Iṣṭakhrī, Ibrāhīm b. Muḥammad. *Kitāb al-masālik wa al-mamālik.* ed. M.J. de Goeje, *BGA*, 2nd edn, 1, Leiden, 1967.

Jaffé, P., ed. *Regesta pontificum romanorum.* (2nd edn G. Wattenbach) 2 vols., Leipzig, 1885–88.

(al-Jāḥiẓ, ʿAmr b. Baḥr). *Tabaṣṣur al-tijāra.* ed. H.H. ʿAbd al-Wahhāb, Damascus, 1351/1932.

"Gahiziana I: Le 'Kitāb al-tabaṣṣur al-tigāra' attribué à Gaḥiẓ," French trans. C. Pellat, *Arabica* 1(1954), pp. 153–65.

al-Jarsīfī, ʿUmar. *Risāla.* See Lévi-Provençal, *Documents arabes.*

Jewish Poets of Spain 900–1250. English trans. D. Goldstein, London, 1965.

al-Khushanī, Muḥammad. *Historia de los jueces de Córdoba por Aljoxaní.* ed. and Spanish trans. J. Ribera y Tarragó, Madrid, 1914.

al-Kindī, Ya'qūb b. Isḥāq. *The Medical Formulary or Aqrabadhin of al-Kindī.* English trans. M. Levy, Madison, 1966.

Lacarra, José María, ed. *Documentos para el estudio de la reconquista y repoblación del Valle del Ebro.* 3 vols., Zaragoza, 1946–52.

Lambert li Tort. *Li Romans d'Alixandre.* ed. H. Michelant, Stuttgart, 1846.

Lanfranco (1206–1226). eds. H.C. Krueger and R.L. Reynolds, 2 vols., Genoa, 1952.

Lévi-Provençal, E., ed. *Documents arabes inédits sur la vie sociale et économique en occident musulman au moyen âge: Trois traités hispaniques de ḥisba.* Cairo, 1955.

Lex Visigothorum. ed. C. Zeumer, *MGH,* Leges (in quarto), I. 1, Hanover, 1892.

The Libelle of Englyshe Polycye. A Poem on the Use of Sea Power, 1436. ed. G. Warner, Oxford, 1926.

Liber iurium reipublicae genuensis. ed. M.E. Ricotti, *Historiae patriae monumenta,* VII, Turin, 1854.

Liber miraculorum S. Bertini Abbatis. Acta Sanctorum, September 5, vol. II, Antwerp, 1748, pp. 595–604.

Liber miraculorum Sancte Fidis. ed. A. Bouillet, Paris, 1897.

Liber pontificalis. ed. L. Duchesne, 3 vols., Paris, 1955.

Liutprand of Cremona. *Opera.* ed. J. Becker, *MGH,* Scriptores in usum scholarum, Hanover-Leipzig, 1915.

Llibre del repartiment de Valencia. ed. A. Ferrando i Francés, Valencia, 1979.

The Mabinogion. English trans. J. Gantz, London, 1976.

Madurell Marimón, J. and García Sanz, A., eds. *Comandes comerciales barcelonesas de la baja edad media.* Barcelona, 1973.

Mañueco Villalobos, M., ed. *Documentos de la Iglesia Colegial de Santa María la Mayor de Valladolid (siglo XIII, 1201–1280).* Valladolid, 1920.

al-Maqqarī, Aḥmad b. Muḥammad. *Analectes sur l'histoire et la littérature des arabes d'Espagne.* ed. R. Dozy, 2 vols., Leiden, 1855–60.

Nafḥ al-ṭīb min ghuṣn al-Andalus al-raṭīb. 10 vols., Cairo, 1949.

The History of the Mohammaden Dynasties in Spain. English trans. Pascual de Gayangos, 2 vols., London, 1840.

Azhār al-riyāḍ fi akhbār al-'iyāḍ. II, Cairo, 1359/1940.

al-Maqrīzī, Taqī al-Dīn Aḥmad. *Mawā'iz wa al-i'tibār bi-dhikr al-khiṭaṭ wa al-'athār.* Bulaq, 1270/1853–4.

Martin of Savona, *Il Cartulario del notaio Martino, Savona, 1203–1206.* ed. D. Puncuh, Genoa, 1974.

Martín Rodríguez, José Luis, ed. "Portazgos de Ocaña y Alarilla," *AHDE* 32(1962), pp. 519–26.

Mas Latrie, Louis de, ed. "Documents sur l'histoire de l'Algérie et de l'Afrique septentrionale pendant le moyen âge: Relations avec Pisa," *Bibliothèque de l'Ecole de Chartes* 10(1848–9), pp. 134–54.

Traités de paix et documents divers concernant les relations de chrétiens avec les arabes de l'Afrique septentrionale au moyen âge. Paris, 1866.

al-Mas'ūdī, 'Alī b. Ḥusayn. *Murūj al-dhahab (Les praires d'or).* ed. and French trans. C. Barbier de Meynard, Paris, 1861.

Kitāb al-tanbīh wa al-ishrāf. ed. M.J. de Goeje, *BGA*, 2nd edn, VIII, Leiden, 1967.

Historical Encyclopedia. English trans. A. Sprenger, London, 1841.

Math vab Mathonwy. ed. and English trans. W.J. Gruffydd, Cardiff, 1928.

Méry, Louis and Guindon, F., eds. *Histoire analytique et chronologique des actes et des délibérations du corps et du conseil de la municipalité de Marseille depuis le Xe siècle jusqu'au nos jours*. I, Marseilles, 1841.

Molina, Luis., ed. and Spanish trans. *Una descripción anónima de al-Andalus*. 2 vols., Madrid, 1983.

Mones, H., ed. "Waṣf al-jadīd li-Qurṭuba al-islamiyya," *Madrid: MDI* 13(1965–6), pp. 164–81.

Montaiglon, Anatole de, ed. *Recueil général et complet des fabliaux des XIIIe et XIVe siècles*. I, Paris, 1872.

Moses b. Maimon. *Glossary of Drug Names*. English trans. F. Rosner, Philadelphia, 1979.

Kovets teshuvot ha-Rambam ve-iggerotav. ed. A. Lichtenberg, Leipzig, 1859 (reprint 1969).

Letters of Maimonides. English trans. L.D. Stitskin, New York, 1977.

Responsa. ed. Joshua Blau, 3 vols., Jerusalem, 1957–61.

Mouynès, G. ed. *Inventaire des archives communales. Ville de Narbonne*. Narbonne, 1871.

Müller, Joel, ed. *Die Responsen der spanischen Lehrer des 10. Jahrhunderts*. Berlin, 1889.

Teshuvot geonei mizrah u-ma'arav [*Responsen der Lehrer des Osten und Westens*). Berlin, 1888 (reprint Jerusalem, 1966).

Muñoz y Romero, Tomás, ed. *Colección de fueros municipales y cartas puebles de los reinos de Castilla, León, Corona de Aragón, y Navarra*. I, Madrid, 1847 (reprint 1971).

al-Muqaddasī, Muḥammad b. Aḥmad. *Aḥsan al-taqāsīm fi ma'rifat al-aqālīm*. ed. M.J. de Goeje, *BGA*, 2nd edn, III, Leiden, 1967.

Description de l'occident musulman au IVe = Xe siècle. ed. and French trans. C. Pellat, Paris, 1950.

Muratori, Ludovico Antonio, ed. *Antiquitates italicae medii aevi sive dissertationes*. IV, Rome, 1741.

Nāsir-i Khusraw. *Nāser-e Khosrow's Book of Travels* (*Safarnāma*). English trans. W.M. Thackston, Albany, 1986.

Notker the Stammerer. *De Carolo Magno*. ed. P. Jaffé, *Monumenta carolina*. IV, *Bibliotheca rerum germanicarum*. Berlin, 1867.

al-Nuwayrī, Aḥmad b. 'Abd al-Wahhāb. *Historia de los musulmanes de España y Africa por en-Nuguarí*. ed. and Spanish trans. M. Gaspar Remiro, I, Granada, 1917.

Oberto Scriba de Mercato (*1186*). ed. M. Chaiudano, Genoa, 1940.

Oberto Scriba de Mercato (*1190*). eds. M. Chaiudano and R. Morozzo della Rocca, Genoa, 1938.

Pegolotti, Francesco Balducci. *La pratica della mercatura*. ed. Allan Evans, Cambridge, Mass., 1936.

Peter the Venerable. *Adversus iudeorum inveteratam duritiem*. ed. Y. Friedman, Corpus Christianorum: Continuatio Mediaevalis, 58; Turnhout, 1985.
Petrus Alfonsi, *The "Disciplina clericalis" of Petrus Alfonsi*. English trans. P.R. Quarrie, London, 1977.
Petrus Guillelmus. *Miracula beati Aegidii*. ed. P. Jaffé, *MGH*, Scriptores (in folio), XII, Hanover, 1856.
Pliny, *Natural History*. ed. and English trans. H. Rackham, Cambridge, Mass., 1983.
Portugaliae monumenta historica: Diplomata et chartae. I, Lisbon, 1867.
Portugaliae monumenta historica: Leges et consuetudines. I, Lisbon, 1856.
Potthast, A., ed. *Regesta pontificum romanorum*. Berlin, 1874–5.
Procopius of Caesaria. *Bellum gothicum*. ed. and English trans. H.B. Dewing, London, 1919.
Pryor, John H., ed. *Business Contracts of Medieval Provence; Selected "Notulae" from the Cartulary of Giraud Amalric of Marseilles, 1248*. Toronto, 1981.
al-Qalqashandī, Aḥmad b. ʿAlī. *Ṣubḥ al-ʿasha fī kitābāt al-inshāʾ*. Spanish trans. L. Seco de Lucena, Valencia, 1975.
al-Qazwīnī, Zakarīya b. Muḥammad. *Athār al-bilād wa akhbār al-ʿibār*. Beirut, 1380/1960.
Qudama b. Jaʿfar. *Kitāb al-kharāj*. ed. M.J. de Goeje, *BGA*, 2nd edn, VI, Leiden, 1967.
Raoul de Cambrai. *Chanson de Geste*. eds. M.P. Meyer and A. Longnon, Paris, 1882.
al-Rāzī, Aḥmad. *Anales palatinos del califa de Cordoba al-Ḥakam II, por ʿIsā b. Aḥmad al-Rāzī*. Spanish trans. E. García Gómez, Madrid, 1967.
"La 'Description de l'Espagne' d'Aḥmad al-Rāzī," ed. E. Lévi-Provençal, *Al-Andalus* 18(1953), pp.51–108.
Recueil des historiens de Gaules et de la France. XVI, Paris, 1878.
Regné, Jean. *History of the Jews in Aragon. Regesta and Documents, 1213–1327*. Jerusalem, 1978.
Richard the Pilgrim, *Chanson d'Antioch, composée au XIIe siècle par Richard le pèlerin*. ed. L. de Saint-Aulaire, Paris, 1862.
Roger of Hoveden. *Cronica*. (ed. W. Stubbs), 4 vols., London, 1868–71.
al-Saḥnūn, ibn Saʿīd al-Tanūkhī. *Mudawwana al-kubrā*. Cairo, 1323/1905.
al-Sakhāwī, Muḥammad. b. ʿAbd al-Raḥmān. *ʿIlān bi-l-tawbīkh limān dhamma al-taʾrīkh*. Damascus, 1349/1931.
Salmon, *Liber magistri Salmonis sacri palatii notarii (1222–1226)*. ed. Arturo Ferretto, *ASLSP* 36(1906).
al-Saqaṭī, Muḥammad b. Abī Muḥammad. *Kitāb al-faqīh al-ajall al-ʿālim al-ʿārif al-awḥad (Un manuel hispanique de ḥisba)*. eds. G.S. Colin and E. Lévi-Provençal, Paris, 1931.
"El kitāb fī ādāb al-ḥisba de al-Saqaṭī," Spanish trans. P. Chalmeta, *Al-Andalus* 32(1967), pp.125–62, 359–97; 33(1968), pp.143–95, 367–434.
Scheler, A., ed. "Trois traités de lexicographie latine du XIIe au XIIIe siècle," *Jahrbuch für romanische und englische Literatur* 6(1865).

Sendra Cendra, Ma. Dolores. *Aranceles aduaneros de la Corona de Aragón (siglo XIII)*. Valencia, 1966.

al-Shaqundī, Ismāʿīl b. Muḥammad. *Risāla*. (in Maqqarī, *Analectes*) Spanish trans. E. García Gómez, *Elogio del Islam español (Risāla fī faḍl al-Andalus)*.; French trans. A. Luya, "Le 'Risāla' d'as-Saḳundī," *Hespéris* 22(1936), pp.133–81.

al-Silafī, Aḥmad b. Muḥammad. *Akhbār wa al-tarājim andalusiyya*. ed. I. ʿAbbās, Beirut, 1963.

The Song of Roland. English trans. D.L. Sayers, London, 1976.

The Theodosian Code. English trans. C. Pharr, Princeton, 1952.

Theodulfus. *Versus contra iudices*. ed. E. Dümmler, *MGH*, Poetae latini, I.2, Berlin, 1881.

Thorpe, L., trans. *Two Lives of Charlemagne*. London, 1969.

Traducción española de un manuscrito anónimo del siglo XIII sobre la cocina hispano-magribī. Spanish trans. A. Huici Miranda, Madrid, 1966.

Tucci, Raffaele di. "Documenti inediti sulla spedizione e sulla mahona dei Genovesi a Ceuta (1234–1237)," *ASLSP* 64(1935), pp.273–340.

al-ʿUdhrī, Aḥmad b.ʿUmar b. al-Dilāʾī. "Nuṣūs ʿan al-Andalus," *Tarḍīʿ al-akhbār wa tanwīʿ al-ʿāthār*. ed. A.A. al-Ahwānī, Madrid, 1960.

"La cora de Ilbīra (Granada y Almeria) en los siglos X y XI, segun al-ʿUdhrī," Spanish trans. M. Sánchez Martínez, *Cuadernos de historia de Islam* 7(1975–6), pp.5–137.

La cora de Tudmīr segun al-ʿUdhrī [s. XI]: aportaciones al estudio geográfico-descriptivo del S.E. peninsular. Spanish trans. E. Molina López, Granada, 1972.

al-ʿUmarī, Ibn Faḍl Allah. *Masālik al-abṣār fī mamālik al-amṣār*. French trans. M. Gaudefroy-Demombynes, *L'Afrique moins l'Egypte*. Paris, 1927.

Usamah b. Munqidh. *Kitāb al-ʿitibār*. (*Ousāma ibn Mounḳidh, un émir syrien au premier siècle des croisades (1095–1188)*.) ed. H. Derenbourg, 2 vols., Paris, 1886–93.

Usatges de Barcelona. eds. R. d'Abadal y Vinyals and F. Valls Taberner, Barcelona, 1913.

Vitas sanctorum patrum Emeretensium. ed. A. Maya Sánchez, Corpus Christianorum: Series latina, 116; Turnhout, 1992. Also ed. and English trans. J.N. Garvin, Washington, D.C., 1946.

al-Wansharīsī, Aḥmad b. Yaḥyā. *Miʿyār al-muʿrib wa al-jāmiʿ al-maghrib*. ed. M. Ḥajjī, 13 vols., Rabat-Beirut, 1401/1981.

"La pierre de touche des fétwas de Aḥmad al-Wanscharīsī," Selected passages summarized in French by E. Amar, *Archives marocainnes* 12(1908); 13(1909).

Yaḥyā b. ʿUmar. *Kitāb aḥkām al-sūq*. ed. F. Dashraoui, Tunis, 1975. Also ed. M.A. Makkī, *Madrid:MDI* 4(1956), pp.59–151.

"Unas 'ordenanzas del zoco' del siglo IX," Spanish trans. E. García Gómez, *Al-Andalus* 22(1957), pp.253–316.

al-Yaʿqūbī, Aḥmad. *Kitāb al-buldān*. ed. M.J. de Goeje, *BGA*, 2nd edn, VII, Leiden, 1967.

al-Yāqūt, ibn 'Abd Allah al-Hamawī. *Mu'jām al-buldān.* [*Jacut's Geographisches Worterbuch*] ed. F. Wüstenfeld, Leipzig, 1873.

La España musulmana en la obra de Yaqut. ed. and Spanish trans. G. 'Abd al-Karīm, Granada, 1974.

Yepes, A. *Coronica general de la Orden de San Benito.* Valladolid-Pamplona, 1609–21.

al-Zuhrī, ibn 'Abd Allah Muḥammad. "Kitāb al-dja'rāfiyya," ed. M. Hadj-Sadok, *Bulletin des études orientales* 21(1968), pp.111–310.

"Extrait de la description de l'Espagne tiré de l'ouvrage du géographe anonyme d'Almeria," ed. R. Basset, *Homenaje a Don Francisco Codera.* Zaragoza, 1904, pp.619–47.

SECONDARY LITERATURE

'Abbādī, Aḥmad. *Los esclavos en España. (al-Ṣaqāliba fī Isbānīya.)* Madrid, 1953.

'Abd al-Karīm, Gamal. "Alejandría y al-Ṣilafī, nexo cultural entre Oriente y al-Andalus," *Cuadernos de historia del Islam* 7(1975–6), pp. 111–51.

Abiad, M. "Origine et développement des dictionnaires biographiques arabes," *Bulletin d'études orientales* 31(1979), pp. 7–15.

Abu-Lughod, Janet. *Before European Hegemony. The World System A.D. 1250–1350.* Oxford, 1989.

Abulafia, David. "Asia, Africa, and the Trade of Medieval Europe," *Cambridge Economic History of Europe.* 2nd edn, Cambridge, 1987, pp. 402–73.

"Catalan merchants and the Western Mediterranean, 1236–1300: Studies in the Notarial Acts of Barcelona and Sicily," *Viator* 16(1985), pp. 209–42.

"The Pisan *Bacini* and the Medieval Mediterranean Economy: A Historian's Viewpoint," *Papers in Italian Archeology* 5(1985), pp. 287–302.

The Two Italies: Economic Relations between the Norman Kingdom of Sicily and the Northern Communes. Cambridge, 1977.

Abun-Nasr, Jamil M. *A History of the Maghrib.* 2nd edn, Cambridge, 1975.

Agus, I.A. *Urban Civilization in Pre-Crusade Europe. A Study of Organized Town Life.* 2 vols., Leiden, 1965.

Ahmad, Aziz. *History of Islamic Sicily.* Edinburgh, 1975.

Airaldi, Gabriela. "Groping in the Dark: The Emergence of Genoa in the early Middle Ages," *Miscellanea di studi storici II. (Collana storica di fonti e studi).* Genoa, 1983, pp. 9–17.

Al-Azmeh, A. "Barbarians in Arab Eyes," *Past and Present* 134(1992), pp. 3–18.

Alemany Bolufer, José. "La geografía de la península ibérica en los escritores árabes," *Revista del centro de estudios históricos de Granada y su reino* 9(1919), pp. 109–72; 10(1920), pp. 1–29, 121–84; 11(1921), pp. 1–39.

Alfau de Solalinde, J. *Nomenclatura de los tejidos españoles del siglo XIII.* Madrid, 1969.

Allouche, I.S. "La vie économique et sociale à Grenade au XIVe siècle," *Mélanges d'histoire et d'archéologie de l'occident musulman. Hommage à Georges Marçais.* II, Algiers, 1957, pp. 7–12.

Bibliography

Alvazes de Morales, C. "Pesos y medidas en un manuscrito árabe sobre materia medica del siglo XI," *Cuadernos de historia del Islam* 8(1977), pp. 161–5.

Antoniadis-Bibicou, H. *Recherches sur les douanes a Byzance*. Paris, 1963.

Antuña, M. "Ibn Hayyān de Córdoba y su historia de la España musulmana," *Cuadernos de historia de España* 4(1945), pp. 5–71.

Arié, Rachel. "Considérations sur la vie économique dans l'Espagne musulmanau cours du bas moyen âge," *Akten des VII Kongresses für Arabistik und Islamwissenschaft (Gottingen, 1974)*. Gottingen, 1976, pp. 47–58.

La España musulmana (siglos VII–XV). Barcelona, 1982.

"La vie économique de l'Espagne musulmane," *Wirtschafts-geschichte des vorderen Orients in islamischer Zeit*. Leiden, 1977, pp. 239–54.

Ashtor, Eliyahu. "Banking Instruments between the Muslim East and the Christian West," *Journal of European Economic History* 1(1972), pp. 553–73.

"Catalan Cloth on the Late Medieval Mediterranean Markets," *Journal of European Economic History* 17(1988), pp. 227–57.

"Gli ebrei nel commercio mediterraneo nell'alto medioevo (sec. X–XI)," *Gli Ebrei nell'alto medioevo*. Settimane di studio del Centro italiano di studi sull'alto medioevo, XXVI, Spoleto, 1980, pp. 401–64.

The Jews of Moslem Spain. 3 vols., Philadelphia, 1973–84.

The Levant Trade in the Later Middle Ages. Princeton, 1973.

"Prix et salaires dans l'Espagne musulmane aux Xe et XIe siècles," *Annales:ESC* 20(1965), pp. 664–79.

"Quelques observations d'un orientaliste sur la thèse de Pirenne," *JESHO* 13(1970), pp. 166–94.

"Recent Research on Levantine Trade," *Journal of European Economic History* 14(1985), pp. 361–85.

"Il regime portuario nel califato," *La navigazione mediterranea nell'alto medioevo*. Settimane di studio del Centro italiano di studi sull'alto medioevo, XXV, Spoleto, 1978, pp. 651–84.

"Republiques urbaines dans le proche orient à l'époque des croisades," *Cahiers de civilisation médiévale* 18(1975), pp. 117–31.

Attman, A. *The Bullion Flow between Europe and the East, 1000–1750*. Göteborg, 1981.

Avila, María Luisa. *La sociedad hispano-musulmana al final del califato (aproximación a un estudio demográfico)*. Madrid, 1985.

Ayalon, David. "Aspects of the Mamluk Phenomenon," *Der Islam* 53(1976), pp. 196–225.

"On the Eunuchs in Islam," *Jerusalem Studies in Arabic and Islam* 1, Jerusalem, 1979, pp. 67–124.

Bach, Erik. *La cité de Gênes au XIIe siècle*. Copenhagen, 1955.

Bachrach, Bernard S. *Jews in Barbarian Europe*. Lawrence, Kansas, 1977.

Badr, A. "Al-andalusiyyūn wa al-maghāriba fī al-Quds," *Awrāq* 4(1981), pp. 125–39.

Baer, Yitzhak F. *A History of the Jews in Christian Spain*. 1, Philadelphia, 1961.

Balard, Michel. "Escales génois sur les routes de l'orient méditerranéan au XIVe siècle," *Recueils de la Société Jean Bodin* 32(1974), pp. 243–59.

"Remarques sur les esclaves à Gênes dans la seconde moitié du XIIIe siècle," *Mélanges d'archéologie et d'histoire de l'Ecole française de Rome* 80(1968), pp. 627–80.

Balbi, Giovanna. "La schiavitù a Genova tra i secoli XII e XIII," *Mélanges offerts à René Crozet*. II, Paris, 1966; pp. 1025–9.

Ballesteros y Beretta, Antonio. *Historia de España y su influencia en la historia universal*. II, Barcelona, 1920.

Sevilla en el siglo XIII. Seville, 1913.

Banti, Ottavio. "I rapporti tra Pisa e gli stati islamici dell'Africa settentrionale tra l'XI e il XIV secolo," *Le ceramiche medievali delle chiese di Pisa*. Pisa, 1983, pp. 9–26.

Bardenhewer, L. *Der Safranhandel im Mittelalter*. Bonn, 1914.

Barkai, Ron. *Cristianos y musulmanes en la España medieval (el enemigo en el espejo)*. Madrid, 1984.

Barbour, Nevill. "Al-Andalus en las crónicas inglesas de los siglos doce y trece," *Madrid: MDI* 13(1965–6), pp. 137–48.

"L'influence de la géographie et de la puissance navale sur le destin de l'Espagne musulmane et du Maroc," *ROMM* (1970), pp. 45–54.

"The Influence of Sea Power on the History of Muslim Spain," *Madrid: MDI* 14(1967), pp. 103–11.

"The Significance of the Word 'Maurus' with its derivatives 'Moro' and 'Moor', and of other terms used by medieval writers in Latin to describe the inhabitants of Muslim Spain," *Actas de IV Congreso de estudios árabes e islámicas*. Leiden, 1971, pp. 253–66.

Barceló, Miguel. "Alguns problemes d'història agrària mallorquina suggerits pel text d'al-Zuhrī," *Recerques* (Barcelona) 8(1978), pp. 27–49.

"Expedicions militars i projectes d'atac contra les illes orientales d'al-Andalus," *Sobre Mayūrqa*. Palma, 1984, pp. 59–75.

"Un estudio sobre la estructura fiscal y procedimientos contables del emirato omeya de Córdoba (138–300/755–912) y el califato (300–66/912–76)," *Acta mediaevalia*. 1985, pp. 45–72.

"El hiato en las acuñaciones de oro en al-Andalus, 127–316/744(5)–936(7)," *Moneda y crédito* 132–5(1975), pp. 33–71.

"La qüestió del documents d'un suposat acord entre 'Alī b. Mujāhid de Dānya i el bisbe Guislabert de Barcelona," *Sobre Mayūrqa*. Palma, 1984, pp. 13–25.

"Why and How did Andalusian Coins travel to Europa during the Emirate and the Caliphate from 98/716–17 to 403/1012–13," *ROMM* 36(1983), pp. 5–18.

Bautier, R.H. "Notes sur l'histoire économique médiévale dans l'archives italiennes," *Mélanges d'archéologie et d'histoire de l'Ecole française de Rome* 58(1946), pp. 291–307; 60(1948), pp. 181–210.

"Les relations commerciales entre l'Europe et l'Afrique du Nord et l'équilibre économique méditerranéen du XIIe au XIVe siècle," *Bulletin philologique et historique* (1953–4), pp. 399–416.

"Sources pour l'histoire du commerce maritime en Méditerranée du XIIe au

XVe siècle," *Actes du IVème colloque international d'histoire maritime (Paris, 1959)*. Paris, 1962, pp. 137–77.

Benaboud, M. "'Asabiyya and Social Relations in al-Andalus during the Period of the Taifa States," *Hespéris-Tamuda* 19(1980–1), pp. 5–45.

Ta'rīkh al-siyyāsī wa al-ijtimā'ī al-Ishbīliyya. Tetuan, 1983.

"Tendances économiques dans al-Andalus durant la période des Etats-Taifas," *Bulletin économique et social du Maroc* 151–2(1983), pp. 5–34. English version: "Economic Trends in al-Andalus during the period of the Taifa States," *Islamic Studies* 26(1987), pp. 1–30.

Bensch, Stephen. "From Prizes of War to Domestic Merchandise: Slaves in the Towns of Eastern Iberia," Unpublished paper presented at the annual meeting of the Medieval Academy of America, Princeton, NJ, May, 1991.

Bernis Madrazo, Carmen. "Tapiceria hispano-musulmana (siglos IX–XI)," *Archivo español de arte* 27(1954), pp. 189–211.

Berti, Graziella and Tongiorgi, Liana. *Arte islamica in Italia: i bacini delle chiese pisane*. Rome-Pisa, 1983.

"I bacini ceramici delle chiese della provincia di Pisa con nuove proposte per la datazione della ceramica spagnola tipo pula," *Faenza* 60(1974), pp. 67–79.

I bacini ceramici medievali delle chiese di Pisa. Rome, 1981.

"I bacini ceramici di S. Michele di Castello-Villa a Roggio (Pescaglia-Lucca)," *Faenza* 60(1974), pp. 76–84.

"Bacini ceramici su alcune chiese della campagna Luccese," *Faenza* 59(1973), pp. 4–15.

"Bacini ceramici su edifici religiosi e civili delle province di Pistoia, Firenze e Siena," *Faenza* 61(1975), pp. 123–35.

"Ceramiche decorate (XI-XIV secolo) di importazione da vari centri del Mediterraneo e di produzione locale sulla base della documentazione in Toscana," *La céramique médiévale en Méditerranée occidentale*. Paris, 1980, pp. 83–91.

Ceramiche importate dalla Spagna nell'area pisana dal XII al XV secolo. Florence, 1985.

"Per lo studio dei bacini delle chiese di Pisa: Rassegna di recenti contributi alla storia della ceramica," *Le ceramiche medievale delle chiese di Pisa*. [Biblioteca del Bollettino storico pisano, collana storica 25], Pisa, 1983.

Berti, Graziella and Tongiorgi, Ezio. *Ceramiche importate dalla Spagna nell'area pisana dal XII al XV secolo*. Florence, 1985.

Beshir, B.J. "Fatimid Military Organization," *Der Islam* 55(1978), pp. 37–56.

Bishai, Wilson B. "Negotiations and Peace Agreements between Muslims and Non-Muslims in Islamic History," *Medieval and Middle Eastern Studies in Honor of A.S. Atiya*. Leiden, 1972, pp. 50–61.

Bishko, Julian. "Sesenta años después: *La Mesta* de Julius Klein a la luz de la investigación subsiguente," *Historia, Instituciones, Documentos* (Seville) 8(1981), pp. 9–57.

Blake, H. "The 'Bacini' of North Italy," *La céramique médiévale en Méditeranée occidentale*. Paris, 1980, pp. 93–111.

Bloch, Marc. "Le problème d'or au moyen âge," *Annales d'histoire économique et sociale* 19(1933), pp. 1–34.
Blum, André. *On the Origin of Paper*. New York, 1934.
Bohannan, Paul and Dalton, George, eds. *Markets in Africa*. Chicago, 1962.
Boissonade, P. "Les études relatives à l'histoire économique de l'Espagne et leur résultats," *Revue de synthèse historique*. (Paris), 1913, pp. 62–83, 145–55.
Bolens, Lucie. *Agronomes andalous du moyen âge*. Geneva, 1981.
La cuisine andalouse, un art de vivre: XIe-XIIIe siècle. Paris, 1990.
"Henné et koḥl: Le corps peint du rituel nuptial chez les hispano-arabes du moyen âge," *Razo* 7(1987), pp. 63–79.
"Les parfums et la beauté en Andalousie médiévale (XIe-XIIIe siècle)," *Les soins de beauté. Actes du IIIe colloque international, Grasse (avril, 1985)*. Nice, 1987, pp. 145–69.
"The Use of Plants for Dyeing and Clothing: Cotton and Woad in al-Andalus: A Thriving Agricultural Sector (5th/11th-7th/13th centuries)," *The Legacy of Muslim Spain*. (ed. S.K. Jayyusi), Leiden, 1992, pp. 1000–15.
"La viticulture d'après les traités d'agronomie andalous (XIe-XIIe siècles)," *L'Andalousie du quotidien au sacré (XIe-XIIIe siècles)*. Aldershot, 1991, pp. 1–7.
Bolin, Sture. "Mohammed, Charlemagne, and Ruric," *Scandinavian Economic History Review* 1(1953), pp. 5–39.
Borlandi, F. "Note per la storia della produzione e del commercio di una materia prima: il guado nel medio evo," *Studi in onore di Gino Luzzatto*. 1, Milan, 1950, pp. 297–326.
Borouiba, Rachid. "Monnaies et bijoux trouvés à la Qal'a des Bani Hammad," *ROMM* 8(1970), pp. 67–77.
Bosch Vilá, Jacinto. "Algunas consideraciones sobre 'al-tagr' en al-Andalus y la división político-administrativa de la España musulmana," *Etudes d'orientalisme dédiées à la mémoire de Lévi-Provençal*. Paris, 1962, pp. 23–33.
Ben al-Jatīb y Granada. Madrid, 1980.
Los Almorávides. Tetuan, 1956.
La Sevilla islámica 712–1248. Seville, 1984.
Bosworth, C.E. *The Islamic Dynasties*. Edinburgh, 1967.
Bouayed, M.A. "Le port de Hunayn, trait d'union entre le Maghreb central et l'Espagne au moyen âge," *Relationes de la península ibérica con el Magreb (siglos XIII-XVI)*. (eds. M. García-Arenal and M.J. Viguera), Madrid, 1988. pp. 325–59.
Bovill, E.W. *The Golden Trade of the Moors*. 2nd edn, Oxford, 1970.
Braudel, Ferdinand. *The Mediterranean and the Mediterranean World in the Age of Philip II*. 2 vols., New York, 1966.
Braulio, Justel. "Nuevo fondo de manuscritos árabes en la Biblioteca Nacional," *Madrid:MDI* 20(1979–80), pp. 96–143.
Brett, Michael. "Ifrīqiya as a Market for Saharan Trade from the 10th to the 12th C. AD," *Journal of African History* 10(1969),.pp. 347–64.
"Islam and Trade in the 'Bilād al-Sūdān' 10th-11th c.," *Journal of African History* 24(1983), pp. 431–40.

Bridbury, A.R. *England and the Salt Trade in the Later Middle Ages*. Oxford, 1955.

Brockelmann, C. *Geschichte der arabischen Litteratur*. Supplement 1, 3 vols., Leiden, 1937–42.

Brown, Peter. "Mohammed and Charlemagne by H. Pirenne," *Daedalus* 103(1974), pp. 25–33.

Bruno, Federico. "Le convenzioni commerciali e la marina savonese dai tempi piu antichi sino alla fine del secolo XIV," *Atti della Societá savonese di storia patria*. (Savona) 1924.

Brunschvig, Robert. *La Berbérie orientale sous les Hafṣides*. Paris, 1947.

Buckley, R.P. "The Muḥtasib," *Arabica* 39(1992), pp. 59–117.

Bulliet, Richard W. *The Camel and the Wheel*. Cambridge, Mass. 1975.

"A quantitative approach to medieval Muslim biographical dictionaries," *JESHO* 13(1970), pp. 195–211.

Burns, Robert Ignatius. *Islam under the Crusaders: Colonial Survival in the 13th-century Kingdom of Valencia*. Princeton, 1973.

"Jaume I and the Jews of the Kingdom of Valencia," *Jaime I y su época: X Congresso de historia de la Corona de Aragón*. Zaragoza, 1980, pp. 245–322.

"The Paper Revolution in Europe: Crusader Valencia's Paper Industry," *Pacific Historical Review* 50(1981), pp. 1–30.

"Piracy as an Islamic-Christian Interface in the Thirteenth Century," *Viator* 11(1980), pp. 165–78.

"Renegades, Adventurers, and Sharp Businessmen: The 13th-century Spaniards in the Cause of Islam," *Catholic Historical Review* 58(1972), pp. 341–66.

Society and Documentation in Crusader Valencia. Princeton, 1985.

Byrne, Eugene H. "Commercial Contracts of the Genoese in the Syrian Trade of the Twelfth century," *Quarterly Journal of Economics* 31(1916–17), pp. 128–70.

"Easterners in Genoa," *JAOS* 38(1918), pp. 176–87.

Genoese Shipping in the Twelfth and Thirteenth Centuries. Cambridge, Mass, 1930.

"Genoese Trade with Syria in the 12th Century," *AHR* 25(1920), pp. 191–219.

Cabona, I. and D., Gardini, A., Mannoni, T., Milanese, M. "Contributi dell'archeologia medievale ligure alle conoscenze dei prodotti ceramici nel Mediterraneo occidentale," *La céramique médiévale en Méditerranée occidentale*. Paris, 1980, pp. 113–23.

Cagiano de Azevedo, M. "Le navi nella documentazione archeologica," *La navigazione mediterranea nell'alto medioevo*. Settimane di studio del Centro italiano di studi sull'alto medioevo, xxv, Spoleto, 1978, pp. 413–27.

Cahen, Claude. "Commercial Relations between the Near East and Western Europe from the 7th to the 11th century," *Islam and the Medieval West*. (ed. K. Semaan), Albany, 1980, pp. 1–25.

"Douanes et commerce dans les ports méditerranéens de l'Egypte médiévale d'après le 'Minhādj d'al-Makhzūmī'," *JESHO* 7(1964), pp. 217–314.

"Ports et chantiers navals dans le monde méditerranéen musulman jusqu'aux croisades," *La navigazione mediterranea nell'alto medioevo*. Settimane di studio del Centro italiano di studi sull'alto medioevo, xxv, Spoleto, 1978, pp. 300–13.

"Quelques problèmes concernant l'expansion économique musulmane au haut moyen âge," *L'Occident e l'Islam nell'alto medioevo*. Settimane di studio del Centro italiano di studi sull'alto medioevo, xii, Spoleto, 1965, pp. 381–432.

Caiger-Smith, A. *Lustre Pottery: Technique, tradition, and innovation in Islam and the Western World*. London, 1985.

Caille, Jacques. "Les marseillais à Ceuta au XIIIe siècle," *Mélanges d'histoire et d'archéologie de l'occident musulmane: Hommage à Georges Marçais*. Algiers, 1957. pp. 21–31.

Canard, M. "Ibrāhīm b. Ya'qūb et sa relation de voyage en Europe," *Etudes d'orientalisme dédiées à la mémoire de E. Lévi-Provençal*. ii, Paris, 1962, pp. 503–8.

Canto García, A. and A.M. Balaguer, "Al-Andalus y los carolingios, un singular testimonio monetario," *Gaceta numismatica* 85(1987), pp. 41–9.

Carande, Ramon. "La huella económica de las capitales hispano-musulmanas," *Moneda y crédito* 29(1949), pp. 3–19.

"El puerto de Málaga y la lana de Menorca en la edad media (dos estudios de F. Melis)," *Moneda y crédito* 64(1958), pp. 11–24.

Sevilla, fortaleza y mercado. Seville, 1972.

Carbonell, Antonio. "La minería y la metalurgia entre los musulmanes de España," *Boletín de la academia de ciencias, bellas letras, y nobles artes de Córdoba* 25(1929), pp. 179–217.

Carlé, María del Carmen. "Mercaderes en Castilla (1252–1512)," *Cuadernos de historia de España* 21–2(1954), pp. 146–328.

Carus-Wilson, Eleanora. "The Woollen Industry," *Cambridge Economic History of Europe*. (eds. M. Postan and E. Rich) ii, Cambridge, 1952, pp. 55–429; 2nd edn, Cambridge, 1987, pp. 614–92.

Casaretto, Pier Francesco. "La moneta genovese in confronto con le altre valute mediterranee nei secoli XII e XIII," *ASLSP* 55(1928), pp. 1–225.

Castro, Américo. "Unos aranceles de aduanas del siglo XIII," *Revista de filología española* 8(1921), pp. 1–29, 325–56; 9(1922), pp. 266–76; 10(1923), pp. 113–36.

Chalmeta Gendrón, Pedro. "An Approximate Picture of the Economy of al-Andalus," *The Legacy of Muslim Spain*. (ed. S.K. Jayyusi), Leiden, 1992, pp. 741–58.

"Bilan et tendances des recherches (1967–1987) al-Andalus (occidentale)," *L'Arabisant* 26(1987), pp. 17–28.

"Facteurs de la formation des prix dans l'Islam médiéval," *Actes du premier congrès d'histoire et de la civilisation du Maghreb*. i, Tunis, 1979, pp. 111–37.

"La ḥisba en Ifrīqiya et al-Andalus: étude comparative," *Cahiers de Tunisie* 18(1970), pp. 87–105.

"La Méditerranée occidentale et al-Andalus de 934 à 941: les données d'Ibn Ḥayyān," *Rivista degli studi orientali* 50(1976), pp. 337–51.

"Précisions au sujet du monnayage hispano-arabe (dirham qāsimī et dirham arbaʿīnī)," *JESHO* 24(1981), pp. 316–24.

El señor del zoco en España: edades media y moderna, contribución al estudio de la historia del mercado. Madrid, 1973.

"Sources pour l'histoire socio-économique d'al-Andalus: Essai de systématisation et de bibliographie," *Annales islamologiques* 20(1984), pp. 1–14.

"Treinta años de historia hispana: El tomo V del *Muqtabas* de Ibn Ḥayyān," *Hispania* 35(1975), pp. 665–76.

Chazen, Robert. *Church, State, and the Jew in the Middle Ages*. New York, 1980.

Chiaudano, Mario. *Contratti commerciali genovesi del secolo XII: Contributo alla storia dell' "accomendatio" e della "societas"*. Turin, 1925.

Chica Garrido, Margarita la. "Referencias árabes a las costas de la península ibérica en la edad media," *Saitabi* 24(1974), pp. 55–63.

Childs, Wendy R. *Anglo-Castilian Trade in the Later Middle Ages*. Manchester, 1978.

Cipolla, Carlo M. *Money, Prices, and Civilization in the Mediterranean World, 5th–17th C*. Princeton, 1956.

"Sans Mahomet, Charlemagne et inconcevable," *Annales: ESC* 17(1962), pp. 130–6.

Citarella, A.O. "Patterns in Medieval Trade: The Commerce of Amalfi before the Crusades," *Journal of Economic History* 28(1968), pp. 53–5.

"A Puzzling Question concerning the Relations between the Jewish Communities of Christian Europe and those represented in the Geniza documents," *JAOS* 91(1971), pp. 390–7.

"The Relations of Amalfi with the Arab World before the Crusades," *Speculum* 42(1967), pp. 299–312.

Cohen, H.J. "The Economic Background and Secular Occupations of Muslim Jurisprudents and Traditionists in the Classical Period of Islam," *JESHO* 13(1970), pp. 16–61.

Colin, G.S. "Filaha (in the Muslim West)," *EI2* II, pp. 901–2.

Coll i Alentorn, M. "La crónica de Sant Pere de les Puelles," *II Colloqui d'historia del monaquisme catala*. Santas Creus, 1967, pp. 35–50.

Collins, Roger. *Early Medieval Spain: Unity in Diversity, 400–1000*. London, 1983.

Colom, F.S. "Navegaciones mediterraneas (s. XI–XVI): valor del puerto de Mallorca," *Navigazioni mediterranea e connessioni continentali*. (ed. R. Ragosta), Naples, 1982, pp. 15–74.

Coniglio, Guiseppe. "Amalfi e il commercio amalfitano nel medioevo," *Nuova rivista storica* 28–9(1944–5), pp. 100–14.

Constable, O.R. "Genoa and Spain in the twelfth and thirteenth centuries," *Journal of European Economic History* 19(1990), pp. 635–56.

Corcos-Abulafia, David. "The Attitude of the Almohadic Rulers towards the Jews" [in Hebrew], *Zion* 32(1967), pp. 137–60.

Corda, Mario. "Pisa, Genova, e l'Aragona all'epoca di Giacomo I nelle fonti narrative," *Jaime I y su época: X Congresso de historia de la Corona de Aragón*. Zaragoza, 1980, pp. 579–88.

Cornu, Georgette. "Les géographes orientaux des IXe et Xe siècles et al-Andalus," *Sharq al-Andalus* 3(1986), pp. 11–19.

Cossio, José María de. "Cautivos de moros en el siglo XIII," *Al-Andalus* 7(1942), pp. 49–112.

Courtois, Christian. "Les rapports entre l'Afrique et la Gaule au début du moyen âge," *Cahiers de Tunisie* 2(1954), pp. 127–45.

"Remarques sur le commerce maritime en Afrique au XIe siècle," *Mélanges d'histoire et d'archéologie de l'occident musulmane. Hommage à Georges Marçais.* II, Algiers, 1957, pp. 51–9.

Cowdrey, H.E.J. "The Mahdia Campaign of 1087," *English Historical Review* 362(1977), pp. 1–29.

Crone, Patricia. *Meccan Trade and the Rise of Islam*. Princeton, 1987.

Curtin, Philip D. *Cross-Cultural Trade in World History*. Cambridge, 1984.

Cutler, Anthony. *The Craft of Ivory: Sources, Techniques, and Uses in the Mediterranean World, AD 200–1400*. Washington, DC, 1985.

Dalton, George. "Comments on Ports of Trade in Early Medieval Europe," *Norwegian Historical Review* 11(1978), pp. 102–8.

"Karl Polanyi's Analysis of Long-Distance Trade and his wider Paradigm," *Ancient Civilization and Trade*. (eds. J.A. Sabloff and C.C. Lamberg-Karlovsky), Albuquerque, 1975, pp. 63–132.

Davillier, Charles. *Notes sur les cuirs de Cordoue, guadamaciles d'Espagne, etc.* Paris, 1878.

Day, John. *The Medieval Market Economy*. Oxford, 1987.

Dennett, D.C. "Pirenne and Muhammad," *Speculum* 23(1948), pp. 167–90.

Desimini, C. and Belgrano, L.T. "Atlante idrografico del medioevo posseduto dal Prof. Tammar Luxoro," *ASLSP* 5(1867), pp. 7–270.

Devisse, Jean. "La question d'Awdaghust," *Tegdaoust I; Recherches sur Aoudaghost*. (eds. J. Devisse, D. Robert, S. Robert), Paris, 1970, pp. 109–54.

"Routes de commerce et échanges en Afrique occidentale en relation avec la Méditerranée: Un essai sur le commerce africain médiéval du XIe au XVIe siècle," *Revue d'histoire économique et sociale* 50(1972), pp. 42–73, 357–97.

Di Tucci, Raffaele. *Studi sull'economia genovesi del secolo decimosecondo: la nave e i contratti marittimi*. Turin, 1933.

Dodds, J.D., ed. *Al-Andalus: The Art of Islamic Spain*. New York, 1992.

Doehaerd, Renée. "Méditerranée et économie occidentale pendant le haut moyen âge," *Cahiers d'histoire mondiale* 1(1954), pp. 571–93.

"Les réformes monétaires carolingiennes," *Annales: ESC* 7(1952), pp. 13–20.

Dolley, R.H.M. "A Spanish Dirham found in England," *Numismatic Chronicle* 17(1957), pp. 242–3.

Dotson, J.E. "A Problem of Cotton and Lead in Medieval Italian Shipping," *Speculum* 57(1982), pp. 52–62.

Dozy, Reinhart. *Dictionnaire détaillé des noms des vêtements chez les arabes*. Amsterdam, 1845.

Glossaire des mots espagnols et portugais dérivés de l'arabe. 2nd edn, Leiden, 1869.

Histoire des musulmans d'Espagne. 4 vols., Leiden, 1861. (revised edn E. Lévi-Provençal, 3 vols., Leiden, 1932).

Supplément aux dictionnaires arabes. 2 vols., Leiden, 1881.

Drury, Thomas. "The Image of Alfonso VI and his Spain in Arabic Historians," Ph.D. dissertation, Princeton University, 1973.

Dubler, C.E. *Über das Wirtschaftsleben auf der iberischen Halbinsel vom XI zum XIII Jahrhundert*. Geneva, 1943.

Dufourcq, Charles-Emmanuel. "Aperçu sur le commerce entre Gênes et le Maghrib au XIIIe siècle," *Economies et sociétés au moyen âge: Mélanges offerts à Edouard Perroy*. Paris, 1973, pp. 721–36.

"A propos de l'Espagne catalane et le Maghreb aux XIIIe et XIVe siècles," *Revue d'histoire et de civilisation du Maghreb* 2(1967), pp. 32–53.

"Berbérie et Ibérie médiévales: un problème de rupture," *Revue historique* 240(1968), pp. 293–324.

"Commerce du Maghrib médiéval avec l'Europe chrétienne et marine musulmane données connues et petitiques en suspen," *Actes du I Congrès d'histoire et de la civilisation du Maghreb*. 1, Tunis, 1979, pp. 161–7.

"Les communications entre les royaumes chrétiens ibériques et les pays de l'occident musulman dans les derniers siècles du moyen âge," *Les Communications dans la péninsule ibérique au moyen âge*. Paris, 1981, pp. 29–44.

L'Espagne catalane et le Maghrib aux XIIIe et XIVe siècle. Paris, 1966.

"La question de Ceuta au XIIIe siècle," *Hespéris* 42(1955), pp. 67–127.

"Les relations du Maroc et de la Castille pendant la première moitié du XIIIe siècle," *Revue d'histoire et de civilisation du Maghreb* (Algiers) 5(1968), pp. 37–62.

La vie quotidienne dans l'Europe médiévale sous domination arabe. Paris, 1978.

Dufourçq, C.H. and Gautier-Dalché, J. *Histoire économique et sociale de l'Espagne chrétienne au moyen âge*. Paris, 1976.

Dunlop, D.M. *The History of the Jewish Khazars*. Princeton, 1954.

"The *Kitāb al-maḥabbah* of Lisān al-Dīn Ibn al-Khaṭīb," *Actas del I Congreso de historia de Andalucía*. Cordoba, 1978. pp. 125–130.

"Sources of Gold and Silver in Islam according to al-Ḥamdānī," *Studia islamica* 8(1957), pp. 29–50.

Duplessy, Jean. "La circulation des monnaies arabes en Europe occidentale du VIIIe au XIIIe siècle," *Revue numismatique*, 5th series, 18(1956), pp. 101–63.

Dupont, André. *Les relations commerciales entre les cités maritimes de Languedoc et les cités méditerranéennes d'Espagne et d'Italie du Xe au XIIIe siècle*. Nîme, 1942.

Duprat, Eugène. "Les relations de la Provence et du Levant du Ve siècle aux croisades," *Séances et travaux du Congrès français de la Syrie*. Jan. 1919, Fasc. II, pp. 75–98.

Ebersolt, Jean. *Orient et occident: recherches sur les influences byzantines et orientales en France avant les croisades*. Paris, 1928.

Edwards, John. "'Development' and 'Underdevelopment' in the Western Mediterranean: The Case of Córdoba and its Region in the Late Fifteenth and Early Sixteenth Centuries," *Mediterranean Historical Review* 2(1987), pp.3–45.

Ehrenkreutz, Andrew S. "Another Orientalist's Remarks concerning the Pirenne Thesis," *JESHO* 15(1972), pp. 94–104.

"The Place of Saladin in the Naval History of the Mediterranean Sea in the Middle Ages," *JAOS* 75(1955), pp. 100–16.

"Studies in the Monetary History of the Near East in the Middle Ages; the Standard of Fineness of some types of Dinars," *JESHO* 2(1959), pp. 126–61.

"Studies in the Monetary History of the Near East in the Middle Ages; the Standard of Fineness of Western and Eastern Dinars before the Crusades," *JESHO* 6(1963), pp. 243–77.

Elshayyal, Gamal al-Dīn. "The Cultural Relations between Alexandria and the Islamic West in al-Andalus and Morocco," *Madrid:MDI* 16(1971), pp. 61–9.

Epalza, Mikel de. "Costas alicantinas y costas magrebíes: el espacio marítimo musulmán según los textos árabes," *Sharq al-Andalus* 3(1986), pp. 25–31.

Moros y moriscos en el levante peninsular [*Sharq al-Andalus*]: *Introducción bibliográfica*. Alicante, 1983.

Epstein, S. *Wills and Wealth in Medieval Genoa 1150–1250*. Cambridge, Mass., 1984.

Epstein, S. *An Island for itself, Economic development and social change in late medieval Sicily*. Cambridge, 1992.

Fabrège, Frédéric. *Histoire de Maguelone*. Paris and Montpellier, 1894–1900.

Face, Richard D. "Secular History in twelfth-century Italy: Caffaro of Genoa," *Journal of Medieval History* 6(1980), pp. 169–84.

Ferrandis Torres, José. *Cordobanes y guadamecíes; Catálogo ilustrado de la exposición. Sociedad de amigos de arte*. Madrid, 1955.

Ferreira Priegue, E. "El papel de Galicia en la redistribución de productos andaluces visto a traves de los archivos ingleses," *Actas del II Coloquio de historia medieval andaluza: Hacienda y comercio, Sevilla, 8–10 de abril, 1981*. Seville, 1982, pp. 241–7.

Galicia en el comercio marítimo medieval. La Coruña, 1987.

Fierro, Ma. Isabel. "Sobre la adopción del titulo califal por 'Abd al-Raḥmān III," *Sharq al-Andalus* 6(1988), pp. 33–42.

Finot, Jules. *Etude historique sur les relations commerciales entre la Flandre et l'Espagne au moyen âge*. Paris, 1899.

Fischel, W.J. *The Jews in the Economic and Political Life of Medieval Islam*. reprint London, 1969.

"The Spice Trade in Mamluk Egypt," *JESHO* 1(1958), pp. 157–74.

Freehof, Soloman B. *The Responsa Literature and a Treasury of Responsa*. New York, 1973.

Freeman-Grenville, G.S.P. *The Muslim and Christian Calendars*. New York, 1963.

Frothingham, Alice W. *Lustreware of Spain*. New York, 1951.

Fryde, E.B. "Italian Maritime Trade with Medieval England (c. 1270–1530)," *Recueils de la Société Jean Bodin* 32(1974), pp. 291–337.

Fuentes Guerra, R. "Panorama económico-industrial del califato de Córdoba," *Actas del I Congreso de estudios árabes e islámicas*. Madrid, 1964, pp. 433–9.

García, Arcadi. "Contractes comercials vigatans de principis del segle XIII," *Ausa* (Vich) 43(1963), pp. 321–9.

García de Valdeavellano, Luis. "Economía natural y monetaria en León y Castilla durante los siglos IX, X, y XI," *Moneda y crédito* 10(1944), pp. 28–46.

"El mercado. Apuntes para su estudio en León y Castilla durante la edad media," *AHDE* 8(1931), pp. 210–405.

El mercado en León y Castilla durante la edad media. 2nd edn., Seville, 1975.

"La moneda y la economía de cambio en la península ibérica desde el siglo VI hasta mediados del siglo XI," *Moneta e scambi nell'alto medioevo*. Settimane di studio del Centro italiano di studi sull'alto medioevo, VIII, Spoleto, 1961, pp. 203–30.

Sobre los burgos y los burgueses de la España medieval. Madrid, 1960.

García Arenal, Mercedes. "Algunos manuscritos de 'fiqh' andalusíes y norteafricanos pertenecientes a la Real Biblioteca de el Escorial," *Al-Qantara* 1(1980), pp. 9–26.

"Los moros en las Cántigas de Alfonso X el Sabio," *Al-Qantara* 6(1985), pp. 133–52.

García Franco, Salvador. *La lengua náutica en la edad media*. Madrid, 1947.

García Gómez, Emilio. "A propósito de Ibn Ḥayyān," *Al-Andalus* 11(1946), pp. 395–423.

"Tejidos, ropas y tapicería en los *Anales de al-Hakam II* por 'Isā Rāzī," *Boletín de la Real Academia de la historia* 156(1970), pp. 43–53.

Gari, Blanca. "El reino de Granada y la política comercial genovesa en la península ibérica en la segunda mitad del siglo XIII," *Relaciones exteriores del reino de Granada. IV Coloquio de historia medieval andaluza*. Almeria, 1988, pp. 287–96.

Gariel, E. *Les monaies royales de France sous la race carolingienne*. Strasbourg, 1883.

Garrard, Timothy F. "Myth and Metrology: The Early Trans-Saharan Gold Trade," *Journal of African History* 23(1982), pp. 443–61.

Gateau, A. "Quelques observations sur l'intérêt du voyage d'Ibn Jubair pour l'histoire de la navigation en Méditerranée au XIIe siècle," *Hespéris* 36(1949), pp. 289–312.

Gautier, E.F. "L'or du Soudan dans l'histoire," *Annales d'histoire économique et sociale* 32(1935), pp. 113–23.

Gautier-Dalché, J. "Islam et chrétienté en Espagne au XIIe siècle: Contibution à l'étude de la notion de frontière," *Hespéris* 47(1959), pp. 183–217.

"Monnaie et économie dans l'Espagne du nord et du centre (VIIIe a XIIIe siècle," *Hespéris-Tamuda* 3(1963), pp. 63–74.

"Les peages dans les pays de la Couronne de Castille: état de la question, réflexions, perspectives de recherches," *Les communications dans la péninsule ibérique au moyen âge* (*Actes du Colloque de Pau, 28–29 mars, 1980*). Paris, 1981, pp. 73–8.

Gazulla, F.D. "La redención de cautivos entre los musulmanes," *BRABLB* 13(1928), pp. 321–42.

Gibert de Vallve, Soledad. "La ville d'Almeria a l'époque musulmane," *Cahiers de Tunisie* 18(1970), pp. 61–72.

Giese, W. "Cuero de Córdoba y guadalmeçí," *Revista de la filología española* 12(1925), pp. 75–6.

Gil, Moshe. "The Radhanite Merchants and the Land of Radhan," *JESHO* 17(1974), pp. 299–328.

Gioffré, Domenico. "Uno studio sugli schiavi a Genova nel XIII secolo," *ASLSP* n.s. 9(1969), pp. 321–5.

Gisbert, Josep A. "La ciudad de Denia y la producción de cerámicas vidriadas con decoración estampillada," *Sharq al-Andalus* 2(1985), pp. 161–74.

Glick, Thomas F. *Islamic and Christian Spain in the Early Middle Ages*. Princeton, 1979.

"Muhtasib and Mustasaf: A Case Study of Institutional Diffusion," *Viator* 2(1971), pp. 59–81.

Glick, Thomas F. and Pi-Sunyar, O. "Acculturation as an Explanatory Concept in Spanish History," *Comparative Studies in Society and History* 2(1969), pp. 136–54.

Goitein, S.D. "Bankers' Accounts from the 11th century AD," *JESHO* 9(1966), pp. 28–68.

"The Beginnings of the Kārim Merchants and the Character of their Organization," *Studies in Islamic History and Institutions*. Leiden, 1968, pp. 351–60.

"The Biography of Judah Ha-Levi in the Light of the Cairo Geniza Documents," *Proceedings of the American Academy for Jewish Research* 28(1959), pp. 41–56.

"Commercial and Family Partnerships in the Countries of Medieval Islam," *Islamic Studies* 3(1964), pp. 315–37.

"The Documents of the Cairo Geniza as a Source for Islamic Social History," *Studies in Islamic History and Institutions*. Leiden, 1968, pp. 279–95.

"L'état actuel de la recherche sur les documents de la Geniza du Caire," *Revue des études juives* 118(1959–60), pp. 9–27.

"The Exchange Rate of Gold and Silver Money in Fatimid and Ayyubid Times; A Preliminary Study of the Relevant Geniza Material," *JESHO* 8(1965), pp. 1–46.

"From Aden to India: Specimans of the Correspondence of India Traders of the 12th century," *JESHO* 23(1980), pp. 43–66.

"Glimpses from the Cairo Geniza on Naval warfare in the Mediterranean and on the Mongol Invasion," *Studi orientalistici in onore de Giorgio Levi della Vida*. 1, Rome, 1956, pp. 393–408.

"Judeo-Arabic Letters from Spain (early 12th century)," *Orientalia Hispanica; Studies in Honor of F.M. Pareja*. Leiden, 1974, pp. 331–50.

"The Main Industries of the Mediterranean Area as reflected in the Records of the Cairo Geniza," *JESHO* 4(1961), pp. 168–97.

A Mediterranean Society. The Jewish Communities of the Arab World as Portrayed in the Documents of the Cairo Geniza. 5 vols. Berkeley, 1967–88.

"Mediterranean Trade preceeding the Crusades: Some Facts and Problems," *Diogenes* 59(1967), pp. 47–62.

"The Rise of the Near Eastern Bourgeoisie in Early Islamic Times," *Cahiers d'histoire mondiale* 3(1957), pp. 583–604.

"Slaves and Slavegirls in the Cairo Geniza Records," *Arabica* 9(1962), pp. 1–20.

"The Tribulations of an Overseer of the Sultan's Ships: A Letter from the Cairo Geniza (written in Alexandria in 1131)," *Arabic and Islamic Studies in Honor of H.A.R. Gibb.* Cambridge, Mass., 1965, pp. 270–84.

"La Tunisie du XIe siècle à la lumière de documents de la Geniza du Caire," *Etudes d'orientalisme dédiées à la memoire de Lévi-Provençal.* II, Paris, 1962. pp. 559–79. English translation: "Medieval Tunisia: The Hub of the Mediterranean. A Geniza Study," *Studies in Islamic History and Institutions.* Leiden, 1968, pp. 308–28.

"The Unity of the Mediterranean World in the 'Middle' Middle Ages," *Studia islamica* 12(1960), pp. 29–42.

Golb, Norman and Omeljan, Pritzak. *Khazarian Hebrew Documents of the tenth century.* Ithaca, 1982.

Golvin, Lucien. "Note sur l'industrie du cuivre en occident musulman au moyen âge," *Cahiers de linguistique, d'orientalisme, et de slavistique* 1–2(1973), pp. 117–26.

Gómez Moreno, Manuel. *Iglesias mozárabes: arte español de los siglos IX a XI.* Madrid, 1919.

"La loza dorada primitiva de Málaga," *Al-Andalus* 5(1940), pp. 383–98.

El Panteón real de las Huelgas de Burgos. Madrid, 1946.

González Martí, M. *Cerámica del levante español: siglos medievales.* Barcelona-Madrid, 1944–52.

González Mínguez, César. *El portazgo en la edad media. Aproximación a su estudio en la Corona de Castilla.* Bilbao, 1989.

González Palencia, Angel. *Aspectos sociales de la España árabe.* Madrid, 1946.

Los mozárabes de Toledo en los siglos XII y XIII. 3 vols., Madrid, 1926–8.

Grant, Michael. *The Ancient Mediterranean.* New York, 1969.

Greif, A. "The Organization of Long-Distance Trade: Reputation and Coalitions in the Geniza Documents and Genoa during the 11th and 12th centuries." Ph.D. Dissertation, Northwestern University, 1989.

Grierson, Philip. "Carolingian Europe and the Arabs: The Myth of the Mancus," *Revue belge de philologie et d'histoire* 32(1954), pp. 1059–74.

"Commerce in the Dark Ages: A Critique of the Evidence," *Transactions of the Royal Historical Society* 9(1959), pp. 123–40.

Medieval European Coinage. I, Cambridge, 1986.

"Muslim Coins in 13th-century England," *Studies in Honor of George C. Miles.* Beirut, 1974, pp. 387–91.

"Numismatics and History," *Historical Association: General Series.* London, 1951.

Grohmann, A. "Ṭirāz," *Encyclopedia of Islam*. 1st edn, Leiden, 1913–42, IV.2, pp. 785–3.

Groom, Nigel. *Frankincense and Myrrh, a Study of the Arabian Incense Trade*. London, 1981.

Grunebaum, Gustave E. von. *Medieval Islam: A Study in Cultural Orientation*. 2nd edn, Chicago, 1962.

"The Structure of the Muslim Town," *Islam. Essays in the Nature and Growth of a Cultural Tradition*. London, 1961, pp. 141–58.

Gual Camarena, Miguel. "Aranceles de la Corona de Aragón en el siglo XIII," *VI Congreso de la historia de la Corona de Aragón (1957)*. Madrid, 1959, pp. 209–220.

"El comercio de telas en el siglo XII hispano," *Anuario de historia económica y social* 1(1968), pp. 85–106.

"Origenes y expansion de la industria lanera catalana en la edad media," *Atti della seconda settimana di studio, Istituto F. Datini*. (ed. M. Spallanzani), Florence, 1976, pp. 511–23.

"Para un mapa de la industria textil hispana en la edad media," *Anuario de estudios medievales* 4(1967), pp. 109–68.

"Para un mapa de la sal hispana en la edad media," *Homenaje a Jaime Vicens Vives*. I, Barcelona, 1965, pp. 483–97.

"Peaje fluvial del Ebro (siglo XII)," *Estudios de la edad media de la Corona de Aragón* 8(1967), pp. 155–88.

"Tarifas hispano-lusas de portazgo, peaje, lezda, y hospedaje (siglos XI y XII)," *Anuario de estudios medievales* 9(1974–9) pp. 365–92.

Vocabulario del comercio medieval. Tarragona, 1968.

Guerrero Lovillo, José. *Las Cántigas: Estudio arqueológico de sus miniaturas*. Madrid, 1949.

Guichard, Pierre. "Le peuplement de la région de Valence aux deux premiers siècles de la domination musulmane," *Mélanges de la Casa de Velázquez* 5(1969) pp. 103–57.

Structures sociales "orientales" et "occidentales" dans l'Espagne musulmane. Paris, 1977.

Guillen Robles, F. *Málaga musulmana*. 2 vols. Malaga, 1880. (reprint Malaga, 1984).

Gutkind, E.A. *Urban Development in Southern Europe: Spain and Portugal*. New York, 1967.

al-Hajji, Abdurrahman A. "Andalusia e Italia altomedievale," *Rivista storica italiana* 79(1967), pp. 158–73.

Andalusian Diplomatic Relations with Western Europe during the Umayyad Period. Beirut, 1970.

Halphen, L. "La conquête de la Méditerranée par les européens au XIe et au XIIIe siècles," *Mélanges d'histoire offerts à Henri Pirenne*. I, Brussels, 1926, pp. 175–80.

Hamada, Fadhel. "Unos aspectos del desarollo económico en la época de los reyes de taifas," *Actas del IV Coloquio hispano-tunecino (Palma, 1979)*. Madrid, 1983, pp. 155–61.

Hamarneh, S.K. and Sonnedecker, G. *A Pharmaceutical View of Abulcasis Alzahrāwī in Moorish Spain.* Leiden, 1963.

Hamblin, William. "The Fatimid Navy during the Early Crusades: 1099–1124," *The American Neptune* 46(1986), pp. 77–83.

Handler, Andrew. *The Zirids of Granada.* Coral Gables, Florida. 1974.

al-Hassan, Aḥmad Y. "Iron and Steel Technology in medieval Arabic sources," *Journal for the History of Arabic Science* 2(1978), pp. 31–43.

al-Hassan, Aḥmad Y. and Hill, D.R., *Islamic Technology: An Illustrated History.* Cambridge, 1986.

Haverkamp, A. "Zur Sklaverei in Genua während des 12. Jahrhunderts," *Geschichte in der Gesellschaft: Festschrift für Karl Bosl.* Stuttgart, 1974, pp. 160–215.

Hazard, Harry W. *The Numismatic History of Late Medieval North Africa.* New York, 1952.

Heers, Jacques. *Esclaves et domestiques au moyen âge dans le monde méditerranéen.* Paris, 1981.

"Les hommes d'affaires italiens en Espagne au moyen âge: Le marché monétaire," *Fremde Kaufleute auf der iberischen Halbinsel.* (ed. H. Kellenbenz), Cologne-Vienna, 1970, pp. 74–83.

"Le royaume de Grenade et la politique marchande de Gênes en occident (XVe siècle)," *Le moyen âge* 63(1957), pp. 87–121.

"Les relations commercials entre Gênes et le royaume d'Aragon vers le milieu du XVe siècle," *IV Congreso de Historia de la Corona de Aragón. Actas y Comunicaciones.* II, Barcelona, 1970, pp. 1–14.

"Types de navires et spécialisation des trafics en Méditerranée a la fin du moyen âge," *Le navire et l'économie maritime du moyen âge au XVIIIe siècle principalement en Méditerranée.* Paris, 1958, pp. 107–17.

Hendy, Michael. "From Public to Private: The Western Barbarian Coinages as a Mirror of the Disintegration of Late Roman State Structures," *Viator* 19(1988), pp. 29–78.

Herlihy, David. *Pisa in the Early Renaissance.* New Haven, 1958.

Hernández Jiménez, Félix. "El camino de Córdoba a Toledo en la época musulmana," *Al-Andalus* 24(1959), pp. 1–62.

Herrero Carretero, C. *Museo de telas medievales: Monasterio de Santa María la Real de Huelgas.* Madrid, 1988.

Heyd, W. *Histoire du commerce du Levant au moyen âge.* 2 vols., Leipzig, 1885.

Higounet, Charles. "Les fôrets de l'Europe occidentale du Ve au XIe siècle," *Agricoltura e mondo rurale in occidente nell'alto medioevo.* Settimane di studio del Centro italiano di studi sull'altro medioevo, XIII, Spoleto, 1966, pp. 343–98.

Hillgarth, J.N. *The Spanish Kingdoms 1250–1516.* I, Oxford, 1976.

Hinojosa Montalvo, J. "Las relaciones comerciales entre Valencia y Andalucia durante la baja edad media," *Actas del II Coloquio de historia medieval andaluza: Hacienda y comercio. Sevilla, 8–10 de abril, 1981.* Seville, 1982, pp. 249–67.

Hinz, Walther. *Islamische Masse und Gewichte umgerechnet ins metrische System.* Leiden, 1955 (revised edn Leiden-Köln, 1970).

Hirschberg, H.Z. *A History of the Jews in North Africa*. 2nd edn, Leiden, 1974.
Hocquet, J.-C. *Le sel et la fortune de Venise*. (vol. II, *Voiliers et commerce en Méditerranée, 1200–1650*.) Lille, 1979.
Hodges, Richard. *Dark Age Economics. The Origins of Towns and Trade, AD 600–1000*. New York, 1982.
"Ports of Trade in Early Medieval Europe," *Norwegian Archeological Review* 11(1978), pp. 97–101.
Hodges, Richard and Whitehouse, David. *Mohammad, Charlemagne and the Origins of Europe*. Ithaca, 1983.
Hoenerbach, Wilhelm. *Araber und Mittelmeer: Anfange und Probleme arabischer seegeschichte*. Kiel, 1967.
"La navigación omeya en el Mediterraneo y sus consecuencias político-culturales," *Miscelanea de estudios árabes y hebraicos Universidad de Granada* (1953), pp. 77–98.
Hoover, Calvin B. "The Sea Loan in Genoa in the 12th Century," *Quarterly Journal of Economics* 40(1925–26), pp. 495–529.
Horton, Mark. "The Swahili Corridor," *Scientific American* Sept. 1987, pp. 86–93.
Hourani, A. and Stern, S.M. *The Islamic City*. Oxford, 1970.
Houston, J.M. "Urban Geography of Valencia: The Regional Development of a Huerta City," *Transactions of the Institute of British Geographers* 15(1951), pp. 19–35.
Huici Miranda, Ambrosio. *Historia política del imperio almohade*. 2 vols., Tetuan, 1956–7.
"The Iberian Peninsula and Sicily," *Cambridge History of Islam*. 2A, Cambridge, 1970, pp. 406–39.
Humphreys, S.C. "History, Economics, and Anthropology: The Work of Karl Polanyi," *History and Theory* 8(1969), pp. 165–212.
Hurst, J.G. "The Export of Spanish Lustreware to North-West Europe," *La céramique médiévale en Méditerranée occidentale*. Paris, 1980, p. 372.
"Spanish Pottery imported into Medieval England," *Medieval Archeology* 21(1977), pp. 69–105.
Idris, Hady Roger. *La Berbérie orientale sous les Zirides*. 2 vols., Paris, 1962.
"Commerce maritime et kirāḍ en Berbérie orientale d'après un recueil inédit des fatwās médiévales," *JESHO* 4(1961), pp. 225–39.
"Les tributaires en occident musulmane médiévale d'après le *Mi'yār* d'al-Wansharīsī," *Mélanges d'islamologie: Volume dédié à la mémoire de Armand Abel*. Leiden, 1974, pp. 172–96.
Imamuddin, S.M. "Business Contracts in Muslim Spain," *Journal of the Pakistan Historical Society* (1962), pp. 282–301.
"Coins in Umayyad Spain, 711–1031," *Dacca University Studies* 9(1959), pp. 49–65.
"Commercial Relations between Muslim Spain and Christian Countries in the 9th and 10th centuries," *Journal of the Asiatic Society of Pakistan* 3(1958), pp. 1–13.
"Commercial Relations of Spain with Ifriqiyah and Egypt in the 10th century," *Islamic Culture* 38(1964), pp. 9–14.

The Economic History of Spain under the Umayyads (711–1031). Dacca, 1963.

Iradiel Muragarren, P. *Evolución de la industria textil castellana en los siglos XIII–XVI*. Salamanca, 1974.

James, Margery. *Studies in the Medieval Wine Trade*. (ed. E.M. Veale), Oxford, 1971.

Jayyusi, Salma Khadra, ed. *The Legacy of Muslim Spain*. Leiden, 1992.

Jenkins, Marilyn, "Medieval Maghribī Ceramics. A Reappraisal of the Pottery Production of the Western Regions of the Muslim world." Ph.D. Dissertation, New York University, 1978.

"Medieval Maghribī Lustre-painted Pottery," *La céramique médiévale en Méditerranée occidentale*. Paris, 1980, pp. 335–42.

Joncheray, M.J.P. "Le navire de Bataiguier," *Archeologia* 85 (1975), pp. 42–8.

Kahane, Henri and Kahane, Renée. "Notes on the Linguistic History of *sclavus*," *Studi in onore di Ettore Lo Gatto e Giovanni Maver*. Rome, 1962, pp.345–60.

Kamen, H. "The Decline of Spain: A Historical Myth," *Past and Present* 81(1978), pp.24–50.

Kassis, Hanna. "Muslim Revival in Spain in the 5th/11th Century," *Der Islam* 67(1990), pp.78–110.

Katz, Soloman. *The Jews in the Visigothic and Frankish Kingdoms of Spain and Gaul*. Cambridge, Mass, 1937.

Khadduri, Majid. *War and Peace in the Law of Islam*. Baltimore, 1955.

Khalis, Saleh. *La vie litteraire à Séville au XIe siècle*. Algiers, 1966.

Khallāf, M. ʿAbd al-Wahhāb. *Qurṭuba al-islāmiyya fī al-qarn al-ḥādī ʿashara al-mīlādī al-khāmis al-ḥijrī*. Tunis, 1984.

Klein, Julius. *The Mesta: A Study in Spanish Economic History (1273–1836)*. Cambridge, Mass, 1920.

King, P.D. *Law and Society in the Visigothic Kingdom*. Cambridge, 1972.

Kramers, G.H. "Geography and Commerce," *The Legacy of Islam*. (eds. T. Arnold and A. Guillaume), Oxford, 1931, pp.79–107.

Kreutz, Barbara. "Ships, Shipping, and the Implications of Change in the Early Medieval Mediterranean," *Viator* 7(1976), pp.79–109.

Krueger, Hilmar Carl. "The Commercial Relations between Genoa and North-West Africa in the Twelfth Century." Ph.D. Dissertation, University of Wisconsin, 1931.

"Early Genoese Trade with Atlantic Morocco," *Medievalia et humanistica* 3(1945), pp.3–15.

"Economic Aspects of Expanding Europe," *Twelfth-century Europe and the Foundations of Modern Society*. (ed. M. Clagett), Madison, 1961, pp.59–76.

"Genoese Merchants, their Associations and Investments, 1155–1230," *Studi in onore di Amintore Fanfani*. 1, Milan, 1962, pp.413–26.

"Genoese Merchants, their Partnerships and Investments, 1155–1164," *Studi in onore di Armando Sapori*. Milan, 1957, pp.257–72.

"Genoese Shipowners and their Ships in the 12th century," *The American Neptune* 47(1987), pp.229–39.

"Genoese Trade with North-West Africa in the Twelfth century," *Speculum* 8(1933), pp.377–95.
Navi e proprietà navale a Genova, seconda metà del secolo XII. Genoa, 1985.
"Post-war Collapse and Rehabilitation in Genoa (1149–1162)," *Studi in onore di Gino Luzzatto.* 1, Milan, 1949, pp.117–28.
"The Routine of Commerce between Genoa and North-West Africa during the Late Twelfth century," *The Mariner's Mirror* 19(1933), pp.417–38.
"The Wares of Exchange in the Genoese-African Traffic of the Twelfth century," *Speculum* 12(1937), pp.57–71.
Kurdian, H. "Kirmiz," *JAOS* 61(1941), pp.105–7.
Lacarra, José María. "Un arancel de aduanas del siglo XI," *Actas del primer congreso internacional de pirenéistas.* San Sebastián, 1950, pp.5–20.
"Aspectos económicos de la sumisión de los Reinos de Taifas (1010–1102)," *Colonización, parias, repoblación, y otros estudios.* Zaragoza, 1981, pp.43–76.
"Dos tratados de paz y alianza entre Sancho el de Peñalén y Moctádir de Zaragoza 1069–1073," *Colonización, parias, repoblación, y otros estudios.* Zaragoza, 1981, pp.79–94.
"Panorama de la historia urbana española," *Estudios de alta edad media española.* Valencia, 1971, pp.27–65.
Lacave, J.L. "España y los judíos españoles," *Revue des études juives* 144(1985), pp.7–25.
Ladero Quesada, M.A. "Almojarifazgo sevillano y comercio exterior de Andalucía en el siglo XV," *Anuario de historia económica y social* 2(1969), pp.69–115.
"Las aduanas de Castilla en el siglo XV," *Revue internationale d'histoire de la banque* 7(1973), pp.83–110.
Lamm, Carl Johan. *Cotton in Medieval Textiles of the Near East.* Paris, 1937.
Lane, Arthur. "Early Hispano-Moresque Pottery: A Reconsideration," *Burlington Magazine* 88(1946), pp.246–52.
Early Islamic Pottery. London, 1947.
Lane, Frederic C. "The Economic Meaning of the Invention of the Compass," *AHR* 68(1963), pp.605–17.
"The Economic Meaning of War and Protection," *Venice and History: Collected Papers of Frederick C. Lane.* Baltimore, 1966, pp.383–98.
Lapidus, I. *Muslim Cities in the Later Middle Ages.* Cambridge, Mass, 1967.
Laroui, A. *The History of the Maghrib; An Interpretative Essay.* Princeton, 1977.
Latham, J.D. "Some Observations on the Bread Trade in Muslim Malaga (ca. AD 1200)," *Journal of Semitic Studies* 29(1984), pp.111–22.
Latour, A. "Paper: A Historical Outline," *Ciba Review* 6(1947–49), pp.2630–40.
Laurent, Henri. *Un grand commerce d'exportation au moyen âge: la draperie des Pays-Bas en France et dans les pays méditerranéens [XIIe-XVe siècle].* Liège-Paris, 1935.
Le Clair, Edward E. "Economic Theory and Economic Anthropology," *American Anthropologist* 64(1962), pp.1179–203.
Leggett, W.F. *The Story of Linen.* New York, 1955.
Leix, Alfred. "Dyes of the Middle Ages," *Ciba Review* 1(1937), pp.19–21.

Lenker, M.K. "The Importance of the Rihla for the Islamization of Spain." Ph.D. Dissertation, University of Pennsylvania, 1982.

Lesch, Alma. *Vegetable Dyeing*. New York, 1970.

Le Tourneau, Roger. *The Almohad Movement in North Africa in the 12th and 13th centuries*. Princeton, 1969.

Fez in the Age of the Marinids. Norman, Oklahoma, 1961.

Levasseur, P.E. *Histoire du commerce de la France*. 1, Paris, 1911.

Lévi-Provençal, E. *Las ciudades y las instituciones urbanas del occidente musulman en la edad media*. Tetuan, 1950.

"Un échange d'ambassades entre Cordoue et Byzance au IXe siècle," *Byzantion* 12(1937), pp. 1–24.

L'Espagne musulmane au Xème siècle: Institutions et vie sociale. Paris, 1932.

Histoire de l'Espagne musulmane. 3 vols., Paris, 1950–3.

Inscriptions arabes d'Espagne. Paris, 1931.

Islam d'occident; Etudes d'histoire médiévale. Paris, 1948.

"Le Kitāb nasab Quraysh de Musʿab al-Zubayrī," *Arabica* 1(1954), pp. 92–5.

"La política africana de ʿAbd al-Raḥmān III: El conflicto entre las influencias Omeya y Fatimī en el Maghrib," *Al-Andalus* 11(1946), pp. 351–78.

"La vie économique de l'Espagne musulmane au Xe siècle," *Revue historique* 167(1931), pp. 305–23.

Lévi-Provençal, E., García Gómez, E., Oliver Asín, J. "Novedades sobre la batalla llamada de al-Zallāqa (1086)," *Al-Andalus* 11(1950), pp. 111–55.

Levillian, Léon. "Etudes sur l'abbaye de St. Denis à l'époque mérovingienne," *Bibliothéque de l'école de Chartres* 91(1930), pp. 5–65.

Examen critique des chartes mérovingiennes et carolingiennes de l'abbaye de Corbie. Paris, 1902.

Lewicki, Tadeusz. "Les écrivains arabes du moyen âge au sujet des pierres précieuses et des pierres fines en territoire africain et de leur exploitation," *Africana Bulletin* 7(1967), pp. 49–68.

"L'état nord-africain de Tahert et ses relations avec le Soudan occidental à la fin du VIIIe et au IXe siècle," *Cahiers d'études africaines* 8(1962), pp. 513–35.

"Traits d'histoire du commerce transsaharien. Marchands et missionaires ibadites en Soudan occidental et central au cours des VIIIe-XIIe siècles," *Etnografia polska* 8(1964), pp. 291–311.

"Les voies maritimes de la Méditerranée dans le haut moyen âge d'après les sources arabes," *La navigazione mediterranea nell'alto medioevo*. Settimane di studio del Centro italiano di studi sull'altro medioevo, xxv, Spoleto, 1978. pp. 439–70.

Lewis, Archibald R. "Mediterranean Maritime Commerce: AD 300–1100 Shipping and Trade," *La navigazione mediterranea nell'alto medioevo*. Settimane di studio del Centro italiano di studi sull'altro medioevo, xxv, Spoleto, 1978, pp. 481–501.

Naval Power and Trade in the Mediterranean AD 500–1100. Princeton, 1951.

"Northern European Sea Power and the Straits of Gibraltar, 1031–1350 AD," *Order and Innovation in the Middle Ages: Essays in Honor of Joseph R. Strayer*. Princeton, 1976. pp. 139–65.

The Northern Seas: Shipping and Commerce in Northern Europe. AD 300–1100. Princeton, 1958.
Lewis, Archibald and Runyan, Timothy. *European Naval and Maritime History 300–1500.* Bloomington, 1985.
Lewis, Bernard. *The Muslim Discovery of Europe.* New York, 1982.
The Political Language of Islam. Chicago, 1988.
Lieber, A.E. "Eastern Business Practices and Medieval European Commerce," *Economic History Review* 21(1968), pp. 230–43.
Linder Welin, U.S. "Spanish-Umaiyad Coins found in Scandinavia," *Numismatiska Meddelanden* 30(1965), pp. 15–25.
Lisciandrelli, Pasquale. "Trattati e negoziazioni politische della Repubblica di Genova (958–1797)," *ASLSP* n.s. 1(1960).
Lister, F.C. and R.H. Lister. *Andalusian Ceramics in Spain and New Spain: A Cultural Register from the third century BC to 1700.* Tucson, 1987.
Lloyd, T.H. *Alien Merchants in England in the High Middle Ages.* New York, 1982.
Llubía Munné, Luis M. *Cerámica medieval española.* Barcelona, 1967.
Lluis y Navas Brusi, Jaime. "Observaciones sobre la amonedación legal de los musulmanes de España," *Madrid:MDI* 4(1956), pp. 47–78.
Lomax, D.W. *The Reconquest of Spain.* New York, 1978.
Lombard, Maurice. "Arsenaux et bois de marine dans la Méditerranée musulmane (VIIe-XIe siècles)," *Le navire et l'économie maritime du moyen âge au XVIIIe siècle principalement en Méditerranée.* (ed. M. Mollat), Paris, 1958, pp. 53–106.
The Golden Age of Islam. Oxford, 1975.
"Mahomet et Charlemagne," *Annales:ESC* 3(1948), pp. 188–99.
Les métaux dans l'ancien monde du Ve au XIe siècle. Paris, 1974.
Monnaie et histoire Alexandre à Mahomet. Paris, 1971.
"L'or musulman du VIIe au XIe siècles," *Annales:ESC* 2(1947), pp. 145–60.
"Un problème cartographié: Le bois dans la Méditerranée musulmane (VIIe-XIe siècles)," *Annales:ESC* 14(1959), pp. 234–54.
Les textiles dans le monde musulman du VIIe au XIIe siècle. Paris, 1978.
Longpérier, Adrien D. "Monnaie andalouse trouvée à contres," *Revue numismatique* n.s. 8(1963), pp. 14–16.
Lopez, R.S. "Alfonso el Sabio y el primer almirante de Castilla genovés," *Cuadernos de historia de España* 14(1950), pp. 5–16.
"L'attività economica di Genova nel Marzo 1253 secondo gli atti notarili del tempo," ASLSP 64(1934), pp. 166–270.
"Aux origines du capitalisme génois," *Annales d'histoire économique et sociale* 9(1937) pp. 429–54.
"Back to Gold, 1252," *Economic History Review* 2nd series, 9(1956–57), pp. 219–40.
"China Silk in Europe in the Yuan Period," *JAOS* 72(1952), pp. 72–6.
The Commercial Revolution of the Middle Ages 950–1350. New York, 1971.
"Concerning Surnames and Places of Origin," *Medievalia et humanistica* 8(1954), pp. 6–16.

"The Dollar of the Middle Ages," *Journal of Economic History* 3(1951), pp. 209–34.

"East and West in the Early Middle Ages: Economic Relations," *Relazioni del X Congresso internazionale di scienze storiche*. III, Rome, 1955, pp. 113–63.

Genova marinara nel duecento: Benedetto Zaccaria, ammiraglio e mercante. Milan, 1932.

"I genovesi in Africa occidentale nel medioevo," *Studi sull'economia genovese nel medioevo*. Turin, 1936, pp. 3–61.

"Majorcans and Genoese on the North Sea Route in the 13th century," *Revue belge de philologie et d'histoire* 29(1951), pp. 1163–79.

"Market Expansion: The Case of Genoa," *Journal of Economic History* 24(1964), pp. 445–64.

"Mohammed and Charlemagne: A Revision," *Speculum* 18(1943), pp. 14–38.

"The Origin of the Merino Sheep," *Joshua Starr Memorial Volume*. New York, 1953, pp. 161–8.

"Il predominio economico dei genovesi nella monarchia spagnola," *Giornale storico e letterario della Liguria* 11(1936), pp. 65–74.

"Profil du marchand génois," *Annales:ESC* 3(1958), pp. 501–15.

"Silk Industry in the Byzantine Empire," *Speculum* 20(1945), pp. 1–42.

"Still Another Renaissance?" *AHR* 57(1951), pp. 1–21.

"The Trade of Medieval Europe: The South," *Cambridge Economic History of Europe*. (eds. M. Postan and E. Rich) II, Cambridge, 1952. pp. 257–354; 2nd edn Cambridge, 1987, pp. 306–401.

"The Unexplored Wealth of the Notarial Archives in Pisa and Lucca," *Mélanges d'histoire du moyen âge dédiés à la mémoire de Louis Halphen*. Paris, 1951, pp. 417–32.

Lopez, R.S. and Raymond, I.W. *Medieval Trade in the Mediterranean World*. New York, 1955.

López Ortiz, P. José. "Fatwas granadinos de los siglos XIV y XV," *Al-Andalus* 6(1941), pp. 73–127.

"Formularios notariales de la España musulmana," *La ciudad de Dios* (1926), pp. 260–72.

López de Coca Castañer, E.J. "Comercio exterior del reino de Granada," *Actas del II Coloquio de historia medieval andaluza. Hacienda y comercio. Sevilla, 8–10 de Abril. 1981*. Seville, 1982, pp. 335–77.

Lowick, N.M. "The Kufic Coins from Cuerdale," *The British Numismatic Journal* 46(1977), pp. 19–28 (reprinted in N.M. Lowick, *Islamic coins and trade in the medieval world*. London, 1990).

MacDonald, Gerald J. "Spanish Textile and Clothing Nomenclature in -án, -í, and -ín," *Hispanic Review* 44(1976), pp. 57–78.

Mackay, Angus. "Comercio/mercado interior y la expansión económica del siglo XV," *Actas del II Coloquio de historia medieval andaluza: Hacienda y comercio. Sevilla, 8–10 de Abril, 1981*. Seville, 1982, pp. 103–23.

Spain in the Middle Ages: From Frontier to Empire, 1000–1500. London, 1977.

Makkī, Maḥmūd. "Ensayo sobre las aportaciones orientales en la España musulmana," *Madrid:MDI* 11(1963), pp. 7–140.

Malanima, Paolo. "Pisa and the Trade Routes to the Near East in the Late Middle Ages," *Journal of European Economic History* 16(1987), pp. 335–56.
Malowist, Marian. "Quelques observations sur le commerce de l'or dans le Soudan occidental au moyen âge," *Annales:ESC* 5–6(1970), pp. 1630–6.
Malpica Cuello, Antonio. "Regimen fiscal y actividad económica de las salinas del reino de Granada," *Actas del II Coloquio de historia medieval andaluza: Hacienda y comercio. Sevilla, 8–10 de Abril, 1981*. Seville, 1982, pp. 393–403.
Mann, Jacob, ed. "The Responsa of the Babylonian Geonim as a Source of Jewish History," *Jewish Quarterly Review* 7(1916–17), pp. 457–90.
Texts and Studies in Jewish History and Literature. 2 vols. Cincinnati, 1931–35.
Marçais, George. "Les villes de la côte algérienne et la piraterie au moyen âge," *Annales de l'Institut d'études orientales. Faculté des lettres de l'Université d'Alger* 13(1955), pp. 118–42.
Martínez, María del Carmen. *Los nombres de tejidos en castellano medieval*. Granada, 1989.
Martínez Caviró, Balbina. *La loza dorada*. Madrid, 1983.
Martínez Montavez, Pedro. "La economia de la España omeya," *Hispania* 25(1965), pp. 429–40.
"Islam y cristianidad en la economia mediterranea de la baja edad media," *XIII Congreso internacional de ciencias históricas*. Moscow, 1970, pp. 1–14.
Mas Latrie, Louis de. *Relations et commerce de l'Afrique septentrionale en Maghreb avec les nations chrétiennes au moyen âge*. Paris, 1886.
Masiá de Ros, Angeles. *La Corona de Aragón y los estados del norte de Africa; Politica de Jaime II y Alfonso IV en Egipto, Ifriquía, y Tremcén*. Barcelona, 1951.
Mateu y Llopis, F. "El hallazgo de 'pennies' ingleses en Roncevalles," *Principe de Viana* 11(1950), pp. 201–10.
"Hallazgos numismáticos musulmanes," *Al-Andalus* 12(1947), pp. 481–4.
Mauny, Raymond. "Découvert à Gao d'un fragment de poterie émaillée du moyen âge musulman," *Hespéris* 39(1952) pp. 514–16.
"La navigation sur les côtes du Sahara pendant l'antiquite," *Revue des études anciennes* 57(1955), pp. 92–101.
Les navigations médiévales sur les côtes sahariennes antérieures à la découverte portugais (1434). Lisbon, 1960.
Tableau géographique de l'ouest africain au moyen âge d'après les sources écrits, la tradition et l'archéologie. Dakar, 1961.
May, Florence Lewis. *Silk Textiles of Spain, 8th–15th century*. New York, 1957.
Mayer, Ernesto. *Historia de los instituciones sociales y políticas de España y Portugal durante los siglos V a XIV*. 1, Madrid, 1925.
Mazzaoui, M. *The Cotton Industry of Medieval Italy*. Cambridge, 1981.
Meiggs, Russell. *Trees and Timber in the Ancient Mediterranean World*. Oxford, 1982.
Melis, Federigo. *Mercaderes italianos en España (siglos XIV–XV)*. Seville, 1976.
"The Nationality of Sea-Borne Trade between England and the Mediterranean around 1400," *Journal of European Economic History* 4(1975), pp. 359–80.

I trasporti e le comunicazioni nel medioevo. Florence, 1984.

Menéndez Pidal, Ramón. *The Cid and his Spain*. London, 1934.

Messier, Roland A. "The Almoravids: West African Gold and the Gold Currency of the Mediterranean Basin," *JESHO* 17(1974), pp.31–47.

"Muslim Exploitation of West African Gold during the Period of the Fatimid Caliphate." Ph.D. Dissertation, University of Michigan, 1972.

Mez, Adam. *The Renaissance of Islam*. London, 1937.

Michel, Francisque Xavier. *Recherches sur le commerce, la fabrication et l'usage des étoffes de soie, d'or et d'argent et autres tissus précieux en occident, principalement en France, pendent le moyen âge*. 2 vols., Paris, 1852–4.

Migeon, Gaston. *Manuel d'art musulman; Arts plastiques et industriels*. Paris, 1927.

Miles, George C. *The Coinage of the Umayyads of Spain*. New York, 1950.

Coins of the Spanish Mulūk at-Tawā'if. New York, 1954.

"The Year 400 AH/1009–1010 AD at the Mint of Cordoba," *Numisma* 17(1967), pp.9–25.

Millás Vallicrosa, J.M. "El cultivo del algodón en la España árabe," *Boletín de la Real Academia de la historia* 139(1956), pp.463–72.

Miquel, André. "L'Europe occidentale dans la relation arabe d'Ibrāhīm b. Ya'qūb, (Xe siècle)" *Annales: ESC* 21(1966), pp.1048–64.

La géographie humaine du monde musulman jusqu'au milieu du XIe siècle. Paris, 1967.

Misbach, Henri L. "Genoese Commerce and the Alleged Flow of Gold to the East, 1154–1253," *Revue internationale d'histoire de la banque* (1970), pp.67–87.

"Genoese Trade and the Flow of Gold 1154–1253." Ph.D. Dissertation, University of Wisconsin, 1968.

Molina, Luis. "Nota sobre 'murūs'," *Al-Qantara* 4(1983), pp.283–300.

Molina López, Emilio. "Algunas consideraciones sobre la vida socio-económica de Almería en el siglo XI y primera mitad del XII," *Actas del IV Coloquio hispano-tunecino (Palma, 1979)*. Madrid, 1983, pp.181–96.

Mollat, M., ed. *Le rôle du sel dans l'histoire*. Paris, 1968.

Mones, Hussein. "Al-jughrāfiya wa al-jughrāfiyūn fī al-Andalus," *Madrid: MDI* 7–8(1959–60), pp.199–359; and 9–10(1961–2), pp.257–372.

"Al-jughrāfiya wa al-jughrāfiyūn fī ma'āṣarū al-Idrīsī," *Madrid: MDI* 11–12(1963–4), pp.7–328.

Moraes Farias, P.F. de. "Silent Trade: Myth and Historical Evidence," *History in Africa* 1(1974), pp.9–24.

Morales Belda, F. *La marina de al-Andalus*. Barcelona, 1970.

"Papel de las disponibilidades forestales en la reconquista del tráfico marítimo de al-Andalus mediterráneo," *Anuario de estudios medievales* 10(1980), pp.173–85.

"La unidad de medida de los itinerarios marítimos en al-Andalus, siglos VIII-XV," *Actas de las jornadas de cultura árabe e islámica (1978)*. Madrid, 1981, pp.165–77.

Moresco, M. and Bognetti, G.P. *Per l'edizione dei notai liguri del secolo XII*. Turin, 1938.

Morral i Romeu, Eulália, and Segura i Mas, Antoni. *La seda en España: Leyenda, poder, y realidad.* Barcelona, 1991.

Morrison, Karl F. "Numismatics and Carolingian Trade: A Critique of the Evidence," *Speculum* 38(1963), pp.403–32.

Muldoon, J. *Popes, Lawyers, and Infidels.* Philadelphia, 1979.

Munro, John H. "The Medieval Scarlet and the Economics of Sartorial Splendor," *Cloth and Clothing in Medieval Europe. Essays in Memory of Prof. E.M. Carus-Wilson.* London, 1983, pp.13–70.

Mut Remola, Enrique. *La vida económica en Lérida de 1150 a 1500.* Lerida, 1953.

Navarro Palazon, J. "Murcia como centro productor de la loza dorada," *III Congresso internazionale sulla ceramica medievale nel Mediterranea occidentale. Siena, ottobre, 1984.* Florence, 1986, pp.129–46.

Neale, W.C. "The Market in Theory and History," *Trade and Market in Early Empires.* (ed. K. Polanyi), New York, 1957, pp.357–72.

Nef, John. "Mining and Metallurgy in Medieval Society," *Cambridge Economic History of Europe.* (eds. M. Postan and E. Rich) II, Cambridge, 1952, pp.430–93; 2nd edn, Cambridge, 1987, pp.693–761.

Nelson, B. "Blancard (the Jew?) of Genoa and the Restitution of Usury in Medieval Genoa," *Studi in onore di Gino Luzzatto.* I, Milan, 1949, pp.96–116.

Neuman, Abraham A. *The Jews in Spain.* Philadelphia, 1942.

Nicolle, David. "Shipping in Islamic Art: Seventh through Sixteenth Century AD," *The American Neptune* 49(1989), pp.168–97.

Noberasco, Filippo. "Savona allo spirare del secolo XII," *Atti della Societá savonese di storia patria* 14(1932), pp.213–55.

Noonan, Thomas S. "Andalusian Umayyad Dirhams from Eastern Europe," *Acta numismatica* 10(1980), pp.81–91.

"Ninth-century dirham hoards from European Russia: A preliminary analysis," in *Viking Age Coinage in Northern Lands.* (eds. M.A.S. Blackburn and D.M. Metcalf), Oxford, 1981, pp.47–117.

North, Douglas C. "Markets and other Allocation Systems in History: The Challenge of Karl Polanyi," *Journal of European Economic History* 6(1977), pp.703–16.

Nykl, A.R. *Hispano-Arabic Poetry*, Baltimore, 1946.

O'Callaghan, Joseph F. *The Cortes of Castile-León, 1188–1350.* Philadelphia, 1989.

A History of Medieval Spain. Ithaca, 1975.

Origo, Iris. *A Merchant of Prato.* New York, 1957.

Otte, Enrique. "El comercio exterior andaluz a fines de la edad media," *Actas del II Coloquio de historia medieval andaluza: Hacienda y comercio. Sevilla, 8–10 de Abril, 1981.* Seville, 1982, pp.193–240.

Pacha, Najet. *Le commerce au Maghreb du XIe au XIVe siècles.* Tunis, 1976.

Pastor de Togneri, Reyna. "La lana en Castilla y León antes de la organización de la Mesta," *Atti della prima settimana di Studio, Istituto F. Datini.* (ed. M. Spallanzani), Florence, 1974, pp. 253–69.

Pariset, Ernest. *Histoire de la soie.* 2 vols., Paris, 1862–5.

Partearroyo, C. "Almoravid and Almohad Textiles," *Al-Andalus: The Art of Islamic Spain.* (ed. J. Dodds), New York, 1992, pp. 105–13.

Pellegrini, G.B. "Terminologia marinara di origine arabe in italiano e nelle lingue europee," *La navigazione mediterranea nell'alto medioevo.* Settimane di studio del Centro italiano di studi sull'altro medioevo, XXV, Spoleto, 1978, pp. 797–841.

Pérès, Henri. *La poesie andalouse en arabe classique au XIe siècle.* Paris, 1953. Spanish trans. M. García Arenal, *Esplendor de al-Andalus.* Madrid, 1983.

Pérez Embid, Florentino. *Bibliografía española de historia marítima (1932–1962).* Seville, 1970.

"Navigation et commerce dans le port de Séville au bas moyen âge," *Le moyen âge* 75(1969), pp. 263–89, 479–502.

Phillips, C.R. "Spanish Merchants and the Wool Trade in the 16th Century" *Sixteenth Century Journal* 14(1983), pp. 259–82.

Phillips, W.D. "Spain's Northern Shipping Industry in the Sixteenth Century," *Journal of European Economic History* 17(1988), pp. 267–301.

Pigeouneau, H. *Histoire du commerce de la France.* Paris, 1885.

Pirenne, Henri. *Medieval Cities; their Origins and the Revival of Trade.* New York, 1956.

Mohammed and Charlemagne. London, 1939.

Pistarino, Geo. "Le donne d'affari a Genova nel secolo XIII," *Miscellanea di storia italiana e mediterranea per Nino Lamboglia.* Genoa, 1978, pp. 157–69.

"Genova e Barcelona: Incontro e scontro di due civiltá," *Atti del I Congresso storico Liguria-Catalogna (14–19 ottobre, 1969).* Bordighera, 1974, pp. 81–122.

"Genova e l'Islam nel Mediterraneo occidentale (secoli XII-XIII)," *Anuario de estudios medievales* 10(1980), pp. 189–205.

"Genova e il Maghreb nel secolo XII," *Italia e Algeria: Aspetti storici di un'amicizia mediterranea.* Milan, 1982, pp. 23–68.

"Genova e l'Occitania nel secolo XII," *Atti del I Congresso storico Liguria-Provenza, Ventimiglia-Bordighera (2–5 ottobre, 1964).* Bordighera, 1966, pp. 64–130.

Testi per lo studio del medio evo in Liguria. Genoa, n.d.

Poncet, J. "Le mythe de la 'catastrophe' hilalienne," *Annales: ESC* 22(1967), pp. 1099–1120.

Posac Mon, Carlos. "Relaciones entre Génova y Ceuta durante el siglo XII," *Tamuda* 7(1959), pp. 159–68.

Postan, M. "Credit in Medieval Trade," *Economic History Review* 1(1927), pp. 234–61.

Power, E. *The Wool Trade in English Medieval History.* Oxford, 1941.

Prieto Vives, A. *Los reyes de taifas. Estudio histórico-numismático de los musulmanes españoles en el siglo V de la hégira.* Madrid, 1926.

Pryor, John H. *Geography, Technology, and War: Studies in the Maritime History of the Mediterranean, 649–1571.* Cambridge, 1988.

"The Medieval Muslim Ships of the Pisan Bacini," *The Mariners Mirror* 76(1990), pp. 99–113.

"Mediterranean Commerce in the Middle Ages: A Voyage under Contract of Commenda," *Viator* 14(1983), pp. 133–94.
"The Origins of the 'Commenda' Contract," *Speculum* 52(1977), pp. 5–37.
"Transportation of Horses by Sea during the Era of the Crusades," *The Mariner's Mirror* 68(1982), pp. 9–27, 103–25.
Rabie, Hassanein. *The Financial System of Egypt*. London, 1972.
Rabinowitz, L. *Jewish Merchant Adventurers: A Study of the Radanites*. London, 1948.
Reglá, J. "El comercio entre Francia y la Corona de Aragón en los siglos XIII y XIV y sus relaciones con el desenvolvimiento de la industria textil catalana," *Actas del primer congreso internacional de estudios pirenaicos, San Sebastian, 1950*. Zaragoza, 1952, pp. 47–65.
Renfrew, Colin. "Trade as Action at a Distance," *Ancient Civilization and Trade*. (eds. J.A. Sabloff, C.C. Lamberg-Karlovsky), Albuquerque, 1975, pp. 3–59.
Renouard, Yves. "Lumiéres nouvelles sur les hommes d'affaires italiens du moyen âge," *Annales: ESC* 3(1955), pp. 63–78.
"Le rôle des hommes d'affaires italiens dans la Méditerranée au moyen âge," *Revue de la Méditerranée* 15(1955), pp. 115–35.
"Un sujet de recherches: L'exportation des chevaux de la péninsule ibérique en France et en Angleterre au moyen âge," *Homenaje a Jaime Vicens Vives*. 1, Barcelona, 1965, pp. 571–7.
"Les voies de communication entre pays de la Méditerranée et pays de l'Atlantique au moyen âge: Problèmes et hypothèses," *Mélanges d'histoire du moyen âge dédiés à la mémoire de Louis Halphen*. Paris, 1951, pp. 587–94.
Reparaz, Gonzalo de. "L'activité maritime et commerciale du royaume d'Aragon au XIIIe siècle," *Bulletin hispanique* 49(1947), pp. 422–51.
Reyerson, K. "Montpellier and the Byzantine Empire: Commercial Interaction in the Mediterranean World before 1350," *Byzantion* 48(1978), pp. 456–76.
Reynolds, Robert L. "Genoese Trade in the late Twelfth century, particularly in Cloth from the Fairs of Champagne," *Journal of Economic and Business History* 3(1930–1), pp. 362–81.
"The Origins of Modern Business Enterprise: Medieval Italy," *Journal of Economic History* 12(1952), pp. 350–65.
Ribera y Tarrago, J. *Disertaciones y opúsculos*. 1, Madrid, 1928.
Riu, Manuel. "The Woolen Industry in Catalonia in the Later Middle Ages," *Cloth and Clothing in Medieval Europe: Essays in Memory of Prof. E.M. Carus-Wilson*. London, 1983, pp. 205–29.
Robbert, L.B. "Twelfth-century Italian Prices: Food and Clothing in Pisa and Venice," *Social Science History* 7(1983), pp. 381–403.
Rodinson, M. *Europe and the Mystique of Islam*. Seattle, 1987.
"Le marchand méditerranéen à travers les âges," *Markets and Marketing as Factors of Development in the Mediterranean Basin*. (ed. C.A.O. Van Nieuwenhuijze), The Hague, 1963, pp. 71–92.
"Le marchand musulman," *Islam and the Trade of Asia*. (ed. D.S. Richards), Philadelphia, 1970, pp. 21–35.

Rörig, F. *The Medieval Town*. Berkeley, 1967.

Roover, Florence Edler de. "Partnership Accounts in twelfth-century Genoa," *Business History Review* 15(1941), pp. 87–92.

Roover, Raymond de. "Economic Thought: Ancient and Medieval Thought," *International Encyclopedia of Social Sciences*. New York, 1968.

Rosenthal, F. *A History of Muslim Historiography*. Leiden, 1968.

Rosselló Bordoy, Guillermo. "Algunas anotaciones sobre la vida económica de las Baleares durante la dominación musulmana," *Boletín de la camera oficial de comercio, industria, y navegación* (Palma) 621(1958), pp. 140–5.

"Un ataifor norteafricano: un ensayo de interpretación iconográfica," *Sharq al-Andalus* 2(1985), pp. 191–205.

"The Ceramics of al-Andalus," in *Al-Andalus: The Art of Islamic Spain*. (ed. J. Dodds), New York, 1992, pp. 97–103.

"Mallorca: Comercio y cerámica a lo largo de los siglos X al XIV," *II Coloquio internacional de cerámica medieval en el Mediterraneo occidental, Toledo, 1981*. Madrid, 1986, pp. 193–238.

Roth, Norman. "Some Aspects of Muslim-Jewish Relations in Spain," *Estudios en homenaje a D. Claudio Sánchez Albornoz*. II, Buenos Aires, 1983, pp. 179–214.

Rotstein, Abraham. "Karl Polanyi's Concept of Non-Market Trade," *Journal of Economic History* 30(1970), pp. 117–26.

Rottenburger, Elizabeth. "Genoese Relations with Mediterranean France and Spain and the Balearic Islands, 1155–1164." MA Dissertation, University of Cincinnati, 1947.

Rouche, M. "Les relations transpyrénéennes du Ve au VIIIe siècle," *Les communications dans la péninsule ibérique au moyen âge (Actes du Colloque de Pau, 28–29 mars, 1980)*. Paris, 1981, pp. 13–20.

Roy, B., Poinssot, P., and Poinssot, O. *Inscriptions arabes de Kairouan*. I, Paris, 1950.

Rozi, A.I. "The Social Role of Scholars ('Ulamā) in Islamic Spain." Ph.D. Dissertation, Boston University, 1983.

Ruiz, Teofilo F. "Burgos y el comercio castellano en la baja edad media: economia y mentalidad," *La ciudad de Burgos. Actas del congreso de historia de Burgos*. Madrid, 1985, pp. 37–55.

"Castilian Merchants in England, 1248–1350," *Order and Innovation in the Middle Ages: Essays in Honor of Joseph R. Strayer*. Princeton, 1976, pp. 173–86.

Crisis and Continuity: Land and Town in Late Medieval Castile. Philadelphia, 1994.

"Expansion et changement: la conquête de Séville et la société castillane (1248–1350)," *Annales: ESC* 34(1979), pp. 548–65.

Sociedad y poder real en Castilla. Barcelona, 1981.

"The Transformation of the Castilian Municipalities: The Case of Burgos 1248–1350," *Past and Present* 77(1977), pp. 3–32.

Ruiz Domenec, J.E. "En torno a un tratado comercial entre las ciudades de Génova y Barcelona en la primera mitad del siglo XII," *Atti del I*

Congresso storico Liguria-Catalogna (14–19 ottobre 1969). Bordighera, 1974, pp. 151–60.

"Las posibilidades que la reflexión histórico-antropológica puede tener en el discernimiento de la expansión marítima de la Corona de Aragón," *Second International Congress of Studies on Cultures of the Western Mediterranean*. Barcelona, 1978, pp. 329–57.

"Ruta de las especias/ruta de las islas: apuntes para una nueva periodización," *Anuario de estudios medievales* 10(1980), pp. 689–97.

"The Urban Origins of Barcelona: Agricultural Revolution or Commercial Development?" *Speculum* 52(1977), pp. 265–86.

Ruzafa García, Manuel. "Las relaciones económicas entre los mudejares valencianos y el reino de Granada en el siglo XV," *Relaciones exteriores del Reino de Granada. IV Coloquio de historia medieval andaluza*. Almeria, 1988, pp. 343–81.

Sabbe, Etienne. "L'importation des tissus orientaux en Europe occidentale au haut moyen âge (IXe et Xe siècles)," *Revue belge de philologie et d'histoire* 15(1935), pp. 811–48, 1261–88.

"Quelques types de marchands des IXe et Xe siècles," *Revue belge de philologie et d'histoire* 13(1934), pp. 176–87.

Salavert, Vicente. "Nuevamente sobre la expansión mediterránea de la Corona de Aragón," *Second International Congress of Studies on Cultures of the Western Mediterranean*. Barcelona, 1978, pp. 359–88.

Sālim, ʿAbd al-ʿAzīz. "Algunos aspectos del florecimiento económico de Almería islámica durante el período de los Taifas y de los Almorávides," *Madrid: MDI* 20(1979–80), pp. 7–22.

Taʾrīkh madīnat al-Mariyya al-Andalusiyya. Alexandria, 1984.

Salzman, L.F. *English Trade in the Middle Ages*. Oxford, 1931,

Samarrai, Alauddin. "Medieval Commerce and Diplomacy: Islam and Europe, AD 850–1300," *Canadian Journal of History* 15(1980), pp. 1–21.

"Some Geographical and Political Information on Western Europe in the Medieval Arab Sources," *The Muslim World* 62(1972), pp. 304–22.

Sāmarrāʾi, Khalīl Ibrāhīm. *ʿAlaqāt al-murabiṭīn bi al-mamālik al-Isbāniyah bi al-Andalus*. Baghdad, 1985.

Sánchez Albornoz, Claudio. *Estampas de la vida en León durante el siglo X*. 3rd edn, Madrid, 1934.

"El precio de la vida en el reino Astur-Leonés hace mil años," *Logos: Revista de la facultad de filosofía y letras de la Universidad de Buenos Aires* 3(1944), pp. 225–64.

"La primitiva organización monetaria de León y de Castilla," *AHDE* 5(1928), pp. 301–45.

Santamaría Arández, Alvaro. "La reconquista de las vías marítimas," *Anuario de estudios medievales* 10(1980), pp. 41–133.

Santillana, D. *Istituzioni di diritto musulmano malichita con riguardo anche al sistema sciafita*. Rome, 1938.

Santos Jener, S. de los. "Monedas carolingias en un tesorillo de dirhemes del emirato cordobés," *Numario hispánico* 5(1956), pp. 79–87.

Saussure, Hermine de. "De la marine antique à la marine moderne," *Revue archéologique* n.s. 10(1937), pp. 90–105.

Sauvaget, J. "Les épitaphes royales de Gao," *Al-Andalus* 14(1949), pp. 123–41.

"Les épitaphes royales de Gao," *Bulletin de l'Institut français de l'Afrique noire* 12(1950), pp. 418–40.

Sauvaire, M.H. "Matériaux pour servir à l'histoire de la numismatique et de la métrologie musulmanes," *Journal asiatique* VIIe série 19(1882), pp. 23–77; VIIIe série 4(1884), pp. 207–321; 7(1886), pp. 394–468; 10(1887), pp. 200–59.

Sawyer, P. "Kings and Merchants," *Early Medieval Kingship*. (eds. P. Sawyer and I.N. Wood), Leeds, 1977, pp. 139–58.

Sayous, André. *Commerce et finance en Méditerranée au moyen âge*. Variorum, London, 1988.

"Les méthodes commerciales de Barcelone au XIIIe siècle, d'après des documents inédits des archives de sa cathédrale," *Estudis universitaris catalans* 16(1931), pp. 155–98.

Scales, Peter. "The Handing over of the Duero Fortresses: 1009–1011 AD (399–401 AH)," *Al-Qantara* 5(1984), pp. 109–22.

Scalia, Giuseppe. "Il carme pisano sull'impresa contro i saraceni del 1087," *Studi di filologia romanza offerti a Silvio Pellegrini*. Padua, 1971, pp. 565–627.

"Contributi pisani alla lotta anti-islamica nel Mediterraneo centro-occidentale durante il secolo XI e nei primi decenni del XII," *Anuario de estudios medievales* 10(1980), pp. 135–41.

Scandurra, Enrico. "The Marine Republics: Medieval and Renaissance Ships in Italy," *A History of Seafaring*. (ed. G. Bass), London, 1972, pp. 205–24.

Scanlon, G.T. "Egypt and China: Trade and Imitation," *Islam and the Trade of Asia*. (ed. D.S. Richards), Philadelphia, 1970, pp. 81–95.

Scerrato, U. and F. Gabrieli. *Gli arabi in Italia*. Milan, 1979.

Schaefer, G. "The Development of Paper-Making," *Ciba Review* 6(1947–9), pp. 2641–9.

Schaube, Adolf. *Handelsgeschichte der romanischen völker des Mittelmeergebiets bis zum ende der kreuzzüge*. Munich–Berlin, 1906.

Schneidman, J. Lee. "The State and Trade in thirteenth-century Aragon," *Hispania* 19(1959), pp. 366–77.

Segura, Cristina. "Almería en el ocaso del dominio musulman," *Hispania* 36(1976), pp. 117–29.

Senac, P. "Contribution à l'étude des relations diplomatiques entre l'Espagne musulmane et l'Europe au Xe siècle: le règne de 'Abd ar-Raḥmān III (912–61)," *Studia islamica* 61(1985), pp. 45–56.

Musulmans et sarrasins dans le sud de la Gaule du VIIIe au XIe siècle. Paris, 1980.

Serjeant, R.B., ed. *The Islamic City*. Paris, 1980.

"Material for a History of Islamic Textiles up to the Mongol Conquest," (Chapter XVII: Textiles and Ṭirāz in Spain) *Ars Islamica* 15(1951), pp. 29–61.

Sesma Muñoz, J. Angel. "El comercio de exportación de trigo, aceite, y lana desde Zaragoza a mediados del siglo XV," *Aragón en la edad media*. Zaragoza, 1977, pp. 201–37.

Lexico del comercio medieval en Aragón [siglo XV]. Zaragoza, 1982.

Shaked, Shaul. *A Tentative Bibliography of Geniza Documents*. The Hague, 1964.

Shatzmiller, Maya. "The Legacy of the Andalusian Berbers in the fourteenth-century Maghreb," *Relaciones de la península ibérica con el Magreb (siglos XIII–XIV)*. (eds. M. García-Arenal and M.J. Viguera), CSIC, Madrid, 1988, pp. 205–6.

"Professions and Ethnic Origin of Urban Labourers in Muslim Spain: Evidence from a Moroccan Source," *Awrāq* 5–6(1982–3), pp. 149–59.

Smith, R.S. "The Early History of the Spanish Sea Consulate," *Politica* 1(1935), pp. 314–24.

Soto i Company, Ricard. "El primer tràfic esclavista a Mallorca," *L'Avenç* 35(1981), pp. 60–5.

Soucek, S. "*Mīnā'*," *Encyclopedia of Islam*. 2nd edn, Leiden 1960–, VII, pp. 66–72.

Spallanzani, M., ed. *Produzione commercio e consumo dei panni di lana (nei secoli XII–XVIII)*. Atti della seconda settimana di studio, Istituto F. Datini. Florence, 1976.

Sprandel, Rolf. "Le commerce de fer en Méditerranée orientale au moyen âge," *Sociétés et compagnies de commerce en orient et dans l'Ocean indien*. Paris, 1970, pp. 387–92.

Spufford, Peter. *Handbook of Medieval Exchange*. London, 1986.

"Le rôle de la monnaie dans la révolution commerciale du XIIIe siècle," *Etudes d'histoire monétaire, XIIe–XIXe siècles*. (ed. John Day), Lille, 1984, pp. 355–95.

Stern, S.M. "An Original Document from the Fatimid Chancery concerning Italian Merchants," *Studi orientalistici in onore di Giorgio Levi della Vida*. Rome, 1956, pp. 529–38.

"Tari," *Studi medievali* 11(1970), pp. 177–207.

Stillman, Norman A. "Aspects of Jewish Life in Islamic Spain," *Aspects of Jewish Culture in the Middle Ages*. (ed. Paul Szarmach), Albany, 1979, pp. 51–84.

"East–West Relations in the Islamic Mediterranean in the Early Eleventh century – A Study in the Geniza correspondence of the House of Ibn 'Awkal." Ph.D. Dissertation, University of Pennsylvania, 1970.

"The Eleventh-century Merchant House of Ibn 'Awkal (A Geniza Study)," *JESHO* 16(1973), pp. 15–88.

The Jews of Arab Lands: A History and a Source Book. Philadelphia, 1979.

"Quelques renseignements biographiques sur Yōsēf Ibn 'Awkal, médiateur entre les communautés juives du Maghreb et les académies d'Irak," *Revue des études juives* 132(1973), pp. 529–42.

Talbi, Mohamed. *L'émirat aghlabide*. Paris, 1966.

"Intérêt des oevres juridiques traitant de la guerre pour l'historien des armées médiévales ifrīkiennes," *Cahiers de Tunisie* 4(1956), pp. 289–93.

Tapia Garrido, J.A. *Almería musulmana*. Almeria, 1986.

Todesca, James J. "The Monetary History of Castile-Leon (ca. 1100–1300) in Light of the Bourgey Hoard," *American Numismatic Society Museum Notes* 33(1988), pp. 129–203.

Torres Balbás, Leopoldo. "Alcaicerías," *Al-Andalus* 14(1949), pp. 431–55.

"Las alhóndigas hispanomusulmanas y el Corral del Carbón de Granada," *Al-Andalus* 11(1946), pp. 447–81.

"Almería islámica," *Al-Andalus* 22(1957), pp. 411–53.

"Bibliography of Spanish Muslim Art, 1936–1946," *Ars Islamica* 15–16(1951), pp. 165–85.

"Cementerios hispanomusulmanes," *Al-Andalus* 22(1957), pp. 131–91.

"Extensión y demografía de las ciudades hispanomusulmanas," *Studia islamica* 3(1955), pp. 37–59.

Torres Delgado, Cristóbal. "El reino nazari de Granada (1232–1492). Aspectos socio-económicos y fiscales," *Actas del II Coloquio de historia medieval andaluza: Hacienda y comercio. Sevilla, 8–10 de Abril, 1981*. Seville, 1982, pp. 297–334.

Tria, Luigi. "La schiavitù in Liguria (ricerche e documenti)," *ASLSP* 70(1947).

Turnau, Irena. "The Diffusion of Knitting in Medieval Europe," *Cloth and Clothing in Medieval Europe: Essays in Honor of Prof. E.M. Carus-Wilson*. London, 1983, pp. 368–89.

Ubieto Arteta, Antonio. *Ciclos económicos en la edad media española*. Valencia, 1969.

Udina Martorell, F. "La expansión mediterranea catalano-aragonesa," *Second International Congress of Studies on Cultures of the Western Mediterranean*. Barcelona, 1978, pp. 209–24.

Udovitch, Avram L. "At the Origins of the Western Commenda: Islam, Israel, Byzantium?" *Speculum* 37(1962), pp. 198–207.

"Commercial Techniques in Early Islamic Trade," *Islam and the Trade of Asia*. (ed. D.S. Richards), Philadelphia, 1970, pp. 37–62.

"Les échanges de marché dans l'Islam médiéval: Théorie du droit et savoir local," *Studia islamica* 65(1987), pp. 5–30.

"Merchants and *Amīrs*: Government and Trade in eleventh-century Egypt," *Asian and African Studies* 22(1988), pp. 53–72.

Partnership and Profit in Medieval Islam. Princeton, 1970.

"Reflections on the Institutions of Credit and Banking in the Medieval Islamic Near East," *Studia islamica* 41(1975) pp. 5–21.

"A Tale of Two Cities: Commercial Relations between Cairo and Alexandria during the second half of the 11th century," *The Medieval City*. (eds. H.A. Miskimin, D. Herlihy, A.L. Udovitch), New Haven, 1977, pp. 143–62.

"Time, the Sea, and Society: Duration of Commercial Voyages on the Southern Shores of the Mediterranean during the High Middle Ages," *La navigazione mediterranea nell'alto medioevo*. Settimane di studio del Centro italiano di studi sull'altro medioevo, XXV, Spoleto, 1978, pp. 503–63.

Unger, Richard W. *The Ship in the Medieval Economy (600–1600)*. London, 1980.

"Warships and Cargo Ships in Medieval Europe," *Technology and Culture* 22(1981), pp. 233–52.

Urvoy, Dominique. *Le monde des ulémas andalous du V/XIe au VII/XIIIe siècle.* Geneva, 1978.

Usher, A.P. "The Origins of Banking: The Primitive Bank of Deposit, 1200–1600," *Economic History Review* 4(1932–4), pp. 391–428.

Uytven, Raymond von. "Cloth in Medieval Literature of Western Europe," *Cloth and Clothing in Medieval Europe: Essays in Memory of Prof. E.M. Carus-Wilson.* London, 1983, pp. 151–83.

Valdeón, Julio. *Alfonso X el Sabio.* Madrid, 1986.

Valdeón, J. et al. "Las relaciones entre Castilla y Francia (siglos XIII–XV)," *Les communications dans la péninsule ibérique au moyen âge. Actes du colloque de Pau, 28–29 mars, 1980.* Paris, 1981, pp. 45–53.

Valls i Subirà, Oriol. "El paper al al-Andalus i a la Corona d'Aragó," *Second International Congress of Studies on Cultures of the Western Mediterranean.* Barcelona, 1978, pp. 441–8.

Vallvé Bermejo, Joaquin. "La agricultura en al-Andalus," *Al-Qantara* 3(1982), pp. 261–97.

"Carthage et Carthagene au VIIIe siècle," *Actas del II Coloquio hispano-tunecino de estudios históricos.* Madrid, 1973, pp. 7–12.

"La emigración andalusí al Magreb en el siglo XIII (despoblación y repoblación en al-Andalus)," *Relaciones de la península ibérica con el Magreb (siglos XIII–XIV).* (eds. M. García-Arenal and M.J. Viguera), CSIC., Madrid, 1988, pp. 87–129.

"España musulmana en el siglo XI: aspectos económicos," *Actas de las jornadas de cultura árabe e islámica (1978).* Madrid, 1981, pp. 197–204.

"La industria en al-Andalus," *Al-Qantara* 1(1980), pp. 209–41.

"El nombre de al-Andalus," *Al-Qantara* 4(1983), pp. 301–55.

"Notas de metrología hispano-árabe: El codo en la España musulmana," *Al-Andalus* 41(1976), pp. 339–54.

"Notas de metrología hispano-árabe II: Medidas de capacidad," *Al-Andalus* 42(1977), pp. 61–121.

"Notas de metrología hispano-árabe III: Pesos y monedas," *Al-Qantara* 5(1984), pp. 147–67.

"Poids et mesures en Espagne musulmane," *Cahiers de Tunisie* 26(1978), pp. 143–54.

Van Beek, G.W. "Frankincense and Myrrh in Ancient South Arabia," *JAOS* 78(1958), pp. 141–51.

Vanacker, Claudette. "Géographie économique de l'Afrique du Nord, selon les autors arabes du IXe siècle au milieu du XIIe siècle," *Annales:ESC* 28(1973), pp. 659–80.

Veale, E.M. *The English Fur Trade in the Later Middle Ages.* Oxford, 1966.

Verlinden, Charles. "A propos de la place des juifs dans l'économie de l'Europe occidentale au IXe et Xe siècles: Agobard de Lyon et l'historiographie arabe," *Storiografia e storia: Studi in onore di Eugenio Dupré Theseider.* Rome, 1977, pp. 21–37.

L'esclavage dans l'Europe médiévale. Bruges, 1955.
"L'Espagne au Xe siècle; aux origines d'une civilisation composite," *Revue des cours et conferences* 38(1936–7), pp. 261–78.
"From the Mediterranean to the Atlantic: Aspects of an Economic Shift (12th–18th c.)," *Journal of European Economic History* 1(1972), pp. 625–46.
"Italian Influence in Iberian Colonization," *The Hispanic American Historical Review* 33(1953), pp. 199–211.
"L'origine de sclavus-esclave," *Bulletin Du Cange: Archivum latinitatis medii aevi* 17(1942), pp. 97–128.
"La place de la Catalogne dans l'histoire commerciale du monde méditerranéen médiéval (avant 1300)," *Revue des cours et conferences* 39 (1937–8), pp. 586–606.
"Les Radaniya et Verdun. A propos de la traite des esclaves slaves vers l'Espagne musulmane aux IXe et Xe siècles," *Estudios en homenaje a D. Claudio Sánchez Albornoz*. II, Buenos Aires, 1983, pp. 105–32.
"Le recrutement des esclaves à Gênes du milieu du XIIe siècle jusque vers 1275," *Fatti e idee di storia economica nei secoli XII-XX. Studi dedicati a Franco Borlandi*. Bologna, 1977, pp. 37–57.
"The Rise of Spanish Trade in the Middle Ages," *Economic History Review* 10 (1940), pp. 44–59.
"La traite des esclaves. Un grand commerce international au Xe siècle," *Etudes de civilisation médiévale (IXe – XIIIe siècles). Mélanges offerts à Edmond-René Labande*. Poitiers, 1974, pp. 721–30.
Vernet, Juan. "La cartografia náutica, Tiene un origen hispano-árabe?" *Madrid: MDI* 1 (1953), pp. 66–91.
"La navegación en la alta edad media," *La navigazione nell'alto medioevo*. Settimane di studio del Centro italiano di studi sull'altro medioevo, xxv, Spoleto, 1978, pp. 323–81.
"El Valle del Ebro como nexo entre oriente y occidente," *BRABLB* 23 (1950), pp. 249–86.
Vernet, Robert. "Les relations céréalières entre le Maghreb et la péninsule ibérique du XIIe au XVe siècle," *Anuario de estudios medievales* 10 (1980), pp. 321–35.
Vicens Vives, Jaime. *An Economic History of Spain*. Princeton, 1969.
Vindry, Georges. "Présentation de l'épave arabe de Batéguier (Baie de Cannes, Provence-orientale)," *La céramique médiévale en Méditerranée occidentale*. Paris, 1980, pp. 221–6.
Viré, François. "Dénereaux, estampilles et poids musulmans en verre en Tunisie," *Cahiers de Tunisie* 4 (1956), pp. 17–90.
Vire, M.M. "Notes sur trois épitaphes royales de Gao," *Bulletin de l'Institut français d'Afrique du Nord* 20 (1958), pp. 368–76.
Vismara, Giulio. "Limitazioni al commercio internazionale nell'imperio romano e nella comunita' cristiana medioevale," *Scritti in onore di Contardo Ferrini*. I, Milan, 1947, pp. 443–70.
Vitale, Vito. "La schiavitù in Liguria," *Bollettino ligustico per la storia e la cultura regionale* 1 (1949), pp. 43–7.

"Vita e commercio nei notai genovesi dei secoli XII e XIII. Parte prima: La vita civile," *ASLSP* 72 (1949).

Wakin, Jeanette A. *The Function of Documents in Islamic Law; The Chapters on Sales from Tahāwī's "Kitāb al-shurūṭ al-kabīr"*. Albany, 1972.

Walker, John. *A Catalogue of the Arab-Byzantine and Post-Reform Umaiyad Coins*. London, 1956.

Wansborough, John. "The Safe-Conduct in Muslim Chancery Practice," *BSOAS* 34 (1971), pp. 20–35.

Wasserstein, David. "Byzantium and al-Andalus," *Mediterranean Historical Review* 2 (1987), pp. 76–101.

"Does Benjamin of Tudela mention Portugal?" *Journal of Semitic Studies* 24 (1979), pp. 193–200.

The Rise and Fall of the Party Kings: Politics and Society in Islamic Spain 1002–1086. Princeton, 1985.

Watson, Andrew. *Agricultural Innovation in the Early Islamic World*. Cambridge, 1983.

"The Arab Agricultural Revolution and its Diffusion, 700–1100," *Journal of Economic History* 34 (1974), pp. 7–35.

"Back to Gold – and Silver," *Economic History Review* 20 (1967), pp. 1–34.

"The Rise and Spread of Old World Cotton," *Studies in Textile History in Memory of Harold B. Burnham*. (ed. V. Gervers), Toronto, 1977, pp. 355–68.

Watt, W.M. *The Influence of Islam on Medieval Europe*. Edinburgh, 1972.

Watt, W.M. and Cachia, P. *A History of Islamic Spain*. Edinburgh, 1965.

Wescher, H. "Cotton and the Cotton Trade in the Middle Ages," *Ciba Review* 6 (1947–9), pp. 2322–60.

Whitehouse, David. "Chinese Porcelain in Medieval Europe," *Medieval Archeology* 16 (1972), pp. 63–78.

"La collezione pisana e le produzioni ceramiche dei paesi circummediterranei nei secoli XI-XV," *Le ceramiche medievali delle chiese di Pisa*. [Biblioteca del Bollettino storico pisano, collana storica 25] Pisa, 1983, pp. 31–6.

"Medieval Pottery in Italy: The Present State of Research," *La céramique médiévale en Méditerranée occidentale*. Paris, 1980, pp. 65–82.

Wickham, C. "The Other Transition: From the Ancient World to Feudalism," *Past and Present* 103 (1984), pp. 3–36.

Wiet, Gaston. "Les marchands d'epices sous les sultans Mamlouks," *Cahiers d'histoire egytienne* 7 (1955), pp. 81–147.

"Tapis égyptiens," *Arabica* 6 (1959), pp. 1–24.

Wittlin, A. "The Development of the Silk Industry," *Ciba Review* 2 (1939), pp. 707–21.

Wolf, Kenneth. *Christian Martyrs in Muslim Spain*. Cambridge, 1988.

Yalaoui, M. "Les relations entre Fātimides d'Ifriqiya et Omeyyades d'Espagne à travers le dīwān d'Ibn Hānī," *Actas del II Coloquio hispano-tunecino de estudios históricos*. Madrid, 1973, pp. 13–30.

Yarrison, James Lee. "Force as an Instrument of Policy: European Military Incursions and Trade in the Maghrib, 1000–1355." Ph.D. Dissertation, Princeton University, 1982.

Zanón, Jesus. "Un itinerario de Córdoba a Zaragoza en el siglo X," *Al-Qantara* 7 (1986), pp. 31–51.

Zeki, Ahmad. "Mémoire sur les relations entre l'Egypte et l'Espagne pendant l'occupation musulmane," *Homenaje a Don Francisco Codera*. Zaragoza, 1904, pp. 455–81.

Zozaya, Juan. "Aperçu général sur la céramique espagnole," *La céramique médiévale en Méditerranée occidentale*. Paris, 1980, pp. 265–96.

"Cerámicas islámicas del Museo de Soria," *Boletín de la asociación española de orientalistas* 11 (1975), pp. 135–48.

"El comercio de al-Andalus con el Oriente: nuevos datos," *Boletín de la asociación española de orientalistas* 5 (1969), pp. 191–204.

INDEX

Aachen, 4
'Abbasids, 3, 5
'Abbadids, 8
'Abd al-Raḥmān I, 3
'Abd al-Raḥmān II, 147, 204
'Abd al-Raḥmān III, 79, 127, 156, 163, 180, 184, 198; declaration of caliphate, 4; minting of gold, 4, 40, 137
'Abd Allah b. Buluggīn al-Zīrī of Granada, 49
'Abd Allah b. Massara, 80
'Abd al-Mu'min, Almohad caliph, 10, 43
Abraham b. Daud, 20, 88
Abraham b. Ezra, 154
Abū 'Abd Allah al-Saraqustī, 131
Abū al-'Abbās, 109–10
Abū al-Faḍl Sāliḥ al-Tāhertī, 90
Abū al-Faraj b. Yūsuf al-Andalusı, 91
Abū al-Fidā, 247
Abū al-Ḥasan al-Jazīrī, 25, 125, 161, 164
Abū al-Ḥasan Qāsim, 77
Abū al-Ḥasan b. Yusha' b. Natan al-Andalusī, 91
Abū al-Khayr al-Ishbīlī, 183–4
Abū al-Khulayf, 93
Abū al-Muṭahhar al-Azdī, 181
Abū 'Alī b. Halas (Bencalas), governor of Ceuta, 125
Abū Bakr Muḥammad b. Mu'āwiya al-Marwānī, 36, 80
Abū Faḍl al-Dimashqī, 52–3, 56, 99, 119, 149–50, 165, 186, 194–5
Abū Ibrahım al-Andalusī, 89
Abū Ibrāhīm al-Andalusī, 91–3
Abū Muḥammad 'Abd Allah al-Fihrī, 174
Abū Yūsuf, Ya'qūb b. Ibrāhīm, 128, 131
Abū Yūsuf Ya'qūb al-Manṣūr, Almohad Caliph 69
Abu-Lughod, J., 12
Abulafia, D., 99, 100
accomendatio, see *commenda*
Adalaxia, wife of Fulco de Castello, 104
Aden, 36, 94, 145, 177, 187, 188
Aḥmad b. Marwān, 109
Aghmat, 201
Agobard of Lyons, 204, 205
agriculture, 4, 229
akhbār, see commercial information
Alarilla, 46, 132
Alboran Sea, 16, 32
Alcacer do Sal, 197
Alexandria, 5, 6, 9, 19, 20, 21, 27, 28, 31, 36, 37, 38, 51, 68, 85, 90, 93, 94, 98, 100, 102, 104, 109, 122, 123, 124, 125, 129, 132, 140, 160, 165, 166, 173, 175, 176, 178, 183, 186, 241, 242, 244, 248, 249, 254, 255
Alfasi, Isaac b. Jacob, 69
Alfonso II of Aragon-Catalonia, 217
Alfonso V of Aragon, 248
Alfonso V of Asturias-Leon, 149
Alfonso VI of Leon-Castile, 45, 49
Alfonso VIII of Castile, 50, 106, 236
Alfonso X of Castile, 227, 249, 250
Algarve, 196, 222, 233, 238
Algeciras, 18, 31, 125

Index

Algiers, 31, 34
ʻAlī b. Mujāhid of Denia, 24, 114, 122, 123, 163
Alicante, 18, 221
Aljustrel, 186
Almaden, 187, 217
Almeria, xxiv, 5, 6, 8, 9, 17, **18–19**, 20, 23, 27, 31, 35, 37, 42, 73–5, 85, 93, 94, 95, 100, 114, 115, 116, 119, 122, 124, 129, 131, 132, 136, 140, 154, 155, 157, 158, 167, 186, 188, 189, 201, 202, 207, 211, 242, 246, **247**, 249, 253; industries and economy, 18–19, 34, 49, 145, 174, 175, 177, 179, 223
Almohads and Almohad period, xxi, xxv, 9, 21, 43, 65, 66, 79, 86, 95–6, 109, 114, 125, 127, 129, 130, 133, 155, 163, 166, 173, 179, 185, 187, 202, 206, 212
Almoravids and Almoravid period, xxv, 9, 50, 65, 66, 84, 93, 114, 127, 130, 133, 137, 163, 166, 173, 178, 185, 188, 202–3, 206
Almuñecar, 220
aloes, 155, 156
Alpujarras, 223
alum, 75–6, 105, 158–9, 192, 212, **231–2**
Amalfi, 41, 97, 178
Amalric of Marseilles, 125, 242
'amān, 64–5; *see also* safe conduct
ambergris, 139, 150, 155, 156, 169, 170
'amīn ʻalā al-wādī (overseer for the river), 117
Anatolia, 158, 223, 232
al-Andalus, as economic center and commercial transfer zone, 2, 16, 51, 138–9, 178, 213, 234, 242, 245; as frontier, 1–2, 6–7, 60 (*see also thughūr*); definition of term, xxiii; identity, 57–8, 57 n.8; marginalization, 13
Andalusia, xxiii, 110, 213, 214, 215, 222, 233, 240, 243, 245, 246, 249, 252, 253, 254, 255
animals, hire and sale, 126, 135, 168; *see also* horses
Anne (ship), of Hampton, 215
Ansaldo Letanelo, 102
antimony, 187–8
Arabia, 152
Aragon, xxiii, 8, 9, 12, 14, 117, 216, 244, 251, 256, 257; *see also* Crown of Aragon
archeological evidence, xxi, 138, 167, 190
Arles, 40, 44, 193, 204
arms and weaponry, 133, 146–7, 229, 238, 256, 257
Arnold, a Catalan merchant, 66, 107
aromatics, 141, 150, 155–6, 170
Arras, 250
arsenic, 155
Ashtor, E. 123, 136
Atlantic Ocean and trade, 14, 67, 110, 170, 240, 245, 252, 253, 258
ʻattābī, 145–6, 175
Awdaghost, 34, 201
ʻAydhab, 94, 165
Ayyubids, 10

bacini, xxi, 24, 25–7 (illustrations), 190–1, 222
Baeza, 172
Baghdad, 1, 3, 5, 146, 169, 170, 212
Bakrī, Abū ʻUbayd ʻAbd Allah, 32, 82, 164, 170, 171, 188, 189
balance of trade, 5, 12, 138–40
Balansiya, *see* Valencia
Balearic Islands, 11, 17, 19, 20, 43, 102, 105, 179, 196, 222, 237, 238, 248
Balearic Sea, 16
Balegaris, 66
Banu Marın, 228
Barbastro, siege of, 61
Barcelona, 6, 10, 17, 44, 48, 67, 97, 98, 102, 106, 107, 117, 132, 218, 225, 230, 243, 246, 248, 249, 253, 254
barley, 136, 141, 142, 161, 162, 163

barr al-ʿidwa, 31
Barsbay, Mamluk sultan, 255
Basques, 204, 252
Bay of Biscay, 14, 212, 230, 243, 250
Bayonne, 244
beans, 142, 161
Benjamin of Tudela, xix, 17, 38, 62, 109, 253
Bernard de Barcellonio, 107
biographical dictionaries, *see tarajim*
Blancardus, 100, 103
Bône, 110
Bonus Johannes Malfiiaster, 100
books, 194–5
Bordeaux, 231, 244
Bougie, 43, 68, 98, 102, 103, 123, 242, 244, 247, 248, 249
Brabant, 215
Braudel, F., 13, 162, 240–1
brazilwood (*baqam*), 35, 74, 154, 156, 157, 171, 175
Brett, M., 206
Bristol, 215, 222, 231, 250
Bruges, 14, 209, 212, 214, 216, 218, 219, 221, 224, 227, 232, 233, 245, 250, 251
Burgos, 45, 180, 237, 243, 252
Burgundy, 251, 252
Burone family, 101
Busir, 92
butter, 161
Byrne, E.H., 100
Byzantium, xxiii, 3, 38, 51, 103, 131, 147, 173, 184, 191, 225, 241, 249, 258; *see also* Constantinople

Caceres, 46, 60
Cadiz, 247, 252
Cairo, *see* Old Cairo
Calatayud, 189
Calatrava, order of, 46
Calendar of Cordoba, 147–8, 178
camphor, 155, 156
Canary Islands, 233
Cántigas de Santa María, 28, 29, 150–3
caraway, 170
Cardona, 66
Carolingians and Carolingian period, 4, 96, 172, 177–8, 193, 199, 204–206
Cartagena, 18, 188
Castile, xxiii, xxiv, 8, 9, 14, 44, 46, 50, 63, 67, 101, 110, 132, 172, 178, 193, 209, 210, 212, 215, 216, 217, 218, 219, 222, 225, 226, 228, 229, 240, 243, 249, 250, 251, 252, 256
Castro Urdiales, 67, 212
Catalonia and Catalans, 8, 9, 12, 22, 67, 101, 102, 103, 104, 105, 220, 237, 238, 242, 244, 248, 250, 253
Celanova, 108
cendal, 178, 179, 180
Centocellas, 199
ceramics, xxi, 138, 143, 146, 152, 167–8, **189–91**, 212, **222–3**
Ceuta, 31, 33, 43, 68, 69, 81, 98, 107, 125, 184, 199, 220, 242, 244, 247, 248
Chad, 158
Chalmeta, P., 48
Champagne, 245
chancery rolls, 209, 215
Charles the Bald, 178
Chaucer, G., 209, 216, 231
cheese, 161
Cherchell, 34
chick peas, 142, 161
Chilperic II, 193
China, 59, 167, 173, 189, 220, 225
Chios, 214
chreokoinonia, 70
Christian merchants, 62–7, 78–9, **96–111**, 241, 245, **248–52**
cinnabar (mercuric sulphide), 77, 186–7
cinnamon, 92, 150, 152, 154, 155, 170, 242
citruses, 183, 221
climate, 140–1, 173, 197, 228
clothing, 176–80
cloves, 152, 154
Coimbra, 148
coins and coinage, 33, 47–8, 147, 165,

Index

Elche, 220
Eleanor of Castile, 221, 250
Eliadar, wife of Soloman of Salerno, 99, 104
England, 210, 251; Iberian trade with, 30, 209, 212, 216, 223, 225, 227, 229, 230, 231, 243, 244, 245, 249, 250, 252
Estella, 194
Eulogius, 96
Evora, 60, 132, 235

fairs, 60, 245
famine, 122, 134, 135, 142, 162, 163, 233
Fatimids and Fatimid period, 4, 11, 32, 131, 168, 181, 190
fatwa materials, xx, 54
Ferdinand and Isabella, 251
Ferdinand III of Castile, 11, 12, 43–4, 213, 244
Ferdinand IV of Castile, 256
Fermo, 179
Fez, 33, 73, 74, 75, 83, 95, 96, 129, 155, 158, 171, 186, 201
figs, 141, 169, 183–4, 198, 209, 211, 212, 220, 221, 222
Fihrī, *see* Abū Muḥammad ʿAbd Allah al-Fihrī
Flanders, 209, 210, 217, 218, 219, 225, 229, 230, 231, 243, 245, 249, 250, 251, 252
flax and linen, 35, 92, 122, 131, 141, 144, 159, 160, 173, 176, 225, 226
Florence and Florentines, 10, 150, 216, 248, 250
foenus nauticum, *see* sea loan
food and foodstuffs, 122, 135, 142, 143, 150, **161–4, 181–5**
France, 169, 204, 209, 210, 218, 225, 229, 242, 244, 245, 251
Francesco di Balduccio Pegolotti, 150, 214, 216, 218, 220, 223, 232, 250
frankincense, 152, 154, 155, 175
frontier, *see thughūr*
fruit juice, 161
fruits, 141, 161, 181, 211, **220–2**, 245, 246, 249; *see also* figs, raisins, dates, citruses
fuero, xx, 46, 60, 106, 108, 132, 176, 180, 184, 193, 199, 235, 236
Fulco de Castello, 101, 102
Fulco, son of Fulco de Castello (Fulchino), 101, 102
Fulco de Predi, 103
funduq (hostelry, trading house), 43, 64, 115, **119–21**, 213, 249
furs, 47, 139, 168, 169, **198–9, 219–20**; *see also* hides, rabbit skins
Fusṭāṭ, *see* Old Cairo

Gabes, 21
Galicia and Galicians, 8, 44, 48, 204, 205, 219, 231, 247
Gao, 34, 188, 190, 201
Gascony, 231, 244
gems, 138, 141, 150, 164–6
Geniza, xx, xxii, 9, 19, 20, 21, 24, 26, 27, 28, 33, 35, 37, 38, 53, **54**, 57, 61, 68, 77, 85, 88, 102, 121, 122, 123, 125, 129, 131, 134, 135, 136, 138, 142, 146, 154, 157, 159, 160, 163, 164, 165, 168, 170, 171, 175, 176, 177, 181, 186, 187, 195, 197, 201, 242, 248, 255
Genoa, xxi, xxii, 10–11, 14, **42–4**, 114, 124, 132, 172, 173, 176, 194, 196, 199, 213, 214, 216, 224, 234, 238, 242, 244, 257; Genoese merchants and trade, 20, 98–105, 217, 220, 243, 246, 247, 248, 249, 250, 252, 254
geographical works, xix, 6, 138, 141, 229
Ghadames, 192
Ghana, 200, 201
ghee, 161
Ghent, 225
ginger, 242
Giovanni Scriba, 99, 101, 172, 179
Glick, T., 49
Goitein, S.D., xx, 57–8, 73, 91, 121–2, 123, 135, 185, 187, 195

Murcia, 34, 50, 106, 109, 156, 172, 179, 180, 188, 216, 223
Musāfir b. Samuel, 77
musk, 155, 156
Muslim merchants, 59–60, **78–85**, 109–10, 241, 244, 248, **252–5**
mustasaf, 118
al-Muwaḥid, *see* Almohad
Muẓaffar, 82
myrobalans, 154
myrrh, 152, 155

Nahray b. Nissim, 53, 64, 90–1, 122, 123, 165, 175, 187
names, xxii, 107–8, 144–6, 226; *see also nisba*
Naples, 173, 178
Narbonne, 194, 225, 232
Nāṣir-i Khusraw, 129
Nasrids and Nasrid period, 12, 63, 110, 142, 164, 183, 211, 220, 221, 222, 224, 227, 246, 247, 249; *see also* Granada
Natan al-Andalusī, 91–2
Natan b. Yūsha' b. Natan al-Andalusī (Abū Sahl), 91–2
Navarre, 8, 9, 44, 67, 210, 218, 219, 256
Niebla, 171, 220
nisba, xxiv, 57, 57 n.7, 92
Normandy, 221
Normans, 10, 11, 35
North Africa, xxiii, 2, 81, 100, 160, 184, 188, 191, 211, 228, 238, 241, 245, 247, 249; *see also* Maghrib
North Sea, 14
notarial contracts, xxi, 42–3, 54, **98–9**, 105, 138, 142, 172, 179, 194, 216, 232, 234, 242, 247
Notker the Stammerer, 172
numismatics and numismatic evidence, xxi, **39–41**, **47–50**, 136
nuts, 164, 221
Nuwayrī, Aḥmad b. 'Abd al-Wahhāb, 134

Oberto Ferrario de Valencia, 108
Oberto Scriba, 179
Ocaña, 46, 132, 183
Ogerio de Cartagenia, 108
Old Cairo (and Cairo), xxiv, 1, 20, 37, 90, 94, 131, 145, 165, 186, 190, 223, 245
olives and olive oil, 38, 92, 109, 141, 161, 162, 169, 181, **182–3**, 198, 209, 211, **213–15**, 244, 245, 252
Oran, 34, 43, 162, 253
Ordoño II of Leon, 48
Otto de Castro, 102
Ottoman Empire, 258
Ottonians, 4
Ouargla, 201

Palermo, 28, 35, 89
Palestine, 61, 235
paper, 47, 138, **194–6**, 212
papyrus, 147
paria, 9 (and n.14), **48–50**, 83, 127, 148
Paris, 14, 144, 218
partnerships, 52, 56, 59, **67–77**, 113
pearls, 35, 92, 164, 165
Pechina, 160, 206
Pegolotti, *see* Francesco di Balduccio Pegolotti
pepper, 75, 92, 150, 154, 155, 170, 242
Persia, 167, 173
Persian Gulf, 5
Peter the Venerable, 195
Peter I of Castile, 237, 251
Peter IV of Aragon, 253
Philip Cavarunco, 102
pilgrims and pilgrimage, 20, 28, 30, 36, 42, 45, 80–1, 109
Pirenne, H., 147
Pisa and Pisans, xxi, xxii, 10–11, 42–3, 69, 105, 107, 114, 124, 129, 132, 145, 190–1, 213, 222, 232, 238, 244, 248, 250, 252
plague, 12, 228, 249
Pliny, 29, 159

Cambridge studies in medieval life and thought
Fourth series

Titles in the series

1 The Beaumont Twins: The Roots and Branches of Power in the Twelfth Century
D. B. CROUCH
2 The Thought of Gregory the Great*
G. R. EVANS
3 The Government of England under Henry I*
JUDITH A. GREEN
4 Charity and Community in Medieval Cambridge
MIRI RUBIN
5 Autonomy and Community: The Royal Manor of Havering, 1200–1500
MARJORIE KENISTON MCINTOSH
6 The Political Thought of Baldus de Ubaldis
JOSEPH CANNING
7 Land and Power in Late Medieval Ferrara: The Rule of the Este, 1350–1450
TREVOR DEAN
8 William of Tyre: Historian of the Latin East*
PETER W. EDBURY AND JOHN GORDON ROWE
9 The Royal Saints of Anglo-Saxon England: A Study of West Saxon and East Anglian Cults
SUSAN J. RIDYARD
10 John of Wales: A Study of the Works and Ideas of a Thirteenth-Century Friar
JENNY SWANSON
11 Richard III: A Study of Service*
ROSEMARY HORROX
12 A Marginal Economy? East Anglian Breckland in the Later Middle Ages
MARK BAILEY
13 Clement VI: The Pontificate and Ideas of an Avignon Pope
DIANA WOOD
14 Hagiography and the Cult of Saints: The Diocese of Orléans, 800–1200
THOMAS HEAD
15 Kings and Lords in Conquest England
ROBIN FLEMING
16 Council and Hierarchy: The Political Thought of William Durant the Younger
CONSTANTIN FASOLT
17 Warfare in the Latin East, 1192–1291
CHRISTOPHER MARSHALL
18 Province and Empire: Brittany and the Carolingians
JULIA M. H. SMITH

* *Also published as a paperback*

19 A Gentry Community: Leicestershire in the Fifteenth Century, *c.* 1422–*c.* 1485
ERIC ACHESON

20 Baptism and Change in the Early Middle Ages, *c.* 200–1150
PETER CRAMER

21 Itinerant Kingship and Royal Monasteries in Early Medieval Germany, *c.* 936–1075
JOHN W. BERNHARDT

22 Caesarius of Arles: The Making of a Christian Community in Late Antique Gaul
WILLIAM E. KLINGSHIRN

23 Bishop and Chapter in Twelfth-Century England: A Study of the *Mensa Episcopalis*
EVERETT U. CROSBY

24 Trade and Traders in Muslim Spain: The Commercial Realignment of the Iberian Peninsula, 900–1500*
OLIVIA REMIE CONSTABLE

25 Lithuania Ascending: A Pagan Empire within East-Central Europe, 1295–1345
S. C. ROWELL

26 Barcelona and its Rulers, 1100–1291
STEPHEN P. BENSCH

27 Conquest, Anarchy and Lordship: Yorkshire, 1066–1154
PAUL DALTON

28 Preaching the Crusades: Mendicant Friars and the Cross in the Thirteenth Century
CHRISTOPH T. MAIER

29 Family Power in Southern Italy: The Duchy of Gaeta and its Neighbours, 850–1139
PATRICIA SKINNER

30 The Papacy, Scotland and Northern England, 1342–1378
A. D. M. BARRELL

31 Peter des Roches: An Alien in English Politics, 1205–1238
NICHOLAS VINCENT

32 Runaway Religious in England, *c.* 1240–1540
F. DONALD LOGAN

**Also published as a paperback*